Drums of Redemption

The Drums of Redemption guides believers through the redemptive promises of God as found in the Bible. The concept of redemption is a pillar in Christian doctrine. This book by Professor Sarma identifies the theological foundation of redemptive history and carefully connects it to the contextual understanding of redemption as found in many African cultures so that they can relate that with God's redemptive purposes. The book is theologically written and crafted with simplicity that is typical of the author. I recommend the book to all theological institutions, churches, homes, and every Christian who desires to live a redemptive life.

Nathan H. Chiroma, PhD
Dean, School of Theology,
Pan Africa Christian University, Kenya

Another excellent resource from Professor Sarma! This New Testament theology considers the main themes of each New Testament book (with the exception of Matthew, Mark, and Luke which are grouped together because of their common material) and applies these themes to the spiritual needs of the African continent. Scholarly, rich, simply written, Scripture-focused, and spiritually uplifting. I highly recommend it.

John Hunt
Evangelical Church Winning All Theological College, Nigeria

African drums are a powerful means of communicating messages to their listeners. Bitrus Sarma employs this symbol to communicate that the drums of redemption are the compelling sound that echoes throughout the New Testament. He does this through listening, tracing, investigating, interpreting, applying, and relating the sound of the drums of redemption in the New Testament. It is a superb contribution to New Testament scholarship. This ground breaking work is serious stuff!

Samuel Waje Kunhiyop, PhD
Head of Postgraduate School,
South Africa Theological Seminary

Drums of Redemption

A New Testament Theology for Africa

Bitrus A. Sarma

© 2023 Bitrus A. Sarma

Published 2023 by HippoBooks, an imprint of ACTS and Langham Publishing.

Africa Christian Textbooks (ACTS), TCNN, PMB 2020, Bukuru 930008, Plateau State, Nigeria
www.actsnigeria.org
Langham Publishing, PO Box 296, Carlisle, Cumbria CA3 9WZ, UK
www.langham.org

ISBNs:
978-1-83973-231-7 Print
978-1-83973-797-8 ePub
978-1-83973-798-5 Mobi
978-1-83973-799-2 PDF

Bitrus A. Sarma has asserted his right under the Copyright, Designs and Patents Act, 1988 to be identified as the Author of this work.

All rights reserved. No part of this publication may be reproduced, stored in a retrieval system or transmitted, in any form or by any means, electronic, mechanical, photocopying, recording or otherwise, without the prior written permission of the publisher or the Copyright Licensing Agency.

Requests to reuse content from Langham Publishing are processed through PLSclear. Please visit www.plsclear.com to complete your request.

Unless otherwise stated, Scriptures taken from the Holy Bible, New International Version®, NIV®. Copyright © 1973, 1978, 1984, 2011 by Biblica, Inc.™ Used by permission of Zondervan.

British Library Cataloguing-in-Publication Data
A catalogue record for this book is available from the British Library

ISBN: 978-1-83973-231-7

Cover & Book Design: projectluz.com

The publishers of this book actively support theological dialogue and an author's right to publish but do not necessarily endorse the views and opinions set forth here or in works referenced within this publication, nor guarantee technical and grammatical correctness. The publishers do not accept any responsibility or liability to persons or property as a consequence of the reading, use or interpretation of its published content.

*To Prof. Scott Cunningham
for the unshakable foundation he laid in my life
in the field of New Testament Greek
and whose hard work is exemplary.*

*To my wife, Sanatu,
whose love, faithfulness, and companionship kept me strong along the years.*

*To the members of We Encourage,
Pasadena Covenant Church, Los Angeles, USA
who are the epitome of Christian love and encouragement;
to all my fellow brothers and sisters who are redeemed in Christ.*

And to our faithful and gracious Father and our Redeemer Jesus Christ be the glory!

Contents

Abbreviations xi
Foreword xiii
Acknowledgments xv
Introduction 1
1 Drums of Redemptive Theology. 9
2 Drums of Theological Horizons in Africa. 25
3 Drums of Redemption in the Synoptic Gospels (1). 43
4 Drums of Redemption in the Synoptic Gospels (2). 61
5 Drums of Redemption in the Synoptic Gospels (3). 77
6 Drums of Redemption in the Gospel of John. 119
7 Drums of Redemption in the Acts of the Apostles 141
8 Drums of Redemption in Romans. 147
9 Drums of Redemption in 1 Corinthians. 165
10 Drums of Redemption in 2 Corinthians. 183
11 Drums of Redemption in Galatians. 191
12 Drums of Redemption in Ephesians 197
13 Drums of Redemption in Philippians 211
14 Drums of Redemption in Colossians. 217
15 Drums of Redemption in 1 and 2 Thessalonians. 233
16 Drums of Redemption in the Pastoral Epistles. 239
17 Drums of Redemption in Philemon 245
18 Drums of Redemption in Hebrews 249
19 Drums of Redemption in James. 259
20 Drums of Redemption in 1 Peter 265
21 Drums of Redemption in 2 Peter and Jude. 271
22 Drums of Redemption in 1, 2, and 3 John 279
23 Drums of Redemption in Revelation. 285
Bibliography 297

Abbreviations

ABRL	The Anchor Bible Reference Library
AJPS	*Asian Journal of Pentecostal Studies*
ATR	African Traditional Religion
BECNT	Baker Exegetical Commentary on the New Testament
JETS	*Journal of the Evangelical Theological Society*
JSNT	*Journal for the Study of the New Testament*
NCBC	The New Cambridge Bible Commentary
NIGTC	The New International Greek Testament Commentary
NT	New Testament
OT	Old Testament
R&E	*Review & Expositor: An International Baptist Journal*
SPCK	Society for the Promotion of Christian Knowledge
WTJ	*Westminster Theological Journal*

Foreword

Most people who are conversant with some of the major developments on the African continent over the last few decades, would, no doubt, concede that these troubling events seem to cast shadows on the existence and mission of the church – or, even more, that of its various "national" governments. These are, indeed, turbulent times, such that even glaring human achievements today seem less glamorous, and fade, when compared to, or judged by, the enormity of the African predicament. What are we to make of all this? What can the church, with its institutions, do to "solve" the perplexing problem, beyond merely stemming the tide?

In this stimulating primer for church and Christian leaders in Africa, and her future leaders in training, Dr. Bitrus Sarma gives a clarion call on the need to return to the founding documents of the Christian faith, and re-commit ourselves to their sustained study. If the future looks bleak to those without such deep-seated commitment, then it must look brighter for those who understand the power behind such a rigorous exercise in the context of leadership training today. And this is where the institutions serving the church *and* society must rise to the challenge of the moment.

Dr. Sarma's *Drums of Redemption* is apt for the task at hand: it presents the unfolding "plan" of God's salvation, in the person and work of Jesus Christ, for humankind. This redemption, he contends, is "drummed" by the Gospels, Acts, Epistles and the Revelation (*Apocalypse*). These major *genres*, or literary classifications, of the New Testament have been studied as witnesses to the drama of salvation, which began with Israel in the Old Testament, and found its culmination in Jesus. The church is both the recipient and herald of this redemption in our distressed world. Each book, or cluster of books, of the New Testament is treated from the angle of God's salvation which the death and resurrection of Christ has "activated" and brought into full realization. How this is done by the New Testament authors, via their texts and the messages conveyed by them, is what this book by its sub-title (*A New Testament Theology for Africa*) seeks to do.

New Testament Theology (NTT), as a sub-set of Biblical Theology (BT) (the other being Old Testament Theology, OTT), may be viewed as the culmination of the task of doing a BT, if we reckon the revelation of God in Christ to be climactic for the present age. While either NTT or OTT can stand alone, NTT almost always presupposes the OT(T) and always orients itself to the main task of BT. Doing a NTT for the church in Africa is always a welcome task, and Dr. Sarma is to be warmly commended for it. This primer will serve the needs of senior BA-level students of theology (and religion) in Africa, as well as entering postgraduate (MA) students. It will provoke discussion without rancor, and set the reader thinking deeply about the present and persisting African situation – to be sure, a part of the global predicament of the church and society.

Why a NTT and why Africa? The answers to this double question are given in the book. But it helps to remind us of the enduring issue or problem of how human history and God's revelation are related. The Bible, from God's revelatory standpoint, answers the "sin problem" of humans in their profane history. Dr. Sarma sees this as captured in the OT "promise" held out to humankind from creation, but which finds its "fulfillment" in Jesus. The meaning and implication of all this are what NTT seeks to help Christians and the church in Africa to understand *and* practice. From this point on, biblical history must provide the matrix for our understanding of Africa – its history, problems, solutions, and future. This timely book ignites and begins the discussion for both students and scholars, and ministers and missioners today.

Randee Ijatuyi-Morphé, PhD
Former Provost & Professor of Biblical Studies,
ECWA Theological Seminary, Jos, Nigeria
Director,
Hokma House, Centre for Biblical Research, Nigeria

Acknowledgments

I owe volumes of gratitude to those who made this work possible. Encouragement to pursue writing this book came with the positive response from Fuller Theological Seminary's Global Research Institute (GRI) and a generous grant. My initial contact with staff of the Center for Missiological Research (CMR) – Prof. Amos Yong, Director, Prof. Samuel Bang, Director of International Services, and Dr. Johnny Ching, Program Manager – gave me much encouragement. They not only worked through my proposal and gave approval but they also labored tirelessly through the cumbersome process of visa application until my wife and I made it to Fuller Theological Seminary to begin a six-month writing project with GRI. Similarly, our first meeting with them was a huge delight as they affectionately welcomed us. Subsequently, Prof. Yong and Dr. Ching ensured that I received the right connections regarding my work. I owe the trio an immense debt of gratitude.

My initial proposal approved by Fuller Theological Seminary's Global Research Institute (GRI) was a commentary on the book of Ephesians titled *Blessed New Humanity in Christ: A Theology of Hope for African Christianity from the Book of Ephesians* (HippoBooks, 2021). But the opportunity given to me spurred me to go beyond the approved proposal and pursue another one of my dreams, namely writing a New Testament theology for Africa. Although the stretch was enormous, to God be the glory for the huge enabling he gave me to finish my initial project and begin the second book within the span of six months at Fuller. Therefore, I would like to thank Prof. Amos Yong, Director, Prof. Samuel Bang, and Dr. Johnny Ching for making my sabbatical quite fruitful. I owe the trio an immense debt of gratitude.

As in *Blessed New Humanity*, I feel it is necessary for me to thank some people who were instrumental in the success of my sabbatical. Pastor John Wipf at the Pasadena Covenant Church played a key role as his bookstore supplied some of the books I needed. Not only did I buy his books, he was willing to have me choose a number of books I wanted for free! What a blessing. Similarly, the following will remain dear and indelible in our memories for their love, hospitality, generosity, and friendship: Rev. Dr. Simon Enwereji and his wife, Carolyn; Mr. and Mrs. Carlos Cevallos, Mr. and Mrs. Dece Leonares; Rev. and Mrs. Uchenna D. Anyawu; Miss Jean Campbell who is rich in faith and in sincere love; and Prof. and Dr. Bulus Galadima whose love and kindness are contagious. Spending a weekend in their house at Biola University provided some much needed relief from my busy writing schedule. And while away from our children, our brother and sister Dr. and Dr. Mrs. Bakari Ibrahim were true parents to our children. We are eternally grateful.

Special thanks goes to Pastor Jim Tyberg, President of We Encourage and Executive Pastor of Pasadena Covenant Church. He and his wife showered us with much love. Their devotion to the Lord, friendship, and love are contagious.

I wish to thank the Board of Governors of Kagoro Theological Seminary (ETSK) for releasing me to proceed on my sabbatical. Their magnanimity offered me a tremendous opportunity to explore resources and connect with scholars who greatly enhanced my research. Equal appreciation goes to all who have contributed to the success of this work but whose names are not mentioned. Their reward is with the Lord. And special thanks to the management, faculty, and staff of ETSK for their support.

I owe a special debt of gratitude to Langham Partnership for promoting biblical literature in the majority world. Thank you for publishing my *Hermeneutics of Mission in Matthew: Israel and the Nations in the Interpretative Framework of Matthew's Gospel* (Langham Monographs, 2015). My huge debt of gratitude goes to all the publishing team in Langham Partnership. It is a huge delight to interact with a few of them like Vivian Doub, Pieter Kwant, Elizabeth Mburu, Mark Arnold and their editorial team. I am thankful to them for their faithful services. They have made a pleasant mark in my heart. Thank you for enriching the church in Africa through your excellent and selfless services. Thank you for your labor of love in the kingdom of God. I trust eternity will celebrate you all.

I thank the pastors and members of ECWA Seminary Church (ESC), Jos, under the leadership of Rev. Solomon Guruza. Their prayer support and encouragements are deeply appreciated.

Finally, my wife, Sanatu, my children and grandchildren have given me incredible support. The company of my wife at Fuller Theological Seminary gave me all the encouragement I needed to keep up with the rigorous demands of research. Her selfless service is eternally appreciated. We thank our children Yambale, David, Rejoice and family, Grace and family, and Esther and family. We cherish your love for us. Karis and Nathan, our grandchildren, always wanted to hear our voice. The Lord bless you!

"LORD, you establish peace for us; all that we have accomplished you have done for us" (Isa 26:12). To God be the glory!

Introduction

"If the Bible was not a living power before the Reformation, it was not because the Bible was chained up and forbidden, as we are told, but because their minds were chained by preconceived ideas, and when they read, they failed to read."

Walter Rauschenbusch[1]

Walter Rauschenbusch wrote the words above from the context of Christianity in social crisis. Like people in first-century Judea, most people in Africa live in a tumultuous environment full of sociopolitical unrest and uncertainties. The larger part of Black Africa resonates with the past epithet "the dark continent." Some of the key issues grappled with include genocide, terrorism, political instability, failed governments, oppression of the poor masses, injustice, lack of value for human life,[2] corruption, divisive ethnicity, spiritual power encounters, family breakdown, rapid erosion of community life and values, armed robbery, kidnapping, abject poverty, environmental degradation, hunger and starvation, *inter alia*.

And like first-century Jews in Judea and diaspora, we hope for messiahs – imaginary political figures capable of eradicating our sociopolitical woes. For example, when President Muhammadu Buhari of Nigeria introduced the slogan "Change" in his political campaign, most Nigerians embraced him as a coming messiah capable of changing the misfortunes of their beloved nation, only to be disappointed after months and years of embarrassing failures. And like first-century Judea, many "prophets" roam our beleaguered cities and towns. A few of these prophets are denouncing the injustices in society. But the majority, like the prophets with lying spirits in the service of King Ahab (1 Kgs 22:19–23), have become praise-singing sycophants of the government and political gladiators for their own personal gain. These prophets say nothing wrong against the corrupt leaders as long as their daily bread is supplied. In the words of the prophet Micah, "As for the prophets who lead my people astray,

---

1. Walter Rauschenbusch, *Christianity and the Social Crisis* (Louisville: Westminster John Knox, 1991), 45.

2. Using Nigeria as an example, the only lives that count are those of rich and powerful persons in society. Lives are destroyed with impunity. The destroyers go free (or even are rewarded). In Nigeria, human lives are cheaper than the lives of goats and cows.

they proclaim 'peace' if they have something to eat, but prepared to wage war against anyone who refuses to feed them" (Mic 3:5). Similarly, a good number of false messiahs in the garb of preachers of the gospel are promising heaven on earth for their followers. Their messages are well concocted opium for escaping the obvious predicaments of poverty and social unrest. They "peddle the word of God for profit" (2 Cor 2:17) and "put on a mask to cover up greed" (1 Thess 2:5). In the words of Peter, "These people are springs without water and mists driven by a storm" (2 Pet 2:17). They are prospering in their lucrative businesses while their nations languish in poverty and sorrows caused by wicked leaders.

But Jesus came to usher in the kingdom of light, peace, and rest in a dark and troubled world (Matt 11:28).[3] His mission was foretold by the prophet Isaiah thus:

> Nevertheless, there will be no more gloom for those who were in distress. In the past he humbled the land of Zebulun and the land of Naphtali, but in the future he will honor Galilee of the nations, by the Way of the Sea, along the Jordan –
>
> The people walking in darkness
>   have seen a great light;
> on those living in the land of deep darkness
>   a light has dawned. (Isa 9:1–2; cf. Matt 4:15–16)

At a recent graduation ceremony of an evangelical seminary in Eastern Nigeria, we all enjoyed the beauty of a school well situated in a terrain adorned with beautiful trees and tall green grasses. During the ceremony, someone gave a brief history of the land now occupied by the school. The entire area had been designated "Evil Forest," never entered by ordinary people because it was a place of "territorial" demons and all kinds of evil spirits. The "gift" of that land on which to build a Bible school could hardly have been considered a blessing when it was released to the Christians. But the church cleared the "Evil Forest" and built a theological school that serves as a beacon of light in the entire region and beyond. And there we were, enjoying one of the best places in the entire city because of the cool breeze that was in sharp contrast to the polluted air in the city.

Similarly, in Matthew 4:15–16 Jesus depicts his mission on earth as the kingdom of light penetrating the world full of darkness, a scenario that is

---

3. The basic structure of his message is the kingdom of God and its ethics. See George Strecker, *Theology of the New Testament*, ed. Friedrich Wilhelm Horn, trans. M. Eugene Boring (Louisville: Westminster, 2000), 255–61.

similar to Africa's "Evil Forest."[4] He came to "those living in the land of the shadow of death" (Matt 4:16). He came as the light of the world (John 8:12) to eliminate darkness and to bring relief to those living in oppression and distress. Jesus states his mission thus: "The Spirit of the Lord is on me, because he has anointed me to proclaim good news to the poor. He has sent me to proclaim freedom for the prisoners and recovery of sight for the blind, to set the oppressed free, to proclaim the year of the Lord's favor" (Luke 4:17–19). And all of the New Testament[5] documents bear witness to Christ's completed work of redemption (*apolutrosis*).[6]

But the question is, how should African Christians understand and apply Christ's redemptive mission as presented in the Bible? Similarly, "is it allowable to see Scripture through the eyes of one particular culture?"[7] In other words, how does the New Testament address Africa's sociopolitical issues? For example, how does the word "Messiah" resonate in the mind of a Christian in Northern Nigeria who daily faces the problem of persecution and the reality of martyrdom? What is the meaning of salvation for the poor and needy in Africa who face starvation, oppression, and injustice? If the New Testament is the good news that the Messiah came in the person of Jesus Christ of Nazareth, what good news does he proclaim to the church in Africa today? And what role does the church – the salt and the light of the world (Matt 5:13–16) and "the pillar and foundation of the truth" (1 Tim 3:15) – play in this good news? As John Stott is reported as saying "all theology is contextual,"[8] that is, inseparably related to cultural and ethnic backgrounds,[9] which precipitates the exploration of the New Testament documents from the African context.

---

4. The New Testament shows that the world is an "evil forest" (1 John 5:19), but the children of God have overcome the world (1 John 5:4).

5. The word "testament" means agreement or covenant. Agreements usually have promises in them. Agreements also contain things to do in order to get the promises. One way to understand the Bible is that it is God's book of agreement with the people he has made. Perhaps the best way to understand the terms "old" and "new" lies in the covenants God made with his people and the prescribed way of relating to him through ceremonies and rituals (old) versus the new way of relating to him through Christ (new) (see Heb 9:1–14).

6. Broadly speaking, redemption is release from slavery or from a position of misfortune. Just as God is Israel's redeemer (Ps 78:35; Isa 41:14; 44:24; 48:17; 54:5–8; 60:16), Jesus is the redeemer of humankind from "the curse of the law" and slavery to sin (Gal 3:13–14).

7. Martin Goldsmith, *Matthew and Mission: The Gospel Through Jewish Eyes* (Carlisle: Paternoster, 2001), ix.

8. John Stott, cited in Goldsmith, *Matthew and Mission*, ix.

9. Goldsmith, ix.

Many decades ago, Byang H. Kato wrote,

> The search for authenticity through culture remains a desirable element in many African societies. The attitude of Christians toward cultural renaissance need not be negative. Culture as a way of life must be maintained. Jesus Christ became a man in order to save men. In becoming incarnate, He was involved in the Jewish culture – wearing their clothes, eating their food, thinking in their thought patterns. But while He went through all that, He was without sin, addressing both Jewish and Gentile people authoritatively as the Son of God. Jesus would not have come to make Africans become American Christians nor to cause Europeans to become Indian Christians. It is God's will that Africans, on accepting Christ as their Savior, become Christian Africans. Africans who become Christians should therefore remain Africans wherever their culture does not conflict with the Bible. It is the Bible that must judge the culture. Where a conflict results, the cultural element must give way.[10]

If Jesus became incarnate in order to save humanity from sin as Kato says, how can the gospel also become incarnate on the African soil? The most important question in contextualization is how to communicate the gospel in such a way that people of different worldviews and cultures understand. According to Noel Weeks, the word "contextualization" is used for a variety of things. "Basically it means the making of Biblical doctrine relevant to a different cultural and historical setting."[11] Weeks provides for us a working definition of contextualization. Beverly Zink-Sawyer says, "When we take a look at the history of preaching since New Testament times, we may be surprised to discover an ever-present concern for communicating the gospel in a manner that will be understood by those who hear."[12]

The point is that the problems and situations in Africa need to be addressed theologically in African thought patterns, values, and circumstances without diluting normative biblical truth. The call is for appropriate contextualization. In the words of Kato, we "Express Christianity in a truly African context, allowing it to judge the African culture and never allow the culture to

---

10. Byang H. Kato, "Theological Issues in Africa," *Bibliotheca Sacra* 133, no. 530 (April–June 1976): 145.

11. Noel Weeks, *The Sufficiency of Scripture* (Carlisle: Banner of Truth Trust, 1977), 76.

12. Beverly Zink-Sawyer, "The Word Purely Preached and Heard: The Listeners and the Homiletical Endeavor," *Interpretation: A Journal of Bible and Theology* 51 (1977): 342.

take precedence over Christianity. To do otherwise would isolate African Christianity from historical Christianity, Biblically based."[13] This statement affirms that the New Testament conveys message(s) for every situation in life, implicitly and explicitly. Just like the African drums speak, and every tone conveys a message or dictates the dance steps, the Bible is God's drums that convey messages and dictate the "dance steps" for Christians and all humanity in their particular cultural milieus.

However, this book does not encourage "Afrocentrism."[14] Africans' indebtedness to Western contributions in biblical Christianity and scholarship cannot be overemphasized. Byang H. Kato rightly reminds us that we must allow biblical Christianity "to judge the African culture and never allow the culture to take precedence over Christianity."[15] Rather, the goal of this book is to present a responsible contextualization of the content of New Testament theology from African perspectives.[16] We affirm that the Bible is normative for all cultures at all times. But theologizing is not. In the words of Goldsmith, "A clear distinction needs to be made between revelation on the one side, and theology or biblical exegesis on the other. While revelation comes from God and is therefore perfectly trustworthy, biblical understanding and theology are human attempts to determine the meaning of Scripture and to formulate this."[17]

---

13. Byang H. Kato, *Theological Pitfalls in Africa* (Kisumu, Kenya: Evangel Publishing House, 1975), 182.

14. See David T. Adamo, *Reading and Interpreting the Bible in African Indigenous Churches* (Benin, Nigeria: Justice Jeco Press and Publishers, 2005). Adamo does well to encourage contextualization of the Bible message in Africa. But I think it is problematic when we charge the West for being "Eurocentric interpreters" of the Bible and then try to correct this "anomaly" by resorting to some kinds of syncretistic practices.

15. Kato, *Theological Pitfalls in Africa*, 182. But why write another book on New Testament theology when there are excellent works in the market? First, Africa is still in dire need of books by African writers. We know that the word of the Lord is normative for all cultures, but applying the biblical text is better done in the context of the people for whom the message is presented. See Jean-Claude Loba-Mkole, "New Testament and Intercultural Exegesis in Africa," *JSNT* 30, no. 1 (September 2007): 7–28. Western writers address situations that usually differ from African contexts. Second, although the West has given us a legacy of rich knowledge of the Bible, examples from Western writers usually come from their own contexts and leave African readers wondering about the meaning of their symbols and illustrations. For example, the names of places, idioms, and cultural values, rather than serving as windows for understanding, usually create a communication gap between the writer and the African reader. Therefore, there is urgent need for New Testament theologies written in the African context.

16. The essence of responsible contextualization is how the living and normative word of God speaks to a given context without the interpreter resorting to syncretism. See for example Bitrus A. Sarma, *Reading the Bible in Africa: Understanding and Applying the Message* (Jos, Nigeria: Yakson, 2015), 213–24.

17. Goldsmith, *Matthew and Mission*, ix.

This statement leads us to the question of methods. New Testament theology is done in a number of ways. One method is systematic presentation of the biblical documents, "laying out the theology of each writer, or indeed of each document, in turn."[18] Another method is a thematic approach, namely, collating related materials under themes like the kingdom of God, salvation, and grace, among others. Biblical theology has also been oriented in a salvation history model in which a single theme is presumed to be the one thread that weaves through the documents of the Bible. Jon M. Isaak has cautioned against the salvation history approach because of its claims that there is "one thread that traverses the NT witnesses and holds them together."[19] Isaak fears that a salvation history model "risks imposing a systematic structure on the NT texts – much like the earlier dogmatic approach."[20] According to Isaak, the matter becomes "troubling especially when the NT texts that do not fit the structure are hindered from speaking for themselves or are silenced completely."[21]

Although all of the above approaches have their merits, a weakness common to them is that the documents of the New Testament are usually treated without adequate contemplation of their relevance to contemporary situations. And even when their contemporary relevance is not totally absent, they often fail to address the African situation because the context is usually rooted in Western and European soils. To avoid the single-pronged methods above and to bring the contemporary significance of each book of the New Testament for African Christianity, the approach of this work is historical, thematic, and theological. This means that the method is both descriptive and constructive.[22] The descriptive (inductive) method allows the biblical data to create the ideas, as much as possible, rather than imposing personal or borrowed notions. Inductive study guarantees a high level of integrity and respect for the biblical text and is following the natural flow of each New Testament book as they present themselves. This approach is based on the premise that each author of the New Testament has a distinctive emphasis regardless of the common themes. For this reason, most of the books of the New Testament are treated separately. Those that are treated together because of their common themes, and to avoid repetition, include the Synoptic Gospels,

---

18. James D. G. Dunn, *New Testament Theology: An Introduction* (Nashville: Abingdon, 2009), viii.

19. Jon M. Isaak, *New Testament Theology: Extending the Table* (Eugene: Cascade, 2011), 15.

20. Isaak, *New Testament Theology*, 15.

21. Isaak, 15.

22. This descriptive and constructive approach is based on the key themes presented in each book of the New Testament in line with the inductive character of biblical theology.

the Pastoral Epistles, 1 and 2 Thessalonians, the Johannine Epistles, and 2 Peter and Jude. The common themes in these books are compared and synthesized.

While combining multiple approaches as highlighted above, I regard redemption as the overarching theme of the New Testament, hence the title of this book. Unarguably, the subject of the New Testament is Jesus Christ, "the pioneer and perfecter of faith" (Heb 12:2). Similarly, the "shared theology"[23] of the New Testament writers is evidently the redemptive work of Jesus whose primary mission is that "he will save his people from their sins" (Matt 1:21). And Paul sums up the gospel as "Christ died for our sins according to the Scriptures" (1 Cor 15:3). The basic idea of redemption is to buy back. Biblical redemption is atonement for human sins through the death of Jesus Christ on the cross of Calvary. The new song of the four living creatures and the twenty-four elders is, "You are worthy to take the scroll and to open its seals, because you were slain, and with your blood you purchased for God persons from every tribe and language and people and nation" (Rev 5:9; cf. 14:4). Jesus came to redeem and to heal a broken world. Lost humanity is recovered and delivered through the blood of Christ. For "by his wounds we are healed" (Isa 53:5; cf. 1 Pet 2:24). Healing is broadly used to mean renewal, restoration, and recreation. Jesus came to heal our sin-infected world. He came to heal our fractured world. Therefore, this book explores the redemptive mission of Jesus as the undergirding theological framework of the New Testament. God's redemptive mission in the world through his Son Jesus Christ is for the restoration and transformation (*metamorphosis*) of the world. He came as Messiah. Therefore, the New Testament is a testament of life, peace, hope, healing, and restoration. The New Testament announces the kingdom of light to a dark and dying world, a world burdened with the load of sin and care (Matt 11:28).

In this work, only key theological themes deemed relevant are addressed. But to provide an overview of an entire book or group, a synopsis is presented before treating the selected themes. The synopsis serves as an introduction to the chapter and summary of the book(s) under study. Because this work focuses on theology, introductory matters such as authorship, date, recipients, occasion, and provenance are not given priority except where these shed some light on the theological themes under study. The themes selected are deemed important for the universal church and especially the church in Africa. In conventional approaches, theological themes often overlooked include the Holy Spirit, power encounters, faith, discipleship, prayer, and family, among others.

---

23. Dunn, *New Testament Theology*, vii.

These themes are included in this volume for their relevance in the African context. For example, the Holy Spirit is treated under the Trinity in both the Synoptic Gospels and the Gospel of John. Similarly, power encounters are treated under the rubric redemption as dominion over evil forces and powers.

The first two chapters focus on redemptive theology and the task of theologizing in Africa. It is hoped that these chapters will serve as vistas for understanding the rest of the book as they form the bedrock upon which the entire work rests. The remaining chapters highlight the major themes in the Synoptic Gospels, the Gospel of John, the Pauline epistles, Hebrews, James, 1 Peter, 2 Peter and Jude, the epistles of John, and the book of Revelation. Each chapter of the book is concluded with questions for review and application. These questions are considered vital for a good grasp and application of each chapter.

Finally, the substance of biblical theology is the biblical text. Therefore, the author has intentionally relied on the biblical text as the primary source and guide for discussion.

1

Drums of Redemptive Theology

> Christ redeemed us from the curse of the law by becoming a curse for us, for it is written: "Cursed is everyone who is hung on a pole." He redeemed us in order that the blessing given to Abraham might come to the Gentiles through Christ Jesus, so that by faith we might receive the promise of the Spirit.
>
> Galatians 3:13–14

The Redemptive Purposes of God in History and Revelation

History is divinely driven for a purpose. According to George Eldon Ladd, "The bond that unites the Old and the New Testament is this sense of the divine in history."[1] This means both Testaments acknowledge that history does not run a course independent of the one who made the heavens and the earth. A divine hand superintends history. God has revealed himself, "and this revelation has occurred in a series of historical events."[2] Biblically, therefore, history is "the unfolding plan of God from the beginning of time."[3] A theological perspective of history sees God's redemptive purposes in the complex matrices of human history. This is known as salvation history (*Heilsgeschichte*). As Roy E. Ciampa articulates, "The history of redemption seeks to uncover the biblical authors' own understanding of the events and their significance within the unfolding

---

1. George Eldon Ladd, *A Theology of the New Testament*, rev. ed. Donald A. Hagner (Grand Rapids: Eerdmans, 1993), 21.
2. Ladd, *Theology of the New Testament*, 21.
3. Isaak, *New Testament Theology*, 36.

narrative context in which they are found."[4] Ciampa means that each biblical author interprets key events in the unfolding history of God's relationship with his creation and his people "by way of narrative-theological structures they used or assumed."[5] Theology is imbedded in biblical narratives because the authors saw God's hand in history.

And this perspective leads us to the concept of revelation. In the words of Alister E. McGrath, revelation is "making known in all its fullness" or "the total disclosure of what had hitherto been obscure or unclear."[6] That is, revelation is making known that which was unknown. The knowledge of God comes from what he has revealed of himself and his purposes in both general and special revelations. McGrath echoes the Christian belief that "God chooses to be known, and makes this possible through self-disclosure in nature and human history."[7] When we read in Genesis 1:1, "In the beginning God created the heavens and the earth," we read part of God's revelation of himself in history. He who created is the one who reveals himself.

Theologically, God's self-disclosure is understood in terms of general and special revelations. The general revelation of God is his self-disclosure in creation or nature. The psalmist declares, "The heavens declare the glory of God; the skies proclaim the work of his hands. Day after day they pour forth speech; night after night they reveal knowledge. They have no speech, they use no words; no sound is heard from them" (Ps 19:1–3). According to the psalmist, God has clearly disclosed himself in nature – in the heavens and the sky – as part of his general revelation. This means that we can gain knowledge of God by observing the natural world God has made. For God "has not left himself without testimony: He has shown kindness by giving you rain from heaven and crops in their seasons; he provides you with plenty of food and fills your hearts with joy" (Acts 14:17). But apart from the natural world, God also chose to use human reason, conscience, moral sense, and providence as part of general revelation. The point is that history always runs a course that is according to God's sovereign purposes, and especially for the redemption of human kind. In the words of Paul,

---

4. Roy E. Ciampa, "The History of Redemption," in *Central Themes in Biblical Theology: Mapping Unity in Diversity*, ed. Scott J. Hafemann and Paul R. House (Nottingham: Apollos, 2007), 254–55.

5. Ciampa, "History of Redemption," 255.

6. Alister E. McGrath, *Christian Theology: An Introduction*. 3rd ed. (Oxford: Blackwell, 2001), 200.

7. McGrath, *Christian Theology*, 200.

> The God who made the world and everything in it is the Lord of heaven and earth and does not live in temples built by human hands. And he is not served by human hands, as if he needed anything. Rather, he himself gives everyone life and breath and everything else. From one man he made all the nations, that they should inhabit the whole earth; and he marked out their appointed times in history and the boundaries of their lands. God did this so that they would seek him and perhaps reach out for him and find him, though he is not far from any one of us. "For in him we live and move and have our being." As some of your own poets have said, "We are his offspring." (Acts 17:24–28)

But God also revealed himself supernaturally. This is God's special intervention in history to make himself known, a knowledge that would not be possible through general revelation. God revealed himself in a special way through the Bible (the written word), theophanies (manifestations of God in human form such as in Gen 18:1–33), angels, prophets, visions, dreams, the Holy Spirit, and Jesus Christ. Samuel Waje Kunhiyop says, "Special revelation refers not to God's revealing of himself in nature but to his unique and personal unveiling of himself through words, acts and events, and ultimately through his personal incarnation in Jesus Christ."[8] According to Kunhiyop, this revelation is "faithfully and accurately recorded in the Scriptures."[9] Regarding Jesus who is God's perfect revelation to humanity, the writer of Hebrews says,

> In the past God spoke to our ancestors through the prophets at many times and in various ways, but in these last days he has spoken to us by his Son, whom he appointed heir of all things, and through whom he made the universe. The Son is the radiance of God's glory and the exact representation of his being, sustaining all things by his powerful word. After he had provided purification for sins, he sat down at the right hand of the Majesty in heaven. (Heb 1:1–3)

God spoke in the past. In this context, speaking is synonymous with revelation. God has now spoken by his Son. The revelation of God in Christ is "a life giving and salvation-bringing self-disclosure of God in Christ."[10] Therefore, from the Christian standpoint, Jesus is the culmination of God's redemptive

---

8. Samuel Waje Kunhiyop, *African Christian Theology* (Nairobi: Hippo, 2012), 22.
9. Kunhiyop, *African Christian Theology*, 22.
10. McGrath, *Christian Theology*, 201.

history. While natural revelation is knowledge about God, in Christ we come to know more about God and to know him personally in a redemptive way. Jesus says, "Now this is eternal life: that they may know you, the only true God, and Jesus Christ, whom you have sent" (John 17:3).

The Roots of Redemptive Theology

According to Donald Hagner, "there is, without doubt, extensive and substantial continuity between Christianity and Judaism."[11] His reasoning is that both Jesus and Paul were "intensely Jewish, as indeed is the entire NT and so too the earliest church and its theology."[12] It follows that there can be no New Testament theology without understanding the Old Testament. Whatever the New Testament says about God and his redemptive scheme for the world are imbedded in the writings of the Old Testament. Dunn makes an important observation here:

> The inexplicit character of the NT writers' beliefs in and about God helps explain why so many expositions of NT theology or the theologies of individual NT writers so often forego a section on God and jump at once into other aspects, often an analysis of the human condition. But it is imperative that a NT theology tackle this subject and make explicit the inexplicit; otherwise the rationale underpinning so many other beliefs and practices will have been lost to view.[13]

Dunn means that the New Testament writers had the Old Testament as their Bible. Their "beliefs in and about God" were clearly "inherited" and formed the integral part and framework of their theology. That framework, according to Dunn, includes God as Creator and Judge, God as one, God of Israel, God as transcendent and immanent (Spirit), angelic intermediaries, and God's wisdom/word.[14] The New Testament writers believed that history is divinely orchestrated by God, and the ultimate purpose is the salvation of humankind. As we quoted Ladd at the beginning, what unites the Old and

---

11. Donald Hagner, "How 'New' Is the New Testament? Continuity and Discontinuity Between the Old Testament (Formative Judaism) and the New Testament (Early Christianity)," *AJPS* 19, no. 2 (2016): 103.

12. Hagner, "How 'New,'" 103–4.

13. Dunn, *New Testament Theology*, 42.

14. Dunn, 42.

the New Testaments is "this sense of the divine activity in history."[15] Evidently, these concepts shaped the theology of the New Testament writers. That is, the New Testament writers did not interpret the redemptive work of Christ from *tabula rasa*.[16]

The issue is of continuity and discontinuity, meaning that the Old Testament is the foundation upon which the New rests as the New Testament regards itself as the fulfillment of the Old Testament promises.[17] Therefore according to Isaak, "NT theology must be a theology of the whole Christian Bible as well. It must be able to integrate the Hebrew Bible (OT) and the early Christian writings (NT) without falling into the trap of reading the OT only for its clues to Jesus' identity."[18] Isaak cautions against reading the Old Testament "only for its clues to Jesus' identity" or through the supersessionist ideology that the church has replaced Israel. Therefore,

> Key to understanding will be the realization that the OT sees itself as incomplete – not in the sense of lacking something, but in the sense of anticipating the day when evil is undone and God's creation purpose is finally realized. In this way, the NT theology must be able to connect with OT's vision for creation.[19]

And the OT's vision for creation is restoration. This means that the history of redemption in the New Testament is the saga of human tragedy and the hope of restoration within the salvific plan and work of God in the history of humankind and the entire creation. When the restoration comes,

> The wolf will live with the lamb,
>   the leopard will lie down with the goat,
> the calf and the lion and the yearling together;
>   and a little child will lead them.
> The cow will feed with the bear,

---

15. Ladd, *A Theology of the New Testament*, 21.

16. Latin for "scraped tablet," meaning a mind before education. However, the focus and scope of this book does not allow for further exploration of the theological frameworks highlighted by Dunn above. Also, it is presumed that most readers already possess some knowledge of the "inherited" theology of the New Testament writers – namely, some basic knowledge of the Old Testament. What we must make explicit, however, is the prophetic hope of Israel as portrayed in the Old Testament, which is treated in the theme of promise and fulfillment in the Synoptic Gospels. See pgs 59–60.

17. See Hagner, "How 'New,'" 99–107. See also Vern S. Poythress, *The Shadow of Christ in the Law of Moses* (Philipsburg: P&R, 1991).

18. Isaak, *New Testament Theology*, 17.

19. Isaak, 17.

> their young will lie down together,
> and the lion will eat straw like the ox.
> The infant will play near the cobra's den,
> and the young child put its hand into the viper's nest.
> They will neither harm nor destroy
> on all my holy mountain,
> for the earth will be full of the knowledge of the LORD
> as the waters cover the sea. (Isa 11:6–9)

To sum all of the above, the full manifestation of God's salvific purposes in Christ does not come in a vacuum. It is embedded in the history of Israel and their hope of salvation. Therefore, the redemptive work of Christ as found in the documents of the New Testament is "inherited theology."[20] And this hope of salvation is more vigorously nurtured and propagated in the prophetic writings. The prophetic hope of redemption is then the basic and most profound historical roots of redemption. For example, some events in the life of Jesus that are interpreted by New Testament writers as fulfillment of prophecy include his virgin birth, Bethlehem as the birth place of the Messiah, the flight to Egypt, John the Baptist as the forerunner of Jesus, the ministry in Galilee, and Jesus's performance of miracles, teaching in parables, and suffering, death, and resurrection.

The Biblical Canon in Redemptive History

The biblical canon is crucial as God's special revelation in redemptive history. For Protestant Christians, the biblical canon is the sixty-six books of the Bible (thirty-nine Old Testament and twenty-seven New Testament). But we are focusing on the books of the New Testament.[21] Perhaps a word about the nature of the New Testament canon is in order here. The literal meaning of canon is "reed" which is used figuratively to mean measuring rod or ruler. The rod or ruler conveys the sense of a norm or standard.[22] The books of the New Testament, like those of the Old Testament, are classified according to their

---

20. Dunn, *New Testament Theology*, 71–96.

21. The "New Testament" is so named for two reasons. First, Heb 8:13 implies a new agreement has come to replace the old. Second, Luke 22:20 indicates that something new has happened in the world. Jesus says, "This cup is the new covenant in my blood, which is poured out for you." (Compare Jer 31:31.)

22. James D. Hernando, *Dictionary of Hermeneutics: Concise Guide to Terms, Names, Methods and Expressions* (Springfield: Gospel Publishing House, 2005), 15.

message or writers. They are called canon "because they constitute the norm for Christian faith in documentary form."[23]

For easier understanding, the New Testament books are classified according to their literary types (genres)[24] and messages. In a broad sense, we have the four Gospels (Matthew, Mark, Luke, and John), the Acts of the Apostles, the letters (Romans to Jude), and the book of Revelation, which is both prophetic and apocalyptic in nature. According to R. Laird Harris,

> There has been no question among the Christian churches since early times as to which books belong in the NT. All branches of Christendom have accepted as authoritative and inspired the current 27 books. They are accepted as authoritative because they are held to be true and immediately inspired of God.[25]

The Nature of New Testament Theology

But what is theology? Geoffrey W. Bromiley says, "Strictly, theology is that which is thought and said concerning God."[26] The *Merriam-Webster Dictionary* defines theology as "the study of religious faith, practice, and experience" or the "study of God and God's relation to the world."[27] The word "theology" is a combination of two Greek words *theos* (God) and *logos* (word). The two words are simplified as the study of God.

And what is *New Testament theology*?[28] According to Leon Morris, the meaning is "far from obvious," partly due to the "different ways of using

---

23. Everett F. Harrison, *Introduction to the New Testament*, rev. ed. (Grand Rapids: Eerdmans, 1971), 97.

24. In the ancient world, all genres have basic characteristics. See Charles B. Puskas, *Introduction to the New Testament* (Peabody: Hendrickson, 1987), chs. 6–8 for a treat of the different genres from the Gospels to Revelation.

25. R. Laird Harris, "Canonicity," in *The Zondervan Pictorial Bible Dictionary*, ed. Merrill C. Tenney (Grand Rapids: Zondervan, 1963), 145.

26. Everett F. Harrison, Geoffrey W. Bromiley, and Carl. F. H. Henry, eds., *Baker's Dictionary of Theology* (Grand Rapids: Baker,1960), 518; cited in Leon Morris, *New Testament Theology* (Grand Rapids Academic Books, 1986), 10.

27. "Theology," *Merriam-Webster Dictionary* Online, https://www.merriam-webster.com/dictionary/theology.

28. We have gone beyond the arguments regarding the legitimacy of New Testament theology, as Heikki Räisänen states in *Beyond New Testament Theology: A Story and a Program* (London: SCM, 1990). One of the key issues is whether or not the New Testament authors had a "formed theology." I. Howard Marshall's response is, "Nevertheless, the difficulty of the task is not in itself an argument against the attempt to reconstruct theology from works that are not specifically theological." I. Howard Marshall, *New Testament Theology: One Gospel, Many*

theology."²⁹ One example of this complexity that Morris discusses is found in Rudolf Bultmann's *Theology of the New Testament* in which Bultmann not only sees different "theologies" of the many authors of the New Testament by designating them theology of Paul, theology of John and the like, but also "expressly differentiates the teaching of Jesus from theology."³⁰ According to Bultmann,

> *The message of Jesus* is a presupposition for the theology of the New Testament rather than a part of that theology itself. For New Testament theology consists of the unfolding of those ideas by means of which Christian faith makes sure of its own object, basis, and consequences. But Christian faith did not exist until there was a Christian kerygma; i.e., a kerygma proclaiming Jesus Christ.³¹

Bultmann means that the message of Jesus cannot be equated with theology and that we have more than one theology. So Dunn asks, "And so, should we speak of *theologies* (plural) rather than theology (singular), or does the title (NT theology) suggest a search for the shared theology of (all) the NT writers, assuming that they had such a (singular) theology"?³² Going by Geoffrey Bromiley's definition that "theology is that which is thought and said concerning God,"³³ it is not difficult to conclude that the different perspectives about God presented by the authors of the New Testament could be termed theology of the New Testament. After all, even modern authors who see distinctive theologies in the New Testament title their books *theology* (singular) of the New Testament rather than *theologies* (plural). Therefore, rather than seeing theologies in the New Testament, we see each author as an essential *contributor* to New Testament theology. Therefore, the different theological perspectives found in each book form a coherent whole as canon of the New Testament on the subject of God's redemptive purposes unfolded in the person and works of Jesus Christ the Messiah. Similarly, instead of seeing "*The message of Jesus* as presupposition for the theology of the New Testament rather than

---

Witnesses (Downers Grove: IVP Academic, 2004), 22. Those wishing to go back to Räisänen's arguments and Howard's response may do so.

29. Morris, *New Testament Theology*, 9.

30. Morris, 9.

31. Rudolf Bultmann, *Theology of the New Testament*, trans. Kendrick Grobel (New York: Scribner, 1951), 3, emphasis original.

32. Dunn, *New Testament Theology*, vii, emphasis original. See also Gerhard Hasel, *New Testament Theology: Basic Issues in the Current Debate* (Grand Rapids: Eerdmans, 1978), 140–41.

33. Harrison, Bromiley, and Henry, eds., *Baker's Dictionary of Theology*, 518; cited in Morris, *New Testament Theology*, 10.

a part of that theology itself" according to Bultmann, it is more reasonable to regard the Gospels as theological narratives.

The second challenge in doing New Testament theology has to do with methodology or the "mismatch of method and goals."[34] Leon Morris says, "It seems that almost every New Testament theologian sees his task differently from the way it appears to other practitioners of the art."[35] And numerous volumes interacted with for this work affirm the observation made between 1967 and 1976 that no two authors "agree on the nature, function, method and scope of NT theology."[36] Even with a "mismatch of methods and goals," it is still hoped that my "liberty" to follow my own method remains true to the documents of the New Testament and relevant for African readers.

The New Testament is the continuation of the "redemptive-historical storyline of Scripture,"[37] namely, the account of God's salvific purposes as revealed in his dealings with the human race. As one author put it succinctly,

> As a discipline, NT theology is one segment of the larger enterprise called Biblical theology, which seeks to trace the origins and growth of Biblical teaching and to set forth the various types of doctrine apparent in the different writers. New Testament theology and Biblical theology, accordingly, could be classed among the traditional departments of theology as historical theology; though at the same time they belong essentially to the department of exegetical theology, for their primary task is to furnish a correct grammatico-historical explanation of the teaching of each Biblical writer and to clarify as far as possible the genesis and development of each distinct concept in the canonical Scriptures.[38]

And it is important for us to clarify from the onset that "New Testament Theology is not different from the theology in the whole of Scripture, but rather it emphasizes those characteristics that are prominent in the writings of the New Testament. The same goes for the theologies of Paul, John, etc."[39]

---

34. See editor's preface on the back cover of A. K. M Adam, *Making Sense of New Testament Theology: "Modern" Problems and Prospects*, Studies in American Biblical Hermeneutics 11 (Macon: Mercer University Press, 1995).

35. Morris, *New Testament Theology*, 9–10.

36. Morris, 10; citing Hasel, *New Testament Theology*, 9–10.

37. G. K. Beale, *A New Testament Biblical Theology: The Unfolding of the Old Testament in the New* (Grand Rapids: Baker Academic, 2011), xii.

38. Reformed Books Online, "New Testament Theology," https://reformedbooksonline.com/new-testament-theology/.

39. Reformed Books Online, "New Testament Theology."

New Testament biblical theology is the presentation of the whole counsel of God as represented by the twenty-seven books of the New Testament. Theology of the New Testament is Christocentric theology that focuses on God's salvific purposes for the world through Christ's redemptive death. The goal of redemption is the healing and transformation of creation and humanity in particular. In other words, the death and resurrection of Jesus are the remedy for the tragedy of the fall and its effects (Gen 3). How is that remedy portrayed in the Synoptic Gospels, Johannine literature, Acts of the Apostles, Pauline letters, Hebrews, and general epistles? And how does the message of each book speak to the situation of African Christians and society? These are some of the motivating questions for writing this book. Meanwhile, we will focus on the quest for the historical Jesus because no New Testament studies can ignore this quest.

The Quest for the Historical Jesus and Redemption

> Popular culture always picks and chooses from the cafeteria of the philosophers' recommendations.
>
> Charles Colson[40]
>
> Anyone who doesn't know how to fasten a seat belt is either an idiot or an alien.
>
> Bruce N. Fisk[41]

We are neither idiots nor aliens (although many students of the Bible in Africa are still aliens in the area of biblical criticism). Therefore, I ask that we fasten our seat belts here because we have entered turbulent terrain. It is permissible, and even desirable, that once in a while we leave our "comfortable matrix" and thrust ourselves "into the harsh world of biblical criticism," to use the words of Fisk.[42] The reason for daring to enter this theological jungle is that the influence of biblical criticism, especially the quest for the historical Jesus, is enormous for faith and practice. The quest borders on the "rediscovery

---

40. Charles Colson, *The Good Life: Seeking Purpose, Meaning, and Truth in Your Life* (Wheaton: Tyndale House, 2005), 110.

41. Bruce N. Fisk, *A Hitchhiker's Guide to Jesus: Reading the Gospels on the Ground* (Grand Rapids: Baker Academic, 2011), 14.

42. Fisk, *Hitchhiker's Guide to Jesus*, 15.

of Jesus"[43] regarding the historicity and authenticity of the gospel narratives. Did Jesus really exist? And if he actually did, is he the one portrayed in the Gospels and other New Testament writings? The simple question is, "Can the biographies of Jesus be trusted?"[44] There are so many publications now about the life of Jesus that, in the words of Marshall, "Jesus has found his way onto the station bookstall, even though there is a strange reluctance on the part of Western European man to enter his church."[45] Put in simple terms, people on the street in Europe are willing to grab a copy of a book about the life of Jesus, but the same people are not interested in entering a church!

The old quest for the historical Jesus could be traced back to the history of religions school of thought or "the critical reconstruction of the life of Jesus."[46] According to Dunn, "Up until the nineteenth century the four Gospels had been considered equally valid sources for historical information about Jesus. By harmonizing the different accounts and weaving them together a single picture could be formed. But now intensive study led to a revised estimate."[47] The results of this "revised estimate" are what we now consider the quest for the historical Jesus. The quest seeks to establish the reliability or otherwise of the Gospels.

Bultmann is one of the theologians who popularized the quest for the historical Jesus. By his approach to biblical theology from existentialist philosophy, he maintained that the goal of New Testament theology is self-actualization. He separated the Jesus of faith from the Jesus of history. Unlike those who maintained the historical model in doing New Testament theology, Bultmann doubted the use of history in regard to matters of faith. According to Isaak, for Bultmann valuable theological experience must transcend history, "where people self-actualize in spite of their miserable historical situation. What *is* historical is each person's responsibility to rise above her or his situation, not whether this or that story of Jesus really happened as narrated

---

43. See I. Howard Marshall, *I Believe in the Historical Jesus* (Grand Rapids: Eerdmans, 1977), ch. 1.

44. Lee Strobel, *The Case for Christ: A Journalist's Personal Investigation of the Evidence for Jesus* (Grand Rapids: Zondervan, 2016), 27.

45. Marshall, *I Believe*, 11.

46. Dunn, *New Testament Theology*, 39. For a comprehensive treatment of the quest for the historical Jesus, see N. T. Wright, *Jesus and the Victory of God*, vol. 2: *Christian Origins and the Question of God* (London: SPCK, 1996), chs. 1–3. Treated in these chapters are the first quest, the renewed quest represented by the Jesus Seminar, and the "third" quest.

47. Dunn, *New Testament Theology*, 39.

in the NT."[48] This means that the authenticity of the narratives of the Gospels is not an issue because we cannot be sure of their historicity. Bultmann says, "I do indeed think that we can know *almost nothing* concerning the life and personality of Jesus, since the early Christian sources show no interest in either, are moreover fragmentary and often legendary; and other sources about Jesus do not exist."[49] Moreover, Bultmann says, "I am personally of the opinion that Jesus did not believe himself to be the Messiah, but I do not imagine that this opinion gives me a clearer picture of his personality."[50] This means that Bultmann did not believe that the Gospel writers were interested in facts, therefore their writings are virtually unhistorical. This situation is made worst by lack of independent sources or witnesses that could repudiate or substantiate the claims of the writers of the Gospels. Similarly, Jesus did not claim to be the Messiah, according to Bultmann's opinion.

This opinion takes us to the roots. The historical-critical lenses of reading the Bible developed during the Enlightenment period with its emphasis on science and reason.[51] Using scientific and historical methods of inquiry, the historical-critical practitioners established four major tools for scrutinizing the historicity of the Gospel narratives. The earliest tools include *source criticism, form criticism, textual criticism,* and *redaction criticism.* Source criticism is the method of Gospel criticism that raises the question of sources. What were the literary (written) sources or oral traditions used by the Gospel writers? Or were there literal sources available from which the Gospel writers derived their materials? Form critics ask, what form did the Gospel stories take before they were written down? They presume that for a considerably long period of oral tradition, the gospel message passed down by word of mouth from the disciples of Jesus to the early church and circulated as isolated units of sayings. As time went by, these oral traditions went through natural selection according to the *Sitz im Leben* (life setting) of the early church communities. Redaction criticism (German *Redaktionsgeschichte*, meaning "editing history") is concern with the editorial work of the Gospel writers (or evangelists). The assumption is that the Gospel writers edited the stories they received as those stories suited their own purposes or congregations. Textual critics compare variations in extant original

---

48. Isaak, *New Testament Theology*, 12, emphasis original.

49. Rudolf Bultmann, *Jesus and the Word* (New York: Charles Scribner's Sons, 1958), 8, emphasis added.

50. Bultmann, *Jesus and the Word*, 9.

51. See Bitrus A. Sarma, *Reading the Bible in Africa: Understanding and Applying the Message* (Jos, Nigeria: Yakson, 2015), 64–68.

manuscripts to figure out which reading is probably the original or closer to the original.[52] The implication of these criticisms is that there is room for skepticism about the authenticity of the documents we call the New Testament.

Building on all of the above, Bultmann developed the concept of *demythologizing* in which the New Testament reader is asked to peel away the ancient mythological layers that wrap the Gospels "so that they too can make courageous decisions of faith, just as the first followers of Jesus did."[53] In other words, the early Christians did not believe in what actually happened; their faith rose above their wretched experiences. As absurd as that might sound, that is courageous faith – believing the unreal!

It is important to remember that disbelief about the reliability of the Gospel narratives regarding the life of Jesus gave rise to the quest for the historical Jesus. While many scholars, covering a wide spectrum of opinions contributed to the debate, Bultmann, who is rated as "probably the most influential New Testament scholar of the twentieth century,"[54] stretched the search almost to its elastic limits by claiming that we can know almost nothing regarding the life of Christ.

In recent history, a revival of the quest for the historical Jesus began with Robert Funk. In 1985, Funk, a New Testament scholar, led the way in what is today known as the Jesus Seminar. The mission of Funk was

> to rewrite the story of Jesus. This new story would be stripped of its biblical moorings: a God who creates the universe and who brings all things to conclusion at some time in the future. Moreover, no longer would the story of Jesus be tied to the idea of divine revelation.[55]

According to Funk,

> What we need is a new fiction that takes as its starting point the central event in the Judeo-Christian drama [Jesus] and reconciles that middle with a new story that reaches beyond old beginnings and endings [creation and eschatology]. In sum, we need a new narrative of Jesus, a new gospel, if you will, that places Jesus

---

52. See Harold J. Greenlee, *Introduction to New Testament Textual Criticism*, rev. ed. (Peabody: Hendrickson, 1995).

53. Isaak, *New Testament Theology*, 12.

54. Marshall, *I Believe*, 12.

55. See Mark D. Roberts "The Birth of Jesus: Hype or History?" Mark D. Roberts (blog) 2011. http://www.patheos.com/blogs/markdroberts/series/the-birth-of-jesus-hype-or-history/. http://www.patheos.com/blogs/markdroberts/series/the-birth-of-jesus-hype-or-history/.

differently in the grand scheme, the epic story. Not any fiction will do.... The fiction of Revelation keeps many common folk in bondage to ignorance and fear. We require a new, liberating fiction, one that squares with the best knowledge we can now accumulate and one that transcends self-serving ideologies.[56]

Evidently, Funk presupposed that the idea of divine revelation is one of the "biblical moorings" that must be rejected because it is a "fiction." Instead, Funk generates a new fiction, "one that squares with the best knowledge we can now accumulate and one that transcends self-serving ideologies." The problem is whether Funk's fiction actually "transcends self-serving ideologies." And that problem comes to light when the method of determining the historicity of the deeds and sayings of Jesus at the Jesus Seminar was by *majority votes* cast with colored beads by the participants. Can we discover the historical Jesus through the democratic fashion of majority votes?

In their search for the historical Jesus, some scholars conclude that Jesus was "ultimately the seditious 'King of the Jews' whose promise of liberation from Rome went unfulfilled in his brief life time."[57] But the charge is unwarranted. First, the Gospels would refute that claim because Jesus asked his arresters, "Am I leading a rebellion?" (Matt 26:55; Mark 14:48; Luke 22:52). Second, according to Aslan, Jesus promised liberation of the Jews from Rome. Again, this is not the testimony of the Gospels as Jesus repeatedly shows that his kingdom is not of this world. The Gospels repeatedly portray him as savior from sins (Matt 1:21; Mark 10:45; Luke 19:10). Aslan is right that the central theme of Jesus's message in his brief three-year ministry is the promise of the kingdom. "Practically everything Jesus said or did in the gospels served the function of publicly proclaiming the Kingdom's coming."[58] But as for Aslan's equation of this kingdom with usurping the Roman government and restoring the kingdom of Israel, nothing could be further from the truth. We must add that Jesus not only spoke about the kingdom of God as present but as future as well.[59]

Similarly, Aslan believes it was the early Christian church that "preferred to promulgate an image of Jesus as a peaceful spiritual leader rather than a

---

56. Robert Funk, opening remarks in the first Jesus Seminar, 1985, quoted in Roberts "Birth of Jesus."

57. Reza Aslan, *Zealot: The Life and Times of Jesus of Nazareth* (New York: Random House, 2013), front flap.

58. Aslan, *Zealot*, 116.

59. Barry D. Smith, *Jesus' Twofold Teaching about the Kingdom of God*, New Testament Monograph, 24, ed. Stanley E. Porter (Sheffield: Sheffield Phoenix Press, 2009).

Drums of Redemptive Theology 23

politically conscious revolutionary."[60] Admittedly, Jesus said he did not come to bring peace on earth but division (Luke 12:51). But that statement must be understood from the context and what his entire life portrayed. If the followers of Jesus were to be identified as peacemakers (Matt 5:9), and if he asked for forgiveness for his executors (Luke 23:34), what image would characterize him?[61]

Contrary to popular opinions, we must admit, as Peter Stuhlmacher rightly points out, that the main source of our knowledge of Jesus Christ is the Gospels. "Therefore, a reconstruction of Jesus' work will depend on the question of how the tradition in the Gospels is to be judged."[62] Stuhlmacher gives three errors to avoid in describing the preaching of Jesus. The first error is reconstructing "the preaching of Jesus by autonomously choosing and arbitrarily arranging the sources."[63] Stuhlmacher reiterates that the main source for understanding Jesus is the four Gospels. But many scholars choose the apocryphal Gospels from the second century which "offer only secondary enlargements on and additions to the Gospel tradition."[64] The caution is that there are no sufficient reports about Jesus outside of the Gospels. So "sparse" sources should be used with care. The point is that biblical theology of the New Testament must rely on the Gospels.

The second error to be avoided is using a reconstructed picture of the so-called historical Jesus created by a hypothetical scientific method and presenting such as normative "regarding Jesus' life and work."[65] The third error, according to Stuhlmacher, is

> to consider the testimony of the Synoptic Gospels concerning the historically unique work of Jesus to be Christologically less significant than that of the Gospel of John or the apostolic letters. This attitude fails to recognize that it is these very Synoptic Gospels which invite us to think of God's work of salvation in and through

---

60. Aslan, *Zealot*, front flap.

61. Scholars who want to discredit the Gospels ignore all of the traditional understandings of the text and opt for "novel" meanings and make bizarre claims. They assert that the disciples or rather the early church put words in Jesus's mouth. A careful reading of these theologians reveals, however, that they are the ones who put words in the mouth of Jesus's disciples and the early church because they choose to ignore all the testimony of the early church and follow their own methods of inquiry, even if those methods include casting ballots to figure out what Jesus had really said.

62. Peter Stuhlmacher, *How to Do Biblical Theology* (Allison Park: Pickwick, 1995), 18.

63. Stuhlmacher, *How to Do Biblical Theology*, 17.

64. Stuhlmacher, 17.

65. Stuhlmacher, 17.

Christ in a historically concrete way and to avoid reflecting upon this work of God only in dogmatic abstractions.[66]

And what are the implications of the quest for the historical Jesus for African biblical theology and African Christianity in general? Most African universities and theological institutions still live in the past. Instead of being at the cutting age, they tend to mimic Western scholarship uncritically. To this effect, Hegalian-Bultmannian approaches to biblical theology are still in vogue in some African universities and seminaries. It is not uncommon to hear a professor deliver lectures about JEDP or Q source as though these have passed the hypothetical stages and become verifiable realities. This kind of scholarship is sure to derail African scholarship and the church in Africa. If doing scholarship from the standpoint of skepticism, unbelief, and rejection of revelation did not save the Western world, will it save Africa?

We conclude here that a Jesus reconfigured through the lenses of twentieth or twenty-first century scholars, whatever the tools used and however noble the intentions, cannot give us a better historical Jesus than the one "constructed" by the eyewitnesses[67] and their successors. African scholars cannot afford to theologize on the shaky foundations of unbelief.[68]

Questions for Review and Application

1. What are the roots of redemptive theology?
2. What is the nature of New Testament Theology?
3. What is the origin of the quest for the historical Jesus?
4. How does the quest for the historical Jesus strengthen faith in Jesus?
5. How does the quest for the historical Jesus weaken faith in Jesus?
6. Why must African scholars understand and respond appropriately on issues regarding the quest for the historical Jesus?
7. How has this chapter increased your faith in the historical Jesus?

---

66. Stuhlmacher, 17–18.

67. Richard Bauckham argues persuasively that the Gospels are eyewitness accounts of the life and ministry of Jesus. See Richard Bauckham, *Jesus and the Eye Witnesses: The Gospels as Eyewitness Testimony* (Grand Rapids: Eerdmans, 2006).

68. *The Da Vinci Code* and the Jesus Seminar, popularized in recent times in print and media, are results of the new search for the historical Jesus and are designed to erode faith in the Jesus of the Gospels. Although not documented, it is not hard to imagine those whose faith has diminished as a result of *The Da Vinci Code* and the Jesus Seminar.

2

Drums of Theological Horizons in Africa

A trajectory of any discipline is important because the present is gauged by the past, and the future is predicted based on the past and the present. In other words, both progress and regress are measured through proper retrospection.

A Brief History of Biblical Theology

Historically, though Christians did theology from the early church through the Middle Ages,[1] Wolfgang J. Christmann (1597–1631) first used the term "biblical theology" in print in 1629.[2] But the emerging discipline was established through the publication in 1643 of *Theologia biblica* by Henricus à Diest.[3] Pioneers of biblical theology "collated and organized" Bible verses around some themes or topics in support of certain traditional doctrines of the church. They did this by gathering verses from both the Old and New Testaments to back the theme under study, for example the Holy Spirit. They would usually devote a chapter to the Old Testament and another to the New Testament. To support the doctrine under study, they cited the contributions of "significant figures" in the history of the church. Then they concluded their work by applying the

---

1. The medieval period classified as the early and late Middle Ages cannot be dated with precision. Broadly speaking, it is a period between the fifth and the fifteenth centuries, that is, from the fall of the Western Roman Empire to the Renaissance and the Age of Discovery. But some begin counting the Middle Ages from AD 284.
2. Isaak, *New Testament Theology*, 1.
3. Isaak, 1.

theology to contemporary church life.[4] What guided the discourse on biblical theology in this era was the traditional doctrines of the Christian dogmas or creeds.[5] According to Ladd, biblical study in the Middle Ages "was completely subordinated to ecclesiastical dogma."[6] This means that biblical theology was never pursued as a separate discipline from systematic theology. The theology of the Bible was used in support of church traditions. The concern was, "Not the Bible alone, historically understood, but the Bible as interpreted by church tradition was the source of dogmatic theology."[7]

But the Reformers had a different approach to the Bible. They saw dogmatic theology as unbiblical and believed that theology "must be founded on the Bible alone."[8] According to the Reformers, dogmatic theology must be "the systematic formulation of the teachings of the Bible."[9] That means going back to the original languages and using a grammatical-historical approach in determining the meaning of the text. Allegorical interpretation was discarded in favor of the literal sense of the Bible.[10] Scripture alone (*Sola Scriptura*) must be the yardstick for doing Christian theology.

The pietistic movement in Germany was a reaction to what they perceived as the "scholastic and dry" theological enterprise, "serving the purposes of doctrine alone."[11] Philip J. Spener (1635–1707) spearheaded the pietistic quest and promoted the idea that biblical theology ought to nurture "the individual lives of believers." And "his basic criterion for sound theology was personal significance"[12] as against the "arid quality of rationalism."[13] Those who followed Spener's method launched a home Bible study movement that spread throughout Germany among Reformation churches. This period is known in church history as German Romanticism and was a "reaction against the aridity of reason" of the Enlightenment which focused on human reason,[14] "complimented by an emphasis upon epistemological significance of human

---

4. Isaak, 1.
5. Isaak, 1–2.
6. Ladd, *Theology of the New Testament*, 1.
7. Ladd, 1.
8. Ladd, 1.
9. Ladd, 1.
10. Ladd, 2.
11. Isaak, *New Testament Theology*, 2.
12. Isaak, 2.
13. McGrath, *Christian Theology*, 96.
14. For more on the Enlightenment, see Bitrus A. Sarma, *Reading the Bible in Africa* (Jos, Nigeria: Yakson, 2014), chapter 6.

feelings and emotions."[15] Thus, "Romanticism retained the emphasis upon the individual, but supplanted a concern with reason by a new interest in the imagination and personal feeling."[16]

Another reactionary movement against dogmatic approaches was rationalistic in nature. This movement was in the eighteenth century, still in Germany, and led by scholars like Johann P. Gabler (1753–1826).[17] The argument of the rationalists was that biblical theology is not to be pursued in the service of dogma. Unlike Spener, the concern of the rationalists was not for the personal significance of the biblical text. Rather, they "argued that science should be the determining criterion for sound theology."[18] Gabler saw human reason as a sufficient guide to "determine the *universal* truths from the biblical narrative and these could be and should be separated from the time-bound *particularities* of the ancient Near Eastern culture out of which the Bible emerged. The resultant truth, distilled from the raw material, was real biblical theology."[19] Gabler delivered a famous speech in 1787 at the University of Aldorf in which he argued for a complete separation between biblical theology – which he saw as primarily descriptive, historical, and scientific – from dogmatic theology, "that which was prescriptive, religious, and churchly."[20] Gabler's proposal eventually put an "iron curtain" between biblical theology and doctrinal theology.[21] The result was that biblical theology was separated from the church and pursued in the universities.[22]

Isaak describes how, by the nineteenth century, especially in academia, the history of religion (*Religionsgeschichte*) approach to biblical theology dominated the scene. More and more scholars wrote Old and New Testament theology from historical perspectives. Their concerns centered on the development of Israel's religion or the historical development of early Christianity. Typical questions included Israel's concept of God in comparison to her pagan neighbors; the development of the concept of monotheism in Israel; the settlement of Canaan; and sources of the Old Testament books we have today,

---

15. McGrath, *Christian Theology*, 98.
16. McGrath, 98.
17. Isaak, 2.
18. Isaak, *New Testament Theology*, 2.
19. Isaak, 2, emphasis original.
20. Isaak, 2.
21. Isaak, 3.
22. Isaak, 3.

among others.[23] This purely historical quest gave rise to the separation of the Old Testament from the New Testament such that "the OT prophets were allowed to speak for themselves, without the NT adding anything to them."[24] Similarly, New Testament scholars focused on the historical development of Christianity. The questions raised by scholars in this period included how Jesus came to understand his mission; when he came to think of himself as the Messiah; the nature of Paul's struggle with Judean and Hellenistic Judaism; the formation of the Christian canon and orthodoxy; and the sources behind the New Testament books.[25]

While this historical quest had some benefits, theological issues were largely ignored. The focus was more on the development of religion as a social phenomenon "within a historical model of cause and effect."[26] The heyday of this period was in the 1950s in the works of Gerhard von Rad, who majored on the Old Testament, and Rudolf Bultmann, who majored on the New Testament.[27]

According to Isaak, conservative scholars wrote biblical theology in this period as well, but they tended to widen the existing gap and tension between dogmatics and the historical approach. Those who pursued biblical theology in academia saw their task as merely a descriptive discipline

> primarily interested in how humanity developed and articulated its thinking about God. Dogmatic theology, on the other hand, came to be associated with those in churchly institutions, who had much less interest in historical questions. For these scholars, theology was a confessional or normative discipline, setting out how God is to be known and worshipped by human beings.[28]

This was the "crisis of Biblical Theology," in the words of Brevard S. Childs in 1970, describing the wedge between theological and historical concerns in doing biblical theology.[29] All of this history leads us to the relevance of New Testament theology in Africa.

---

23. Isaak, 3.
24. Isaak, 3.
25. Isaak, 3.
26. Isaak, 3.
27. Isaak, 4.
28. Isaak, 4.
29. Isaak, 4.

The Need for New Testament Biblical Theology in Africa

As highlighted in the introduction, there is a growing need for the right interpretation and application of the normative word of God among people groups all over the world. This means that "theology is never done in a cultural vacuum."[30] The one faith we profess, as Amos Yong puts it succinctly, is expressed in "changing contexts and forms."[31] This is true for the church in Africa. In 1994, Harvey J. Sindima wrote, "The challenge that indigenous Christianity has taken very seriously is to make Christianity authentically African. The process involves deep theological reflection."[32] This deep reflection has been ongoing. Emmanuel A. Obeng said that contextualization of the Christian message in Africa has been the concern of African Christianity during the last few decades. "This has led to what is known as African Christian Theology."[33] Many African scholars have taken the challenge to write a theology that is African. These have, however, tended toward the delineation of numerous theological issues in Africa.[34] Although this approach has some merits, most of these authors seem to address the current theological issues without biblical grounding. Biblical theology engages issues from a biblical standpoint. Biblical theology allows the Bible to speak rather than theological discourse that tends to focus on issues from philosophical, psychological, sociological, anthropological, or political perspectives. As Obeng well observes, there are "few substantial works on biblical studies."[35] Unfortunately, the few scholars who have attempted interpreting the New Testament in Africa seem to focus on methods rather than the actual content of the New Testament.[36] Although methods are primary, they do not furnish the reader with the actual content of the New Testament.

---

30. Emiola Nihinlola, *Theology Under the Mango Tree: A Handbook of African Christian Theology* (Ikeja, Lagos: Fine Print & Manufacturing, 2013), 15.

31. Amos Yong, *Renewing Christian Theology: Systematics for a Global Christianity* (Waco, : Baylor University Press, 2014), 7.

32. Harvey J. Sindima, *Drums of Redemption: An Introduction to African Christianity* (Westport: Greenwood, 1994), 153.

33. Emmanuel A. Obeng, "Emerging Concerns for Biblical Scholarship in Ghana," in *Interpreting the New Testament in Africa*, ed. Mary N. Getui, Tinyiko Maluleke, and Justin Ukpong (Nairobi: Action, 2001), 35.

34. Examples include Samuel Ngwewa, Mark Shaw, and Tite Tienou, eds., *Issues in African Christian Theology* (Nairobi/Kampala/Dar es Salaam: East African Educational Publishers, 1998); Kunhiyop, *African Christian Theology*; Bénézet Bujo, *African Theology in Its Social Context*, trans. John O'Donovan (Nairobi: Paulines Publications Africa, 1992); and K. Gordon Molyneux, *African Christian Theology: The Quest for Selfhood* (San Francisco: Mellen Research University Press, 1993).

35. Obeng, "Emerging Concerns," 35.

36. See Getui, Maluleke, and Ukpong, eds., *Interpreting the New Testament*.

For this reason, there remains a dearth of works done in biblical theology of the New Testament from an African perspective. This work is an attempt to fill in this lacuna.

While we admit that, "Biblical theology is primarily a descriptive discipline,"[37] there is a need to explain that theology from the African context. For example, how does Paul's concept of the "new Adam" as the redeemed and united body of Christ[38] affect our understanding of kinship and ethnicity? If God has chosen us *in Christ*[39] "before the creation of the world" (Eph 1:4), how does that influence our racial and tribal inclinations? Therefore, this work is an attempt to apply the New Testament to the great spiritual needs of our continent. From a biblical standpoint, Christians in Africa must carry on the incarnational ministry of Jesus Christ for the healing of our world which Mark Labberton well describes as "confused, violent and capricious."[40]

Basic Presuppositions for Biblical Theology in Africa

If the center of gravity of Christianity has shifted from Europe and the West to Latin America, sub-Saharan Africa, "and other parts of the southern continents," as Andrew F. Walls said about two decades ago, "This means that Third World Theology is now likely to be the representative Christian theology."[41] What will that representative Christian theology represent? This section is aimed at articulating the basic presupposition for theologizing in Africa. But I would like to begin with the provocative words of Screwtape in *The Screwtape Letters* by C. S. Lewis.[42]

---

37. Ladd, *Theology of the New Testament*, 20.

38. See for example, L. J. Kreitzer, "Adam and Christ," in *Dictionary of Paul and His Letters*, ed. Gerald F. Hawthorne, Ralph P. Martin, and Daniel G. Reid (Downers Grove: InterVarsity, 1993), 9–15.

39. Thomas R. Schreiner well says, "One of the most significant elements of Paul's Christology is his teaching about being 'in Christ.'" *New Testament Theology: Magnifying God in Christ* (Nottingham: Apollos, 2008), 314.

40. Mark Labberton, *The Dangerous Act of Worship: Living God's Call to Justice* (Downers Grove: InterVarsity, 2007), 56.

41. Andrew F. Walls, *The Missionary Movement in Christian History: Studies in the Transmission of Faith* (Maryknoll: Orbis, 1996; reprint, 2009), 9–10.

42. In a fictional novel written in the form of a letter, C. S. Lewis uses plots and characters to address important theological issues. The satirical language is aimed at spurring Christians to serious thinking and actions. In this letter, Screwtape is Satan himself. His nephew is Wormwood. Screwtape speaks about what he would do to divert the attention of Christians from the main issues of the Christian faith.

My Dear Wormwood,

The real trouble about the set your patient is living in is that it is *merely* Christian. They all have individual interests, of course, but the bond remains mere Christianity. What we want, if men become Christians at all, is to keep them in the state of mind I call "Christianity And." You know – Christianity and the Crisis, Christianity and the New Psychology, . . . If they must be Christians let them at least be Christians with a difference. Substitute for the faith itself some Fashion with a Christian coloring. . . .

But the greatest triumph of all is to elevate this horror of the Same Old Thing into a philosophy so that nonsense in the intellect may reinforce corruption in the will. It is here that the general Evolutionary or Historical character of modern European thought (partly our work) comes in so useful. The Enemy [God, in Screwtape's reckoning] loves platitudes. Of a proposed course of action He wants men, so far as I can see, to ask very simple questions; is it righteous? is it prudent? is it possible? Now if we can keep men asking "Is it in accordance with the general movement of our time? Is it progressive or reactionary? Is it the way that History is going?" they will neglect the relevant questions. . . . As a result, while their minds are buzzing in this vacuum, we have the better chance to slip in and bend them to the action *we* have decided on.

Your affectionate uncle

Screwtape[43]

If Screwtape were writing to his nephew Wormwood in an African context, the kind of Christianity he would wish is Christianity and African traditional religion – a syncretic kind of faith. The aim is to erode faith in Christ and to promote reliance on other sources in addition to Christ for salvation and protection.

Similarly, a dominant feature of scholarship is that "nonsense in the intellect," in the words of Screwtape, has reinforced "corruption in the will" such that the questions theologians wrestle with border on the "general movement of our time" rather than the simple questions "is it righteous? is it prudent? is it possible?" As scholars wrestle in their vacuum, Screwtape and his nephew

---

43. C. S. Lewis, *The Screwtape Letters* (New York: Macmillan, 1961), 126–30; cited in John MacArthur, Jr., *Our Sufficiency Is in Christ: Three Deadly Influences that Undermine Your Spiritual Life* (Dallas: Word, 1991), 5–17.

Wormwood "have the better chance to slip in and bend them" to the action they have decided on, namely eroding their faith. But for biblical theology to take roots and flourish in Africa, certain presuppositions are foundational.

Presuppositions are the beliefs or assumptions we live with and that color the way we interpret the world around us.[44] Presuppositions are primary because they tend to determine the course of our lives. There are presuppositions that have shaped the course of history even when they have not been proven. For example in New Testament studies, the majority of scholars believe in Markan priority and the Q source even when the "evidences" remain hypothetical. The number of volumes that have appeared to defend the Markan priority and the existence of the Q source are incredible. To demonstrate that "established" premises could have been built on sand, recent studies by a research team unravel another mystery – that Mark made use of Matthew and Luke![45]

The following proposals are hoped to serve as guardrails for theologizing in Africa.

Belief in the Inspired and Infallible Word of God

African biblical theology must be grounded on the fact that the Bible is the inspired and infallible word of God. Although the writings of the New Testament "differ from one another in literary genre, and the individual genres – Gospels, letters and apocalypses – are notoriously hard to define in terms of their characteristics,"[46] God speaks to us through them all. To remain true to Scripture, we must affirm that "All Scripture is God-breathed and is useful for teaching, rebuking, correcting and training in righteousness, so that the servant of God may be thoroughly equipped for every good work" (2 Tim 3:16–17). Similarly, the apostle Peter wrote, "Above all, you must understand that no prophecy of Scripture came about by the prophet's own interpretation of things. For prophecy never had its origin in the human will, but prophets,

---

44. According to Norman Perrin, modern hermeneutical discussion highlights the influence of presuppositions on exegesis. This means that the exegete's presuppositions color his or her exegesis. See Norman Perrin, *Parable and Gospel*, ed. K. C. Hanson (Minneapolis: Fortress, 2003), 35.

45. See David B. Peabody, Lamar Cope, and Allan J. McNicol, eds., *One Gospel from Two: Mark's Use of Matthew and Luke, A Demonstration by the Research Team of the International Institute for Renewal of Gospel Studies* (New York: Trinity Press International, 2002). This research examines and rejects the long held view that Mark and Q were the sources for the Gospels of Matthew and Luke. Instead, it is Mark who derived his materials from both Matthew and Luke. Who knows what research will reveal in the next few years?

46. Marshall, *New Testament Theology*, 21.

though human, spoke from God as they were carried along by the Holy Spirit" (2 Pet 1:20–21). Liberal theology has eroded the faith of both believers and unbelievers in the God of the Bible.[47] But no biblical theology that takes seriously the biblical narrative, especially the New Testament witness, will undermine or ignore the place of the Holy Spirit in guiding the writers of the Bible.

Likewise, those who believe the inspired and infallible word of God will let the Bible speak on issues rather than human philosophies that are peddled as the word of God. It is the Bible that sheds light on issues and exposes error. To do otherwise is to cease to do biblical theology in the right mode.

Belief in the Holy Spirit

Correct grammatical-historical interpretation of the Bible does not preclude the role of the Holy Spirit. The Holy Spirit is the author of the Bible (2 Tim 3:16–17). As we engage in the interpretation of the Bible, we must remember the words of the apostle Paul,

> What we have received is not the spirit of the world, but the Spirit who is from God, so that we may understand what God has freely given us. This is what we speak, not in words taught us by human wisdom but in words taught by the Spirit, explaining spiritual realities with Spirit-taught words. The person without the Spirit does not accept the things that come from the Spirit of God but considers them foolishness, and cannot understand them because they are discerned only through the Spirit. The person with the Spirit makes judgments about all things, but such a person is not subject to merely human judgments, for,
>
> "Who has known the mind of the Lord
>   so as to instruct him?" (1 Cor 2:12–16)

If the Bible is "spiritually discerned," is it possible to interpret the Bible correctly without the leading of the same Spirit?

---

47. See J. Gresham Machen, *Christianity and Liberalism* (Grand Rapids: Eerdmans, 1923; reprint, 2002). But the gap between liberalism and evangelicalism is narrowing too fast today as too many so-called evangelicals wear liberal garments for recognition and acceptance. The trouble is that the evangelicals never seem to be fully accepted in the camp of the liberals until they are prepared to renounce their evangelical heritage altogether. But even with that, these prodigals, unlike the one in Jesus's parable, never return to their father.

Belief in God's Existence and Sustenance of the Created Universe

Commenting on the "megatrend" of subjectivism in the postmodern world, Millard J. Erickson says, "In a sense Christianity, and specifically Christian theology, is or should be a counterculture."[48] Aspects of the subjectivism of postmodernism, according to Erickson, include rejection of foundationalism, rejection of realism, and adoration of pluralism,[49] pragmatism,[50] interpretative imagination, and "broader manifestations of irrationalism."[51] An aspect of foundationalism rejected by postmodernism is the idea of a transcendent God and "all metanarratives" because "postmodernism exposes metanarratives as projects of power and dominion."[52] But African theological enterprise must be grounded in unshakable faith in the living God, both transcendent and immanent. "For this is what the high and lofty One says – he who lives forever, whose name is holy: 'I live in a high and holy place, but also with the one who is contrite and lowly in spirit, to revive the spirit of the lowly and to revive the heart of the contrite'" (Isa 57:15). Why would it be thought necessary to assert this? The elevation of reason above faith, beginning from the Enlightenment, is responsible for the current situation whereby some scholars treat the Bible like any other human literature. And the outcome is perilous. Faith in God and his word is eroded. But like the writer of Hebrews says, "For we also have had the good news proclaimed to us, just as they did; but the message they heard was of no value to them, because they did not share the faith of those who obeyed" (Heb 4:2). Therefore, African scholars must combine knowledge with faith.

> In the same vein, African Biblical Theology must affirm the truth that the earth is the Lord's and the fullness thereof (Ps 24:1). The biblical narrative affirms: "In the beginning God created the heavens and the earth" (Gen 1:1). And God the Creator sustains

---

48. Millard J. Erickson, *Where Is Theology Going: Issues and Perspectives on the Future of Theology* (Grand Rapids: Baker, 1994), 54.

49. See for instance, D. A. Carson, *The Gagging of God: Christianity Confronts Pluralism* (Leicester: Apollos, 1996). According to Carson, philosophical pluralism, which is the dominant feature of the secular world, asserts that "any notion that a particular ideological or religious claim is intrinsically superior to another is *intrinsically* wrong." *Gagging of God*, 19, emphasis added.

50. J. A. Ilori defines pragmatism as "an attitude, a method, and a philosophy that uses the practical consequences of ideas and beliefs as a standard for determining their worth and truth." J. A. Ilori, *Moral Philosophy in African Context*, 2nd ed. (Zaria, Nigeria: Ahmadu Bello University Press, 1994), 24. According to pragmatism, *truth* is anything that *works*. And what works is the best guide for human behavior.

51. Erickson, *Where Is Theology Going*, 55–60.

52. Richard Bauckham, *Bible and Mission: Christian Witness in a Postmodern World* (Grand Rapids: Baker Academic, 2003), 88.

the universe He has made. It is too simplistic to believe in atheistic evolution which asserts that the world is the product of blind chance. For it actually takes more faith to believe in atheistic evolution than to believe in God the Creator. African theologians cannot afford to believe that we are mere products of chance and the descendants of primates simply because some people think so.[53]

Belief in the Great Commission

Mission is "the program of Jesus."[54] W. D. Davies and Dale C. Allison rightly say, "Universal Lordship means universal mission."[55] Davies and Allison mean that the universal authority God bestowed on Jesus after his resurrection (Matt 28:18) is translated into universal mission. "The disciples' central responsibility is to reproduce themselves."[56] This applies to every believer. Therefore, biblical theology that is African must be missional theology. All the New Testament writers were missionaries to the core. They wrote in the context of mission. They saw themselves as people involved in the mission of God. The academia-mission dichotomy that is prevalent today must have been a foreign idea to Jesus and his disciples. Paul was a missionary par excellence. He wrote in the context of missions. Therefore, theologians in Africa must see themselves as pioneer missionaries involved in the ministry of the kingdom rather than settled academicians whose main work is to debate on the latest fads in the global theological market.

Belief in the Spirit World

John M. Frame reasons that "the doctrine of angels rebukes the smallness and impersonalism of our cosmology."[57] According to him, modern science claims the discovery of a larger universe that was unknown to the ancients. "But they have a much smaller view of the universe of persons, having abandoned belief

---

53. Francisco J. Ayala, *Am I a Monkey? Six Big Questions about Evolution* (Baltimore: John Hopkins University Press, 2010).

54. David L. Turner, *Matthew*, BECNT, ed. Robert W. Yarbrough and Robert H. Stein (Grand Rapids: Baker Academic, 2008), 689.

55. W. D. Davies and Dale C. Allison, *The Gospel According to Matthew*, The New International Critical Commentary on the Holy Scriptures of the Old and New Testaments (London: T&T Clark, 1997), 684.

56. Turner, *Matthew*, 689.

57. John M. Frame, *The Doctrine of the Christian Life* (Phillipsburg: P&R, 2008), 254.

in God and in angels."[58] The Bible affirms that the spirit world is real. Spirit beings are incorporeal, yet they exist. Paradoxically, the incorporeal world is tangible. There are good angels that serve God and are "ministering spirits sent to serve those who will inherit salvation" (Heb 1:14). There are also fallen angels that have "lost their place in heaven" (Rev 12:8). These are also called demons or evil spirits. Therefore, African biblical scholars must affirm the presence of the spirit world. If God is real, the spirit world must be real because God is Spirit (John 4:23). Satan and demons are not mere products of human imagination. They exist. Therefore, any theological enterprise that ignores the premise of the biblical worldview merely acts as judge of the Bible. Reverent scholarship must respect the biblical worldview. This is foundational in doing New Testament theology in Africa.

Belief in the God of Miracles

Many scholars dismiss miracles. According to David Wenham and Steve Walton, "Presuppositions about miracles have been among the dominant factors in historical studies of Jesus, with rationalist assumptions about the impossibility of miracles being openly aired by some of the most influential scholars, e.g. Schweizer, Bultmann."[59] For example they regard the miracles in the Gospels as merely "symbolic" and are "designed to mean more than they say: they transcend past events in the story of Jesus and enter one's own life, encouraging personal experiences with Jesus or making such experience intelligible."[60] But rather than merely symbolic explication of miracle stories as Luz portrays, the Bible affirms that miracles happen; and they happen even today. The early church relied on the power of the Holy Spirit to witness and do miracles (Acts 4:31; 13:9–12). God can use – and does use – believers who are filled with the Holy Spirit to perform miracles to the glory of his name. Therefore, seeing miracles as something that might have happened in the early church but has no relevance in the twenty-first century is denying the power of God.

---

58. Frame, *Doctrine*, 254.

59. David Wenham and Steve Walton, *Exploring the New Testament*, vol. 1: *The Gospels and Acts* (London: SPCK, 2001), 133.

60. Ulrich Luz, *The Theology of the Gospel of Matthew*, trans. J. Bradford Robinson (Cambridge: Cambridge University Press, 1995), 67.

While some scholars in the Western world have concluded that Bible stories about miracles are not true, we in Africa must not only believe but also prove that the Bible stories are true and that miracles happen. We can participate in the Bible stories in real ways as we see God work in our midst beyond the ordinary in healing the sick and breaking the chains of oppression in the African society.

Avoiding the Dichotomy Between Faith and Practice

African biblical scholars must demonstrate that there is a correlation between theological conviction(s) and our way of life. Any theology that does not govern the way we think and act is mere intellectual knowledge. In Jesus's parable of the two builders (Matt 7:24–27), the foolish builder is one who failed to apply the instructions he heard. Doing theology without a corresponding lifestyle is foreign to biblical writers and the saints who preceded us. "Watch your life and doctrine closely," says Paul to the young pastor and theologian Timothy. "Persevere in them, because if you do, you will save both yourself and your hearers" (1 Tim 4:16). African theologians cannot afford to ignore moral integrity.

In this regard, and contrary to the practice of some scholars, African theologians must avoid the tendency to rely on what they *feel* about a text. Rather, the emphasis must be on what the text really says and how it is to be applied. God does not instruct us based on how we feel. He instructs us based on his eternal truth, perfect wisdom, and good, pleasing, and perfect will (Rom 12:2). Therefore, African Christians must discard the world's preoccupation with feelings and embrace truth. God feels, but he is not entrapped in emotions and feelings. Truth matters.

Avoiding an Unhealthy Dichotomy Between the Old and New Testaments

The propensity of some biblical scholars to build a dichotomy between the Old and New Testaments appears superfluous because from a Christian standpoint, there is no New Testament without the Old, while the Old is incomplete without the New.[61] This was our starting point in chapter one of this book on the roots of redemptive history. As G. K. Beale points out, "The NT sees that

---

61. See David L. Baker, *Two Testaments, One Bible: The Theological Relationship Between the Old and the New Testaments*, 3rd ed. (Downers Grove: InterVarsity, 2010).

the OT episodes point forward to events to come in the new covenant era."[62] This means that the New Testament writers saw the Old Testament as the right launching pad for the interpretation of the Jesus event – his birth, ministry, death, and resurrection. Therefore, New Testament biblical theology that is African must take seriously the concept of continuity and prophecy fulfillment embedded in the two Testaments. For example, the coming of Christ was a fulfillment of biblical prophecies. Similarly, many New Testament doctrines such as sacrifice, atonement, redemption, law, and grace have meaning only in the light of the Old Testament. In other words, the primary source for doing New Testament theology is the sixty-six books of the Old and New Testaments. While priority may be given to the content of the New Testament, this content is understood primarily in the light of the Old Testament.

Avoiding the Dichotomy Between Body and Spirit

God is not only concerned about souls going to heaven. The body contains the soul and the spirit. A sick body affects the soul and vice versa. Africans understand life in a holistic way. For example, in some African traditional religions, the farm is connected with the god of rain just as the domestic animals produce well by the help of the god of fertility. This holistic outlook is not alien to the Old and New Testament Scriptures. God chose Israel as his treasured possession and gave them land flowing with milk and honey. The narrative in Matthew 25:31–46 describes the eschatological division between the goats and the sheep. The commendation and eternal reward for the sheep is based solely on social action – caring for the hungry, the sick, the naked, and those in prison. Therefore, New Testament biblical theology must view life holistically as the Bible does. Biblical theology of the New Testament must be able to address every aspect of life in the African context. This means that "the Bible is read within the religious as well as the economic, social and political contexts of Africa."[63] The situation in which believers in Christ sell their conscience because of poverty is unacceptable, especially if it is the failure of the church leaders to help their members excel in the economic world. In

---

62. G. K. Beale, *Handbook on the New Testament Use of the Old Testament: Exegesis and Interpretation* (Grand Rapids: Baker Academic, 2012), 58.

63. Jean-Claude Loba-Mkole, "Bible Translation and Inculturation Hermeneutics," in *Biblical Texts and African Audiences*, ed. Ernst R. Wendland and Jean-Claude Loba-Mkole (Nairobi: Action, 2004), 44; citing J. Ukpong, "Developments in Biblical Interpretations in Africa: Historical and Hermeneutical Directions," in *The Bible in Africa: Translations, Trajectories, and Trends*, ed. Gerald O. West and Musa W. Dube (Leiden/Boston/Köln: Brill), 11–28.

a nutshell, a robust Christianity in Africa requires that African Christians understand and apply the message of the Bible in their own context in all life situations.

Avoiding Pride and Arrogance

The propensity for pride among theologians is high.[64] Instead of upholding the integrity of the Bible, they rely on their pedigrees. They know all the Greek, Hebrew, Latin, Aramaic, and all the other ancient and dead languages. They know the theological jargon that most Christians don't. They can argue theological points with eloquence and persuasion. For example, they can argue, from the Bible, that homosexuality is not a sin and that the Bible does not condemn it. And with the resurgence of paganism in Africa, some university professors – who also profess faith in Christ – are leading the way in reviving African traditional religions (ATRs). Recently an ATR professor proudly argued, to the applause of audience and students, that the practices of witchcraft and divination and consulting mediums and spiritist are not wrong because even the priests and leaders of Israel consulted the Urim and the Thummim! He cited the example of King Saul in 1 Samuel 28:3–20 to support his argument but ignored all the warning passages (Lev 19:31; 20:6; 2 Kgs 21:6; Isa 8:19–22; Jer 27:9–10; Mal 3:5). Using his professorial weight, he twisted the text to serve his purpose. And he claimed that he, too, is a pastor in an evangelical church.

There is need for solemn warning here. Paul says, "We know that 'We all possess knowledge.' But knowledge puffs up while love builds up. Those who think they know something do not yet know as they ought to know. But whoever loves God is known by God" (1 Cor 8:1–3). Theologians who are filled with the Holy Spirit will be full of God's love as well and cannot be puffed up by their academic achievements because they will "consider them garbage" for the surpassing greatness of knowing Christ Jesus (Phil 3:8). This means that authentic and acceptable scholarship before the Lord is one done in the spirit of humility, reverence, and the fear of the Lord. Scholars must not focus on building monuments here on earth – great books, great names, and great intellectual influence – without corresponding treasure in heaven. The word of the Lord reminds us,

---

64. And a common problem with intellectualism is that it makes people adamant in their wrongs. They cling to their erroneous views backed by pedigrees.

> If anyone builds on this foundation using gold, silver, costly stones, wood, hay or straw, their work will be shown for what it is, because the Day will bring it to light. It will be revealed with fire, and the fire will test the quality of each person's work. If what has been built survives, the builder will receive a reward. If it is burned up, the builder will suffer loss. (1 Cor 3:12–15)

Doing theology with a proud and arrogant spirit is building on the foundation using hay and straw.

A Strong Demonstration of Character, Conviction, Competence, and Confidence

African theologians must be known for good character, competence, conviction, and confidence.

Why is character important for our emerging theologians in Africa? In the postmodern world of narcissism, "the fixation on self," God is now "put in the inferior position, the position of the servant; and the individual human holds the superior position, the position of the lord. The human decides what is good and right and true. It is the human's wishes that are to be respected and met."[65] Erickson calls this fixation upon self-gratification "inverted theology."[66] Inverted theology lacks respect or concern for God's commands. Today many theologians lack any sense of respect for God's commands. They lack moral fortitude. But Paul urged Timothy to watch his life and doctrine closely (1 Tim 4:16). The world is not dying for theologians; the world is dying for Christians who live like Jesus. These Christians must be people who live with their theological convictions, whether they are theologians or not. The Bible is the primary text for theology par excellence. Every Christian derives his or her faith and practice from it. And to the extent they practice what they believe, they will touch the world around them and receive their reward from God in accordance with their practice. Christian theologians without the character of the one they are *theologizing* about are certainly unworthy of their calling.

Similarly, African theologians must demonstrate conviction. Conviction is standing by one's persuasion or beliefs. A person of conviction is courageous in the face of danger and distractions (2 Tim 4:1–5). The need for conviction among all evangelical scholars is precipitated by much that is problematic

---

65. Erickson, *Where Is Theology Going*, 84.
66. Erickson, 84.

theologically in the global market. What is at stake is evangelical theology. For example, within some evangelical organizations people who do not accept basic tenets of evangelical Christianity like the inspiration of the Bible and salvation in Christ alone are included, yet evangelical views are not reciprocally accommodated by theologically liberal groupings. This situation calls for conviction and courage on the part of emerging biblical theologians in Africa and beyond. Evangelical scholars must guard against the follies and unbiblical orientation of ungodly scholars.

Competence is another requirement for African theologians. "Not that we are competent in ourselves to claim anything for ourselves, but our competence comes from God" (2 Cor 3:5). Christ is our sufficiency. If deep grounding in the word of God is the prerequisite for "correctly handling the word of truth" (2 Tim 2:15), Africa stands the risk of losing out. As one who has taught in some theological institutions in Nigeria, my lament is that many students run away from the languages such as Greek and Hebrew and opt for other disciplines that do not require these languages. This means that Africa will be lacking in competent exegetes of the word of God. That is digging our theological graves.

Finally, confidence and faith in God are primary. Issuing stern warnings to potential apostates, the writer of Hebrews says, "See to it, brothers and sisters, that none of you has a sinful, unbelieving heart that turns away from the living God" (Heb 3:12), and

> Therefore, since the promise of entering his rest still stands, let us be careful that none of you be found to have fallen short of it. For we also have had the good news proclaimed to us, just as they did; but the message they heard was of no value to them, because they did not share the faith of those who obeyed. (Heb 4:1–2)

Faces of unbelief stare at us as we read Bible scholars whose works reflect philosophic skepticism and the spirit of the Enlightenment, elevating reason above faith and rejecting the authenticity of Scripture. African scholars must demonstrate faith and confidence in the God of the Bible.

Questions for Review and Application

1. Why is there a need for New Testament theology in Africa?
2. What is the main thrust of Screwtape's letter to Wormwood?
3. Why are presuppositions important?

4. What are the six key beliefs that ought to characterize scholarship in Africa?
5. What four things must African scholars avoid?
6. Why are the virtues of character, conviction, competence, and confidence important for African scholars?
7. How can the Christian scholar maintain proper balance between spiritual life and academics?

3

Drums of Redemption in the Synoptic Gospels (1)

It is really foolish to expect others to agree with our truth or to not feel offended when we speak our truth. When something is true, however . . . well, it's true, and you can't change it.

Steve Brown[1]

Scrambling for acceptability in the world, the church is embellishing the gospel with anything and everything but the truth.

John MacArthur, Jr[2]

The word "gospel" is rooted in the Anglo-Saxon language and is derived from two words that mean "good" and "news" from which we have "good news." The Gospels present the ministry of Jesus as the good news to humankind. The Gospels summarize the life of Jesus from birth, ministry, suffering, death, and resurrection. "Jesus did many other things as well. If every one of them were written down, I suppose that even the whole world would not have room for the books that would be written" (John 21:25).

Carl R. Holladay is right that a casual reading of the canonical Gospels shows that Matthew, Mark, and Luke are alike and that they differ from John's Gospel.[3] The first three books, Matthew, Mark, and Luke, present the life of Jesus with so much similarity in arrangement of materials, content, and tone that they are referred to as the *Synoptic* Gospels from a Greek word that means

---

1. Steve Brown, *A Scandalous Freedom: The Radical Nature of the Gospel* (New York: Howard, 2004), 180.

2. MacArthur, *Our Sufficiency*, back flap cover.

3. Carl R. Holladay, *Introduction to the New Testament*, ref. ed. (Waco, TX: Baylor University Press, 2017), 43.

"seeing together." The reason for separating John from Matthew, Mark, and Luke can be summarized by tabulating the "peculiarities" and "coincidences" among the four Gospels as provided by Harrison.[4]

	Peculiarities	Coincidences
Mark	7%	93%
Matthew	42%	58%
Luke	59%	41%
John	92%	8%

On the one hand, the table shows that John shares only 8 percent of material in common with the rest of the Gospels. On the other hand, Mark has only 7 percent of materials that are peculiar to him. He shares 93 percent of his materials with Matthew and Luke. Hence, they "see together."

The Gospels appear first in the New Testament canon because "they fittingly occupy a place at the forefront of the New Testament, since they record what happened at the 'beginning.'"[5] This placement does not necessarily mean that they were the first to have been written.

But who were the writers of these Gospels? Why did they write the Gospels? When did they write? To whom did they write? A common feature of writing in the first century was that some authors did not always include their name on the books they wrote. In other words, the books were anonymous. According to the early tradition of the church, Matthew and John were believed to be among the disciples of Jesus. Mark and Luke were not, but they were closely associated with the disciples. However, authorship and date issues are largely debated among theologians and Bible scholars today. Determining the precise dates of writing are not quite feasible. But though no precise dates can be assigned to the writing of the Synoptic Gospels, it is believed that they were written sometime after the death and resurrection of our Lord Jesus Christ. Just as Luke says in his introduction, each one of these writers wanted to write an accurate account of the life of Jesus Christ for the church in order to strengthen their faith.

The Synoptic Problem

In relating the Gospels to each other, modern biblical criticism concentrates on possible explanations for the similarities and differences in the contents

---

4. Harrison, *Introduction to the New Testament*, 143.
5. Harrison, 137.

of these narratives. This is the Synoptic problem.[6] The two examples below should suffice as illustrations.

Table 1: The Calling of Matthew, the Tax Collector[7]

Matthew 9:9–13	Mark 2:13–17	Luke 5:27–31
[9] As Jesus went on from there, he saw a man named Matthew sitting at the tax collector's booth. "Follow me," he told him, and Matthew got up and followed him. [10] While Jesus was having dinner at Matthew's house, many tax collectors and sinners came and ate with him and his disciples. [11] When the Pharisees saw this, they asked his disciples, "Why does your teacher eat with tax collectors and sinners?" [12] On hearing this, Jesus said, "It is not the healthy who need a doctor, but the sick. [13] But go and learn what this means: 'I desire mercy, not sacrifice.' For I have not come to call the righteous, but sinners."	[13] Once again Jesus went out beside the lake. A large crowd came to him, and he began to teach them. [14] As he walked along, he saw Levi son of Alphaeus sitting at the tax collector's booth. "Follow me," Jesus told him, and Levi got up and followed him. [15] While Jesus was having dinner at Levi's house, many tax collectors and sinners were eating with him and his disciples, for there were many who followed him. [16] When the teachers of the law who were Pharisees saw him eating with the sinners and tax collectors, they asked his disciples: "Why does he eat with tax collectors and 'sinners'?" [17] On hearing this, Jesus said to them, "It is not the healthy who need a doctor, but the sick. I have not come to call the righteous, but sinners."	[27] After this, Jesus went out and saw a tax collector by the name of Levi sitting at his tax booth. "Follow me," Jesus said to him, [28] and Levi got up, left everything and followed him. [29] Then Levi held a great banquet for Jesus at his house, and a large crowd of tax collectors and others were eating with them. [30] But the Pharisees and the teachers of the law who belonged to their sect complained to his disciples, "Why do you eat and drink with tax collectors and sinners?" [31] Jesus answered them, "It is not the healthy who need a doctor, but the sick."

What is responsible for the close parallels between the Gospels as noted in the table above, "especially considering that the Gospels were likely written in

---

6. See for example Mark Goodacre, *The Synoptic Problem: A Way Through the Maze* (New York: Sheffield Academic Press, 2001).

7. See H. E. Cardin, *Synoptic Gospels*, 3-4

different places at different times?"[8] Could the authors have copied from each other? And if so, who copied from the other? Or was there a common source from which they derived their materials?

Table 2: The Healing of the Blind Men [Man][9]

Matthew 20:29–34	Mark 10:46–52	Luke 18:35–43
[29] As Jesus and his disciples were leaving Jericho, a large crowd followed him. [30] Two blind men were sitting by the roadside, and when they heard that Jesus was going by, they shouted, "Lord, Son of David, have mercy on us!" [31] The crowd rebuked them and told them to be quiet, but they shouted all the louder, "Lord, Son of David, have mercy on us!" [32] Jesus stopped and called them. "What do you want me to do for you?" he asked. [33] "Lord," they answered, "we want our sight."	[46] Then they came to Jericho. As Jesus and his disciples, together with a large crowd, were leaving the city, a blind man, Bartimaeus (which means "son of Timaeus"), was sitting by the roadside begging. [47] When he heard that it was Jesus of Nazareth, he began to shout, "Jesus, Son of David, have mercy on me!" [48] Many rebuked him and told him to be quiet, but he shouted all the more, "Son of David, have mercy on me!" [49] Jesus stopped and said, "Call him." So they called to the blind man, "Cheer up! On your feet! He's calling you."	[35] As Jesus approached Jericho, a blind man was sitting by the roadside begging. [36] When he heard the crowd going by, he asked what was happening. [37] They told him, "Jesus of Nazareth is passing by." [38] He called out, "Jesus, Son of David, have mercy on me!" [39] Those who led the way rebuked him and told him to be quiet, but he shouted all the more, "Son of David, have mercy on me!" [40] Jesus stopped and ordered the man to be brought to him. When he came near, Jesus asked him, [41] "What do you want me to do for you?"

---

8. Cardin, 4.
9. Cardin, 5-6.

³⁴ Jesus had compassion on them and touched their eyes. Immediately they received their sight and followed him.	⁵⁰ Throwing his cloak aside, he jumped to his feet and came to Jesus. ⁵¹ "What do you want me to do for you?" Jesus asked him. The blind man said, "Rabbi, I want to see." ⁵² "Go," said Jesus, "your faith has healed you." Immediately he received his sight and followed Jesus along the road.	"Lord, I want to see," he replied. ⁴² Jesus said to him, "Receive your sight; your faith has healed you." ⁴³ Immediately he received his sight and followed Jesus, praising God. When all the people saw it, they also praised God.

From the above table, how can we account for the differences in "minor historical details"[10] in these parallel accounts? To answer this question and similar ones, some theories and hypothesis have been advanced. But it is important to know from the outset that although these hypotheses are sometimes assumed to be true, they remain intellectual conjectures since they have not been proven beyond any reasonable doubt.

And what are the speculations or hypotheses regarding the parallel accounts? These include the single (or common) source theory, miscellaneous sources, and literary dependence sources.[11] Until the eighteenth century, "Matthew was regarded as the first writer, the other two being derived from him in some way and to some degree."[12] Some thought that Mark was an abbreviation of Matthew. And the chief concern in Synoptic studies was harmonizing the differences. But in the eighteenth century, the concern shifted from the differences to the similarities in the Synoptic Gospels. The first of these views was held by B. F. Westcott and Arthur Wright who thought that the

---

10. Cardin, 4.
11. Holladay, *Introduction to the New Testament*, 50–53.
12. Harrison, *Introduction to the New Testament*, 142. See also Holladay, *Introduction to the New Testament*, 54–55 for the Two Gospel Hypothesis, Two Source Hypothesis, and Four Source Hypothesis. According to the Two Gospel hypothesis, formulated by Johann Jakob Griesbach in 1789–1790, Matthew wrote first. Luke used Matthew, and Mark copied from both Matthew and Luke. The Two Source theory, however, holds that Mark wrote first while both Matthew and Luke got their materials from Mark and a second source called Q. This Q source is no longer extant, but accounts for the materials that are common in Matthew and Luke but absent in Mark, so the theory goes. This theory is called Markan priority because it holds that Mark was the first to write his Gospel. A "refinement" from the Markan priority is that there are four sources rather than two to account for the materials unique to Matthew and Luke. So it is believed that apart from Mark and Q, both Luke and Matthew used independent sources tagged L and M.

oral traditions of the church regarding the life and ministry of Christ developed into a fixed form through repetition.[13] This theory accounts for the similarities in the Synoptic Gospels. The writers of the Synoptics made their own "special contributions" on the existing oral traditions according to "the particular aim of each writer."[14] Another theory is called *immediate dependence* in which it is thought that the Synoptics depended on each other's accounts to produce their work.[15] Although this theory could account for the similarities, it does not explain the differences. Similarly, there is no conclusive evidence that Matthew and Luke saw each other's work.[16] A third theory is called *mediate dependence* or *Urevanelium* theory. This theory holds that there was one primitive Gospel from which the three Synoptics copied their materials. But the difference between the materials remains the weakness of this position. And what could have happened that caused such a source to disappear?[17]

The *fragmentary theory* is traced to Schleiermacher and postulates that the sayings and deeds of Jesus were "preserved in separate, detached forms" in the beginning, and the Gospel writers drew their materials from these sources.[18] Whenever they used the same fragment, their accounts agreed with each other. The divergence came whenever they used different fragments. But the problem is the "structural unity between the various accounts. We could not expect any such agreement in the order of events as the Gospels present."[19] The point is that if the Gospel stories were "preserved in separate, detached forms" as speculated, it is difficult to account for the structural similarities among them.

Another theory that has had huge impact is called *Two Document Hypothesis*. This theory is that Mark was the first to write his Gospel, and Matthew and Luke drew their materials from Mark. But there was another unknown source named Q (German *Quelle*, meaning source). It is assumed that the materials common to Matthew and Luke but absent in Mark were derived from Q. "Between these two sources the great bulk of the Synoptics is accounted for."[20] This position is also called *Markan priority*. "Justification for the priority of Mark is based on a comparative study of the first three Gospels

---

13. Harrison, *Introduction to the New Testament*, 144.
14. Harrison, 144.
15. Harrison, 145.
16. Harrison, 145.
17. Harrison, 145.
18. Harrison, 145–46.
19. Harrison, 145–46.
20. Harrison, 147.

which takes note of their contents, language, and sequence of narrative."[21] Mark is "shorthand" from which Matthew and Luke expanded. But as we noted in chapter 2 regarding presuppositions, the Markan priority has been questioned and rejected by some recent scholarship.

Finally, there is the *Four Document Hypothesis* proposed by B. H. Streeter. His proto-Luke hypothesis holds that Luke made a first draft and later incorporated this draft in his finished work.[22] Streeter's view is that prominent centers of Christianity contributed to the origins of the Gospels. Streeter believed that Mark originated from Rome as early as AD 60. The source Q came from Antioch as early as AD 50. And M, which was the source for Matthew, came from Jerusalem around AD 65. The fourth document L, Luke's private source, came from Caesarea around AD 60. The final stages in the formation of Matthew and Luke occurred in Antioch and Corinth between AD 80 and AD 85 respectively.[23]

From the theories above the world of scholarship is generally agreed that Mark could have been the first to write his Gospel and that others derived their sources from him plus the non-extant source Q. The debate goes on. But as Holladay pointed out, the dominant positions today are the Two Gospel and the Two Source Hypotheses.[24]

The approach of this study is inductive delineation of the major themes of the Synoptic Gospels that have relevance for faith and practice for African Christianity. Like Harrison well observed, the Gospels are messages. Therefore, "To say they are biographies or histories is to ignore the testimony of the caption [the Gospels]. Granted that biographical and historical material is found here, yet this material must be viewed as part of a spiritual message."[25] Therefore, we now turn to the messages of the Synoptic Gospels.

---

21. Harrison, 147. See also Goodacre, *Synoptic Problem*, 23.

22. Harrison, 149.

23. Harrison, 150.

24. Holladay, *Introduction to the New Testament*, 68. See also Goodacre, *Synoptic Problem*, 23. According to Goodacre (*Synoptic Problem*, 23),

> Even in Great Britain and the United States, where the Synoptic Problem is still often openly discussed, the Two Source Theory is accepted without question by the vast majority of scholars in the discipline. If one were to take off the shelf at random almost any contemporary book on the Gospels, that book is likely to assume the correctness of the Two Source Theory. It is a matter that is simply taken for granted in much of the scholarship, a mindset that does not often get suspended, even for a moment.

25. Harrison, *Introduction to the New Testament*, 137. See also John Stott, *Men with a Message: In Introduction to the New Testament and Its Writers*, rev. Stephen Motyer (Suffolk: Evangelical Literature Trust, 1994).

The Synopsis of Matthew, Mark, and Luke
Matthew

The aim of this section is to see what Marshall calls "Matthew's theological story."[26] As noted above, the sequence here is Matthew, Mark, and Luke. This sequence follows the canonical order and has nothing to do with hypotheses regarding which Gospel was first and which one followed.[27] This general overview is meant to provide a vista into the thrust of the Gospel of Matthew. We begin with the purpose of the Gospel of Matthew. While John clearly states his purpose for writing his Gospel (John 20:31), Matthew does not state his purpose openly. However a general purpose is perceived, namely, "to set forth such a knowledge of Jesus and his work as to make possible an intelligent decision for him and the gospel."[28] Scholars have also come to believe that Matthew wrote his Gospel as a teaching manual for the church; and this purpose can be deduced from his emphasis on teaching in connection with the Great Commission (Matt 28:16–20).[29] That teaching occupies a central place can be seen in the Sermon on the Mount (5–7) and the many things Jesus taught his disciples and hearers in parables. The Sermon on the Mount is a "harmonious masterpiece of ethical and religious teaching."[30]

Apart from the catechetical setting, some scholars see the Gospel of Matthew containing liturgical (church worship) material, citing as an example the length of the Lord's Prayer (Matt 6:9–13) compared to Luke (11:2–4). According to Johnson, "Both the catechetical and the liturgical settings could have helped influence the shape of this Gospel."[31] In any case, we must bear in mind that issues about setting are mostly "imaginative extrapolation" to use the words of Johnson, that "help us *reconstruct* the situation that the Gospel's form *seems* to presuppose."[32] But do we have the right tools to adequately reconstruct the settings of the Gospels, having been separated from the scene by a wide margin of two thousand years?

---

26. Marshall, *Concise New Testament Theology*, 33.

27. The fluidity of scholarship in this direction suggests that holding onto a particular theory regarding dating without substantial evidence is a fallacy.

28. Harrison, *Introduction to the New Testament*, 173.

29. Harrison, 173.

30. Raymond E. Brown, *An Introduction to the New Testament*, ABRL (New York: Doubleday, 1997), 178.

31. Luke Timothy Johnson, *The Writings of the New Testament: An Introduction*. rev. ed. (Minneapolis: Fortress, 1999), 190.

32. Johnson, *Writings of the New Testament*, 190, emphasis added. What scholars say about the context or setting of any NT book should be taken cautiously as they are mere intelligent guesses.

Most scholars recognize the well-structured nature of the Gospel of Matthew, which "gives evidence of careful composition."[33] Discourse markers in Matthew (7:28; 11:1; 13:53; 19:1; 26:1) provide a neat outline of the major discourses or sayings of Jesus around particular themes. For example, chapters 5–7 are the Sermon on the Mount which centers on discipleship. Chapter 10 majors on mission; chapter 13 is on the parables of Jesus; chapter 18 is on relationships; and chapters 24–25 form Jesus's discourse about the future.[34]

Perhaps a panoramic view will be helpful here. The Gospel of Matthew begins with preliminaries such as the genealogy,[35] the infancy (nativity) narrative, John the Baptist, Jesus's baptism, the temptation, and the beginning of his ministry (Matt 1–4). "The manifesto of the teacher" (4:12–7:29) is within a block that marks "the foundations of the kingdom."[36] Perhaps the most moving section in the entire Gospel of Matthew is chapters 8–9 in which the miracles of Jesus authenticate his mission. The kingdom of God has come on earth in power, and the forces of darkness give way. Evidently, faith (mentioned five times in this section) is an important element in receiving the kingdom and its blessings. Matthew 11:1–13:52 reveals growing opposition and hostility toward the Christ. And Jesus responds by denouncing, in the strongest terms possible, those cities that did not receive the good news of the kingdom, even when they saw the miraculous powers displayed in their midst. Filled with righteous indignation, "Jesus began to denounce the towns in which most of his miracles had been performed, because they did not repent. 'Woe to you, Chorazin! Woe to you, Bethsaida! For if the miracles that were performed in you had been performed in Tyre and Sidon, they would have repented long ago in sackcloth and ashes'" (11:20–21).

The identity of Jesus as the Messiah seems to have been kept hidden from the people until we come to the section of Matthew 13:53–17:27. Key among these are the confession of Peter (16:13–20) and the transfiguration (17:1–13).[37] Jesus reveals himself as the Son of Man who is "going to come in his Father's

---

33. Ladd, *Theology of the New Testament*, 218.

34. Ladd, 218.

35. The family trees (genealogies in Matthew and Luke) speak eloquently about the family, and by extension marriage. God designed the propagation of the human race in and through the important institution of marriage. Jesus's origin is traced through a family line of males and females as ordained by God.

36. David Hill, *The Gospel of Matthew*, The New Century Bible Commentary (Grand Rapids: Eerdmans, 1972; reprint, 1990), 88.

37. According to Donald Macleod, "The idea of the divine sonship is also central to three of the great crises in Jesus' life: the baptism, the temptation and the transfiguration." *The Person of Christ: Contours of Christian Theology* (Downers Grove: InterVarsity, 1998), 101.

glory with his angels, and then he will reward each person according to what they have done" (16:27).

Only in the Gospel of Matthew is the church mentioned.[38] God revealed to Peter that Jesus is the Christ, the Anointed one, and upon that truth Jesus will build his church (*ekklēsia*) (16:18). Similarly, unresolved disputes between individuals in the community of disciples are to be brought to the church (18:17).

The large block of Jesus's teaching in Jerusalem (Matt 19:1–25:46) constitutes the climax of his earthly ministry. Jesus teaches about marriage and divorce (19:1–12). He blesses children (9:13–15). He also teaches about riches and the kingdom of God (Matt 19:16–30).

The final section of Matthew (26–28) is the passion of Christ – arrest, trial, crucifixion, death, and resurrection. The passion of Christ is shared by all the Synoptic Gospels. Jesus's death is for the remission of the sins of the world (Matt 20:28; Mark 10:45), a theology that is transmitted in the rest of the New Testament (1 Tim 2:5–6; Heb 9:15). Because of the significance of the passion narrative, and especially the death of Christ, we will comment on it further as we examine the theology of the Gospel of John.

Mark

Mark, who is believed to have been the disciple of the apostle Peter, is thought to have written his Gospel in Rome to Roman readers. His primary purpose was to show the importance of the redemptive work of Christ (10:45). The Gospel of Mark is a fast-moving drama of the life and ministry of Jesus the Messiah, the Son of God. A panoramic view of Mark's Gospel (Greek *euangelion*)[39] provides some clues to the important themes in the book and paves the way for discussion of these theological themes.

Mark introduces his Gospel as "the good news about Jesus the Messiah, the Son of God" (1:1). Mark's theological narrative comes from the beginning of his Gospel. Jesus is the long awaited Messiah (cf. Matt 11:3). And after a brief prologue, Mark is quick to announce the Messiah's forerunner and his mission (Mark 1:2–13). Mark evokes Isaiah 40:3 to say that John the Baptist's ministry is preparatory to the coming of the Messiah.

---

38. Harrison, *Introduction to the New Testament*, 172.

39. According to Ladd, the term "gospel" as it is used to describe a genre of literature originates from Mark's use of the word (Mark 1:1), "whether or not Mark intended it." Ladd, *Theology of the New Testament*, 229.

The success of John's ministry as forerunner of Christ is evident because, "The whole Judean countryside and all the people of Jerusalem went out to him. Confessing their sins, they were baptized by him in the Jordan River" (Mark 1:5). John baptizes Jesus also, whom John describes as more powerful than himself, the straps of whose sandals John was unworthy to stoop down and untie (1:7). And at the baptism of Jesus, he sees "the Spirit descending on him like a dove," signifying the Spirit's power not only to fill Jesus for ministry but to also bring ultimate healing to the land (1:10). And God himself speaks from heaven, "You are my Son, whom I love; with you I am well pleased" (1:11). After the baptism "the Spirit sent him out into the wilderness," and Jesus is there forty days, "being tempted by Satan" (1:12–13). This event is narrated by all the Synoptic Gospels (cf. Matt 4:1–11; Luke 4:1–13). Jesus's victory is the victory of the Son of God.

After Jesus returns from the wilderness, he begins his ministry by preaching the good news of God. He calls upon the people to repent and believe the good news, for "The time has come," and "The kingdom of God has come near" (Mark 1:15). His mission in Galilee (1:16–8:26), which R. Alan Cole christened "the kingdom of God in Galilee,"[40] begins with calling the first disciples (1:16–20). His ministry in the region is characterized by demonstrations of miraculous powers such as casting out demons (evil spirits), healing the sick, feeding the five thousand, and raising the dead, among others as well as praying in solitary places, appointing the twelve disciples, and teaching in parables, and the growing opposition of the authorities (see 3:22–30; 7:1–23). One important element in Jesus's healing ministry is that he often associates healing with the faith of the healed. Faith is essential for healing to take place.

At the climax of his Galilean ministry, Jesus's identity as Messiah is openly confessed by Peter (Mark 8:27–30), but Jesus warns his disciples not to tell anyone (cf. Matt 16:20). This is often referred to as the messianic secret.[41] Then Jesus goes on to predict his death at the hands of the authorities: "he must be killed and after three days rise again" (Mark 8:31). While this is disturbing news, and Peter (and the rest) could not take it, Jesus knew that it was Satan instigating Peter to oppose his arrest and execution (8:32–33). Therefore, Jesus tells the disciples that "Whoever wants to be my disciple must deny themselves and take up their cross and follow me" (8:34). That is the way to finding true

---

40. R. Alan Cole, *The Gospel According to Mark: An Introduction and Commentary*, Tyndale New Testament Commentaries, rev. ed. (Leicester: Inter-Varsity, 1989), 111.

41. David K. Lowery, "A Theology of Mark," in *A Biblical Theology of the New Testament*, ed. Roy B. Zuck (Chicago: Moody, 1994), 74.

life (8:34–38). The culmination of the revelation of Jesus as the Messiah among the disciples is the transfiguration (9:2–13).

From Mark 9:14–10:52, Jesus travels from Galilee to Jerusalem. Along the way, Jesus heals a demon-possessed boy (9:14–29), settles the disciples' argument regarding the greatest in the kingdom of God (9:33–37), and makes astonishing remarks about someone who was doing miracles in his name but "was not one of us" (9:38). According to Jesus, "No one who does a miracle in my name can in the next moment say anything bad about me, for whoever is not against us is for us" (9:39–40). Jesus also taught about not causing others to sin (9:42–50); divorce (10:1–12); the little children (10:13–16); and more. And for the second time and third times, Jesus foretells his death (9:30–32; 10:32–34). These times Peter learned to keep quiet.

As his earthly ministry draws to a close, Jesus engages in open confrontation with the authorities in Jerusalem (Mark 11:1–13:34). His triumphal entry into Jerusalem raises eyebrows (11:1–11). He adds to the growing hostility by entering the temple and clearing out those who are buying and selling there (11:15–17). Therefore, "The chief priests and the teachers of the law heard this and began looking for a way to kill him, for they feared him, because the whole crowd was amazed at his teaching" (11:18). From this time onward, we see growing opposition culminating in the event of the Passover, arrest, crucifixion, and burial of Jesus (14:1–16:8).

Luke

The Gospel of Luke and the Acts of the Apostles are regarded as "one work in two volumes."[42] Although many scholars treat them as such,[43] they are separate here in order to treat Luke along with the other Gospels as they together center on Jesus, while the Acts of the Apostles tells the story of the growing church under the influence of the Holy Spirit using the instrumentality of the apostles. In the Gospels, Jesus gives the Great Commission. In the Acts of the Apostles, the disciples fulfill the Great Commission.

Luke penned his narrative to one "most excellent Theophilus" (Luke 1:3). There are divergent views about the identity of Theophilus. Conjectures include

---

42. See T. D. Proffitt, III, "Luke-Acts," *Missional and Messianic Bible Commentary*, pre-publication draft, used by author's permission, 2018, 406.

43. See also Morris, *New Testament Theology*. He also treats Acts as the second volume of Luke. While the approach may have some advantages, each book has a particular focus; therefore, bringing the themes together appears muddied. It is for this reason that I separate Luke and Acts by treating Luke along with the Synoptic Gospels.

a government official, "a patron or would-be patron; or a spiritual seeker, or an attorney (given Paul's predicaments)."[44] Other scholars speculate that Theophilus was not a real person but anyone who loves God and desires a deeper knowledge of him. At any rate, Theophilus was a person to whom Luke felt indebted "to write an orderly account" so that he "may know the certainty of things" he had been taught (1:3–4). Given the universalistic outlook of the Gospel of Luke, scholars believe that the author wrote to present Jesus as both the Savior of Israel and of the entire human race. Luke 4:18 seems to set the agenda of the entire Gospel as the "good news to the poor" that reaches all kinds of people who have all kinds of concerns – including the marginalized people in the society such as women and children. Similarly, the Gospel of Luke presents Christ as the ideal man, "the Son of Man."

Luke 1–2 might be regarded as an elaborate prelude. After his statement of purpose (1:1–4), Luke narrates the births and childhoods of John the Baptist and of Jesus Christ (1:5–2:52). Luke's infancy narrative of Jesus is more elaborate than that of Matthew. The birth of John the Baptist is also unique material as the other two Synoptics skip it. According to Bock, Luke's "first two chapters serve as an overture to the Gospel, revealing the major themes that Luke will develop throughout his portrayal of Jesus."[45] John the Baptist comes through an extraordinary birth that heralds the supernatural birth of the Savior. Similarly, unique stories in Luke include the visit of the shepherds, the praising of the angels, the presentation of Jesus at the temple, and the young Jesus in the temple (2:8–52).

Similarly, the ministry of John the Baptist is highlighted in Luke 3:1–20 in more detail. Luke also gives an account of the baptism of Jesus and his temptation (3:21–4:13). Unlike Matthew, Luke does not open his Gospel with the genealogy of Jesus (cf. Matt 1:1–17). He reserves his genealogy for much later (Luke 3:23–38).

Jesus's public ministry in Galilee spans Luke 4:14–9:50. The materials here are much the same as the other Synoptics, with important highlights such as the calling of the twelve, miraculous healings, emphasis on faith, and teaching in parables, among other aspects. Darrell L. Bock sees 8:4–9:17, a section of the Galilean ministry, as "the call to faith and Christology."[46] Christ's authority is

---

44. Proffitt, *Missional and Messianic Bible Commentary*, 406.

45. Darrell L. Bock, *Luke*, The IVP New Testament Commentary, ed. Grant R. Osborne, D. Stuart Briscoe, and Haddon Robinson (Downers Grove: InterVarsity, 1994), 33–34.

46. Bock, *Luke*, 145.

authenticated by a series of miracles such as control of nature, exorcisms, and finally in the commissioning of disciples to preach the message of the kingdom.

According to Luke 9:51–19:57, Jesus moves from Galilee to Jerusalem, teaching along the way. The last week of Jesus, spent in and near Jerusalem (19:28–23:56), is called "the passion week." The sad story of the passion week ends with the glowing story of the resurrection, appearances, and ascension of the Lord (Luke 24:1–53).

In the Gospel of Luke, "great emphasis is placed on prayer, the Holy Spirit, the role of women in the ministry of Jesus, and God's forgiveness of sins."[47] Other important theological themes in Luke include the kingdom of God, repentance, Son of God and Son of Man, Son of David, eschatology, the Christ, the Lord, the passion of Christ, and salvation history.

"Son of David, Son of Abraham" and "Son of Adam, Son of God"

Matthew and Luke trace the redemptive roots of Jesus in Israel's genealogical records. It is also possible to see an "apologetic element" in Matthew as he opens his narrative with the book (*biblos*) of the genealogy (*geneseos*) of Jesus Christ, tracing his roots to David, the iconic leader of the house of Israel.[48] These are iconic figures in Israel's history. According to Marshall, "His genealogical tree roots him in the Jewish people (starting from Abraham) and in its royal line (through David)."[49] But beyond mere apologetics, the theological undertones are clear. The promised deliverer of the nation of Israel must have his place properly secure in the ancestral line of Israel.[50] This genealogy seems to tally with the tradition that Matthew wrote primarily to a Jewish audience, thus he demonstrated from Old Testament prophesies that Jesus is the Messiah, the king of the Jews (see Matt 2:1–6, 15; 21:5; 26:54; 27:9). According to Leonhard Goppelt, "anticipation of the coming of the Son of David was the predominant messianic hope of the people and the teachers."[51] As *the* Son of

---

47. "Introduction" (to Luke) in *The Holy Bible*, New International Version, with Concordance, Dictionary, Maps and Other Bible Study Resources (Minto: Bible Society in Australia, 1973, 1978, 1984), 721.

48. See Bitrus A. Sarma, *Hermeneutics of Missions in Matthew: Israel and the Nations in the Interpretative Framework of Matthew's Gospel* (Carlisle: Langham Monographs, 2015), 82.

49. Marshall, *Concise New Testament Theology*, 33.

50. In the book of Ezra, all the priests who returned from Babylon but could not trace their ancestral descent were excluded from service in the temple because they were considered unclean (Ezra 2:61–62).

51. Leonhard Goppelt, *Typos: The Typological Interpretation of the Old Testament in the New*, trans. Donald H. Madvig (Grand Rapids: Eerdmans, 1982), 83.

David, he therefore qualifies as Israel's Messiah who saves from sin and heals from disease (9:27; 15:22; 20:31).[52] But why does Matthew refer to Jesus also as son of Abraham? John D. Hardy says,

> Matthew's use of 'son of Abraham' is the only time in the NT when the title is applied to Jesus. Its use in the heading points the reader back to Genesis 12:1–3, where Abraham is called to become the father of Israel (cf. Matt. 3:8–9). The call included a number of promises, but it is the promise of universal blessing that Matthew has in view.[53]

Similarly, there is a place for women and Gentiles in the genealogy because of the inclusion of four women, three of them Gentiles – Tamar, Rahab, and Ruth – and Bathsheba. "The four women mentioned had irregular union and/or were non-Jews. This foreshadows Jesus's own unusual birth and the inclusion of Gentiles in the people of God."[54]

Luke equally presents this genealogical orientation in affirming the authenticity of Jesus as the Messiah (Luke 3:23–38). After he narrates the baptism of Jesus (3:21–22), Luke dives into the genealogy, beginning with Joseph and going all the way back to "the son of Adam, the son of God" (3:38), thus authenticating the voice from heaven which said, "You are my Son, whom I love; with you I am well pleased" (3:22). Paul John Isaak says that the words in verse 22 echo Isaiah 42:1 and "remind us of Jesus' heavenly roots, namely, that Jesus is the true Son of God."[55] But as Joseph's son, Luke traces Jesus's "earthly family tree" as well (3:23–38). Luke's genealogy shows that Jesus is both divine and human. Jesus is both Son of God and Son of Man. And since Adam represents the human race, Luke, like Matthew, shows that Jesus came to redeem the entire human race.

John the Baptist and Herald of the Messiah

John the Baptist, the older cousin of Jesus (Luke 1:36), appears on the scene as a forerunner of the Messiah, fulfilling the Old Testament prophecy in Isaiah 40:3. Jesus calls John the greatest of the prophets (Matt 11:11). His status in

---

52. Sarma, *Hermeneutics of Missions in Matthew*, 88, emphasis original.
53. John D. Hardy, "Mission in Matthew," in *Mission in the New Testament: An Evangelical Approach*, ed. William J. Larkin, Jr. and Joel F. Williams (Maryknoll: Orbis, 2005), 126.
54. Marshall, *Concise New Testament Theology*, 33.
55. Paul John Isaak, "Luke," in *Africa Bible Commentary*, ed. Tokunboh Adeyemo (Nairobi: WordAlive, 2006), 1212.

the Synoptics is that of a forerunner (Matt 3:3; 11:10; Mark 1:2–10; Luke 3:1–6; 7:26–27).[56] John called people to repent so that their sins might be forgiven (Matt 3:5–12; Mark 1:4–8; Luke 3:1–28), "encouraging those who were waiting for the Messiah and challenging others who may have been oblivious about that (see Luke 1:16–17, 76–79)."[57] The Gospels record that John's ministry attracted large crowds. Many of these people became John's disciples (Matt 9:14; Luke 11:1; John 1:25, 34–35; cf. Acts 19:1–7).

John the Baptist appeared on the scene in an atmosphere of political turmoil – including armed bandits, political zealots, religious zealots, and a lot more.[58] The clamor for political freedom was loud. But John knew that Jesus is "the Lamb of God" whose mission was to take "away the sins of the world" (John 1:29).[59] The effective remedy for the world's social crisis is deliverance from our number one malady – sin.

Promise and Fulfillment in God's Redemptive Scheme

All of the Synoptic Gospels and the Gospel of John were written within the framework of promise and fulfillment (Matt 1:22–23; 3:1–3; 5:17; 26:24; Mark 7:6; 9:13; 11:17; Luke 3:4; 4:17–21; 7:27; 24:44–47; John 12:14–15, 38; 13:18; 15:25). The fulfillment motif runs throughout the narratives and includes the virgin birth, the ministry of John the Baptist, and the ministry, suffering, death, and resurrection of Jesus the Messiah. The significance of the promise and fulfillment motif in the Gospels is that the Old Testament serves as "a Messianic Primer" because "the doctrine of the Messiah in the OT is at the heart of the promise-plan of God."[60] This means that the Gospels not only see the plan of salvation in the Old Testament but also actively anticipated the Messiah. Jesus as the Messiah fulfills the law (Matt 5:17)[61] and everything else written

---

56. Sarma, *Hermeneutics of Missions in Matthew*, 2015, 108.

57. Yong, *Renewing Christian Theology*, 132.

58. Richard A. Horsley and John S. Hanson, *Bandits, Prophets, and Messiahs: Popular Movements at the Time of Jesus* (New York: Winston, 1985).

59. Thomas D. Lea, *The New Testament: Its Background and Message* (Nashville: Broadman and Holman, 1996), 180.

60. Walter C. Kaiser, Jr., *Toward Rediscovering the Old Testament* (Grand Rapids: Zondervan, 1987), 101.

61. See Esther Yue L. Ng, "Matthew 5:17–22 and 'A Tale of Two Missions,'" in *New Testament Theology in the Light of the Church's Mission: Essays in Honor of I. Howard Marshall*, ed. Jon C. Laansma, Grant R. Osborne, and Ray Van Neste (Eugene: Cascade, 2011), 103–21.

concerning him (Luke 24:44–47). The concept of promise and fulfillment is elaborated in the next chapter under the rubric "promise of the kingdom."

The next chapter takes us to some of the key theological issues in the Synoptic Gospels. But we will first go through questions for review and application.

Questions for Review and Application

1. What is the "Synoptic problem"?
2. How would you explain the similarities between Matthew, Mark, and Luke?
3. What do Matthew and Luke mean by "Son of David, Son of Abraham" and "Son of Adam, Son of God"?
4. Why is the concept of promise and fulfillment important in the Gospels?
5. How has this chapter increased your knowledge of the Synoptic Gospels?
6. In what ways has this chapter increased your faith in Christ?

4

Drums of Redemption in the Synoptic Gospels (2)

At that time Jesus said, "I praise you, Father, Lord of heaven and earth, because you have hidden these things from the wise and learned, and revealed them to little children. Yes, Father, for this is what you were pleased to do.

"All things have been committed to me by my Father. No one knows the Son except the Father, and no one knows the Father except the Son and those to whom the Son chooses to reveal him."

Matthew 11:25–27

God's nature is what it is, not what we think it is or what we hope it is.

Steve Brown[1]

Key Theological Themes in the Synoptic Gospels

The Synoptic Gospels are narratives. In the words of Bock, "How does one extract theology from a narrative?"[2] We respond that in the Synoptic Gospels theology is interwoven in the narrative scheme as the writers perceive the hand of God in the events they narrate. The Synoptic Gospels, for instance, present the Father, the Son, and the Holy Spirit at work in God's redemptive scheme. Often ignored by scholars, we will treat them as of first importance here because the three persons are primary in the work of redemption. They are never offered as theological treaties but as important parts of the gospel narrative.

---

1. Brown, *Scandalous Freedom*, 36.
2. Bock, *Luke*, 33.

Redemptive Work of the Father

According to Larry W. Hurtado,

> The God of the New Testament is described almost entirely in terms of God's acts of creation, calling, sending forth prophets, rescuing and vindicating, giving commandments, judging and punishing, and most importantly God's acts in Jesus, sending him forth, handing him over to redemptive death, and raising him and exalting him to superlative glory. So theologizing about "God" in the NT is essentially making inference based on God's acts.[3]

While Hurtado sees God described almost entirely in terms of his works, the Gospels portray him in relation to his Son and his people in addition to his acts. The Synoptic Gospels portray the distinctive roles of the Father in relation to the work of salvation. These roles are enumerated as follows:

The Father Is the Father of Jesus Christ

Jesus refers to God as his Father in all of the Gospels (Matt 7:21; 10:32–33; 26:39; Mark 8:38; 14:36; Luke 9:26; 10:22; 23:46; John 5:17; 20:17). Jesus is the *begotten* Son of God (John 3:16). This is a complex theological concept, misunderstood by some religions that see the Father and Son relationship in human biological terms. But the Bible does not teach that God is the Father of our Lord Jesus Christ in the human biological sense. (See the concept of the virgin birth in relation to the work of the Holy Spirit below.) Rather, God exists eternally in three persons – Father, Son, and Holy Spirit. For example, in the baptismal formula, the Father, the Son, and the Holy Spirit are mentioned together (Matt 28:19–20). Similarly, Jesus said,

> And I will ask the Father, and he will give you another advocate to help you and be with you forever – the Spirit of truth. The world cannot accept him, because it neither sees him nor knows him. But you know him, for he lives with you and will be in you. (John 14:16–17)

This remains a mystery. While God is the Father of the human race in a generic way, and Father to the disciples (Matt 6:9, 32; 18:14; Mark 11:25; Luke 11:13), God is Father to Jesus in a unique way. When Jesus called God his Father, the Jews charged that he was claiming equality with God. "For this reason they tried all the more to kill him; not only was he breaking the

---

3. Larry W. Hurtado, *God in the New Testament,* Library of Biblical Theology (Nashville: Abingdon, 2010), 35.

Sabbath, but he was even calling God his own Father, making himself equal with God" (5:18). Jesus did not deny the charge but insisted that "I and the Father are one" (John 10:30).

Revealing this unique relationship, Jesus said, "All things have been committed to me by my Father. No one knows who the Son is except the Father, and no one knows who the Father is except the Son and those to whom the Son chooses to reveal him" (Luke 10:22; also Matt 11:27). Furthermore, he said, "Whoever acknowledges me before others, I will also acknowledge before my Father in heaven. But whoever disowns me before others, I will disown him before my Father in heaven" (Matt 10:32–33).

The Father Is the Father of the Disciples

Not only is God the Father of the entire human race and of the Jews, he is the Father of the disciples of Jesus Christ. This designation is given more frequently in Matthew and Luke than in Mark (Matt 5:16; 6:9–15, 26; 10:20; Mark 11:25; Luke 6:36; 11:1–4). The disciples stand in a special relationship with God when they pray. They should address God as their Father (Matt 6:9). As children of their Father, they are also light bearers in the world (Matt 5:16). Their Father in heaven takes special interest in fending for their needs provided they "seek first his kingdom and his righteousness" (Matt 6:32–33). Similarly, they enjoy the special privilege of the Spirit of their Father speaking through them when they stand trial "before governors and kings as witnesses to them and to the Gentiles" (Matt 10:18).

Another dimension of the disciples' special relationship with God as their Father is that "your Father has been pleased to give you the kingdom" (Luke 12:32). The primary reason for the coming of Jesus the Messiah, the Son of God, is to usher in the kingdom. The disciples who have embraced the message of the kingdom have become its heirs. They need not worry about their personal needs anymore because their Father is interested in their well-being. Therefore, Jesus said, "Sell your possessions and give to the poor. Provide purses for yourselves that will not wear out, a treasure in heaven that will never fail, where no thief comes near and no moth destroys. For where your treasure is, there your heart will be also" (Luke 12:33–34).

The Father Is the Sender of the Angels

Angels play significant roles in the Gospel narratives, especially in Matthew and Luke. They appear as God's messengers. An angel appeared to Joseph in a dream on several occasions (Matt 1:20–24; 2:13, 19–20). An angel named Gabriel also appeared to Mary and Zechariah (Luke 1:11–20, 26–38). Angels brought good tidings to the shepherds regarding the birth of Jesus Christ (Luke 2:8–15). Matthew records that an angel came down from heaven and rolled away the stone that covered Jesus's tomb (Matt 28:2–4) and that same angel told the women that Jesus had risen from the dead (Matt 28:5–7). During Jesus's time of ordeal at Gethsemane, "An angel from heaven appeared to him and strengthened him" (Luke 22:43). The writer of Hebrews confirms that all angels are "ministering spirits" (Heb 1:14).

The Father Is the Sender of the Son[4]

Jesus states explicitly that he did not come on earth by his own choice alone. The Father sent him (Matt 10:40; Mark 9:37; Luke 9:48; cf. John 5:36–37; 6:44; 8:16, 42; 12:49; 17:25). The Father sent him on the mission of seeking the lost sheep of Israel (Matt 15:24) and to give his life as a ransom for many (Matt 20:28). According to Luke 4:18b–19, "He has sent me to proclaim freedom for the prisoners and recovery of sight for the blind, to set oppressed free, to proclaim the year of the Lord's favor." Because Jesus came from the Father, "whoever rejects me rejects him who sent me" (Luke 10:16).

The Father Is the Lord of the Harvest

According to Matthew 9:38 and Luke 10:2 (cf. John 4:35–38), God the Father is the Lord of the harvest. The harvest is the world of lost humanity, who are likened to sheep without a shepherd, "When he saw the crowds, he had compassion on them, because they were harassed and helpless, like sheep without a shepherd" (Matt 9:36). Therefore, the mission of Jesus is the mission of God in the harvest field. One of the primary responsibilities of the disciples of Jesus is to, "Ask the Lord of the harvest, therefore, to send out workers into his harvest field" (Matt 9:38).

Redemptive Work of the Son

The subject of the Synoptic Gospels is Jesus Christ who came as the Savior of the world. The questions "Who do people say I am?" and "Who do you say I am?" (Mark 8:27–29; cf. Matt 16:13–17) border on "the topic of Christology, or the person of Christ."[5] As ways of contextualizing, some African scholars

---

4. See Sarma, *Hermeneutics of Mission in Matthew*, 31–35.

5. Timothy Palmer, *Christian Theology in an African Context* (Bukuru, Nigeria: Africa Christian Textbooks, 2015), 73.

depict Jesus as "Chief," or "King," or "Proto-Ancestor."[6] The problem, however, is that when the concept of "ancestor" is used in Africa to refer to Jesus, he is likely to be equated with African ancestral spirits as well. Jesus is not one of the departed spirits of African ancestors. But what do the Synoptic Gospels say about the person of Christ?

Jesus Is the Servant-Messiah

The most important theological understanding regarding the life of Jesus is in relation to his work as the Messiah. The word "messiah" is derived from the Hebrew *mashiakh* and the Greek *christos*, both meaning anointed. The English rendition of the Hebrew is "Messiah" and the Greek is "Christ." The title "Christ" or "Messiah" is used repeatedly in all four Gospels (Matt 2:4; 11:2–6; 16:16–20; 22:42–44; Mark 1:1; 14:61–62; Luke 2:11; 3:15–16; 20:41–43; 22:67–68; 24:26; John 1:41; 4:25–26; 11:27; 20:31). According to Ladd, the title and concept "is the most important of all the Christological concepts historically if not theologically, because it became the central way of designating the Christian understanding of Jesus."[7]

Similarly, the concept of the Messiah is important because Judaism can only be understood in terms of their hope of the coming Messiah from the line of David (Matt 22:42).[8] But the Jews were expecting a zealot-like Messiah, one who would liberate them from Gentile dominion. In other words, they anticipated "a revolutionary freedom fighter, working for Israel's liberation like a Zealot."[9] But Jesus was "a contradiction, *an* enigma, a disappointment for many" because "He did not fulfill the popularly recognized messianic texts; he was not an unambiguous king (2 Sam 7:11–16), and he was not a sword-wielding liberator (Ps 45:4–5)."[10]

---

6. Palmer, *Christian Theology*, 73–75.
7. Ladd, *Theology of the New Testament*, 133.
8. Jesus's response to their belief was,

    "How is it then that David, speaking by the Spirit, calls him 'Lord'? For he says, 'The Lord said to my Lord: "Sit at my right hand until I put your enemies under your feet."' If then David calls him 'Lord,' how can he be his son?" No one could say a word in reply, and from that day on no one dared to ask him any more questions. (Matt 22:43–46)

9. Isaak, *New Testament Theology*, 37.
10. Isaak, 37.

Contrary to Jewish expectations, Jesus came as the foretold Servant-Messiah (Isa 42:1; Matt 12:18) or the servant of the Lord (Isa 52:13–53:12).[11] The servanthood of the Messiah is attested by his loyalty and humble submission to the will of God, doing his work with gentleness of spirit such that, "He will not quarrel or cry out; no one will hear his voice in the streets. A bruised reed he will not break, and a smoldering wick he will not snuff out, till he has brought justice through to victory" (Matt 12:19–20; see Isa 42:2–3). Jesus also authenticated his claims as the expected Messiah through the miraculous works he performed (Matt 11:2–6). One of the charges against Jesus that led to his prosecution and death was his unwavering claim to be the Christ (Matt 26:62–64; Mark 14:60–62; Luke 23:35).

Jesus Is the Savior from Sin
But Jesus is not only the suffering servant of the Lord. As the Messiah, Jesus's specific mission was the salvation of his people from their sins (Matt 1:21). As Hardy well says, "The redemptive nature of that mission is a significant concept for Matthew."[12] This salvation includes his power to forgive sins. The Synoptic Gospels all record the same confrontation with Jesus over his authority to forgive sins (Matt 9:1–8; Mark 2:1–12; Luke 5:17–26). Although "his people" (Matt 1:21) could be understood narrowly as the people of Israel, the Gospels demonstrate that the salvation Jesus brought is universal in scope. Not only does his genealogy include Gentiles, the Great Commission (Matt 28:18–20; Mark 16:15–16) extends to the entire world. The universal scope of salvation in Christ is that, "Salvation is found in no one else, for there is no other name under heaven given to mankind by which we must be saved" (Acts 4:12). As Jesus declared, "I am the way and the truth and the life. No one comes to the Father except through me" (John 14:6).

Jesus Is "the Mediator of Revelation"[13]
According to Matthew 11:25–27, Jesus's uniqueness as the Son of God is that he alone possesses intimate knowledge of the Father. Jesus said, "All things have been committed to me by my Father. No one knows the Son except the

---

11. For a good treatment on the servant of the Lord, see Stephen G. Dempster, "The Servant of the Lord," in *Central Themes in Biblical Theology: Mapping Unity in Diversity*, ed. Scott J. Hafemann and Paul R. House (Nottingham: Apollos, 2007), 128–78.

12. Hardy, "Mission in Matthew," 126.

13. James D. G. Dunn, *Jesus and the Spirit: A Study of Religious and Charismatic Experience of Jesus and the First Christians as Reflected in the New Testament* (Grand Rapids: Eerdmans, 1997), 31.

Father, and no one knows the Father except the Son and those to whom the Son chooses to reveal him" (11:27). The Son of God chooses to reveal the Father to some. And these include "little children" (11:25). The point is that Jesus is in the Father, and the Father is in him (John 14:10). That is why Jesus can reveal the Father to whom he chooses.

Jesus Is the Teacher and Prophet

The popular understanding of Jesus is that he is the teacher (rabbi or *didaskalos*). He regarded himself as a teacher (Matt 10:24–25; cf. John 13:13–15). His disciples, acquaintances, close associates, and even his enemies (e.g., the Pharisees and the teachers of the law) call him "Teacher," as is seen in all the Gospels (Matt 8:19; 9:11; 12:38; 22:24; Mark 4:38; 5:35; 10:17; Luke 7:40; John 1:38; 3:2; 8:4; 11:28–29; 20:16). Jesus is teacher or rabbi because he *teaches* his disciples and all who come to him to listen. He is a teacher par excellence, and "the crowds were amazed at his teaching, because he taught as one who had authority, and not as their teachers of the law" (Matt 7:28–29). Jesus taught both in parables and in plain language. And the content of his message is the principles and ethos of the kingdom of God that he had come to inaugurate.

Besides his teaching ministry, Jesus regarded himself as a prophet and was also recognized as such by those who heard him and saw his works (Matt 21:11, 46; Luke 7:16; 13:33; 24:19). But Jesus's prophetic ministry was not well received in his hometown (Matt 13:57–58; Mark 6:4; Luke 4:24). And their unbelief in him limited the miracles Jesus did among them.

Jesus Is the Son of Man

The Gospels portray Jesus as a genuine human being. The title "Son of Man" appears in all of the Synoptic Gospels (Matt 8:20; 10:23; 19:28; Mark 2:10–11, 28; 8:31; 9:9; 14:21; Luke 5:24; 9:26; 22:48). As we saw above, he is the Messiah who saves from sin (Matt 1:21). And his association as the king of the Jews right from the beginning depicts him as the shepherd of Israel in the Davidic line or the Davidic shepherd-king in fulfillment of Zechariah 13:7.[14] The Magi from the east seek Jesus as king of the Jews (Matt 2:1–6). The people also refer to him as king when he enters Jerusalem (Matt 21:1–9). According to Marshall, this title is in reference to his future role as judge, and the motif of the king or messiah as a shepherd of the people appears in the motif of compassion

---

14. For elaborate treatise on the Davidic shepherd-king, see Sarma, *Hermeneutics of Mission in Matthew*, 82.

for the sheep without a shepherd (Matt 9:36) and in the last judgment scene (Matt 25:32–33).[15]

The kingship of Jesus underscores his humanity. The Son of Man motif in the Gospels is rooted in the prophetic tradition, especially in Ezekiel (e.g., Ezek 2:1–8; 3:4–9, 17–19) and Daniel (e.g., Dan 7:13; 8:17). The title "son of man" appears ninety-three times in the book of Ezekiel. God almost always addresses the prophet as "son of man" when he is going to give him a new message. However in Daniel, it is the angel Gabriel who addresses Daniel as "son of man" (Dan 8:16–17). And this is the only time Daniel is addressed as "son of man." The first use of "son of man" in Daniel is in a vision in which he saw "one like a son of man, coming with the clouds of heaven." This one who resembles the son of man "approached the Ancient of Days and was led into his presence" (Dan 7:13). According to Arthur J. Ferch,

> Within the setting of Dan 7:9–10, 13–14 the SM is an individual, eschatological, celestial being with messianic traits. Though characterized by divine attributes, Dan 7 does not teach a ditheism for the Danielic being assumes a role subordinate to the Ancient of Days. Whereas the manlike figure is a celestial being, he is, nevertheless, set apart from the heavenly creatures referred to in Dan 7:10. While the SM resembles a human being, he is also distinct from the "saints of the Most High" who are human beings with whom he, nevertheless, enjoys a solidarity, for he shares with them throughout perpetuity the kingship given him by the Ancient of Days.[16]

Darrel L. Bock acknowledges that the title "Son of Man" is, "One of the most complex issues in New Testament studies." He says,

> The usage in Daniel is not technically speaking a title, but is a description of a human figure who approaches God to receive dominion. In other words, there is no reference to "the" Son of Man here; only the imagery is present. It should not be ignored, however, that the presence of this figure with this description makes the passage capable of generating a title. Its later history in the NT, 1 Enoch, and 2 Esdras indicates this. The relevant passages

---

15. Marshall, *New Testament Theology*, 112.

16. Arthur J. Ferch, "The Apocalyptic 'Son of Man' in Daniel 7," (Dissertation for the doctor of theology, Andrews University, Seventh-day Adventist Theological Seminary, April 1979), 4. https://digitalcommons.andrews.edu/cgi/viewcontent.cgi?article=1047&context=dissertations.

appear in 1 Enoch 46:37; 48:4–10; 62:3–9, 14; 63:11; 69:27–29, and 2 Esdras 13. The uses in Enoch point to a revealer (46:3), a judge (62:1–5), a universal ruler (62:12–13), an object of worship (69:29; 62:6–7), and an authority and judge (48:5; 62:6, 9). The image is one of authority derived from Daniel 7. It also is to be noted that the association of this figure with coming on the clouds is an image suggesting divinity.[17]

The puzzle surrounding the "son of man" in Daniel may remain unresolved for a while as speculation regarding this enigmatic figure continues to increase – each view further compounding his identity. Meanwhile a safer, and probably more authentic, route is to explore the Son of Man in the Gospels by allowing the texts to speak for themselves. First, the Son of Man displays the characteristics of any human being because he "came eating and drinking, and they say, 'Here is a glutton and a drunkard, a friend of tax collectors and sinners'" (Matt 11:19; cf. Luke 7:34). Second, as a son of man who was subject to the suffering of humanity, especially the poor and downtrodden, Jesus was homeless. He said, "Foxes have dens and birds have nests, but the Son of Man has no place to lay his head" (Matt 8:20 // Luke 9:58). Finally, the Son of Man is subject to betrayal, suffering, and death (Matt 17:22–23; 20:18–19; Mark 14:21; Luke 18:30–33).

But that is not the only portrait of the Son of Man. He is the Lord of the Sabbath (Matt 12:8 // Luke 6:5), an authority never before claimed by any earthly rabbi or priest. This Son of Man also has authority to send out his angels who will "weed out of his kingdom everything that causes sin and all who do evil" (Matt 13:41). When he comes back "in his Father's glory with his angels . . . then he will reward each person according to what they have done" (Matt 16:27; cf. 24:31). In addition, the Son of Man has authority to forgive sins (Mark 2:5–11; Luke 5:18–24). Those who hear him utter the words of forgiveness to the paralytic conclude that Jesus is a blasphemer because he dared to claim what is God's prerogative. Similarly, he "came to seek and to save the lost" (Luke 19:10; cf. Matt 1:21). Above all, the Son of Man is now the one who sits in his glorious throne at the right hand of the Mighty One (Matt 19:28; 26:64; Mark 14:62; Luke 22:69). All these verses indicate that the designation "Son of Man" goes beyond an ordinary son of man who is subject to humanity's limitations and ills.

---

17. Darrell L. Bock, "The Son of Man in Luke 5:24," *Bulletin for Biblical Research* 1 (1991): 111.

In summary, the Son of Man in the Synoptic Gospels is certainly messianic because Jesus portrays himself as one endowed with authority not only to forgive sins but to also share in the glory and authority of his Father as judge of the twelve tribes of Israel (Matt 19:28) and "all the nations" of the world (Matt 25:31–32).

Jesus Is the Son of God

We come to yet another Christological title that is contentious within and outside Christianity.[18] According to D. A. Carson,

> in the New Testament "Son of God" is not a *terminus technicus*, as the Latins say – a technical term that always carries the same associations. It always presupposes some sense of deriving from God, or of acting like God, or both, but the domains of such acting are pretty diverse. Bible readers should exercise special pains not to succumb either to unjustified reductionism, in which one particular usage is read into every occurrence, or to "illegitimate totality transfer," in which the entire semantic range of the expression is read into every occurrence. Context must decide.[19]

Carson's trajectory of the use of the title underlines the fact that

> New Testament writers are constantly drawing lines between, on the one hand, Old Testament persons, institutions, and events, and, on the other hand, Jesus. Thus Jesus is the true Manna, the bread from heaven; he is the Passover Lamb; he is the True Vine; when he is "lifted up" to die, this recalls the lifting up of the serpent in the wilderness; he is the ultimate High Priest; he himself is the Temple of God. So it should not come as a surprise that Jesus is

---

18. One of the biblical doctrines that Muslims misunderstand and vehemently attack is the Son of God. In Islamic conception, Son of God is understood in human biological terms of a conjugal union between male and female. Hence the vehement protest in the Qur'an (6:101; 72:3). In Islam, God is unbegotten and does not beget others (112:3). According to the Qur'an (9:30), whoever says that Jesus is the Son of God is eternally damned. For this reason, according to Rick Brown, "Seekers and believers from Muslim backgrounds regularly single out the term 'Son of God' as the biggest obstacle to reading the Gospel." Rick Brown, "Delicate Issues in Mission: Explaining the Biblical Term 'Son(s) of God' in Muslim Contexts," *International Journal of Frontier Mission* 2, no. 3 (Fall 2005): 91, http://biblicalmissiology.org/wp-content/uploads/2012/02/91-96Brown_SOG.pdf.

19. D. A. Carson, *Jesus the Son of God: A Christological Title Often Overlooked, Sometimes Misunderstood, and Currently Disputed* (Wheaton: Crossway, 2012), 74.

declared to be the ultimate Davidic King, and thus the Son of God (as each Davidic king was declared Son of God in turn).[20]

But our goal here is to make a quick survey of testimonies from the Synoptic Gospels regarding the title. According to the Gospels, not only is the Messiah the Son of Man, he is also the Son of God (Matt 14:33; 16:16; Mark 1:1; 15:39; Luke 1:32-35; 22:69-70). At the baptism of Jesus (Matt 3:17; Luke 3:22), for example, "regal and servant categories come together as the divine voice spoke about Jesus for the first time," in the words of Darrell L. Bock.[21] He sees the Son of God in Matthew 3:17 and Luke 3:22 as references to Psalm 2:7 and Isaiah 42:1, "bringing together the king and the servant imagery" which continue in Luke 4:18-19.[22]

Satan tests Jesus, asking him to prove his entitlement to this extraordinary title (Matt 4:3 // Luke 4:3). And even demons which Jesus exorcises from people recognize him as the Son of God (Matt 8:29; Mark 3:11-12; 5:7; Luke 4:41). His disciples were able to acknowledge and to worship him as Son of God (Matt 14:33; 16:16). This relationship between Jesus and the Father is explicitly expressed in Matthew 11:25-27. No one else enjoys the intimacy and knowledge of the Father except the Son to whom "all things have been committed" by the Father (11:27).

But it is not only the Father and the Son who are active in the work of redemption. We now turn to the redemptive work of the Holy Spirit in the Synoptic Gospels.

Redemptive Work of the Holy Spirit

The least discussed person in the Trinity among scholars is the Holy Spirit. His distinctive role in the mission of God is often ignored, especially when looking at the Gospels. For example, Hurtado says, "Reflecting the influence of the OT particularly, NT references rather consistently represent the Spirit as a power that originates in 'God' and is given to humans. That is, the divine Spirit is typically distinguished from the human spirit or soul."[23] But if we are to take the witness of the Gospels at face value, the Holy Spirit's active and critical role in the life of Jesus cannot be bypassed.

---

20. Carson, *Jesus the Son of God*, 74-75.
21. Darrell L. Bock, "A Theology of Luke-Acts," in *A Biblical Theology of the New Testament*, ed. Roy B. Zuck (Chicago: Moody, 1994), 103.
22. Bock, "Theology of Luke-Acts," 103.
23. Hurtado, *God in New Testament Theology*, 77-78.

The Holy Spirit Caused the Virgin Birth of Christ

Speaking about Matthew's narrative of the virgin birth, Craig S. Keener says, "If the genealogy indicates that Joseph descended from King David, this narrative explains in what sense this son of David (1:20) became Jesus' legal father by adoption."[24] Many people conclude that the concept of the virgin birth is mythological and scientifically impossible.[25] But as Keener rightly points out, whether the account of the miraculous conception of Jesus through the Holy Spirit "makes historical sense rests largely on one's presuppositions."[26] The Synoptic Gospels affirm that the Holy Spirit was instrumental in the miraculous conception of the Messiah (Matt 1:18; Luke 1:35). Keener's question for the doubters is significant: "Would anyone whose logic was not shaped by the Enlightenment thought doubt that of all the miraculous births of history, the Messiah's should be the most miraculous?"[27] This means that if miraculous births are recorded in history – for example the birth of Samson whose mother, the wife of Manoah, was barren (Judg 13) – is it not reasonable that the birth of the Messiah should be the most extraordinary? Therefore, evangelical scholars must not be sidetracked by those who regard the Gospel narratives as unhistorical.

The Holy Spirit Baptizes

In Matthew, Mark, and Luke, John the Baptist's testimony about Jesus emphasizes the coming kingdom.[28] He contrasts his ministry with that of the coming Messiah. The power of the coming one is demonstrated in the mode of baptism. John said, "I baptize you with water for repentance. But after me will come one who is more powerful than I, whose sandals I am not worthy to carry. He will baptize you with the Holy Spirit and fire" (Matt 3:11; cf. Mark 1:7–8; Luke 3:16). While John used ordinary water for his baptism, Jesus utilizes both water and the Holy Spirit.

The Holy Spirit is not only the one through whom believers in Christ are to be baptized. He played a key role at Jesus's baptism (Matt 3:16; Luke 3:21–22).

---

24. Craig S. Keener, *Matthew*, The IVP New Testament Commentary, ed. Grant R. Osborne (Downers Grove: InterVarsity, 1997), 57.

25. Daryl E. Witmer, "Isn't the virgin birth of Jesus Christ mythological and scientifically impossible?" Christian Answers.net (2011), https://christiananswers.net/q-aiia/virginbirth.html; Roberts, "Birth of Jesus."

26. Keener, *Matthew*, 57.

27. Keener, 57.

28. John D. Hardy, *Anointed with the Spirit: The Holy Spirit's Empowering Presence* (Phillipsburg: P&R, 2008), 57.

But the ministry of the Holy Spirit's baptism is explicated in John 3:1–8. The Spirit's baptism causes the new birth.

The Holy Spirit Anoints and Empowers for Mission

The Spirit anointed Jesus, empowering him for the mission of God such as casting out demons and preaching the good news of the kingdom (Matt 12:18, 28; Luke 4:18–19). In the account of Luke 3:21–22, we read:

> When all the people were being baptized, Jesus was baptized too. And as he was praying, heaven was opened and the Holy Spirit descended on him in bodily form like a dove. And a voice came from heaven: "You are my Son, whom I love; with you I am well pleased."

Hardy says we must not overlook Luke's accent on prayer in the text. "The clause reminds us both of Jesus' teaching that the Father gives the Spirit without measure to those who ask him and of the Jerusalem church's experience at Pentecost."[29] According to Hardy, *"God grants the Spirit's empowerment in answer to prayer and in proportion to need."*[30]

Similarly, the Holy Spirit is the one given the task of aiding the disciples as he speaks through them (Matt 10:19–20; Luke 12:11–12). The prophets also spoke through the Holy Spirit, hence he is the Spirit of prophecy (Matt 22:43–44; Mark 12:36). This means that the prophetic mission was carried out through the power of the Holy Spirit.

The empowerment motif is clear in Matthew 12:15–21.

> Aware of this, Jesus withdrew from that place. A large crowd followed him, and he healed all who were ill. He warned them not to tell others about him. This was to fulfill what was spoken through the prophet Isaiah:
>
> "Here is my servant whom I have chosen,
>   the one I love, in whom I delight;
> *I will put my Spirit on him,*
>   *and he will proclaim justice to the nations.*
> He will not quarrel or cry out;
>   no one will hear his voice in the streets.

---

29. Hardy, *Anointed with the Spirit*, 90.
30. Hardy, 90, emphasis original.

> A bruised reed he will not break,
>> and a smoldering wick he will not snuff out,
> till he has brought justice through to victory.
>> In his name the nations will put their hope." (Matt 12:15–21,
>> emphasis added)

In other words, the Holy Spirit is the one who empowered Jesus for his mission of proclaiming justice to the nations. In the words of Turner, "This text, already alluded to at Jesus's baptism (3:17; cf. 17:5), speaks of the Lord's beloved servant as one who is enabled by the Spirit to proclaim justice to the nations."[31]

The Holy Spirit Leads

Both Matthew and Luke record that Jesus *was led* by the Spirit to be tempted by the devil (Matt 4:1). Luke narrates that after his baptism, "Jesus, full of the Holy Spirit, left the Jordan and was led by the Spirit into the wilderness, where for forty days he was tempted by the devil" (Luke 4:1–2). Both Gospels stress the *leading* of the Holy Spirit. They portray that Jesus's journey to the desert to be tempted by the devil was not accidental. God planned it, and it was accomplished through the leading of the Holy Spirit. The English rendering "he was tempted by the devil" (Luke 4:2) does not take into account the continuous sense of the Greek participle *pairazomenos* (being tempted) as is rightly translated in some English versions. This means that Jesus's entire period in the wilderness was marked by temptations, culminating in the three temptations at the end. It follows that Jesus was able to endure the wilderness experience of temptations, hunger, and thirst because the Holy Spirit who led him empowered him to withstand the ordeals.

The Holy Spirit Can Be Blasphemed Against

In Matthew 12:31–32 (cf. Mark 3:28–30), "Jesus warns of the unforgiveable sin."[32] The slanderous charges the Pharisees made against Jesus were blasphemous. The miraculous works done by Jesus were works of the Holy Spirit who empowered him. But the Pharisees attributed them all to the prince of demons. Because the Spirit plays such a critical role in the redemptive work of God, blasphemy against him is never forgiven. Jesus says, "Anyone who speaks a word against the Son of Man will be forgiven, but anyone who speaks

---

31. Turner, *Matthew*, 316.
32. Turner, 322.

against the Holy Spirit will not be forgiven, either in this age or in the age to come" (Matt 12:32). Mark renders the blasphemer as "guilty of eternal sin" (Mark 3:29).

Christians have always wondered what blasphemy of the Holy Spirit could mean for the believer. Can a true Christian blaspheme against the Holy Spirit? What sin could a Christian commit that amounts to blasphemy against the Holy Spirit? Is every act of unbelief unforgiveable? Turner's position is worthy of our consideration. According to Turner,

> Matthew 12 centers on the Spirit-empowered miracles of Jesus, which should have been viewed as evidence of his messianic status (12:23) and his authority to forgive sins on earth (9:6). But the Pharisees' response to this goes well beyond unbelief. They slander the Spirit's ministry to Jesus by accusing him of collaborating with the very forces he is overpowering (12:29). This is the unforgiveable sin. Whether it can be committed today is debatable, but putative current examples must recapitulate the essence of the situation narrated in Matt. 12. It would therefore be wise for expositors to exercise caution in broadly applying this text to unbelief in general. Ultimate unbelief in Jesus is unforgiveable, but the point of 12:24–32 is not so much to narrate unbelief despite clear evidence that Jesus is the Messiah as it is to stress the slanderous attempt to portray this messianic evidence as demonic evidence.[33]

Turner means that the issue in the text is not unbelief in general but the slanderous attitude and actions of the Pharisees. Similarly, Turner says that although ultimate unbelief in Jesus leads to eternal condemnation, we must not conclude that "those who do not immediately believe the gospel have an unalterable state of unforgiveable doom."[34]

Questions for Review and Application

1. What is it that prevented Jesus from doing many miracles in his own town?

---

33. Turner, 323–24.
34. Turner, 324.

2. If miracles do happen today, why is it that we do not see a repeat of what we see in the Gospels? And what could be the hindrance for miracles today?
3. What roles did the Father, Son, and Holy Spirit play in the work of redemption according to the Synoptic Gospels?
4. Can we call Jesus "Our Ancestor" as some African scholars suggest? Why or why not?
5. Why must African Christians emphasize the work of the Holy Spirit?

5

Drums of Redemption in the Synoptic Gospels (3)

> Once, being asked by the Pharisees when the kingdom of God would come, Jesus replied, "The coming of the kingdom of God is not something that can be observed, nor will people say, 'Here it is,' or 'There it is,' because the kingdom of God is in your midst."
>
> Luke 17:20–21

Redemption as Entry in the Kingdom of God[1]

The kingdom of God[2] "is the main theological theme in the teaching of Jesus,"[3] represented as both present and future.[4] When Jesus taught his disciples how to pray, he showed that the first thing that must characterize their longing is God's kingdom (Matt 6:9–10). Similarly, instead of running after what the Gentiles crave and are anxious about, the disciples are to "seek first [God's] kingdom and his righteousness and all these things will be given to you as well" (Matt 6:33). And from the numerous texts regarding the kingdom, it is apparent that the kingdom of God is an overarching theme in the Gospels. This means that Jesus's life and ministry revolved within the framework of the kingdom of God. Therefore, the kingdom of God is pivotal in understanding the mission

---

1. This chapter is an abridged reproduction of Bitrus A. Sarma, *People of the Kingdom: Spiritual Leadership Formation for Holistic Transformation in Africa* (Jos, Nigeria: Yakson, 2014), ch. 1.

2. For the concept of the kingdom of God in ancient Israel, see Perrin, *Parable and Gospel*, ch. 1.

3. Marshall, *New Testament Theology*, 78.

4. See Ladd, *Presence of the Future*.

of Jesus who depicts the kingdom of heaven as the light of God penetrating into the dark world (cf. Matt 4:16–17). Wright asks, "What, then, is central to the understanding of the kingdom?"[5] These topics are discussed below.

The Dilemma of the Kingdom in Modern Perception

The kingdom of God is of primary importance in the New Testament.[6] We see this importance in the preaching of John the Baptist and of Jesus at the commencement of their ministries. In other words, this importance is demonstrated in the earliest *kerygma* of both John and Jesus (Matt 3:1–2; 4:17). Both John the Baptist and Jesus Christ preached repentance in preparation for the coming kingdom of God.[7]

But the proclamation of the coming kingdom in Jesus and the early church's *kerygma* remains a challenge in modern thought. In the year 1945, after the end of World War II, the German theologian Helmut Thielicke stood in the ruins of the University Chapel in Hamburg as he preached on the Lord's Prayer. Thielicke wrestled with the question of the coming of the kingdom of God and came to this rather pessimistic conclusion:

> We must not think of it as a gradual Christianization of the world which will increasingly eliminate evil. Such dreams and delusions, which may have been plausible enough in more peaceful times, have vanished in the terrors of our man-made misery.... Who can still believe today that we are developing toward a state in which the kingdom of God reigns in the world of nations, in culture, and in the public life of the individual? The earth has been ploughed too deep by the curse of war, the streams of blood and tears have swollen all too terribly, injustice and bestiality have become all too

---

5. Wright, *Jesus and the Victory of God*, 223.

6. See Schreiner, *New Testament Theology*, 41. According to James D. G. Dunn, "The centrality of the kingdom of God (*basileia tou theou*) in Jesus' preaching is one of the least disputable, or disputed, facts about Jesus." James D. G. Dunn, *Christianity in the Making*, vol. 1: *Jesus Remembered* (Grand Rapids: Eerdmans, 2003), 383.

7. See Mark Saucy, "The Kingdom-of-God Sayings in Matthew," *Bibliotheca Sacra* 151 (April-June 1994): 177. Repentance "conditioned the whole kingdom proclamation." And Saucy cites Floyd V. Filson that this repentance is "unconditional turning to God, or unconditional turning from all that is against God, not merely that which is downright evil, but that which in a given case makes total turning to God impossible." Floyd V. Filson, *A Commentary on the Gospel according to St Matthew*, 2nd ed. (London: Black, 1975), 226.

cruel and obvious for us to consider such dreams to be anything but bubbles and froth.[8]

In a world of terrorism, who will not identify with Thielicke that "The earth has been ploughed too deep by the curse of war, the streams of blood and tears have swollen all too terribly, injustice and bestiality have become all too cruel and obvious"? Through many decades of violence caused by *Boko Haram* – an Islamic terrorist group that claims to oppose Western education and promotes evangelism by gun and bomb blasts – and Fulani herdsmen in Northern Nigeria, we have lived with the terrifying noise of gun shots and bomb explosions. We have lived with the ugly sight of maimed and charred bodies, burned beyond recognition, of men and women made in the image of God, irrespective of their religious creed. We have lived with the wailing of women and children, the horrors written on the faces of men and women in refugee camps, and the general uncertainty of life day after day. But Thielicke's conclusion is something else. Should we resign and accept the fate that God no longer rules "in the world of nations, in culture, and in the public life of the individual?" Should we not regard Thielicke's conclusion as a sweeping generalization? Doesn't God have a remnant who might yet be catalysts for world transformation?

Ryken identifies with Thielicke as he also speaks about the difficulty of believing that the kingdom of God will ever come. This pessimism increases as the world witnesses more poverty, injustice, crime, war, terrorism, and many other social vices. Seeing all this, we admit with Ryken that, "The Gospel seems to make little progress from one day to the next. The wicked triumph while the righteous go about in chains. When we see all this we do not stop praying for the kingdom, but we want to ask God, 'When will your kingdom come?'"[9] So "when, if ever, will God's kingdom come?"[10] The question posed by Ryken is important, especially in the face of global terrorism. But having said that, let us briefly look at the promise and fulfillment of the kingdom according to Scripture.

---

8. Helmut Thielicke, *Our Heavenly Father* (Grand Rapids: Baker, 1980), 60, 62, quoted in Philip Graham Ryken, *When You Pray: Making the Lord's Prayer Your Own* (Phillipsburg: P&R, 2000), 8.

9. Ryken, *When You Pray*, 77.

10. Ryken, 78.

The Promise of the Kingdom

All the events in the life of Jesus fulfilled the promises of Scripture. According to Luke 24:44, "He said to them, 'This is what I told you while I was still with you: Everything must be fulfilled that is written about me in the Law of Moses, the Prophets and the Psalms.'" Jesus came to usher in the kingdom of God (Matt 4:17). First, let us understand the terms "kingdom of heaven" or "kingdom of God."[11] The idiom "the kingdom of God" does not occur in the Old Testament, but the concept is found throughout the prophetic writings.[12] The Old Testament expresses God's kingship as both present and future. God is Israel's king as well as king of all the earth, "but the kingdom is always Israel's."[13] However, both John the Baptist and Jesus rejected the particularistic idea of the kingdom, especially as represented in Judaism.[14]

In the past discussions about the kingdom of God, especially among scholars, have centered on what the kingdom meant, especially with regards to time. The concepts of "consistent eschatology" and "realized eschatology" became dominant positions for those who believe that Jesus spoke about the kingdom of God either as a future event or the kingdom as a wholly present reality respectively.[15] However today few scholars argue against the position that Jesus proclaimed the message of the kingdom as both present and future, especially after careful inductive study of the Gospels. Therefore, Ladd's saying "the presence of the future" is most appropriate. And for some, "The kingdom of heaven is associated with the church because the church is the realization of the kingdom of heaven. The church brings the heavenly rule to the earth through the heavenly ministry of Christ."[16] But we do not intend to focus on

---

11. Davies and Allison see no significant distinction between the kingdom of God and the kingdom of heaven in Matthew. Davies and Allison, *Gospel According to Matthew*, 187. Similarly Craig S. Keener says, "Some earlier dispensationalists contrasted the kingdom of heaven and the kingdom of God, but few hold this view today, and it is no longer a necessary part of modern dispensationalism." Keener, *Matthew*, 41. Although Matthew's preferred rendering is the "kingdom of heaven," this study employs the two expressions as interchangeable terms. Robert H. Gundry, however, believes that Matthew's preferred term "heaven" is his expression of the *universality* of the dominion by Jesus and the Father. Robert H. Gundry, *Matthew: A Commentary on His Literary and Theological Art* (Grand Rapids: Eerdmans, 1982), 8.

12. Ladd, *Theology of the New Testament*, 58.

13. Ladd, 62.

14. Ladd, 62.

15. See the discussion on the debate over eschatology in George Eldon Ladd, *The Presence of the Future: The Eschatology of Biblical Realism*, rev. ed. (Grand Rapids: Eerdmans, 1974), 3–42.

16. John Pester, "The Building of the Church as the Reality of the Kingdom of the Heavens Through the Heavenly Ministry of Christ in the Gospel of Matthew," *Affirmation & Critique: A Journal of Christian Thought* 23, no. 1 (Spring 2018): 24.

these theological debates. Our primary focus is to look at the "new principle – the reign of God – introduced into the world by our Lord Jesus Christ and destined to transform all areas of human society."[17]

The Fulfillment of the Kingdom

The Synoptic Gospels, along with the Gospel of John, announce the dawn of the kingdom of God.[18] The Gospels show that the coming of Jesus is the fulfillment of Old Testament prophecies (cf. Matt 2:6 // Mic 5:2; Matt 4:13–16 // Isa 9:1–6). In the Judean wilderness, John the Baptist saw his job description as one who was preparing the way for the Lord. He baptized people for repentance in view of the coming kingdom. Then Jesus came. He was baptized by John and was immediately led by the Holy Spirit to the wilderness to be tempted by the devil (Matt 4:1–11; Luke 4:1–13). After he overcame the devil, he came back and began preaching the kingdom of heaven. Jesus "appointed twelve – designating them apostles – that they might be with him and that he might send them out to preach" (Mark 3:14). But one of them was a betrayer! Many others followed Jesus; among them were those who "ate the loaves and had your fill" (John 6:26–27).

Jesus came to establish the kingdom that God promised to the people of Israel through the prophets, a kingdom that would embrace the whole world. In the Gospels, the kingdom of God is "expectation realized."[19] As Dunn rightly points out, "Not only does Jesus proclaim the kingdom's nearness; equally thematic is the note of fulfillment."[20] Therefore, Christ's coming ushered in the rule of God in the world. This dynamic concept of the rule of God is the integrating center of Jesus's message and mission.[21] We find this central message in the Beatitudes. God rules in the community of the believers. The kingdom is within the heart (Luke 17:20–21) and yet has outward manifestations (Matt 7:24–27; Luke 6:46–49).

---

17. Ladd, *Presence of the Future*, 4.
18. Paul Woods, "First Among Equals: Christian Theology and Modern Philosophy," *Transformation* 34, no. 3 (2016): 165. According to Woods, "Firstly, the kingdom of God includes but is bigger than the Church; God acts beyond the Church, in human society. The kingdom seeks to control all areas of life and represent the dominion of God in every sphere of human endeavor."
19. Dunn, *Christianity in the Making*, 439.
20. Dunn, 437.
21. Ladd, *Presence of the Future*, xi.

But how do we participate in the coming of the kingdom? Since Jesus taught his disciples to pray, "Your kingdom come," every generation of Christians must seek to understand the meaning of the phrase and its practical application for their own time. Here is the key. Jesus concluded the Sermon on the Mount with the following:

> Therefore everyone who hears these words of mine and puts them into practice is like a wise man who built his house on the rock. The rain came down, the streams rose, and the winds blew and beat against that house; yet it did not fall, because it had its foundation on the rock. But everyone who hears these words of mine and does not put them into practice is like a foolish man who built his house on sand. The rain came down, the streams rose, and the winds blew and beat against that house, and it fell with a great crash. (Matt 7:24–27; cf. Luke 6:46–49)

The issue borders on practical application of the message of the kingdom. John B. Carpenter is right that in Matthew 25:31–46, "it comes as no surprise that the criterion of judgment is one not of profession but of practice."[22] Believers are the salt and light of the world (Matt 5:13–16). Jesus intended that his followers should "make the teaching about God our Savior attractive" (Titus 2:10).[23] But the fulfillment of the promised kingdom with the coming of Christ does not mean the consummation or the eternal state yet. We are rather referring to the time between Jesus's first coming and the consummation and our role to make the world a better place for humanity in this interim period. What Jesus teaches in the Gospels is the totality of life devoted to kingdom purposes. To usher in the kingdom of God includes sowing the seed of the kingdom through good works (Matt 5:16), proclaiming the good news (Matt 24:14), praying for the kingdom (Matt 6:5–13; Luke 11:1–4), storing treasures in heaven (Matt 6:19–21), carrying the cross (Matt 16:24; Luke 9:23), and making disciples of all nations (Matt 28:19–20). All of this calls for the ultimate commitment of every true believer in Christ.

---

22. John B. Carpenter, "The Parable of the Talents in Missionary Perspective: A Call for an Economic Spirituality," *Missiology: An International Review* 25, no. 2 (April 1997): 166.

23. The failure of the church to act as salt and light in a decayed and dark world has had a profoundly negative effect and impact. Believers must be reminded that just as God jealously guards his kingdom by using his children in the world, Satan also jealously protects his kingdom and fights hard to keep it by using his own messengers. When light fails to shine, darkness will prevail.

Therefore, we may argue that the reason we are not seeing the kingdom come as God intended and are seeing the world remaining in a mess is that the church is doing too little to promote the kingdom of God. If we gauge the things we treasure by what we really desire and pursue, "for which we plan and prepare and to which we devote time and energy,"[24] we would probably come to the conclusion that we are not doing enough for the kingdom of God. Moreover, with the multiplication of tares among the wheat and the cheapening of the gospel message for temporal gains by those who "masquerade as servants of righteousness" (2 Cor 11:14–15) and "put on a mask to cover up greed" (1 Thess 2:5), the church is fast losing relevance in a world plagued by sin. And this issue leads to the next point.

The Kingdom Expressed in Ethical Principles

As we saw above, what Jesus considers crucial about the kingdom of God is how his followers *practice* the message of the kingdom. For example, one of the problems of the teachers of the law and the Pharisees is that "they do not practice what they preach" (Matt 23:3). Richard B. Hays says, "The Sermon on the Mount calls for a life of uncompromising rigor in discipleship."[25] Jesus concludes the Sermon on the Mount by stressing that a theoretical knowledge is of no use to any person or community (Matt 7:24–27). Therefore, knowledge alone lacks the power to transform. To usher in the kingdom, followers of the Messiah must put into practice the values of the kingdom.

In Matthew 5:1–12 (cf. Luke 6:20–26), Jesus presents the core values of the kingdom of God. These core values are the moral principles or ethical standards by which the disciples live. They are the Beatitudes, which D. A. Carson calls "the norms of the kingdom."[26] Carson sees the Beatitudes as "the witness of the kingdom" because, "The righteousness of the life you live will attract attention, even if that attention regularly takes the form of opposition."[27] The Beatitudes speak of unique ethical standards for the children of the kingdom.[28] Each

---

24. Robin Gamble, *The Irrelevant Church* (Eastbourne: Monarch, 1991), 94.

25. Richard B. Hays, *The Moral Vision of the New Testament: A Contemporary Introduction to New Testament Ethics* (Waterloo: T&T Clark, 1996), 97.

26. D. A. Carson, *The Sermon on the Mount: An Exposition of Matthew 5–7* (Carlisle: Paternoster, 2013), 22, 24.

27. Carson, *Sermon on the Mount*, 33.

28. In the words of D. Martyn Lloyd-Jones, the Beatitudes follow a "spiritual logical sequence." D. Martyn Lloyd-Jones, *Studies in the Sermon on the Mount* (Nottingham: Inter-Varsity, 1976; repr. 2009), 46.

Beatitude begins with the word "blessed." The word "blessed" (Greek *makarios*) can mean happy or carefree. But since mourning is not the mark of a carefree person, we need to understand happiness from Jesus's perspective. Daniel N. Doriani points out that Jesus "does not have ordinary happiness, the happiness that comes from food or entertainment, in mind. Jesus's 'happy' disciples are poor and hungry; they mourn and suffer persecution. For disciples, happiness means wholeness and integrity even in the darkest hour."[29] Let us briefly examine each Beatitude.

The poor in spirit are those "who know they have no righteousness of their own."[30] These people "recognize that they are completely and utterly destitute in the realm of the spirit. They recognize their lack of spiritual resources and therefore their complete dependence on God."[31] According to Jones, "There is no one in the kingdom of God who is not *poor in spirit*."[32] The basic meaning of poverty in spirit is "emptying."[33] We must be emptied of self before God fills us. To see an example of this self-emptying, we might look at two people who went to pray – a Pharisee and a tax collector (Luke 18:9–13). The Pharisee came to God full of himself. He did not pray to God but prayed about himself. The tax collector was poor in spirit because he recognized his emptiness. Equally, by recognizing their poverty, the prostitutes and tax collectors were going ahead of the Pharisees and teachers of the law into the kingdom of heaven (Matt 21:31–32). God is always pleased with people who are poor in spirit. Isaiah 66:2 says, "These are ones I look on with favor: those who are humble and contrite in spirit, and who tremble at my word." According to A. W. Tozer,

> The way to deeper knowledge of God is through the lonely valleys of soul poverty and abnegation of all things. The blessed ones who possess the Kingdom are they who have repudiated every external thing and have rooted from their hearts all sense of possessing. These are the "poor in spirit."[34]

---

29. Daniel N. Doriani, *Matthew*, vol. 1, Matthew 1–13, Reformed Expository Commentary (Phillipsburg: P&R, 2008), 106.
30. Mark E. Ross, *Let's Study Matthew* (Edinburgh: Banner of Truth Trust, 2009), 41.
31. Carson, *Sermon on the Mount*, 95.
32. Jones, *Studies in the Sermon on the Mount*, 46, emphasis original.
33. Jones, 46.
34. A. W. Tozer, *The Pursuit of God* (Camp Hill: Christian Publications, 1993), 23.

Those who mourn are people "who grieve over their lack of righteousness."[35] This is not ordinary mourning such as in time of bereavement but "a more fundamental kind of mourning."[36] According to Leon Morris,

> Perhaps we should bear in mind that typically the worldly take a light hearted attitude to the serious issues of life, a fact that is evident in our modern pleasure-loving generation. In their seeking after self-gratification and pleasure they do not grieve over sin or evil. Because they do not grieve over what is wrong in themselves, they do not repent; and because they do not grieve over the wrong they share with others in the communities in which they live, they take few steps to set things right.[37]

These people are not moved by the plight of the poor and the unfortunate in the society. "It may be that Jesus is saying that our values are wrong and that it is those who mourn in the face of the evils that are part and parcel of life as we know it, those who mourn over the way God's cause is so often neglected and his people despised, who are the truly blessed ones."[38] Morris speaks powerfully to our African context in which evil seems to be celebrated rather than mourned and definite steps taken to address it. People usually condone evil because they are either guilty of the same thing and are unwilling to repent or will do the same if given the opportunity.

The meek humble themselves before the Lord. Meekness is not weakness.[39] Tozer says, "The meek man is not a human mouse afflicted with a sense of his own inferiority."[40] Meek people are those "who, being neither proud nor arrogant, humble themselves under the mighty hand of God and claim nothing for themselves."[41] Kapolyo rightly says, "The meek do get angry, but at the right time, and not because of wounded pride. They humbly place all their abilities and emotions under God's complete control and do not allow their personal circumstances, however adverse, to disturb their peace."[42] And why will these

---

35. Ross, *Let's Study Matthew*, 46.

36. Leon Morris, *Gospel According to Matthew*, Pillar of the New Testament Commentary (Cambridge, UK/Grand Rapids: Eerdmans, 1992), 97.

37. Morris, *Gospel According to Matthew*, 97.

38. Morris, 97.

39. Joe Kapolyo, "Matthew," in *Africa Bible Commentary*, ed. Tokunboh Adeyemo (Nairobi: WordAlive, 2006), 1118.

40. Tozer, *Pursuit of God*, 104.

41. Ross, *Let's Study Matthew*, 46.

42. Kapolyo, "Matthew," 1118.

people inherit the earth? If we look at the earth as the new heaven and the new earth (Rev 21:1) as Kapolyo sees it, God "knows they will not spoil it for their own selfish appetites . . . since they already possess everything in Christ (2 Cor 6:10)."[43] While Kapolyo rightly suggests that the earth Jesus spoke about is the renewed world, it is probably correct to say that even in this life, it is not always those who push their way to the top who "inherit the earth." God often fights for the cause of those who are slighted or treated disrespectfully simply because they choose not to assert themselves or "fight" for their rights. The meek person leans on the Lord and is never put to shame. "He knows he is weak and helpless as God has declared him to be, but paradoxically, he knows at the same time that he is, in the sight of God, more important than angels. In himself, nothing; in God, everything."[44]

Those who hunger and thirst for righteousness are people who "intensely long for that righteousness of life that is pleasing to God."[45] The kingdom that both John the Baptist and Jesus announced is the kingdom of righteousness. The new kingdom, as opposed to the kingdom of darkness, is a kingdom with a set of good values. One of them is genuine repentance. John the Baptist and Jesus began preaching by calling people to repent. Turning away from a former way of life is a mark of true repentance. John told those who repented to "produce fruit in keeping with repentance" (Matt 3:8). In other words, there must be evidence of genuine repentance. Faith in Jesus is not a matter of the heart only as some people claim. The fruit must be evident to all. For instance, John told the soldiers not to extort money from people or engage in any inhuman treatment of civilians (Luke 3:14). The tax collectors must not collect more than required (Luke 3:12–13). They were all now in the kingdom of God and must practice the ethics of the kingdom. John the Baptist speaks powerfully to the African situation. We must renounce all forms of corrupt practices in both private and public squares.

The merciful are kind to the undeserving. Hays calls this Beatitude "the hermeneutic of mercy."[46] Mercy is "one of the most important character qualities that Jesus seeks to inculcate in those who heed his words."[47] The mercy of God is a theme that runs throughout Scripture. Because our God is merciful,

---

43. Kapolyo, 1118.
44. Tozer, *Pursuit of God*, 104–5.
45. Ross, *Let's Study Matthew*, 46.
46. Hays, *Moral Vision*, 99.
47. Hays, 99. Hays says Jesus cites Hos 6:6 in emphasizing the subject of mercy (Matt 9:13; 12:7).

he forgives sins (Ps 130:1–4), and he expects his children to practice the same. If God were to keep a record of sins, no one could stand. Showing mercy includes the ability to forgive people who offend us even if they choose not to apologize. But we can also show mercy to people who owe us material things like money. Jesus illustrates the need to show mercy to the undeserving through the parable of the unmerciful servant (Matt 18:21–35).[48] He uses material things like money to draw home the spiritual truth of forgiveness.

Those who are pure in heart are so spiritually connected to Jesus that they are able to "see" him. R. T. France suggests that this Beatitude is based on Psalm 24:3–6.[49] The text reads,

> Who may ascend the mountain of the LORD?
>> Who may stand in his holy place?
> The one who has clean hands and a pure heart,
>> who does not trust in an idol
>> or swear by a false god.
>
> They will receive blessing from the LORD
>> and vindication from God their Savior.
> Such is the generation of those who seek him,
>> who seek your face, God of Jacob. (Ps 24:3–6)

Zion is the hill of the Lord, the holy city. In the holy city is the temple of the Lord. The prerequisite for standing in this holy place is "clean hands and a pure heart." This psalm is like an abridged version of Psalm 15:1–5:

> LORD, who may dwell in your sacred tent?
>> Who may live on your holy mountain?
>
> The one whose walk is blameless,
>> who does what is righteous,
>> who speaks the truth from their heart;
> whose tongue utters no slander,
>> who does no wrong to a neighbor,
>> and casts no slur on others;
> who despises a vile person
>> but honors those who fear the LORD;
> who keeps an oath even when it hurts,

---

48. See Warren Carter, "Resisting and Imitating the Empire: Imperial Paradigms in Two Matthean Parables," *Interpretation* (July 2002): 260–72.

49. R. T. France, *The Gospel of Matthew*, The New International Commentary on the New Testament (Grand Rapids: Eerdmans, 2007), 168.

> and does not change their mind;
> who lends money to the poor without interest;
> who does not accept a bribe against the innocent.
>
> Whoever does these things
> will never be shaken.

"Clean hands and a pure heart" are the equivalent of "whose walk is blameless" and "who does what is righteous." All forms of perversity spring from the heart. Therefore Jesus says, "But the things that come out of a person's mouth come from the heart, and these defile them. For out of the heart come evil thoughts – murder, adultery, sexual immorality, theft, false testimony, slander. These are what defile a person" (Matt 15:18–20). Because of the crucial role the heart plays in running our lives, the Bible says, "Above all else, guard your heart, for everything you do flows from it" (Prov 4:23).

Peace makers will be called the children of God. Peace is a rare commodity in a world full of strife and violence. But Jesus is the Prince of Peace (Isa 9:6). And because he is the Prince of Peace, his disciples must also work to keep the peace in a world ruined by violent conflicts. But how can they bring peace in the world? The primary means of establishing true peace in the world is preaching the gospel of peace. Paul tells the believers at Ephesus, and of course all believers, to stand firm "with your feet fitted with the readiness that comes from the gospel of peace" (Eph 6:15). It is the gospel of Christ that "destroyed the barrier, the dividing wall of hostility" and brought "peace to you who were far away and peace to those who were near" (Eph 2:14, 17).

Christians who proclaim the gospel of Jesus Christ are the true peacemakers. Any religion that claims to be a religion of peace and yet fills the world with violence and bloodshed is an agent of the murderer and father of lies, Satan (John 8:44). It is a counterfeit religion and is not connected with the God of peace. Not only do Christians preach peace, but they also seek to "live at peace with everyone" (Rom 12:18).[50]

Finally, those who are persecuted because of righteousness are blessed. This is a clear warning from Jesus that the persecution of believers is inevitable and

---

50. For example, the truth that remains hidden to the rest of the world is that Christians in Nigeria have never at any time calculated and launched an attack against people of other faiths. And although terrorists have always been the aggressors and attackers, Christians never fought back in most of the attacks. One example is the many bombings that left hundreds of Christians and non-Christians dead and many more maimed on 20 May 2014 in Jos, Nigeria. But any time Christians act in self-defense, the world believes the propaganda by terrorist media outfits that Christians were the aggressors. The Christians' pursuit of genuine peace is always used against them.

that the coming of the kingdom of light does not necessarily guarantee a good reception. Jesus says, "This is the verdict: Light has come into the world, but people loved darkness instead of light because their deeds were evil. Everyone who does evil hates the light, and will not come into the light for fear that their deeds will be exposed" (John 3:19–20). The haters of light are sure to persecute the bearers of light. But instead of mourning, Jesus says, "Rejoice and be glad, because great is your reward in heaven, for in the same way they persecuted the prophets who were before you" (Matt 5:12). Doriani rightly says,

> The call to rejoice in persecution demands that we reappraise our values. Jesus asks us to detach ourselves from this age and recalibrate our ideas about time. We should tell ourselves, "Our time on earth is short; eternity is long. If we endure insults or privation in this life, they are short-lived in comparison to eternity. If we should die because of persecution, then we meet the Lord and taste his goodness earlier than anticipated."[51]

In summary, the disciples' righteousness must be expressed as beyond that of Pharisaic and rabbinic righteousness (Matt 5:20). Righteousness that God accepts involves taming anger (Matt 5:21–26), taming sexual fashions (5:27–30), keeping our word (5:33–37), turning the other cheek (5:38–42),[52] and loving the enemy (5:43–48). Loving the enemy is a critical issue in the context of radicalization of Islam in the world and in the quest to establish theocratic government in Northern Nigeria under *shari'a* law. Yusufu Turaki well says, "The movement of some Muslims toward militancy and classical Islam and their longing for a return to the days of the Caliphate have served to aggravate suspicion, conflict and violence."[53]

The Kingdom Explained in Parables

It is said that parables are earthly stories with heavenly meaning. According to Klyne R. Snodgrass, Jesus's parables are "fictional descriptions taken from everyday life" and "focus mostly on humans."[54] Although they focus on humans,

---

51. Doriani, *Matthew*, 133.
52. See Sunday Bobai Agang, *No More Cheeks to Turn?* (Nairobi: WordAlive, 2017).
53. Yusufu Turaki, *Tainted Legacy: Islam, Colonialism and Slavery in Northern Nigeria* (McLean: Isaac Publishing, 2010), 173.
54. Klyne R. Snodgrass, *Stories with Intent: A Comprehensive Guide to the Parables of Jesus* (Grand Rapids: Eerdmans, 2008), 18.

we must also recognize that "Jesus' parables are theocentric."[55] Snodgrass means that although the parables are intended to change behavior and create disciples, "they do so by telling about God and his kingdom, the new reality God seeks to establish on earth."[56] Jesus spoke in parables to explain the nature of the kingdom of God. Key among the parables of the kingdom are the following:

The parable of the sower (Matt 13:1–22)

Jesus uses the parable of the sower to indicate the kind of responses people have when they hear the message of the gospel. People are likened to the hard road, shallow soil on rock, thorny places, and good soil. As Jesus explains,

> When anyone hears the message about the kingdom and does not understand it, the evil one comes and snatches away what was sown in their heart. This is the seed sown along the path. The seed falling on rocky ground refers to someone who hears the word and at once receives it with joy. But since they have no root, they last only a short time. When trouble or persecution comes because of the word, they quickly fall away. The seed falling among the thorns refers to someone who hears the word, but the worries of this life and the deceitfulness of wealth choke the word, making it unfruitful. But the seed falling on good soil refers to someone who hears the word and understands it. This is the one who produces a crop, yielding a hundred, sixty or thirty times what was sown. (Matt 13:19–23)

The parable of the weeds (Matt 13:24–30)

This describes a farmer who sowed good seed in his field but his enemy came and sowed weeds when everyone was sleeping. This shows that in this world, the church is a "mixed community" that consists of good and evil.[57] "This points to the influence of evil in the church."[58] According to the parable, the owner allows the weeds and the wheat to grow together. The appearance of weeds is deceptive because they look like wheat. But the separation comes at harvest time: "At that time I will tell the harvesters: First collect the weeds and

---

55. Snodgrass, *Stories with Intent*, 20.
56. Snodgrass, 20.
57. Snodgrass, 199.
58. Snodgrass, 200.

tie them in bundles to be burned; then gather the wheat and bring it into my barn" (v. 30).

The parable of the yeast (Matt 13:33; Luke 13:20-21)
Jesus uses the parable of the years to illustrate the dynamism and influence of the kingdom of heaven. It grows and expands until the entire world is saturated with the values of the kingdom. "The kingdom of heaven is like yeast that a woman took and mixed into about sixty pounds [about 27 kg] of flour until it worked all through the dough" (Matt 13:33). We can only imagine what the world will look like when more and more people embrace the values of the kingdom such as speaking the truth, loving our neighbors, respecting human life, working hard rather than stealing, and pursuing peace with all people.

The parables of the hidden treasure and the pearl (Matt 13:44-46)
These underscore the inestimable worth of the kingdom of God. Jesus said, "The kingdom of heaven is like treasure hidden in a field. When a man found it, he hid it again, and then in his joy went and sold all he had and bought that field. Again, the kingdom of heaven is like a merchant looking for fine pearls. When he found one of great value, he went away and sold everything he had and bought it." The value one places on the kingdom of God determines the level of one's investment. There is nothing too precious to relinquish or sacrifice for the sake of the kingdom of heaven.

The parable of the net (Matt 13:47-50)
Jesus describes a net that is let down into the lake that caught all kinds of fish and teaches that within the church is a mixed multitude of the good and the bad. However, there will be a day of separation. "This is how it will be at the end of the age. The angels will come and separate the wicked from the righteous and throw them into the blazing furnace, where there will be weeping and gnashing of teeth" (vv. 49-50).

The parable of the unforgiving servant (Matt 18:23-35)
Here Jesus stresses the necessity of forgiveness. The one who refuses to forgive others forfeits God's forgiveness.

> Then the master called the servant in. "You wicked servant," he said, "I canceled all that debt of yours because you begged me to. Shouldn't you have had mercy on your fellow servant just as I had

on you?" In anger his master turned him over to the jailers to be tortured, until he should pay back all he owed.

> This is how my heavenly Father will treat each of you unless you forgive your brother from your heart. (Matt 18:32–36; cf. Matt 6:12, 14–15; Mark 11:25)

The parable of the seed (Mark 4:26–29)

Jesus tells the parable of the seed scattered on the ground about the sometimes unnoticed growth of the kingdom. Jesus said,

> This is what the kingdom of God is like. A man scatters seed on the ground. Night and day, whether he sleeps or gets up, the seed sprouts and grows, though he does not know how. All by itself the soil produces grain – first the stalk, then the head, then the full kernel in the head. As soon as the grain is ripe, he puts the sickle to it, because the harvest has come. (Mark 4:26–29)

The parable of the generous landowner

This parable tells of a landowner and workers who are hired at different times of the day but receive equal pay (Matt 20:1–16) and is anchored in "reversal of fortunes,"[59] namely, "many who are first will be last, and many who are last will be first" (Matt 19:30; cf. 20:16). The parable teaches that "God rewards his servants according to grace," and "those who treat God's grace as his obligation are evil."[60] Similarly, "God's gracious generosity vastly exceeds human merit-based expectations, and his servants will receive a reward appropriate to their work."[61]

---

59. Keener, *Matthew*, 305. According to Turner, the reversal could be seen in three dimensions. First is religious reversal in which tax collectors and sinners who enter the kingdom of God last are preferred by God to the Jewish religious leaders. Second is redemptive-historical reversal in which the hired workers at different times "represent successive epochs in history. Gentiles instead of Jews eventually come into prominence. Third is ecclesiastical reversal in which the disciples who wish to be prominent will be humbled, but those who are humble will be considered truly great (Matt 18:1–4; 20:25–28)." Turner, *Matthew*, 480–81.

60. Keener, *Matthew*, 306.

61. Turner, *Matthew*, 480.

The parable of the wedding banquet (Matt 22:1-14)
Here Jesus shows that the kingdom offer can be rejected. Similarly, counterfeits and impostors are found among those who embrace the kingdom. But they will be revealed and removed at the end.

> But when the king came in to see the guests, he noticed a man there who was not wearing wedding clothes. He asked, "How did you get in here without wedding clothes, friend?" The man was speechless.
>
> Then the king told the attendants, "Tie him hand and foot, and throw him outside, into the darkness, where there will be weeping and gnashing of teeth." For many are invited, but few are chosen. (vv. 11-14)

The parable of the mustard seed (Matt 13:31-32; Mark 4:30-35; Luke 13:18-19)
This parable teaches that while the kingdom invitation is slighted by some, it takes root and blossoms in the soil where it has been planted. Its beginning may look small and insignificant, but it grows large. According to Jesus, though the mustard seed "is the smallest of all your seeds, yet when it grows, it is the largest of garden plants and becomes a tree, so that the birds come and perch in its branches" (Matt 13:32).

The parable of the ten virgins (Matt 25:1-13)
With this parable Jesus underscores the need to prepare for the second coming of the Son of Man. Jesus concludes the parable by saying, "Therefore keep watch, because you do not know the day or the hour" (v. 13).

The parable of the talents (Matt 25:14-30; cf. Luke 19:11-27)
This parable indicates that talents and resources are given to individuals according to their abilities. What counts is faithfulness in the use of the gifts and resources at one's disposal. Each person will be rewarded according to his or her faithfulness and not according to the amount received.

> The man with the two talents also came. "Master," he said, "you entrusted me with two bags of gold; see, I have gained two more."
>
> His master replied, "Well done, good and faithful servant! You have been faithful with a few things; I will put you in charge of many things. Come and share your master's happiness!" (Matt 25:22-23)

The parable also warns against laziness and unfaithfulness in the service of the Lord.

The parable of the vineyard (Matt 21:33–46; Mark 12:1–12; Luke 20:9–19)
The parable of the one who planted a vineyard and rented it out to some tenants is an indictment of Israel for rejecting Jesus the Messiah.

Some of the parables of the kingdom have an eschatological dimension as well (cf. Matt 25:1–30; Luke 19:11–27). And included in the eschatological parables is the concept of recompense.

The Kingdom Entered Through Repentance and Faith

Repentance and faith are prerequisites for entry into the kingdom of God. The Gospels clearly teach that there is no such thing as entering the kingdom of heaven without repentance (Matt 4:17; 11:20–21; 21:32; Mark 1:15; 6:7–12; Luke 13:3–5; 15:7; 16:27–30). For example, Jesus denounced Chorazin and Bethsaida because they saw his miracles but they neither believed or repented. He said, "Woe to you, Chorazin! Woe to you, Bethsaida! If the miracles that were performed in you had been performed in Tyre and Sidon, they would have repented long ago in sackcloth and ashes" (Matt 11:21). Similarly, Jesus spoke to the chief priests and the elders of the people, "For John came to you to show you the way of righteousness, and you did not believe him, but the tax collectors and the prostitutes did. And even after you saw this, you did not repent and believe him" (Matt 21:32). Heaven's jubilation over one sinner who repents underscores the significance of repentance. Jesus said, "I tell you that in the same way there will be more rejoicing in heaven over one sinner who repents than over ninety-nine righteous persons who do not need to repent" (Luke 15:7). Two things stand out regarding repentance and faith.

Repentance Is Renouncing the Sinful Way of Life

In the Bible, repentance and conversion are similar in meaning. Therefore we will treat repentance and conversion as interchangeable terms. Jesus said, "Go into all the world and preach the gospel to all creation. Whoever *believes* and is baptized will be saved, but whoever does not *believe* will be condemned" (Mark 16:15–16, emphasis added). Believing is embracing the gospel message about God's offer of salvation to the world through Christ. A turning from the former sinful way of life is involved in this expression of trust. Therefore, we may define conversion as turning away from sin.[62] Repentance carries the same basic meaning of turning to God (Matt 3:5–12; Luke 3:7–14).[63] It involves "a radical change in the individual's disposition."[64] Faith and repentance are inseparable.[65] The turning to God (1 Thess 1:9) and new behavior (Acts 26:10–20) that Kearsley points out as the fruits of repentance are what conversion means. Both Kearsley and S. S. Smalley cite 1 Thessalonians 1:9 to stress the meaning of conversion and repentance.[66] Both authors see transformation and sanctification involved in repentance and conversion.[67] In ordinary language, transformation is an improved change in appearance or usefulness, while sanctification is beatification of the inner life resulting in outward manifestation of good works. Christian transformation is inner change that involves renewal of the mind in conformity with the perfect will of God (Rom 12:2), while sanctification is the pursuit of holy living. Regarding sanctification, Paul says,

> For you know what instructions we gave you by the authority of the Lord Jesus.
>
> *It is God's will that you should be sanctified*: that you should avoid sexual immorality; that each of you should learn to control your own body in a way that is holy and honorable, not in passionate lust like the pagans, who do not know God; and that in this matter no one should wrong or take advantage of a brother or sister. The Lord will punish all those who commit such sins, as we told you and warned you before. *For God did not call us to be impure, but to live a holy life.* (1 Thess 4:2–7, emphasis added)

Repentance and conversion do not happen until the message of the kingdom of God is proclaimed. John the Baptist and Jesus proclaimed the message of the kingdom and called for repentance from sin as a prerequisite for entry into the kingdom of heaven (Matt 3:1–2; 4:17). Turning away from sin is necessary because sin is "an assault on God."[68] But how does conversion come

---

62. See Samuel Waje Kunhiyop, *Christian Conversion in Africa: The Bajju Experience* (Jos: ECWA Productions, 2005), 2.

63. R. Kearsley, "Repentance," in *New Dictionary of Theology*, ed. Sinclair B. Ferguson and David F. Wright (Downers Grove: InterVarsity, 1988), 580.

64. Kearsley, "Repentance," 580.

65. Kearsley, 580.

66. S. S. Smalley, "Conversion," in *New Dictionary of Theology*, ed. Sinclair B. Ferguson and David F. Wright (Downers Grove: InterVarsity, 1988), 167; Kearsley, "Repentance," 580.

67. Kearsley, "Repentance," 580; Smalley, "Conversion," 167.

68. John Piper, *What Jesus Demands from the World* (Wheaton: Crossway, 2006), 41.

about? Jesus tells us that the work of the Holy Spirit is primary in conversion. Jesus said,

> When [the Holy Spirit] comes, he will prove the world to be in the wrong about sin and righteousness and judgment: about sin, because people do not believe in me; about righteousness, because I am going to the Father, where you can see me no longer; and about judgment, because the prince of this world now stands condemned. (John 16:8–11)

Apart from teaching believers, the Holy Spirit convicts the world of guilt. The Greek word to convict (*elegchō*) used in the text "implies rebuking in such a way as to bring about conviction."[69] Without the Holy Spirit, sinners may live and feel comfortable with their guilt. Their conscience may be so "seared as with hot iron" (1 Tim 4:2) that they no longer feel their lost state. Sin becomes a way of life. But the Holy Spirit makes the sinner see the righteousness of God and his righteous indignation against sinful life.

True conversion involves a radical change of perception about sin and evil, good and righteousness, truth and falsehood. It is "a conscious, deliberate decision to leave sin behind – and a conscious turning to God with a commitment to follow His will for our lives. It is a change of direction, an alteration of attitudes, and a yielding of the will."[70] However the dilemma is that repentance can be superfluous and temporary. In his parable, Jesus likens this repentance to a seed growing in rocky soil. "Those on rocky ground are the ones who receive the word with joy when they hear it, but they have no root. They believe for a while, but in the time of testing they fall away" (Luke 8:13). This is why African Christians must wrestle with the issue of genuine versus fake conversion because it appears that the church is baptizing people who do not show signs of turning away from sin.

Faith Is the Expression of Confidence in the Gift and Power of God

Faith is a subject that lies at the heart of the New Testament.[71] James D. G. Dunn observes that "nearly two-thirds of the references to faith occur in relation to

---

69. Millard J. Erickson, *Christian Theology*, 2nd ed. (Grand Rapids: Baker Academic, 1998), 275–76.

70. Franklin Graham, *Billy Graham in Quotes* (Nashville: Thomas Nelson, 2011), 70.

71. Judith M. Lieu, "Faith and the Fourth Gospel: A Conversation with Teresa Morgan," *Journal for the Study of the New Testament* 40, no. 3 (February, 2018): 289.

miracles."[72] In the "three circles of miracles and discipleship"[73] recorded in Matthew 8:1–10:1, for instance, Turner rightly says, "the overall emphasis is on faith, discipleship, and gentile mission."[74] But most scholars pay little attention to these vital elements in the Gospels. The Gospels speak about faith in more than one sense. Salvation is by faith (Matt 8:5–13; John 3:16). The many who "will come from the east and the west, and will take their places at the feast with Abraham, Isaac and Jacob in the kingdom of heaven" (Matt 8:11) are those who placed their faith in Jesus. That is saving faith. But some believers will turn away from their faith as a result of persecution (Matt 24:9–10). The Gospels also show that many people received what they asked for because they trusted Jesus (cf. Matt 9:21–22; 15:22–28). This is faith that receives from the Lord.

So on the one hand, Jesus is particularly touched by those who demonstrated faith in the power of God and his ability to perform miracles (Matt 8:8–10; 9:2, 27–29; 15:25–28; Mark 5:30–34; Luke 5:18–20; 7:6–9; 17:12–19; 18:35–42). For example, Jesus was touched by the faith of the centurion and exclaimed,

> Truly I tell you, I have not found anyone in Israel with such great faith. I say to you that many will come from the east and the west, and will take their places at the feast with Abraham, Isaac and Jacob in the kingdom of heaven. But the subjects of the kingdom will be thrown outside, into the darkness, where there will be weeping and gnashing of teeth. (Matt 8:10–12)

This kind of faith is salvific. Then Jesus told the centurion, "Go! Let it be done just as you believed it would" (Matt 8:13). Similarly, the woman who was subject to bleeding for twelve years showed an unusual demonstration of faith (Matt 9:20–22; Luke 8:43–48). Others believed that Jesus was able to forgive their sins (Luke 7:37–50). All of these people were commended for their faith.

But on the other hand, unbelief is the most dangerous impediment in the way of the mighty works of God. The Synoptic Gospels portray Jesus's displeasure when he encountered hearts filled with unbelief or little faith, even among his own disciples (Matt 8:23–26; 14:25–31; 16:5–8; 17:15–20; Mark 4:35–41; 16:14; Luke 8:22–25; 12:27–28). According to Luz, "Little faith is faith mingled with fear and doubt. Little faith is the faith of those who would like to believe but cannot."[75] But lack of faith means that faith is virtually absent.

---

72. Dunn, *Jesus and the Spirit*, 74.
73. Turner, *Matthew*, 227.
74. Turner, *Matthew*, 227.
75. Luz, *Theology of the New Testament*, 68.

Lack of faith in Jesus was reason for him not to perform miracles even in his own hometown and among his own people (Matt 13:54–58; Mark 6:4–6). Jesus berated and condemned them for their lack of faith.

The possibility that faith could increase or diminish or fail altogether is clearly taught in the Gospels (Luke 17:5–6; 18:7–8; 22:32–34). Several times the disciples asked Jesus to increase their faith. In response, Jesus told them, "Truly I tell you, if you have faith as small as a mustard seed, you can say to this mountain, 'Move from here to there,' and it will move. Nothing will be impossible for you" (Matt 17:20).

But the dreaded possibility is *failed faith* even among Jesus's followers. The classical example of the possibility of failed faith is Simon Peter. The Lord Jesus foresaw the plan of the enemy to derail Peter from the faith. So Jesus said to him, "Simon, Simon, Satan has asked to sift you as wheat. But I have prayed for you, Simon, that your faith may not fail. And when you have turned back, strengthen your brothers. But he replied, 'Lord, I am ready to go with you to prison and to death'" (Luke 22:31–33). Faith is subject to trial. But like Peter, believers might be presumptuous and think that they are strong enough to stand without recourse to the intercessory prayer of Jesus. Jesus prays for his followers that their faith may not fail.

The Kingdom Expanded through Discipleship[76]

Graham Cray well says, "The greatest good that any person can encounter is to become a follower of Jesus Christ, finding salvation in Him. If we love our neighbors, we will bear witness to them."[77] Primarily, a disciple is one who believes and follows a leader, a philosophy, or a religion. From the calling of the twelve disciples, Jesus made his intentions very clear. The Gospel of Mark sums it up this way, "He appointed twelve – designating them apostles – that they might be with him and that he might send them out to preach and to have authority to drive out demons" (Mark 3:14–15). The first task of Jesus's disciple is *to be* with the Master. Apprenticeship does not happen by proxy. The apprentice must be present and receive instruction from the trainer. The second task of Jesus's disciple is to go on errands: "to send them out to preach and to have authority to drive out demons." This sending is illustrated by

---

76. See Sarma, *People of the Kingdom*, 239–60.

77. Graham Cray, *Disciples and Citizens: A Vision for Distinctive Living* (Nottingham: Inter-Varsity, 2007), 16.

Jesus's commission of the twelve as well as the seventy-two (Matt 10:1–42; Luke 9:1–10; 10:1–17). The errand is fishing for people (Matt 4:19).

This errand means that the mission of Jesus's new community is to disciple the nations (Matt 28:16–20; Mark 16:15–16). Therefore, the Great Commission is essentially "to disciple nations, transform society, and see the glory of the Lord cover the earth."[78] This Commission means that God involves the church in leading the world. Discipleship is the primary means of this involvement; that is, God advances his kingdom on earth through disciple making. True discipleship takes place when the church identifies God's demands for the church and society and equips members to queue into God's program to fulfill those demands. Therefore the relevance of the church must be felt in the family, economy, education, government, arts and media, and science and technology. Regardless of the numerical strength of the church in any given society, if the church is not able to penetrate the areas highlighted above as salt and light, its influence will remain marginal, to say the least. Healing the land invariably involves active participation in all areas of legitimate human endeavor and changing the pagan worldview so that people reflect on and think about issues from a biblical stand point. All of this is a huge responsibility. But God's demands are not burdensome; they are for the salvation, peace, and security of the world. The church advances the kingdom by word and deed. If a church fails to adequately address the moral, social, and spiritual challenges of the society, this failure indicates that church is far from the ideals of the kingdom Jesus proclaimed. Therefore, we will draw a few conclusions here.

First, the goal of Christian discipleship is the transformation of church and society until Christians conform to the image of God and the will of God is done "on earth as it is in heaven" (Matt 6:10). Individual transformation leads to family, community, and national transformation. Every disciple prays and works for this.

Second, discipleship or spiritual formation is the pilgrim's walk. We cannot reach the ultimate until we are all gathered at the feet of Jesus. The implication is that every believer is a disciple. While senior Christians – not necessarily by age – disciple younger Christians in the faith, the senior and mature Christians continue to learn at the feet of Jesus and from fellow Christians as a lifelong process.

Third, effective spiritual formation means that we critically examine the life of Jesus and his teachings as we apply these to contextual and practical life

---

78. Banning Liebscher, *Jesus Culture: Living a Life that Transforms the World* (Shippensburg: Destiny Image, 2009), 59.

situations. If we cannot connect faith with real life situations, we have failed because "faith by itself, if it is not accompanied by action, is dead" (Jas 2:17). Our world needs to see the Christian faith at work.

Fourth, discipleship is modeling lives. It is for this reason that spiritual leadership formation is critical in African Christianity and calls for moral leadership. We need leaders who can say like Paul, "Therefore I urge you to imitate me" (1 Cor 4:16). They boldly tell their followers, "Follow my example, as I follow the example of Christ" (1 Cor 11:1). Beyond this level, however, is the moral leadership in which every Christian must stand above reproach in the community and in the vocation to which God has called him or her. Every Christian has the privilege to lead the world in character. That is moral leadership. It does not require portfolios. It only requires moral excellence.

Fifth, disciple making requires boldness and courage (Matt 10:26-31). Jesus repeatedly said, "Do not be afraid" because he knows that fear is a serious barrier for ministry in a hostile world. Paul asked for prayers that he would declare the word of the Lord *fearlessly* (Eph 6:19). The answer to the early believers' prayers after the threats of authorities was that "they were all filled with the Holy Spirit and spoke the word of God *boldly*" (Acts 4:31, emphasis added). The church in Africa needs this boldness to confront the forces of evil in African society, including terrorism. Without boldness and courage, we cannot survive.

Sixth, disciple making is an enormous task that cannot be done by human wisdom or ingenuity. It is the work of God through his word and the Holy Spirit. Paul says, "He is the one we proclaim, admonishing and teaching everyone with all wisdom, so that we may present everyone fully mature in Christ. To this end I strenuously contend with all the energy Christ so powerfully works in me" (Col 1:28-29). If we follow Paul's example, we will go with his mission statement and transform the church and society.

Finally, discipleship is counting the cost of following the Master. Discipleship means self-denial and carrying one's cross daily to follow the Master (Matt 16:24-25; Luke 9:32; cf. John 12:25-26). To become a disciple of Jesus, one must first count the cost (Luke 14:28-32). The point is that discipleship entails giving up everything to follow the Master, because "those of you who do not give up everything you have cannot be my disciples" (Luke 14:33). Therefore, some who would be disciples apparently did not count the cost and turned away (Matt 8:19-22 // Luke 9:57-60).

Redemption as Dominion Over Evil Forces and Powers

The Gospels show that Satan and evil spirits are real. And their purposes are the antithesis of God's redemptive purposes. Therefore, a sign that Jesus came to usher in the kingdom of God is the driving out of demons and evil spirits in the power of the Holy Spirit.

When Jesus was accused of driving out demons by Beelzebub, the prince of demons, he responded, "If Satan drives out Satan, he is divided against himself. How then can his kingdom stand? And if I drive out demons by Beelzebub, by whom do your people drive them out? So then, they will be your judges. But if it is by the Spirit of God that I drive out demons, then the kingdom of God has come upon you" (Matt 12:26–28). Similarly, when the seventy-two disciples whom Jesus sent out for mission came back with news of successful outreach, saying, "Lord, even the demons submit to us in your name" (Luke 10:17), Jesus declares, "I saw Satan fall like lightning from heaven" (Luke 10:18). This means that Jesus came to heal a broken world plagued by the forces of evil driven by the adversary, Satan, and his allies.

Exorcism as the Mark of the Defeat of Satan and Evil Spirits

According to Marshall, "Jesus' basic teaching is about the rule of God, understood as God's sovereign, gracious power operating through himself to create a sphere of blessing for humankind and to overcome the power of Satan and destroy evil; it will be fully manifested in the near future but is already at work."[79] Therefore, Jesus drove out evil spirits as a demonstration of his power over the evil forces that had held God's children captive.[80] Some people, especially in the West, think that evil spirits no longer exist. But as Clinton E. Arnold well says,

> Evil spirits have not disappeared since Jesus' day; nor have they turned into psychological pathologies. They continue to exist and do all they can to oppose the redemptive work of God in the world. In the same way that Paul dealt with these spirits, we can effectively deal with them. Overcoming them has nothing to do

---

79. Marshall, *Concise New Testament Theology*, 31.

80. For more on Jesus and exorcism, see G. H. Twelftree, "Demon, Devil, Satan," in *Dictionary of Jesus and the Gospels*, ed. Joel B. Green, Scott McKnight, and I. Howard Marshall (Downers Grove: InterVarsity, 1992): 163–72.

with our own strength, but the power and authority of acting in the name of Jesus by virtue of our close relationship with him.[81]

Speaking in terms of mission, power encounters are real because evil spirits have not disappeared since Jesus's day. But the problem is the church's response. A few decades ago, Byang H. Kato said that the devil has many avenues of fighting against Christ's church and knows how best to succeed. Kato predicted that, "Christo-paganism appears to be the area of attack within the next generation."[82] He concluded, "The battle has started."[83] And this battle is more evident in our time. Yusufu Turaki rightly notes,

> In their comparative study of traditional religion and Christianity, most African scholars have ignored the significance of the spiritual powers and forces in traditional religion and culture. But ever since its arrival in Africa, Christianity has engaged in spiritual warfare with the spirit powers and forces that lie behind traditional religion.[84]

According to Turaki, the early missionaries and their converts had "face to face" confrontations with demonic forces "but overcame them by Christ's power."[85] Collaborating the words of Arnold that evil spirits have not disappeared, Turaki says, "The same struggle continues today as we witness how traditional spirituality and power-consciousness are still shaping and moulding African religious thought. It is giving rise to Neopaganism, religious cults and religious syncretism."[86]

As highlighted above, today the church in Africa is at a crossroads. Many African Christians see the return to African traditional religions as a viable alternative when faced with diabolic "powers and principalities." But are the evil powers "arrayed against God and his people"[87] a match to the power of God? How does the New Testament address this challenge? The Bible declares that Christ is

---

81. Clinton E. Arnold, *Acts* (Grand Rapids: Zondervan, 2002), 158.
82. Kato, *Theological Pitfalls in Africa*, 173.
83. Kato, 173.
84. Yusufu Turaki, *The Trinity of Sin* (Nairobi: WordAlive, 2011), 168–69. See also Randee Ijatuyi-Morphé, *Africa's Social Quest: A Comprehensive Survey and Analysis of the African Situation* (Jos, Nigeria: Hokma House, 2011). One of such formidable spiritual powers and forces in Africa which Ijatuyi-Morphé discusses in his book is witchcraft (55–69).
85. Turaki, *Trinity of Sin*, 169.
86. Turaki, 169.
87. Marshall, *New Testament Theology*, 395.

far above all rule and authority, power and dominion, and every name that is invoked, not only in the present age but also in the one to come. And God placed all things under his feet and appointed him to be head over everything for the church, which is his body, the fullness of him who fills everything in every way. (Eph 1:21–23; cf. Matt 10:1; Mark 16:17; Luke 9:1)

African biblical scholars must address the challenge of power encounters by providing biblical answers regarding confrontation with evil forces. In the absence of this effort, popular theology prevails, and the church loses.

Miracles Are the Marks of Redemptive Restoration

While exorcism is a direct defeat of Satan and evil spirits, all miracles play an important role in God's redemptive scheme.[88] Miracles are the visible display of the "finger of God" (Exod 8:19; 31:18; Luke 11:20). The Gospels portray miracles as restoration of the fallen world. When John the Baptist heard in prison what Christ was doing, he sent his disciples to find out if Jesus was the expected Messiah or someone else. Jesus replied,

> Go back and report to John what you hear and see: The blind receive sight, the lame walk, those who have leprosy are cleansed, the deaf hear, the dead are raised, and the good news is proclaimed to the poor. Blessed is anyone who does not stumble on account of me. (Matt 11:4–6)

Clearly, Jesus came to heal a broken world, namely "the people living in darkness" and "those living in the land of the shadow of death" (Matt 4:16). The *light* of Jesus brings recovery of sight to the blind and freedom for the oppressed. The *light* of Jesus comes as "the year of the Lord's favor." This light is demonstrated in the miracles below.

Healing Miracles: Jesus Came to Heal the Sick

Some of the most fascinating sections in the Bible are the narratives of healing miracles in the Gospels. These miracles are a testament that God breaks into human history with power and deliverance. He has come in the person of Jesus

---

88. See Graham Twelftree, *Jesus the Miracle Worker* (Downers Grove: InterVarsity 1999.

to heal the world. Jesus came to address human afflictions through healing.[89] Matthew records that at the beginning of his ministry,

> Jesus went throughout Galilee, teaching in their synagogues, proclaiming the good news of the kingdom, *and healing every disease and sickness* among the people. News about him spread all over Syria, and people brought to him all who were ill with various diseases, those suffering severe pain, the demon-possessed, those having seizures, and the paralyzed, *and he healed them.* (Matt 4:23–24, emphasis added)

Everyone who came to Jesus was healed of his or her sickness. He cured all manner of diseases: lameness, blindness, deafness, fevers, leprosy, and every other ailment that plagued humanity at his time. This healing was a visible sign of the power of God at work in the life of the Son whom the Father sent into the world to not only save the sinful but also to carry their diseases. Everything Jesus did was fulfillment of biblical prophecies. The Gospel of Matthew records, "When evening came, many who were demon-possessed were brought to him, and he drove out the spirits with a word and healed all the sick. This was to fulfill what was spoken through the prophet Isaiah: 'He took up our infirmities and bore our diseases'" (Matt 8:16–17).

Feeding the Hungry: Jesus Cares for the Poor and Needy

Two of the evils in the world are poverty and hunger. Every night, millions of people go to bed hungry. Even in the wealthiest nations, people still beg for bread on the streets. Furthermore, many are homeless. Likewise in first-century Judea, poverty and hunger were widespread social menaces. When the crowds followed Jesus, many of them did so for fish and bread (John 6:25–26). And the feeding of the five thousand miracle is recorded in all of the Gospels (Matt 14:13–21; Mark 6:30–44; Luke 9:10–17; John 6:1–15). According to Marshall,

> Jesus addresses people with needs: physical, social and spiritual. He criticizes Pharisaic religion for its insistence on obedience to the minutiae of the law, its concentration on outward observance

---

89. On the concept of healing ministry, see Alison Fitchett Climenhaga, "Pursuing Transformation: Healing, Deliverance, and Discourse of Development among Catholics in Uganda," *Journal of the International Association for Mission Studies* 35, no. 2 (2018): 204–24. The entire volume is devoted to healing as a natural part of the Christian life, especially in global Pentecostal and charismatic Christianity.

regardless of the attitude of the heart, and its lack of concern for those who do not live up to its standards.[90]

Therefore, the gospel of Christ has special appeal to the African poor because it shows that the Lord is God of the poor.

Calming the Storm and Walking on the Water: Jesus's Power over Nature

One of the miracles of Jesus is calming the storm (Matt 8:23–27; Mark 4:35–41; Luke 8:22–25). By this miracle Jesus demonstrated his power over nature. As the Son of God, Jesus had the power to speak to the natural elements. They must obey him who made them. Similarly, Jesus walked on water (Matt 14:22–33; Mark 6:45–52; cf. John 6:16–21). The two miracles demonstrate the power of God over nature.

Redemption and the Purpose of Prayer

It was John Chrysostom who wrote,

> The potency of prayer has subdued the strength of fire; it has bridled the rage of lions, hushed anarchy to rest, extinguished wars, appeased the elements, expelled demons, burst the chains of death, expanded the gates of heaven, assuaged diseases, repelled frauds, rescued cities from destruction, stayed the sun in its course, and arrested the progress of the thunderbolt. Prayer is an all efficient panoply, a treasure undiminished, a mine that is never exhausted, a sky unobscured by clouds, a heaven unruffled by the storm. It is the root, the fountain, the mother of a thousand blessings.[91]

Prayer occupies a special place in the Synoptic Gospels (Matt 6:7–13; 26:36–44; Mark 9:28–29; 14:32–41; Luke 3:21–22; 6:12–13; 22:39–46). The Gospels teach that prayer is primarily for praise and for communion with God as exemplified in the life of Jesus. For example, Jesus teaches that God's house is a house of prayer (Matt 21:13; Mark 11:17; Luke 19:46; cf. Isa 56:7). Jesus's communion with the Father is recorded in Matthew 11:25–26: "At that time Jesus said, 'I praise you, Father, Lord of heaven and earth, because you have

---

90. Marshall, *Concise New Testament Theology*, 31.
91. John Chrysostom quoted in E. M. Bounds, *E. M. Bounds on Prayer* (New Kensington: Whitaker House, 1997), 34.

hidden these things from the wise and learned, and revealed them to little children. Yes, Father, for this is what you were pleased to do.'" Likewise, it was customary for Jesus to withdraw from people and go to solitary places for a time of communion with his Father (Mark 1:35; Luke 9:28).

Apart from praise and communion with the Father, prayer is a means of asking and receiving. Jesus said,

> Ask and it will be given to you; seek and you will find; knock and the door will be opened to you. For everyone who asks receives; the one who seeks finds; and to the one who knocks, the door will be opened.
>
> Which of you, if your son asks for bread, will give him a stone? Or if he asks for a fish, will give him a snake? If you, then, though you are evil, know how to give good gifts to your children, how much more will your Father in heaven give good gifts to those who ask him! (Matt 7:7–11; cf. Luke 11:9–13; John 14:13–14; 15:7; 16:24)

In the same vein Jesus said,

> Have faith in God. . . . Truly I tell you, if anyone says to this mountain, "Go, throw yourself into the sea," and does not doubt in their heart but believes that what they say will happen, it will be done for them. Therefore I tell you, whatever you ask for in prayer, believe that you have received it, and it will be yours. (Mark 11:22–24)

Asking from the Lord includes intercession, even for an enemy and persecutor. Jesus said, "But I tell you, love your enemies and pray for those who persecute you, that you may be children of your Father in heaven. He causes his sun to rise on the evil and the good, and sends rain on the righteous and the unrighteous" (Matt 5:44–45).

Other components of prayer include asking for the coming of the kingdom of heaven on earth, asking for our daily bread, asking for forgiveness of sins, and asking for deliverance from temptations and the evil one. All these are included in the prayer Jesus taught his disciples: "This, then, is how you should pray: 'Our Father in heaven, hallowed be your name, your kingdom come, your will be done, on earth as it is in heaven. Give us today our daily bread. And forgive us our debts, as we also have forgiven our debtors. And lead us not into temptation, but deliver us from the evil one" (Matt 6:9–13).

From the above, Jesus shows that the kingdom of God advances here on earth when his children pray for it. They ask that God's will be done on earth as it is in heaven. Similarly, asking for daily bread is legitimate. But preoccupation with daily bread is counterproductive, "For the pagans run after all these things, and your heavenly Father knows that you need them" (Matt 6:32). Rather, "seek first his kingdom and his righteousness, and all these things will be given to you as well. Therefore do not worry about tomorrow, for tomorrow will worry about itself. Each day has enough trouble of its own" (Matt 6:33–34).

And because the children of the kingdom are human and often err, they must ask for forgiveness from their Father. As God forgives them, they must also forgive those who sin against them: "And forgive us our debts, as we also have forgiven our debtors" (Matt 6:12). The consequences of refusing to forgive others is illustrated by the parable of the unforgiving servant (Matt 18:21–35).

Finally, as we see from the Lord's Prayer (Matt 6:13), deliverance from temptation comes through prayer (Matt 26:41 // Mark 14:38; Luke 22:40).

Redemption and the Persecution of the Righteous

Persecution is imbedded in the history of the church. But perhaps at no time in Christian history has the church suffered persecution as extreme as now. From open denial of rights and privileges by anti-Christian governments and non-governmental organizations to killings and destruction of lives and properties, Christians all over the world are suffering persecution. In many countries, Christians face death every day of their lives for the sake of Christ. As Paul wrote, "we are considered as sheep to be slaughtered" (Rom 8:36). But why are Christians persecuted, and what should be their response?

Jesus tells his followers that the primary reason the world hates them is that they bear his name. Jesus said, "You will be hated by everyone because of me, but the one who stands firm to the end will be saved" (Matt 10:22; cf. Mark 13:13; Luke 6:22; 21:17). The Fourth Gospel puts it this way,

> If the world hates you, keep in mind that it hated me first. If you belonged to the world, it would love you as its own. As it is, you do not belong to the world, but I have chosen you out of the world. That is why the world hates you. Remember what I told you: "A servant is greater than his master." If they persecuted me, they will persecute you also. If they obeyed my teaching, they will obey yours also. They will treat you this way *because of my name*, for they do not know the one who sent me. If I had not come and

spoken to them, they would not be guilty of sin; but now they have no excuse for their sin. Whoever hates me hates my Father as well. (John 15:18–23, emphasis added)

As the Bible declares, Christians are the children of light. Light interrupts and upsets darkness. Therefore, those who live in darkness hate the children of light. Jesus said,

> This is the verdict: Light has come into the world, but people loved darkness instead of light because their deeds were evil. Everyone who does evil hates the light, and will not come into the light for fear that their deeds will be exposed. But whoever lives by the truth comes into the light, so that it may be seen plainly that what they have done has been done in the sight of God. (John 3:19–21)

And quite often, what fans the flames of persecution is hate preaching and speeches which serve as indoctrination for followers who are against the church. For example some years ago, an Islamic cleric in Northern Nigeria delivered a public address against Christians. Among other hateful speeches, he urged all Moslem soldiers to consider the protection of Islam and the fight against infidels as their primary duty in the armed forces. All soldiers are paid by the government of Nigeria. But the tax-payers' money was to be used to fight against a particular people – Christians. For whatever reason, the cleric urged Moslems to wage war against Christians in Plateau State, Nigeria. He was proud that the Qur'an gives Moslems the liberty and authority to kill the infidels. And not long after, the 7 September 2001 crises began in Jos, Plateau State.[92] The rest is part of our history and daily experience to this day – pregnant women are ripped open; human beings are burned alive; thousands are maimed for life; the internally displaced people (IDPs) number in the hundreds of thousands; those who have lost all earthly relations and belongings are everywhere; and trauma is the daily experience of many.

But how are Christians to respond to persecution? This question is complex. But I will present the biblical data and allow the church to weave through it and come up with a theology of responding to persecution. Here is the biblical data:

---

92. From 7 September 2001, terrorism by Islamists spread throughout our country like wild fire.

Rejoice and be glad!

Jesus said, "Blessed are you when people insult you, persecute you and falsely say all kinds of evil against you because of me. *Rejoice and be glad*, because great is your reward in heaven, for in the same way they persecuted the prophets who were before you." (Matt 5:11–12, emphasis added)

Do not repay evil with evil

Again Jesus said, "You have heard that it was said, 'Eye for eye, and tooth for tooth.' But I tell you, do not resist an evil person. If anyone slaps you on the right cheek, turn to them the other cheek also. And if anyone wants to sue you and take your shirt, hand over your coat as well. If anyone forces you to go one mile, go with them two miles. Give to the one who asks you, and do not turn away from the one who wants to borrow from you." (Matt 5:38–42; cf. Luke 6:27–34)

Love and pray for the enemy!

Jesus said, "You have heard that it was said, 'Love your neighbor and hate your enemy.' But I tell you, love your enemies and pray for those who persecute you, that you may be children of your Father in heaven. He causes his sun to rise on the evil and the good, and sends rain on the righteous and the unrighteous. If you love those who love you, what reward will you get? Are not even the tax collectors doing that? And if you greet only your own people, what are you doing more than others? Do not even pagans do that? Be perfect, therefore, as your heavenly Father is perfect." (Matt 5:43–48)

Be wise as serpents and innocent as doves!

Jesus said, "I am sending you out like sheep among wolves. Therefore be as shrewd as snakes and as innocent as doves." (Matt 10:16)

Flee!

> Jesus instructed, "When you are persecuted in one place, flee to another." (Matt 10:23)

Sell your cloak and buy a sword!

> Then Jesus asked [his disciples], "When I sent you without purse, bag or sandals, did you lack anything?"
>
> "Nothing," they answered.
>
> He said to them, "But now if you have a purse, take it, and also a bag; and if you don't have a sword, sell your cloak and buy one." (Luke 22:35–36)

To say it again, the intention here is to present the biblical data and let the persecuted church in the twenty-first century figure how to apply these teachings from our Lord Jesus Christ. According to the Bible, the church cannot escape persecution in a world that hates God and his people (John 15:18–25). To think that we can be totally free from persecution in this life is open denial of the words of Jesus.

But the church can be proactive. We can minimize the gravity of persecution by helping unbelievers become believers through active evangelism and good works (Matt 5:13–16). Another way to minimize marginalization and persecution is through the practice of Christian unity. A united church tells the world that we belong to God and that he loves us (John 17:20–23). Believers can also be proactive by taking the initiative and leading the way in transforming society rather than reacting to situations and events. Our God is a proactive God. He planned the salvation of sinners before the foundation of the world (Eph 1:3–4). Revelation 13:8 says that Jesus is the Lamb "who was slain from the creation of the world"! We can be proactive in governance (executive, legislative, and judiciary arms), politics, education, science and technology, economics, media, and every other aspect of legitimate human endeavor. Banning Liebscher believes that to heal the land, we must transform culture. And transforming culture takes place in the family, religion, economy, education, government, arts and media, and science and technology. According to Liebscher, "whoever commands and controls those mountains sets the agenda and atmosphere in society."[93]

---

93. Liebscher, *Jesus Culture*, 59.

Another aspect of being proactive is empowering the church, which is a step further from the above. Empowerment goes beyond material possessions but does not exclude them. There are rich business men and women, celebrities, politicians, government officials, and world leaders who have no moral capacity to change a nation for good. So even when they take the mountains above, they have no capacity to transform society. The empowerment we are talking about is of people who are morally upright, have keen vision, are led by the Holy Spirit, and are able to see the future. Those who are morally and spiritually empowered are able to soar above circumstances and can handle any situation. These kinds of people are able to lead the way in transforming society.

But Jesus also commanded his disciples to be innocent as doves (Matt 10:16).[94] The dove represents innocence, purity, and obedience. Similarly, during Jesus's baptism, the dove represented the presence of the Holy Spirit (Luke 3:21–22).

But how can the persecuted church apply the command to be innocent as doves? Is God not endangering the lives of his people the more? Two things are worth mentioning here. First as innocent doves, Christians are the embodiment of peace and reconciliation in a broken world, and to them God committed the awesome and enormous task of reconciling the world to himself. Paul wrote,

> All this is from God, who reconciled us to himself through Christ and gave us the ministry of reconciliation: that God was reconciling the world to himself in Christ, not counting people's sins against them. And he has committed to us the message of reconciliation. We are therefore Christ's ambassadors, as though God were making his appeal through us. We implore you on Christ's behalf: Be reconciled to God. God made him who had no sin to be sin for us, so that in him we might become the righteousness of God. (2 Cor 5:18–21)

Second, the power of the gospel to attract the unbelieving world is in making "the teaching about God our Savior attractive" through our blameless lives (Titus 2:10). Only innocent doves are qualified. Jesus said, "let your light shine before others, that they may see your good deeds and glorify our Father in heaven" (Matt 5:16). The apostle Peter wrote,

---

94. In the Bible, the only birds that were offered for sacrifice were doves and turtledoves. And even the poorest people could afford them (Gen 15:9; Lev 5:7; 12:6; Luke 2:22–24). We wonder why God chose innocent and harmless birds – like doves – for burnt offerings and sin offerings. Perhaps the answer is found in what Jesus did for us: "God made him who had no sin to be sin for us, so that in him we might become the righteousness of God" (2 Cor 5:21).

> Dear friends, I urge you, as foreigners and exiles, to abstain from sinful desires, which wage war against your soul. Live such good lives among the pagans that, though they accuse you of doing wrong, they may see your good deeds and glorify God on the day he visits us. (1 Pet 2:11–12)

Similarly Paul wrote,

> Do everything without grumbling or arguing, so that you may become blameless and pure, "children of God without fault in a warped and crooked generation." Then you will shine among them like stars in the sky as you hold firmly to the word of life. And then I will be able to boast on the day of Christ that I did not run or labor in vain. (Phil 2:14–16)

The word of life that we hold is attractive only when our lives are beyond reproach like doves.

Finally, believers can be proactive by refusing to create room for the enemy to take advantage. This is food for thought. When we give the devil a foothold, he is sure to take the entire body. The enemy is tenacious in holding on to whatever he grabs. Christians must not let the enemy grab what is theirs in the first place, which is part of being wise as serpents and innocent as doves.

Redemption and the Poor, the Oppressed, and the Marginalized

The most important Hebrew words that refer to the poor in the Old Testament are 'ebyon and 'ani. Mounce says 'ebyon is "consistently used to describe the physical poverty of those that are destitute."[95] Such people are the object of genuine concern and care. Similarly, a poor person is "one who has been humbled or afflicted by circumstances, and who, because of current disability, finds himself or herself dependent on others for life's necessities."[96] The New Testament Greek word for poor is *ptōchos* and can literally refer to the economically disadvantaged or figuratively "to the one whose vulnerable state leads to total dependence on God."[97]

Poverty and oppression are real issues in the world. The reason for treating the poor, the oppressed, and the marginalized together is that they are often

---

95. William D. Mounce, "Poor," in *Mounce's Complete Expository Dictionary of Old and New Testament Words* (Grand Rapids: Zondervan, 2006), 521.

96. Mounce, "Poor," 521.

97. Mounce, 521.

the victims of oppression in society (Ezek 22:29; Amos 4:1; 5:12; Zech 7:10). It is the poor who are insulted and discriminated against, and whose wages are denied by the rich (Jas 2:1–7; 5:4). Fortunately, the Bible shows that "God acts when his people are oppressed."[98] For example, God spoke through the prophet Amos,

> You levy a straw tax on the poor
> > and impose a tax on their grain.
> Therefore, though you have built stone mansions,
> > you will not live in them;
> though you have planted lush vineyards,
> > you will not drink their wine.
> For I know how many are your offenses
> > and how great your sins.
>
> There are those who oppress the innocent and take bribes
> > and deprive the poor of justice in the courts. . . .
>
> Therefore this is what the LORD, the LORD God Almighty, says:
>
> "There will be wailing in all the streets
> > and cries of anguish in every public square.
> The farmers will be summoned to weep
> > and the mourners to wail.
> There will be wailing in all the vineyards,
> > for I will pass through your midst,"
> says the LORD. (Amos 5:11–12, 16–17)

Similarly, God told his people through Amos,

> Hear this, you who trample the needy
> > and do away with the poor of the land,
>
> saying,
>
> "When will the New Moon be over
> > that we may sell grain,
> and the Sabbath be ended
> > that we may market wheat?" –
> skimping on the measure,
> > boosting the price
> > and cheating with dishonest scales,

---

98. Agang, *No More Cheeks*, 29.

> buying the poor with silver
>> and the needy for a pair of sandals,
>> selling even the sweepings with the wheat.
>
> The LORD has sworn by himself, the Pride of Jacob: "I will never forget anything they have done.
>
> "Will not the land tremble for this,
>> and all who live in it mourn?
> The whole land will rise like the Nile;
>> it will be stirred up and then sink
>> like the river of Egypt.
>
> "In that day," declares the Sovereign LORD,
>
> "I will make the sun go down at noon
>> and darken the earth in broad daylight.
> I will turn your religious festivals into mourning
>> and all your singing into weeping.
> I will make all of you wear sackcloth
>> and shave your heads.
> I will make that time like mourning for an only son
>> and the end of it like a bitter day. (Amos 8:4–10)

Because the Lord is a just God, oppression of the poor and needy grieves his heart. Therefore, he brings severe judgment on oppressors. He deprives them the enjoyment of their ill-gotten wealth. He brings calamities on them so that they mourn and wail in the land. He turns their hypocritical religious feasts into mourning and all their singing into weeping.

The Gospels speak about the poor, the oppressed, and the marginalized in the society. Samuel Waje Kunhiyop is right that "the poor had a prominent place in Jesus' ministry."[99] When Jesus announced his mission on earth, the poor and the oppressed were in view. Quoting Isaiah 61:1–2, Jesus said, "The Spirit of the Lord is on me, because he has anointed me to proclaim good news to the poor. He has sent me to proclaim freedom for the prisoners and recovery of sight for the blind, to set the oppressed free, to proclaim the year of the Lord's favor" (Luke 4:17–19). Jesus's concern for the poor and needy is demonstrated by feeding the hungry (Matt 14:13–21; Mark 6:30–44; Luke 9:10–17; cf. John 6:1–15). Similarly, according to Matthew 25:31–46, the difference between the

---

99. Samuel Waje Kunhiyop, *African Christian Ethics* (Nairobi: WordAlive, 2008), 146.

sheep and the goats, those on the right and the left respectively, is in caring for the needy of the society.

> He will put the sheep on his right and the goats on his left.
>
> Then the King will say to those on his right, "Come, you who are blessed by my Father; take your inheritance, the kingdom prepared for you since the creation of the world. For I was hungry and you gave me something to eat, I was thirsty and you gave me something to drink, I was a stranger and you invited me in, I needed clothes and you clothed me, I was sick and you looked after me, I was in prison and you came to visit me." (Matt 25:33–36)

Like the poor and needy, children and women were also among the marginalized in first-century Judea and the Roman world. But Jesus reversed this unjust worldview and culture. To enter the kingdom of God, he said, one must be like a little child (Matt 18:1–5), and the kingdom of God belongs to little children (Matt 19:13–14 // Mark 10:13–14). Similarly, women stand out prominently in the Gospels. The Savior of the world came through a woman (Matt 1:18–25; Luke 1:26–35; 2:1–7). Women followed Jesus and supported his ministry (Luke 8:1–3). Mary anointed Jesus with expensive perfume (John 12:3). Women followed and mourned for Jesus when he was led to the cross of Calvary (Luke 23:27). They were the first to witness the empty tomb of the risen Lord (Mark 16:1–6; Luke 24:1–3) and the first to see the risen Lord himself (Matt 28:1–10; Mark 16:1–9). The gospel of Christ is always countercultural.[100]

Redemption as Future Consummation of the Kingdom

The Synoptic Gospels reveal that although the kingdom of God was inaugurated at the coming of Christ the Messiah, it still awaits a future perfect condition or consummation (cf. Matt 12:36–45; 25:31–46; Mark 13:24–27, 32–37), which is the "*eschatological fulfillment* of God's promise of salvation."[101] This will take place at the second coming of the Messiah. According to Cole, the watchfulness

---

100. See David Platt, *Counter Culture: A Compassionate Call to Counter Culture in a World of Poverty, Same-Sex Marriage, Racism, Sex Slavery, Immigration, Abortion, Persecution, Orphans, and Pornography* (Carol Stream: Tyndale House, 2015).

101. Randee O. Ijatuyi-Morphé, *Community and Self-Definition in the Book of Acts* (Bethesda: Academica Press, 2004), 7, emphasis original.

Jesus demands of his followers as they wait for his coming underscores "the moral and spiritual incentive provided by the doctrine of the second coming."[102]

Similarly, the Synoptic Gospels often contrast this age and the age to come (Matt 12:32; Mark 10:29–30; Luke 20:27–38; cf. 1 Cor 2:6–8; 2 Cor 4:3–5; Gal 1:4; 1 Tim 6:19; Titus 2:12–13). This age is characterized by evil. The age to come is the final renewal of all things (Matt 19:28). This is the final redemption of believers in Christ (Luke 22:20–21). The events of the consummation of all things are described as follows:

1. "The Son of Man is going to come in his Father's glory" (Matt 16:27; cf. Mark 13:26 // Luke 21:27). This appearing marks the end of the evil age and the beginning of the age to come.

2. The Son of Man will send out and appear with his angels (Matt 13:41, 49; 25:31; Mark 13:27). The angels will serve as body guards to the Son of Man and herald his coming. They will also be given the authority to gather "his elect from the four winds, from one end of the heavens to the other" (Matt 24:31 // Mark 13:27).

3. The righteous will be separated from the wicked, like sheep from goats (Matt 25:31–46). Jesus said, "This is how it will be at the end of the age. The angels will come and separate the wicked from the righteous and throw them into the blazing furnace, where there will be weeping and gnashing of teeth" (Matt 13:49–50).

4. Rewards will be given according to what each person has done (Matt 16:27; cf. Rom 2:6; Rev 22:12).

5. The wicked will have no share in the kingdom of God. They will endure eternal punishment in hell fire (Matt 13:40–42, 49–50; 25:46) "where there will be weeping and gnashing of teeth" (Matt 8:12; 22:13; 25:30; Luke 13:28).

6. The righteous will enjoy eternal life with God (Matt 19:29; 25:46).

In summary, the consummation of the kingdom is eternal life with God (Mark 10:29–30). Eternal life is the most important preoccupation of those who seek after God (Matt 18:8; 19:16, 29; Mark 10:17; Luke 10:25; 18:18). Eternal life in the kingdom of God is characterized by peace and happiness (Matt 25:21–23). The righteous will share in the inheritance of the kingdom: "Then the King will say to those on his right, 'Come, you who are blessed by

---

102. Cole, *Gospel According to Mark*, 283.

my Father; take your inheritance, the kingdom prepared for you since the creation of the world'" (Matt 25:34).

Questions for Review and Application

1. Why is the kingdom of God such an important concept in the Synoptic Gospels?
2. In what ways did Jesus demonstrate that the kingdom of God has dominion over the evil forces?
3. How can Christians in Africa demonstrate that the gospel has power over evil forces?
4. What good news did Jesus bring for the poor, the oppressed, and the marginalized of the world? And how should the church represent good news to the poor, the oppressed, and the marginalized in the world today?
5. How is the kingdom of God expanded in the world?
6. How can the church in Africa address the issues of poverty, illiteracy, oppression, and marginalization?
7. In what ways are you making the kingdom of God real in your community?

6

Drums of Redemption in the Gospel of John

> I am the light of the world. Whoever follows me will never walk in darkness, but will have the light of life.
>
> — Jesus[1]

> I am the resurrection and the life. The one who believes in me will live, even though they die; and whoever lives and believes in me will never die.
>
> — Jesus[2]

Synopsis of the Gospel of John

One of the most fascinating books of the New Testament is the Gospel of John. A verse that stands out in the book is John 3:16. Similarly, John 14:1–3 has comforted countless troubled souls throughout Christian history, especially those suffering from grief and sorrow caused by the death of loved ones. Likewise, John's theological propositions distinguish him from the Synoptic Gospels. He offers profound theological statements like that contained in John 1:1–4 where he unpacks what it means that Jesus is the Word, the one with God from the beginning.

John alone records the theologically loaded words of Jesus to Nicodemus,

> Very truly I tell you, no one can enter the kingdom of God unless they are born of water and the Spirit. Flesh gives birth to flesh, but the Spirit gives birth to spirit. You should not be surprised at

---
1. John 8:12.
2. John 11:25–26.

my saying, "You must be born again." The wind blows wherever it pleases. You hear its sound, but you cannot tell where it comes from or where it is going. So it is with everyone born of the Spirit. (3:5–8)

When we examined the Synoptic Gospels, we noted that John has a somewhat different orientation in narrating the teaching and events in the life of Jesus Christ. As Marshall well says, "Although some of the events are the same, and others are of a basically similar character, the general way in which they are narrated and the character of the theological argumentation are distinctive. The historical traditions regarding Jesus have been given fresh expression in a different idiom."[3] And F. F. Bruce notes the Fourth Gospel's divergence from the others "in matters of geography, chronology and diction."[4] But there are common themes in the four Gospels that we need not treat as separate theological elements. These include the Son of God, the Son of Man, the Messiah, the Prophet, and the Teacher.

After the prologue, John proceeds with Jesus's pre-Galilean ministry (John 1:15–4:54) that begins with a narrative about the mission of John the Baptist and his testimony regarding Jesus (1:15–34). Like in the Synoptic Gospels, John the Baptist plays his role as forerunner and testifies concerning Jesus (John 1:19–23).

Jesus's pre-Galilean ministry includes the miraculous change of water into wine, which was "the first of the signs through which he revealed his glory; and his disciples believed in him" (John 2:11). Other highlights of this ministry period include the cleansing of the temple in Jerusalem (2:13–22); Jesus's famous encounter with Nicodemus and his teaching on the new birth (3:1–21); Jesus's encounter with the Samaritan woman (4:1–42); and his healing of a royal official's son (4:43–54). This healing is called "the second sign Jesus performed" (4:54) after he began his ministry.

Jesus's Galilean ministry and conflict with the authorities in Jerusalem (John 5:1–10:42) is a long section that records healing the sick on the Sabbath which the leaders thought was against the stipulations of the law (5:1–18); feeding the five thousand with five small loaves and two small fish (6:1–13); going to the Jewish Feast of Tabernacles (7:1–53); and the healing of the man born blind (9:1–20). The section is characterized by growing unbelief regarding the identity of Jesus.

---

3. Marshall, *Concise New Testament Theology*, 187.

4. F. F. Bruce, *The New Testament Documents: Are They Reliable?* Sixth edition (Nottingham: Inter-Varsity, 2000), 66.

We will now focus on the special character of the Gospel of John. For example, while we have the genealogy of Jesus in both Matthew and Luke, this information is virtually absent in the Gospel of John except for the introduction of Jesus as the "Word." Similarly, the way John narrates the ministry of Jesus in terms of geography differs remarkably from Matthew, Mark, and Luke. For example, the Synoptic Gospels present Jesus's ministry primarily in Galilee and then make a climatic move to Jerusalem "for his one fatal visit to that city."[5] John, however, presents Jesus as going back and forth between Jerusalem and Galilee (John 2:13–22; 5:1; 7:1; 10:22; 12:12).

Another unique feature is the prologue: John 1:1–14. John begins his Gospel with some of the most profound theological concepts in the entire Bible – the preexistent and the incarnate Word of God – "In the beginning was the Word. . . . the Word became flesh" (John 1:1, 14). Jesus became human in order to make the Father known to humanity. John says the Word "was with God from the beginning" (1:2).

Another unique feature in the Gospel of John is the absence of exorcisms (casting out demons) among the deeds and signs of Jesus. Instead, Jesus raises Lazarus from the dead (John 11:1–44), a miracle that is not recorded in the Synoptic Gospels. Similarly, parables are absent in the Gospel of John. In their place are long discourses (e.g., 5:19–47; 10:1–38; 14:1–17:26). There are also many figures of speech or metaphors in the Gospel of John which the Synoptics do not record.

Similarly, a distinctive feature of the Gospel of John is the statement of purpose. Although each Gospel writer had a purpose for writing, none of the four writers set his agenda so clearly as John does. According to John, "Jesus performed many other signs in the presence of his disciples, which were not recorded in this book. But these are written that you may believe that Jesus is the Messiah, the Son of God, and that by believing you may have life in his name" (John 20:30–31). This goal could probably account for the different orientation and flavor of the Gospel of John.

Finally, a distinctive feature of the Gospel of John is the issue of dualism. While many scholars point to a dualistic orientation in the Gospel of John, others prefer the concept of "oppositional dualities." According to Miroslav Volf, although "far from being negating of pluralism as both a social fact and a political project, John's kind of oppositional dualities may in fact be the best

---

5. Johnson, *Writings of the New Testament*, 528.

way to preserve social pluralism and make it flourish."⁶ Although Volf's dualism accommodates pluralism, the Gospel of John does not seem to support such a view since exclusivism with regards to salvation is clearly taught in the Gospel (John 14:6). But Volf's "oppositional dualities" are not the primary concern here. In the Gospel of John, contrasts are made between light and darkness, heaven and earth, life and death, and truth and falsehood, among others.

Considering the differences between the Synoptics and the Gospel of John, some have concluded that the Gospel of John is "the *supplement* to the synoptic tradition." Such were the views of the early church writers Eusebius and Augustine.[7] But according to Johnson, the supplementary nature of the Gospel of John should not be understood merely as providing materials that are absent in the Synoptic Gospels. This supplementary role "in a deeper sense" is through "*explicit theological reflection in the form of a story*."[8] This means that John makes explicit the theological themes found in the Synoptics.

But despite the differences noted above, many points of convergence or "resemblance" can be found among the four Gospels. These parallels include a healing requested by an official that Jesus does at a distance (John 4:46–53; Matt 8:5–10; cf. Luke 7:1–10); the healing of a paralytic (John 5:2–9; cf. Matt 9:1–7; Mark 2:1–12; Luke 5:17–26); and the feeding of the multitude through the multiplication of loaves and fish (John 6:1–13; cf. Matt 14:14–21; Mark 6:33–44; Luke 9:12–17). Other similar accounts found in all four Gospels include Jesus walking on the water, John the Baptist's ministry of baptism and his arrest by Herod, Peter's confession, Jesus's purification of the temple in Jerusalem, the anointing of Jesus at Bethany, the triumphal entry into Jerusalem, and the passion of Christ.[9]

And these similarities lead us to some of the theological themes in the Gospel of John.

---

6. Miroslav Volf, "Johannine Dualism and Contemporary Pluralism," *Modern Theology* 21, no. 2 (March 2005): 189–217. https://onlinelibrary.wiley.com/doi/10.1111/j.1468-0025.2005.00282.x.

7. Eusebius, *Ecclesiastical History* III.24.7–13, emphasis added; see also Augustine, *Harmony of the Evangelists* IV.7, V.8.

8. Johnson, *Writings of the New Testament*, 529, emphasis original.

9. Johnson, 529.

Key Theological Themes of the Gospel of John

According to Craig R. Koester, the author of the Gospel of John "is traditionally dubbed 'the theologian' because of the way he leads readers into questions pertaining to God."[10] Similarly, Andreas J. Kösteberger says,

> the Gospel penetrates more deeply into the mystery of God's revelation in his Son than the other canonical Gospels and perhaps more deeply than any other biblical book. From the majestic prologue to the probing epilogue, the evangelist's words are carefully chosen as they must be thoughtfully pondered by every reader of his magnificent work.[11]

Some of the themes found in the Gospel of John have been treated in the Synoptic Gospels.[12]

Redemptive Work of God the Father

Although we have examined the work of the Father in redemption according to the Synoptic Gospels, the Gospel of John adds a twist that is not found in the first three Gospels. These include God the Father's roles as one who draws people to Christ, the one who gives life along with the Son, and the one who gives the Holy Spirit.

The Father Is the Creator

According to Rabbi Jonathan Sacks,

> The link between monotheism and the moral life is that a universe seen as the home of many gods or none is an arena of conflicting forces in which the strong prevail, the weak suffer, the manipulative exploit the vulnerable, and might is sovereign over right. A world without a Judge is one in which there is no reason to expect justice. The human condition becomes a tragic script

---

10. Craig R. Koester, *The Word of Life: A Theology of John's Gospel* (Grand Rapids: Eerdmans, 2008), ix.

11. Andreas J. Kösteberger, *John*, BECNT, ed. Robert Yarbrough and Robert H. Stein (Grand Rapids: Baker Academic, 2004), 1.

12. For example, the designation of God as the Father of our Lord Jesus Christ occurs more in the Gospel of John than in any other Gospel (John 3:35; 5:17–39). Similarly, the Father is conceived as one who sends the Son and the Holy Spirit (John 1:14; 4:34; 5:24–37; 7:16; 15:26; 17:25; 20:21–22). Also, believers in Christ are God's children (John 1:12–13; 11:51–52). But all of this does not constitute a new theological view point.

in which ideals prove to be illusion, revolution a mere change of places in the seats of power, and the ship of hope destined to be wrecked by the cold iceberg of reality.[13]

Johannine cosmology begins with the premise that God created the universe (John 1:1–3; cf. Gen 1:1). Therefore, historic Christian faith teaches that the one true God created the heavens and the earth and all that is in them (Ps 24:1–2). This creation by God gives the world moral moorings. But this understanding is challenged today by Darwinian evolutionary cosmology in which evolution replaces the direct act of God's creative work. On the one hand, biblical cosmology pictures the world as having intrinsic value because God created everything good (Gen 1:31). On the other hand, Darwinian Big Bang (cosmic explosion) cosmology sees the world as a product of chance and therefore without intrinsic value. Darwinism as propagated by secular humanists is that "life began through a cosmic explosion that brought all matter of the universe into being, and then life, in the form of tiny single-celled plants, emerged out of the seas, capturing the energy of the sun."[14] This is to say that "something came from nothing, merely by chance." According to Colson,

> Biology texts offer a variety of explanations of this process, but all are predicated on chance. They claim that through eons and eons of random mutations and natural selection, the complex system of nature and the even more astonishing complexity of human life have evolved. Life is the result, we are told by the National Association of Biology Teachers, of "an unsupervised, impersonal, unpredictable and natural process."[15]

Therefore, Darwinism rejects the concept of an Intelligent Designer.

But according to the Gospel of John, the work of creation is that of the Father and the Son. For "He was with God in the beginning. Through him all things were made; without him nothing was made that has been made. In him was life, and that life was the light of all mankind" (John 1:2–4). Paul says,

---

13. Rabbi Jonathan Sacks, *To Heal a Fractured World: The Ethics of Responsibility* (New York: Schocken, 2005), 173.

14. Colson, *Good Life*, 216.

15. Colson, 216; citing "NABT Unveils New Statement on Teaching Evolution," *The American Biological Teacher* 68, no. 1 (January 1996): 61. According to Colson, "the original NABT statement created such an uproar that the organization subsequently dropped the words *unsupervised* and *impersonal*" (emphasis original). But as Colson well notes, the change was cosmetic because it leaves the words "unpredictable" and "natural" which retains the original meaning.

> The Son is the image of the invisible God, the firstborn over all creation. For in him all things were created: things in heaven and on earth, visible and invisible, whether thrones or powers or rulers or authorities; all things have been created through him and for him. He is before all things, and in him all things hold together. (Col 1:15–17)

The belief of Darwinism that the world happened by some kind of chance through some impersonal force seems ludicrous and nonsensical by contrast to the straightforward biblical narrative regarding the origin of life, "In the beginning God created the heavens and the earth" (Gen 1:1). And chapters 1 and 2 of Genesis go on to explain how the creation of the various elements happened.

The greatest concentration on the cosmos in the Gospel of John is found in chapters 15–17, namely in Jesus's final discourse. First, the world is seen as the earth or the universe. The understanding of the world as the earth is found in passages such as John 1:1–3; 12:25; 13:1; 17:4–6). Hence, Jesus's kingdom "is not of this world" (18:36–37).

Second, the world is equated with humankind (John 8:12; 12:46–47). These are the people of the world who did not recognize the Messiah (1:9–10). This world is a domain full of sin and for which the Lamb of God came (1:29). It is this same world that God sent his only begotten Son to save and that remains in darkness because their deeds are evil (3:16–20). But all responsive hearts recognized that Jesus is the Savior of the world (4:42).

Third, the world is the system that is opposed to truth (John 12:31). Because the world opposes the truth, it is a formidable threat to the believers (15:18–16:33). It hates the believers in Christ with unimaginable intensity. Jesus said,

> I have given them your word and the world has hated them, for they are not of the world any more than I am of the world. My prayer is not that you take them out of the world but that you protect them from the evil one. They are not of the world, even as I am not of it. Sanctify them by the truth; your word is truth. (John 17:14–17)

The world also hates Jesus because he testifies "that its works are evil" (7:7). The world that opposes Jesus and his people is led by Satan, the prince of the world. Jesus said, "Now is the time for judgment on this world; now the prince of this world will be driven out" (12:31; cf. 14:30–31; 16:11).

The Father Is the Father of Jesus Christ

In the Gospel of John, Jesus refers to God as his Father more frequently than all the Synoptic Gospels combined (thirty-nine times in John verses thirty-two times in Matthew, Mark, and Luke). According to the Gospel of John, Jesus stands in a unique, intimate relationship to God as his only begotten Son (John 3:16). Although all believers in Christ are God's children (1:12–13), none shares the same position Jesus enjoys with the Father. As the Son of God, he always decided and acted according to the instructions he received from the Father (8:16). Accordingly, the Father always bore witness to whatever Jesus testified (8:18). Similarly, Jesus spoke only as the Father taught him (8:28). God always glorified Jesus as his Son (8:54). And as the unique Son of God, Jesus knows the Father just as he is also known by the Father (10:15).

Jesus expressed the depth of his relationship with the Father when he said, "I and the Father are one" (John 10:30). And because of this declaration, the Jews picked up stones to stone him "for blasphemy, because you, a mere man, claim to be God" (10:33). As understood by his hearers, Jesus's claim of Sonship went beyond the ordinary claim of God as Father to all Israel. Jesus was claiming exceptional oneness with God, a unique relationship that no other human being can claim. Similarly, when Philip asked Jesus to show them the Father, Jesus responded,

> Don't you know me, Philip, even after I have been among you such a long time? Anyone who has seen me has seen the Father. How can you say, "Show us the Father"? Don't you believe that I am in the Father, and that the Father is in me? The words I say to you I do not speak on my own authority. Rather, it is the Father, living in me, who is doing his work. Believe me when I say that I am in the Father and the Father is in me; or at least believe on the evidence of the works themselves. (John 14:9–11)

The Father Is the Father of Believers

All those who receive Jesus Christ stand in special relationship with the Father as his children. Scripture says,

> He came to that which was his own, but his own did not receive him. Yet to all who did receive him, to those who believed in his name, he gave the right to become children of God – children born not of natural descent, nor of human decision or a husband's will, but born of God. (John 1:11–13)

This is the second birth (3:3–8). In his post-resurrection appearances, Jesus told Mary, "Do not hold on to me, for I have not yet ascended to the Father. Go instead to my brothers and tell them, 'I am ascending to my Father and your Father, to my God and your God'" (20:17).

The Father Is the Sender of the Son
The Gospel of John shows that Jesus did not come for his own mission. The Father sent him (John 4:34; 5:24, 30, 37; 6:38–39, 44; 7:16, 28, 33; 8:16, 18, 26, 29; 9:4; 12:44–45, 49; 13:20; 14:24; 15:21; 16:5). Martin Erdmann says, "Jesus' activity as the one sent by the Father serves as the definitive example for his followers as they seek to fulfill their mission."[16] And everything he did was in accordance with the will of the Father. The task the Father gave Jesus was his food (4:34). Jesus said, "Do not believe me unless I do the works of my Father. But if I do them, even though you do not believe me, believe the works, that you may know and understand that the Father is in me, and I in the Father" (10:37–38). Statements like this infuriated the Jews and they wanted to arrest Jesus, but he escaped them.

The Father Is the Giver of Eternal Life
Jesus spoke about the Father's role in the work of redemption in this manner:

> "Stop grumbling among yourselves," Jesus answered. "*No one can come to me unless the Father who sent me draws them*, and I will raise them up at the last day. It is written in the Prophets: 'They will all be taught by God.' *Everyone who has heard the Father and learned from him comes to me*. No one has seen the Father except the one who is from God; only he has seen the Father. (John 6:39–46, emphasis added)

The text shows that it is the Father who draws people to Christ. According to John 5:21–24, the Father gives eternal life along with the Son. The Father has also entrusted judgment to the Son "that all may honor the Son just as they honor the Father" (5:23). This eternal life that is given by the Father comes through hearing the words of the Son and believing the Father who sent the Son. The one who does so has crossed over from death to life.

---

16. Martin Erdmann, "Mission in John's Gospel and Letters," in *Mission in the New Testament: An Evangelical Approach*, ed. William J. Larkin, Jr. and Joel F. Williams (Maryknoll: Orbis, 2005), 222.

The Father Is the Giver of the Holy Spirit

God the Father gives the Holy Spirit. "For the one whom God has sent speaks the words of God, for God gives the Spirit without limit" (John 3:34). Similarly, Jesus said,

> And I will ask the Father, and he will give you another advocate to help you and be with you forever – the Spirit of truth. The world cannot accept him, because it neither sees him nor knows him. But you know him, for he lives with you and will be in you. I will not leave you as orphans; I will come to you. (John 14:16–18)

According to the text, Jesus will not leave his disciples like orphans. He would surely come back to them through the Holy Spirit whom the Father would send at his request.

The Redemptive Work of the Son of God

Jesus Christ, the Son of God, plays a significant role in the work of redemption. His place in the salvific scheme is outlined below:

The Son Is Christ the Messiah

The messianic titles of Jesus are prominent in the Gospel of John. Like the Synoptic Gospels, the Gospel of John portrays Jesus as the Messiah (John 1:41; 4:25–26, 29; 7:26–27; 9:22; 12:34; 20:31). According to C. H. Dodd, "In none of the Synoptic Gospels, and indeed in no other New Testament writer, do these messianic titles receive such prominence as here."[17]

The Messiah in the Gospel of John is one whom the prophets have written about (John 1:45). He is the Son of Man (1:51; 5:27; 6:27; 8:28; 9:35; 13:31). But Jesus is also the Son of God (1:49; 5:25–26; 19:7; 20:31). He is the prophet (6:14–15; 7:40; 9:17). Jesus is also the Teacher or Rabbi (1:38; 3:2; 8:4; 11:28–29; 13:13–14; 20:16). He is the King of Israel (1:49) and the "Holy One of God" (6:69). "He is the Coming One"[18] (12:13; cf. Matt 11:3; 21:9; Mark 1:24; 11:9; Luke 4:34; 7:19; 13:35).

The messianic hopes of first-century Judea resonate in the Gospel of John. The people "were groaning under the yoke of Rome. They yearned for the

---

17. C. H. Dodd, *The Interpretation of the Fourth Gospel* (Cambridge: Cambridge University Press, 1970), 228.

18. Dodd, *Interpretation of the Fourth Gospel*, 228.

deliverer. They were looking for the coming Messiah."[19] A close examination of John for self-identification by the Jewish leaders shows how much the people were longing for the coming Messiah (John 1:19–22).

The sense of fulfillment and relief by those who recognized Jesus as Messiah is expressed by Andrew. "The first thing Andrew did was to find his brother Simon and tell him, 'We have found the Messiah'" (that is, the Christ) (John 1:41). Similarly even the Samaritans, despised as unclean by the Jews, shared the same messianic hopes as the children of Israel. After her encounter with Jesus, the Samaritan woman told the people in town, "Come, see a man who told me everything I ever did. Could this be the Messiah?" (4:29). And when the people saw and heard Jesus for themselves, they said to the Samaritan woman, "We no longer believe just because of what you said; now we have heard for ourselves, and we know that this man really is the Savior of the world" (4:42).

The Son Is One with God

The Gospel of John brings out the deity of the Son more clearly than the Synoptics by going beyond the title "Son of God." John explains why Jesus is the Son of God – he is one with the Father. John portrays the Messiah as the *Logos* and the one who has been with God from the beginning (John 1:1–3).

There are explicit and implicit statements in the Gospel of John which express that the Messiah is one with God. According to John 1:18, "No one has ever seen God, but the one and only Son, who is himself God and is in closest relationship with the Father, has made him known." This statement parallels Jesus's statement in Matthew 11:27, "No one knows the Son except the Father, and no one knows the Father except the Son and those to whom the Son chooses to reveal him." Similarly, Jesus said, "All that belongs to the Father is mine. That is why I said the Spirit will receive from me what he will make known to you" (John 16:15).

The Son Is the Sign of the Kingdom

John did not record as many miraculous signs as the Synoptic Gospels. And he explains why in John 20:30: "Jesus did many other signs in the presence of his disciples, which are not recorded in this book." In the Fourth Gospel, the manifestation of the kingdom of God is attested by *miraculous signs* (2:11, 23–24; 3:2; 4:54; 6:14; 7:31; 9:16; 11:47; 12:18). Notable among these miraculous signs are changing of water into wine (2:1–11), the multiplication of bread and

---

19. John G. Mitchell, *Let's Revel in John's Gospel* (West Linn: Glory Press, 2000), 15.

fish (6:1–14), opening the eyes of one born blind (9:1–41), and the raising of Lazarus from the dead (11:1–47).

The Son Is the "I Am"

The "I am" sayings in the Gospel of John beg for attention as they reveal something about Jesus's uniqueness as the bearer of eternal life.

Jesus states, "I am the bread of life. Whoever comes to me will never go hungry, and whoever believes in me will never be thirsty" (John 6:35). Jesus's food "endures to eternal life, which the Son of Man will give you" (6:27). And "whoever drinks the water I give them will never thirst. Indeed, the water I give them will become in them a spring of water welling up to eternal life" (4:14). Jesus is the bread "that comes down from heaven and gives life to the world" (6:33–35). Unlike the manna which the Israelites ate in the desert but still eventually died, the bread that Jesus gives sustains life for eternity (John 6:47–58). This bread of life is his body and blood. This "hard teaching" caused many of his disciples to desert him, but not the twelve (John 6:60–69).

Jesus also states, "I am the light of the world. Whoever follows me will never walk in darkness, but will have the light of life" (John 8:12; cf. 9:5). Jesus's light is the light of life, and this light of life contrasts with darkness (John 1:4–5; 3:19; 8:12; 9:4; 11:9–10; 12:35) which people love rather than the light because their deeds are evil (3:20). Jesus is the light of the world because "In him was life, and that life was the light of all mankind" (1:4). As the light of the world, he shows the way to the Father (14:6).

Jesus further states, "I am the gate; whoever enters through me will be saved. They will come in and go out, and find pasture" (John 10:9). This means that life at its fullest is found in him. Jesus thus contrasts himself with those who came before him, thieves and robbers who "come only to steal and kill and destroy" (10:10). The gate of the sheep is also "the good shepherd" who "lays down his life for the sheep" (10:11).

In his next "I am" statement, Jesus states, "I am the resurrection and the life" (John 11:25). Therefore, death does not hold a permanent grip on the one who believes in him. For "The one who believes in me will live, even though they die; and whoever lives by believing in me will never die" (11:25–26).

Jesus then states, "I am the way and the truth and the life. No one comes to the Father except through me" (John 14:6). Jesus means that he alone possesses the keys to the eternal life and is the only way and the only truth. Coming to the Father is impossible apart from Jesus. In God's scheme of salvation, he has made Jesus the only way to be saved. The disciples of Jesus understood that this is what Jesus meant, and they preached the same message (Acts 4:12).

In his final "I am" statement, Jesus says, "I am the true vine (John 15:1). Jesus's followers are the branches. Just as the branches receive their life and nutrients from the vine, followers of Jesus receive their life and spiritual nourishment from him, hence the danger of severing oneself from the vine (15:2–5).

The Son Is the Bearer of Eternal Life

The Gospel of John could be titled the gospel of eternal life (John 3:14–16, 36; 4:13–14, 36; 5:24, 39; 6:27, 40, 54, 68; 10:28; 17:3), "underscoring the permanence of life made available in and through Jesus."[20] At the end of his book, John states the purpose of his writing, "Jesus performed many other signs in the presence of his disciples, which are not recorded in this book. But these are written that you may believe that Jesus is the Messiah, the Son of God, and that by believing you may have life in his name" (20:30–31). Ladd says, "As the Son of God, Jesus has a divinely appointed mission to fulfill. The most frequently reiterated element in his mission is to mediate life to men and women."[21]

But what is eternal life? The word "eternal" in Hebrew and Greek expresses an "indefinitely prolonged" period.[22] John's Gospel defines eternal life as knowing "the only true God, and Jesus Christ," whom God sent (John 17:3). In Jesus is life, "and that life was the light of all mankind" (1:4). This eternal life comes by believing the Son of Man who "must be lifted up, that everyone who believes may have eternal life in him" (3:14–15). And all this comes from God who "gave his one and only Son, that whoever believes in him shall not perish but have eternal life" (3:16). But just as the Father gave the Son, the Son also willingly laid down his life for his friends (15:13). The Son was given the authority to give eternal life along with the Father (4:13–14; 5:21–24, 39–40; 6:33–35, 47–69; 10:10–11, 28; 11:25–26). Therefore, it is the "Father's will that everyone who looks to the Son and believes in him shall have eternal life." For such ones, the Son has power to "raise them up at the last day" (6:40). John's concept of eternal life is also treated in 1 John.

The Son Is Entrusted with the Judgment of the World

Jesus said,

---

20. Köstenberger, *John*, 212.
21. Ladd, *Theology of the New Testament*, 285.
22. Dodd, *Interpretation of the Fourth Gospel*, 144.

> For just as the Father raises the dead and gives them life, even so the Son gives life to whom he is pleased to give it. Moreover, the Father judges no one, but has entrusted all judgment to the Son, that all may honor the Son just as they honor the Father. Whoever does not honor the Son does not honor the Father, who sent him. (John 5:21–23)

According to Kösteberger, "This is a remarkable assertion, since according to the Hebrew Scriptures, judgment is the exclusive prerogative of God (e.g., Gen. 18:25; cf. Judg. 11:27; though see Ps. 2:2)."[23] Jesus tells us why judgment is given to him: "that all may honor the Son just as they honor the Father" (John 5:23). This means that anyone who does not honor the Son dishonors the Father.

The Redemptive Work of the Holy Spirit

In John 1:31–34, the ministry of the Holy Spirit in redemption is spelled out. John the Baptist said,

> "I myself did not know him, but the reason I came baptizing with water was that he might be revealed to Israel."
>
> Then John gave this testimony: "I saw the Spirit come down from heaven as a dove and remain on him. And I myself did not know him, but the one who sent me to baptize with water told me, 'The man on whom you see the Spirit come down and remain is the one *who will baptize with the Holy Spirit.*' I have seen and I testify that this is the Son of God." (emphasis added)

John's testimony is that Jesus, the Son of God, is the one who baptizes with the Holy Spirit. This means that all believers are baptized with the Holy Spirit. But the text is explicit that the baptism of the Holy Spirit is in collaboration with the work of the Son of God.

The Holy Spirit Is the Author of New Birth

According to John 3:1–8, the Holy Spirit is the author of new birth. Jesus tells the puzzled teacher of the law, Nicodemus, that "no one can see the kingdom of God unless they are born again" (3:3). Seeing the kingdom of God means participating in the kingdom at the end of the age, namely, to enjoy eternal

---

23. Köstenberger, *John*, 187–88.

life.[24] And this new birth, according to Jesus, is possible only through the mysterious work of the Holy Spirit (3:5–8).

Similarly, the Holy Spirit is the giver of eternal life. This means that he not only causes new birth, but he himself is the giver of life along with the Father and the Son. Jesus said, "The Spirit gives life; the flesh counts for nothing. The words I have spoken to you – they are full of the Spirit and life" (John 6:63). The Holy Spirit, along with the Father and Son, gives life (3:5–8). Entry into the kingdom of God is possible only through the work of the Holy Spirit. Like the wind, the Spirit works in mysterious ways to cause new birth or regeneration thereby placing believers in the family of God (1:12–13; 3:8).

The Holy Spirit Is the Teacher and the Spirit of Truth
The Holy Spirit is called "the Spirit of truth" whom the world cannot accept (John 14:17).[25] As the Spirit of truth, he guides believers in all truth (16:13). In his first epistle, the apostle John reiterates that the Holy Spirit teaches: "As for you, the anointing you received from him remains in you, and you do not need anyone to teach you. But as his anointing teaches you about all things and as that anointing is real, not counterfeit – just as it has taught you, remain in him" (1 John 2:27).

The Holy Spirit Testifies about Jesus
The Spirit's witness concerning Jesus is cast in a courtroom scene.[26] Jesus said, "When the Advocate comes, whom I will send to you from the Father – the Spirit of truth who goes out from the Father – he will testify about me. And you also must testify, for you have been with me from the beginning" (John 15:26–27). The primary ministry of the Holy Spirit is to bear witness to the mission of Jesus in the world. In other words, the Holy Spirit's ministry is to testify that Jesus is the Son of God who brought the good news of eternal life and secured salvation for humankind by his death, resurrection, and ascension.

But the Holy Spirit is not the only one who testifies about Jesus. The disciples were with Jesus from the beginning of his earthly ministry to the time he was taken up to heaven. No one is better qualified to testify about him on earth. The Holy Spirit who abides in the disciples enables them to bear witness concerning Jesus. John wrote, "For there are three that testify: the Spirit, the water and the blood; and the three are in agreement. We accept

---

24. Köstenberger, 122.
25. Jesus alludes to the fact that the world rejects the light (John 3:19–20).
26. Köstenberger, *John*, 467.

man's testimony, but God's testimony is greater because it is the testimony of God, which he has given about his Son" (1 John 5:7–9).

The Holy Spirit Is the Paraclete and the Abiding Presence
The Greek word *parakletos* means helper, advocate, or counselor. Jesus promised the disciples that he would not leave them alone as orphans. He said, "And I will ask the Father, and he will give you another advocate to help you and be with you forever – the Spirit of truth. The world cannot accept him, because it neither sees him nor knows him. But you know him, for he lives with you and will be in you" (John 14:16–17; cf. 14:25–26; 15:26; 16:7–15).

As the *parakletos*, the Holy Spirit is the abiding presence in the lives of the believers. He will live with them forever. Jesus's departure was better for the disciples in light of the abiding presence of the Holy Spirit. Jesus says,

> but now I am going to him who sent me. None of you asks me, "Where are you going?" Rather, you are filled with grief because I have said these things. But very truly I tell you, it is for your good that I am going away. Unless I go away, the Advocate will not come to you; but if I go, I will send him to you. (John 16:5–7)

The Holy Spirit Convicts the World of Sin
The Holy Spirit also functions as one who convicts the world of sin. Jesus said,

> When [the Holy Spirit] comes, he will prove the world to be in the wrong about sin and righteousness and judgment: about sin, because people do not believe in me; about righteousness, because I am going to the Father, where you can see me no longer; and about judgment, because the prince of this world now stands condemned. (John 16:8–11)

This means that "it is not Jesus who is on trial but the world."[27] The world is guilty of unbelief, "convicted on the basis of Christ's righteousness (or of its lack of unrighteousness) and judged together with the supernatural 'ruler of this world.'"[28] When the Holy Spirit comes, he will convict the world that "masquerades as righteous and suppresses any evidence to the contrary, and such behavior requires the Spirit to expose its guilt."[29]

---

27. Köstenberger, 471.
28. Köstenberger, 471.
29. Köstenberger, 471.

The Holy Spirit Fills the Believers

The reference here is to Jesus's post-resurrection appearance to his disciples recorded in John 20:19–23. The resurrected Jesus came to them and said, "'Peace be with you! As the Father has sent me, I am sending you.' And with that he breathed on them and said, 'Receive the Holy Spirit'" (20:21–22). In this passage, Jesus commissions his disciples to succeed him by continuing with the harvest of the ripe fields (cf. Matt 28:18–20; Luke 24:46–49; John 4:35–38). The filling of the Spirit is implied in John 3:34 and 7:38–39. According to John 14:16–17 (cf. 14:25–26; 15:26; 16:7–15), the Holy Spirit comes in to abide with the disciples. According to Kösteberger, Jesus breathing the Holy Spirit on the disciples is a symbolic promise "of the soon-to-be given gift of the Holy Spirit, not the actual giving of it fifty days later at Pentecost."[30] The symbolic nature of Jesus's action is supported by the fact that the actual coming of the Holy Spirit was on the day of Pentecost (Acts 2:1–21). Similarly, Jesus had earlier indicated that the Holy Spirit would not come until he was glorified (John 16:7).[31]

Redemption and Discipleship in the Community

According to the Gospel of John, four things mark the life of discipleship in the community of believers: faith, service, love, and unity.

The first mark of true discipleship is faith. Faith in the Gospel of John is primarily about believing Jesus is the Messiah (2:11; 7:31; 8:30; 11:45; 12:11, 42; 14:12). Similarly, belief is the means by which one obtains eternal life (1:12–13; 3:16; 20:31). "Whoever believes in the Son has eternal life, but whoever rejects the Son will not see life, for God's wrath remains on them" (3:36). Similarly, Jesus said, "Very truly I tell you, whoever hears my word and believes him who sent me has eternal life and will not be judged but has crossed over from death to life" (5:24).

The second mark of discipleship is service. In this life of service, the disciple's primary allegiance is to the Master, Jesus Christ. In Jesus's own words, "Whoever serves me must follow me; and where I am, my servant also will be. My Father will honor the one who serves me" (John 12:26). And serving the Master involves self-denial: "Anyone who loves their life will lose it, while anyone who hates their life in this world will keep it for eternal life" (John 12:25; cf. Matt 16:24–25; Luke 14:26–27).

---

30. Köstenberger, 574.
31. Köstenberger, 574–75.

But disciples are called to imitate their Master by serving their fellow disciples as well. Jesus set forth the example of service in the community of believers by washing the feet of his disciples (John 13:1–17). So he tells them, "Now that I, your Lord and Teacher, have washed your feet, you also should wash one another's feet. I have set you an example that you should do as I have done for you" (13:14–15). By humbling himself and taking the place of a servant, Jesus became the ultimate example by which his disciples must live.

The third mark of discipleship is love. The community of disciples is to be characterized by love for one another. Jesus said, "A new command I give you: Love one another. As I have loved you, so you must love one another. By this everyone will know that you are my disciples, if you love one another" (John 13:34–35). This concept of love is also treated in the epistles of John.

The fourth mark of true discipleship is unity. Jesus prayed fervently for the unity of the disciples, both present and future.

> My prayer is not for them alone. I pray also for those who will believe in me through their message, that all of them may be one, Father, just as you are in me and I am in you. May they also be in us so that the world may believe that you have sent me. I have given them the glory that you gave me, that they may be one as we are one – I in them and you in me – so that they may be brought to complete unity. Then the world will know that you sent me and have loved them even as you have loved me. (John 17:20–23)

What kind of oneness was Jesus praying for? The oneness Jesus prayed for is exemplified by the church in Acts 2:44–47:

> All the believers were together and had everything in common. They sold property and possessions to give to anyone who had need. Every day they continued to meet together in the temple courts. They broke bread in their homes and ate together with glad and sincere hearts, praising God and enjoying the favor of all the people. And the Lord added to their number daily those who were being saved.

Similarly, "All the believers were one in heart and mind. No one claimed that any of their possessions was their own, but they shared everything they had" (Acts 4:32). As understood by Paul, Jesus prayed for his disciples to maintain "the unity of the Spirit through the bond of peace" (Eph 4:3), "being like-minded, having the same love, being one in spirit and of one mind" (Phil 2:2).

But tribal and denominational sentiments, among other issues, have divided the church in Africa such that we have lost the unity that is a mark of true discipleship. And by our divisive actions, we have lost the other marks of true discipleship as well – faith, service, and love. We have ruined our testimony to the world by our shameful divisions. Consequently, for African Christianity to survive and thrive, we must repent from the sin of divisive ethnicity and denominationalism and embrace unity.

Redemption through the Passion and Resurrection of Christ

John 18–21 is the passion narrative – the trial, crucifixion, death, and resurrection of Jesus. John concludes his Gospel by recounting the conspiracy of the Jewish authorities – chief priests and elders – that resulted in the suffering and death of the Messiah, Jesus Christ. The account is found in all the Gospels – Matthew, Mark, Luke, and John. As is well noted, "No part of the life of Jesus is related in such detail and with such close agreement in the sources" because "The earliest proclamation of Jesus centered on the story of the death and the resurrection. This was the great saving act, the climax of the saving acts in the history of salvation."[32]

But there is another important dimension to the passion narrative. When read through human lenses, it evokes anti-Semitic sentiments because "the Jews as people have been labeled 'Christ-killers.'"[33] A Christmas song that was popular while I was growing up in the village goes like this:

> *Yahudawa suka kashe Yesu*
> *Yahudawa suka kashe Yesu (translation The Jews Killed Jesus)*
> *Allah ya basu dama su je su yi abinda sun ga dama*
> *Allah ya basu iko su je su yi abinda sun ga dama (translation*
>   *But it was God who gave them the permission and power to*
>   *do as they wished)*

The meaning of the song is that the Jews killed Jesus. But it was God who gave them the permission and power to do as they wished. The conspiracy by the small group of elders and chief priests who hated Jesus for his growing

---

32. John L. McKenzie, "The Gospel According to Matthew," *The Jerome Biblical Commentary*, 2 vol., ed. Raymond E. Brown, Joseph A. Fitzmyer, and Roland E. Murphy (Englewood Cliffs: Prentice Hall, 1968), 107.

33. Bruce Vawter, "The Gospel According to John," *The Jerome Biblical Commentary*, 2 vol., ed. Raymond E. Brown, Joseph A. Fitzmyer, and Roland E. Murphy (Englewood Cliffs: Prentice Hall, 1968), 461.

popularity is attributed to the entire Jewish race. Although the declaration of the crowd before Pilate was, "His blood be on us and on our children!" (Matt 27:25), Jesus's response on the cross was, "Father, forgive them, for they do not know what they are doing" (Luke 23:34). When correctly understood, the Jewish authorities in Jerusalem were the "prime movers" of the conspiracy, but the Roman rulers cannot be excused "of criminal complicity in the death of Jesus."[34]

The point is that like in the Synoptic Gospels, Jesus's death was not an accident. It was divinely arranged. God appointed that his Son would suffer injustice, incredible torture, and agony in the hands of human beings he made. God predestined that his Son would die on a cruel cross. All this does not excuse Judas for his betrayal nor the Jewish leaders and Roman authorities for their conspiracy and complicity. But, most importantly, God arranged that his Son would rise from the grave on the third day. And his victory over death secured salvation for sinful humanity. Jesus said, "Just as Moses lifted up the snake in the wilderness, so the Son of Man must be lifted up, that everyone who believes may have eternal life in him" (John 3:14–15). This is the essence of the gospel (cf. 1 Cor 15:1–6). As in the rest of the Gospels, the ultimate victory of the Messiah is the empty tomb (John 20:1–10). Jesus died for the sins of the entire world – Jews and Gentiles. As Vawter well says, "Christians must be profoundly ashamed of the persecutions that have been meted out to the Jews at various times in Christian history in the name of the compassionate Christ."[35]

Redemption as Resurrection of the Righteous in the Last Day

The Gospel of John also contains eschatological expressions. Particularly important is Jesus's use of the "last day" (John 6:39–40, 44, 54; 7:37; 12:48). Kösteberger says, "The repetition of the words 'on the last day' (6:39, 40, 44, 54) accentuates the heavenly, transcendent character of Jesus's mission, conveyed also by the title 'Son of Man.'"[36] Kösteberger observes that "the last day" is a Johannine expression, found in the New Testament only in John. With regards to the resurrection on the last day, Jesus said,

> Very truly I tell you, a time is coming and has now come when the dead will hear the voice of the Son of God and those who hear

---

34. Vawter, "Gospel According to John," 461.
35. Vawter, 461.
36. Kösteberger, *John*, 212.

will live. For as the Father has life in himself, so he has granted the Son also to have life in himself. And he has given him authority to judge because he is the Son of Man.

Do not be amazed at this, for a time is coming when all who are in their graves will hear his voice and come out – those who have done what is good will rise to live, and those who have done what is evil will rise to be condemned. (John 5:25–29)

Most Jews understood the last day in connection with end-time resurrection. They believed that the problem of death would be settled in God's redemptive scheme by resurrection from the dead. This belief is affirmed by Martha who responded to Jesus regarding the resurrection of her brother Lazarus, "I know he will rise again in the resurrection at the last day" (John 11:24). This belief is also congruent with Jesus's teaching in John (5:21, 25–29; 6:39–44, 54). But Jesus's response to Martha was, "I am the resurrection and the life. The one who believes in me will live, even though they die; and whoever lives and believes in me will never die" (11:25–26). This means that believers in Christ, whether they live or die, participate in the resurrection and life that Jesus offers because he is the resurrection and the life.[37] Jesus wanted Martha to shift her focus from the abstract future to the present life that is obtained through him.

Questions for Review and Application

1. Who is Jesus in the Gospel of John? Should believers in Africa refrain from calling Jesus the Son of God because that is offensive to other faiths? Please explain.
2. What is the meaning of "Messiah" in the Gospel of John?
3. What are the works of the Father, the Son, and the Holy Spirit in the Gospel of John?
4. What particular functions does the Holy Spirit play in the world and in the life of the believer?
5. What does Jesus say about unity in John 17:20–23, and how does this apply to Christians in Africa?
6. How does the Gospel of John draw you closer to God?

---

37. Kösteberger, 335–36.

7

Drums of Redemption in the Acts of the Apostles

On one occasion, while [Jesus] was eating with [his disciples], he gave them this command: "Do not leave Jerusalem, but wait for the gift my Father promised, which you have heard me speak about. For John baptized with water, but in a few days you will be baptized with the Holy Spirit."

Then they gathered around him and asked him, "Lord, are you at this time going to restore the kingdom to Israel?"

He said to them: "It is not for you to know the times or dates the Father has set by his own authority. But you will receive power when the Holy Spirit comes on you; and you will be my witnesses in Jerusalem, and in all Judea and Samaria, and to the ends of the earth."

Acts 1:4–8

Then they called them in again and commanded them not to speak or teach at all in the name of Jesus. But Peter and John replied, "Which is right in God's eyes: to listen to you, or to him? You be the judges! As for us, we cannot help speaking about what we have seen and heard."

Acts 4:18–20

Synopsis of the Book of Acts

Many scholars rightly treat the book of Acts as a continuation of the Gospel of Luke and regard it as "Luke's volume two."[1] But because the Synoptic Gospels – Matthew, Mark, and Luke – share so much in common, it is also reasonable that the Acts of the Apostles be treated separately. The Acts of the Apostles records how the disciples continued the work of Christ through the Holy Spirit who is a prominent person in the book. Other prominent themes include the risen Lord Jesus Christ, the author of life; the fellowship of the believers; witnessing; persecution; and Paul's missionary journeys.

The Old Testament is the framework or "source book"[2] for understanding the book of Acts. This means that the book of Acts points out and affirms that all the events recorded regarding Jesus Christ, the Holy Spirit, and the church are fulfillments of the Scriptures and what God has promised his people – namely, his salvific purposes (Acts 1:16; 2:16–21, 25–30, 33, 39; cf. Luke 24:25–49).

Acts tells us how the apostles, led by the Holy Spirit, planted churches beginning in Jerusalem and extending to other parts of the world in fulfillment of Jesus's commission (Matt 28:19–20; Mark 16:15–16). In the book of Acts, we see the stages of the growth of the church as follows:

1. Jerusalem: chapters 1–7
2. Judea, Samaria, and Syria: chapters 8–12
3. Asia Minor and Greece: chapters 13–20
4. To Rome: chapters 20–28

As we have said above, the subject of the Acts of the Apostles is the growth of the church through the work of the Holy Spirit who gives power to witness. Luke who wrote the book explains the purpose: "In my former book, Theophilus, I wrote about all that Jesus began to do and to teach until the day he was taken up to heaven, after giving instructions through the Holy Spirit to the apostles he had chosen" (Acts 1:1–2). Luke recorded what Jesus began to do and to teach until he was taken to heaven. The Gentile believers, the probable recipients of the book, needed to know the historical reliability of Christ's redemptive work. The main focus of Acts is the risen and exalted Christ through whom salvation is offered to all human kind, the same exalted Christ who sent the promised Holy Spirit.

---

1. Wenham and Walton, *Exploring the New Testament*, 267.
2. Wenham and Walton, 267.

Key Theological Themes in the Book of Acts

According to William J. Larkin, Jr., Luke 24:46–48 provides the framework for expounding Luke's theology.[3] Larkin sees the theological message of both Luke and Acts as the suffering, death, and resurrection of our Lord Jesus Christ, of which his disciples were the witnesses, and the preaching of repentance and forgiveness of sins to the nations, beginning in Jerusalem.

God Acts through the Holy Spirit[4]

Pneumatology is prevalent in the Acts of the Apostles.[5] According to Hurtado, "the NT references to the Spirit typically reflect and presuppose experiential phenomena. The Spirit is not simply talked about, and the presence of the Spirit is not simply affirmed as a doctrine; the Spirit is something *experienced*."[6] And perhaps nowhere else in the Bible is the Holy Spirit *experienced* like in the Acts of the Apostles.

Twelftree says, "We could expect the beginning of Acts to shed light on what Luke might contribute to a discussion on the origins of the church."[7] According to Luke, then, the church's origin is traced to the coming of the Holy Spirit. The Spirit's coming is "one of the most important events in the history of the world."[8] Jesus promised the coming of the Holy Spirit (Acts 1:8; cf. John 16:7–8). He commanded the disciples to wait in Jerusalem until they received the Holy Spirit who came on the day of Pentecost, the Jewish Feast of Weeks (Acts 2:1–12).[9] Luke records,

> When the day of Pentecost came, they were all together in one place. Suddenly a sound like the blowing of a violent wind came from heaven and filled the whole house where they were sitting.

---

3. William J. Larkin Jr., *Acts*, IVP New Testament Commentary Series, ed. Grant R. Osborne, D. Stuart Briscoe, and Haddon Robinson (Downers Grove: InterVarsity, 1995), 23.

4. See Graham H. Twelftree, *People of the Spirit: Exploring Luke's View of the Church* (Grand Rapids: Baker Academic, 2009).

5. Robert L. Reymond well notes "the pervasive emphasis on the dominant role of the Holy Spirit in the expansion of the gospel" is found in the book of Acts. *Paul: Missionary Theologian* (Ross-shire: Christian Focus, 2000), 34.

6. Hurtado, *God in New Testament Theology*, 83, emphasis original.

7. Twelftree, *People of the Spirit*, 15.

8. Danny McCain, *Notes on Acts of the Apostles* (Bukuru, Jos: Africa Christian Textbooks, 2001), 29.

9. See Arnold, *Acts*, 14. The word "Pentecost" is a transliteration of the Greek *pentekoste*, meaning fiftieth, that is fifty days after the Passover festival. The Pentecost festival is called the Feast of Weeks (Lev 23:15–21; Deut 16:9–12).

They saw what seemed to be tongues of fire that separated and came to rest on each of them. All of them were filled with the Holy Spirit and began to speak in other tongues as the Spirit enabled them. (Acts 2:1–4)

The Holy Spirit gave the disciples the power (Greek *dunamis*) for witnessing. Subsequently, the Holy Spirit's manifestation on those who believe includes speaking "the word of God boldly" (4:31) and speaking in tongues and prophesying (19:6).

Jesus Is the Exalted Lord and Author of Life

The Christology of Jesus in the book of Acts appears in his titles and work of redemption. The accounts in Acts show that God acts in Christ, the Messiah (Acts 9:22; 18:5). One of the central themes in the Acts is that Jesus is the resurrected and exalted Lord.[10] Similarly, "Acts emphasizes the name of Jesus, signifying his authority and his divinity."[11] He is the Son of God (Acts 9:20). Paradoxically, he is also the suffering servant of Isaiah (Acts 8:27–35; cf. Isa 53:1–12). But "God exalted him to his own right hand as Prince and Savior that he might bring Israel to repentance and forgive their sins" (Acts 5:31).

Jesus is the author of life whom God raised from the dead (Acts 3:15). The exalted Lord is the one who poured his Spirit upon the believers on the day of Pentecost (2:33). "Salvation is found in no one else, for there is no other name under heaven given to mankind by which we must be saved" (4:12).

Repentance and Forgiveness Granted to Jews and Gentiles

Although Acts 5:31 portrays that the exaltation of Christ as Prince and Savior is so that he might give repentance and forgiveness to Israel, the universal outlook of this salvation is apparent (Acts 9:15; 10:45; 11:1, 18; 13:16, 26, 46–48; 14:1, 27; 15:1–19; 26:20, 23; 28:28). Craig S. Keener observes that the Gentile mission was ratified in Acts 15:1–35.[12] God's salvation is for both Jews and the

---

10. Thomas R. Schreiner, *Magnifying God in Christ: A Summary of New Testament Theology* (Grand Rapids: Baker Academic, 2010), 80.

11. Schreiner, *Magnifying God in Christ*, 81.

12. Craig S. Keener, *Acts: An Exegetical Commentary*, vol. 3 (Grand Rapids: Baker Academic, 2014), 2194.

Gentiles. In other words, "people from other nations will join the community of believers."[13] As Schreiner well summarizes,

> Since Jesus is the Christ, the exalted Lord over all, the Son of God, the Prophet, and the Servant of the Lord, he is to be preached and proclaimed to all (Acts 5:42; 8:5, 12; 9:22; 18:5, 28; 28:31). Because Jesus Christ is the universal Lord, salvation is available only through him (4:12). He will judge the living and the dead on the last day (10:42; 17:31). Hence, people receive forgiveness of sins by believing and trusting Jesus Christ the Lord (11:17; 16:31; 19:4; 20:21; 24:24).[14]

Therefore, the book of Acts shows that the suffering and death of Christ were for the forgiveness of sins of all human kind. This is the "major blessing resulting from Jesus' death and resurrection."[15] Repentance and forgiveness are offered freely to all those who believe regardless of race. The blood of Christ is the means by which people are purchased for God (Acts 20:28).

Questions for Review and Application

1. Why did Jesus ask his disciples to wait in Jerusalem? What would have happened if they had not waited as Jesus instructed them?
2. Why is the day of Pentecost important in the history of the church?
3. Why is the book of Acts significant for the church in Africa?
4. How does the book of Acts view Jews and Gentiles in God's purposes of salvation? How does this view address divisive ethnicity in African Christianity?
5. How does your understanding of the theology of the book of Acts draw you closer to God?

---

13. Wenham and Walton, *Exploring the New Testament*, 268.
14. Schreiner, *Magnifying God in Christ*, 82.
15. Wenham and Walton, *Exploring the New Testament*, 268.

8

Drums of Redemption in Romans

I am not ashamed of the gospel, because it is the power of God that brings salvation to everyone who believes: first to the Jew, then to the Gentile. For in the gospel the righteousness of God is revealed – a righteousness that is by faith from first to last, just as it is written: "The righteous will live by faith."

Romans 1:16–17

But now apart from the law the righteousness of God has been made known, to which the Law and the Prophets testify. This righteousness is given through faith in Jesus Christ to all who believe. There is no difference between Jew and Gentile, for all have sinned and fall short of the glory of God, and all are justified freely by his grace through the redemption that came by Christ Jesus. God presented Christ as a sacrifice of atonement, through the shedding of his blood – to be received by faith. He did this to demonstrate his righteousness, because in his forbearance he had left the sins committed beforehand unpunished – he did it to demonstrate his righteousness at the present time, so as to be just and the one who justifies those who have faith in Jesus.

Romans 3:21–26

Synopsis of the Letter to the Romans

Paul is the greatest theologian of the first-century church.[1] Many New Testament scholars begin the study of Paul's theology by exploring the sources

---

1. Michael F. Bird, *A Bird's Eye View of Paul: The man, his mission and his message* (Nottingham: Inter-Varsity, 2008), 20.

of his thought.² Paul, the "converted Pharisee," was indeed "the greatest mind in the New Testament to interpret the person and work of Jesus."³ Our goal here is to provide clues for understanding Paul's great theological insights. Paul had Jewish, Hellenistic, and Christian backgrounds. According to Acts (21:39; 22:3, 25), Paul was a Roman citizen who was born in Tarsus in Cilicia. This background means that Paul was familiar with the culture and worldview of the Greco-Roman world. Paul also grew up according to strict Jewish law, "circumcised on the eighth day, of the people of Israel, of the tribe of Benjamin, a Hebrew of Hebrews; in regard to the law, a Pharisee; as for zeal, persecuting the church; as for righteousness based on the law, faultless" (Phil 3:5–6). Paul was not only a Jew but a Pharisee as well, having obtained his training in Jerusalem under the famous Rabbi Gamaliel (Acts 5:33–40; 22:3). But this Roman citizen and trained Jewish rabbi encountered Jesus on the way to Damascus (Acts 9:1–9). This encounter changed his life.

How much Paul's diverse background influenced his thought is debatable. Did Paul's theology come from his background as a trained Jewish rabbi or from his encounter on the road to Damascus? What some scholars ignore is Paul's own testimony regarding the source of his theology; namely, that his gospel came to him "by revelation from Jesus Christ" (Gal 1:11–12). According to Lea, "Any analysis of Paul's thought that ignores this statement cannot do justice to his theology."⁴ Paul encountered Christ on the road to Damascus and was also taught by the Holy Spirit in Arabia (Gal 1:15–17). The content of Paul's gospel is the death and resurrection of Christ to redeem sinners who were under the curse of the law (Gal 3:13).⁵ Similarly, Paul's interpretation of the Old Testament is in the light of the revelation he received from God. The Greek world in which Paul lived could have aided his philosophical understanding. But these backgrounds were not the ultimate source of his thought.⁶

The origin of the church in the city of Rome is uncertain.⁷ Some think that Peter founded this church. But there is no proof for this claim. And if Peter had founded this church, Paul would most likely have mentioned him in the letter. Perhaps Jews and proselytes from Rome who were in Jerusalem on the day of

---

2. See for example Ladd, *Theology of the New Testament*, ch. 29; Thomas D. Lea, *The New Testament: Its Background and Message* (Nashville: Broadman and Holman, 1996), 334–35.

3. Ladd, *Theology of the New Testament*, 398.

4. Lea, *New Testament*, 334.

5. Lea, 334.

6. Lea, 334.

7. Donald Guthrie, *New Testament Introduction* (Leicester: Apollos, 1990), 403.

Pentecost pioneered the church at Rome (Acts 2:10-11). Similarly, opinions differ about the composition of the membership of the church in Rome. But most scholars agree that it is a mixture of Jews and Gentiles, and the Gentiles were probably in the majority (Rom 15:15-16).

On the occasion and purpose of Romans, it is believed that Paul was on his third missionary journey when he wrote the Letter to the Romans (15:21-28; cf. 1:11-15). Paul gives clues as to the purpose of writing in Romans 15:22-24, 29, 32. He intended to visit Rome, but because he was not sure about the conditions in Jerusalem, he wrote the letter ahead of his visit. Paul wanted "the help of the Roman Christians for his mission to the western parts of the Roman Empire."[8] The place of writing is thought to be Greece.[9] The date of this letter is believed to be somewhere between AD 57 and 59.

As for the content of the book, Paul has interwoven theology with practical pastoral concerns. In some of his books, for example Romans and Ephesians, theology seems to come first before practical application. However in other Pauline writings, a separation of doctrine and practical living are not easily discernible. On the whole, we could say that every concern that the apostle raises or treats is rooted in the overarching framework of seeing that believers live according to their theological convictions such that the two spheres – theology and practice – go together.

Paul's theology is Christocentric. Lea suggests that the frequent phrase in Paul's writings, "in Christ," is an accurate summary of Paul's thought.[10] Paul's main concern in Romans is "salvation for Jews and Gentiles by grace through faith,"[11] as Paul states, "for all have sinned and fall short of the glory of God, and are justified freely by his grace through the redemption that came by Christ Jesus" (Rom 3:23-24). The book of Romans teaches that all of humanity has sinned in Adam,[12] which Paul explains in Romans 5:14-19:

> Nevertheless, death reigned from the time of Adam to the time of Moses, even over those who did not sin by breaking a command, as did Adam, who is a pattern of the one to come.

---

8. Paul J. Achtemeier, Joel B. Green, and Marianne Meye Thompson, *Introducing the New Testament: Its Literature and Theology* (Grand Rapids: Eerdmans, 2001), 300.

9. Guthrie, *New Testament Introduction*, 407.

10. Lea, *New Testament*, 355.

11. Marshall, *Concise New Testament Theology*, 126.

12. Dane C. Ortlund, "What Does It Mean to Fall Short of the Glory of God? Romans 3:23 in Biblical-Theological Perspective," *WTJ* 80 (2018): 121.

But the gift is not like the trespass. For if the many died by the trespass of the one man, how much more did God's grace and the gift that came by the grace of the one man, Jesus Christ, overflow to the many! Nor can the gift of God be compared with the result of one man's sin: The judgment followed one sin and brought condemnation, but the gift followed many trespasses and brought justification. For if, by the trespass of the one man, death reigned through that one man, how much more will those who receive God's abundant provision of grace and of the gift of righteousness reign in life through the one man, Jesus Christ!

Consequently, just as one trespass resulted in condemnation for all people, so also one righteous act resulted in justification and life for all people. For just as through the disobedience of the one man the many were made sinners, so also through the obedience of the one man the many will be made righteous.

According to Simon Gathercole, "A familiar feature in Pauline scholarship is the view that sin as a power, and the concomitant forces of the flesh and death, are the dominant elements in Paul's account of the human plight."[13] The word "flesh" refers to the substance of the body, whether of animals or persons (1 Cor 15:39; 2 Cor 12:7). In its idiomatic use, the word indicates the human race or personhood (Matt 24:22; 1 Pet 1:24). In an ethical and spiritual sense, the Greek word *sarx* translated "flesh" is the lower nature of a person, the seat and vehicle of sinful desires (Rom 7:25; 8:4–9; Gal 5:16–17).[14] In the book of Romans, Paul argues that sin has brought a separation between humankind and God due to humankind's rejection of the knowledge of God (Rom 1:18–30). But God's mercy provided a way of escape, not through the law but through faith in Christ. The one who believes in Christ is justified, sanctified, and dedicated to serve the Lord.

While Romans 1–11 are largely doctrinal, the remaining chapters are rather hands-on application or "practical Christian living."[15] Johnson rightly refers to 12:1–15:3 as "life in the Christian community."[16] The believers in Christ, in

---

13. Simon Gathercole, "'Sins' in Paul," *New Testament Studies* 64 (2018): 143.

14. Jack W. Hayford and David P. Seemuth, *Ephesians and Colossians*, Spirit-Filled Life Commentaries (Nashville: Thomas Nelson, 2005), 50. The NIV 2011 translates *sarx* variously as "sinful nature" (Rom 7:17, 25), "the realm of the flesh" (Rom 8:8), "the flesh" (Rom 8:3; Gal 5:19, 24). The idea is living that is opposed to the will of God and his Spirit or existence apart from God.

15. Lea, *New Testament*, 404.

16. Johnson, *Writings of the New Testament*, 357.

view of God's mercies as elucidated in the doctrinal section, are to offer their bodies "as a living sacrifice" (12:1-2). First, they are to use their spiritual gifts for the service of the Lord and for building one another (12:3-8). Second, they are to demonstrate their love for one another and even for those outside the body of Christ (12:9-21). Third, they are to obey and respect constituted government authorities because they are ordained by God (13:1-7). Believers must owe nothing to anyone except the continuing debt of love (13:8-10) and to be morally upright (13:10-14). Paul finally urges the believers to respect each other's liberty and never become stumbling blocks of one another (14:1-15:13). Like Christ, they are to seek the good of all. Paul concludes the book by sharing his personal plans and final greetings (15:14-16:27).

Key Theological Themes in the Letter to the Romans

The book of Romans has many important theological themes. But we have highlighted key ones below as follows:

The Sinfulness of Humanity and the Need for Redemption

One of the rejected concepts in modern secular psychology is the concept of the sinfulness of the human race. Sigmund Freud and his forebears believed that human beings are born *tabula rasa*, meaning born without sin. This thinking contradicts the biblical account that says,

> Therefore, just as sin entered the world through one man, and death through sin, and in this way death came to all people, because all sinned –
>
> To be sure, sin was in the world before the law was given, but sin is not charged against anyone's account where there is no law. Nevertheless, death reigned from the time of Adam to the time of Moses, even over those who did not sin by breaking a command, as did Adam, who is a pattern of the one to come. (Rom 5:12-14)

Romans 1:18-3:20 is Paul's lengthy argument about the sinfulness of the entire human race.

Moral Depravity as a Manifestation of Sinful Humanity

Theologically, depravity is a state of moral corruption that makes it hard for the depraved person to pursue righteousness. Instead, the natural propensity of the depraved person is toward evil. A classic example of depravity is found in Genesis 6:5, "The LORD saw how great the wickedness of the human race had become on the earth, and that every inclination of the thoughts of the human heart was only evil all the time." Similarly, "Now the earth was corrupt in God's sight and was full of violence. God saw how corrupt the earth had become, for all the people on earth had corrupted their ways" (Gen 6:11–12).

According to Paul, the depraved human race abandons the knowledge of God in nature and in the voice of reason to embrace the inclinations of the sinful nature. They suppress the truth they know.

> The wrath of God is being revealed from heaven against all the godlessness and wickedness of people, who suppress the truth by their wickedness, since what may be known about God is plain to them, because God has made it plain to them. For since the creation of the world God's invisible qualities – his eternal power and divine nature – have been clearly seen, being understood from what has been made, so that people are without excuse.
>
> For although they knew God, they neither glorified him as God nor gave thanks to him, but their thinking became futile and their *foolish hearts were darkened*. Although they claimed to be wise, they became fools and exchanged the glory of the immortal God for images made to look like a mortal human being and birds and animals and reptiles. (Rom 1:18–23, emphasis added)

This text shows that by rejecting the truth, people knew they became darkened in their understanding. A parallel text on this darkening of the mind is Ephesians 4:17–19:

> So I tell you this, and insist on it in the Lord, that you must no longer live as the Gentiles do, in the futility of their thinking. They are darkened in their understanding and separated from the life of God because of the ignorance that is in them due to the hardening of their hearts. Having lost all sensitivity, they have given themselves over to sensuality so as to indulge in every kind of impurity, and they are full of greed.

Three important results of depravity are clearly stated in Romans 1:18–23. They include the following:

1. Exchanging the Truth for a Lie
Romans 1:25 says, "They exchanged the truth of God for a lie, and worshiped and served created things rather than the Creator – who is forever praised.

Amen." This is one of the worst forms of human depravity, namely, rejecting the Creator whom they know,

> since what may be known about God is plain to them, because God has made it plain to them. For since the creation of the world God's invisible qualities – his eternal power and divine nature – have been clearly seen, being understood from what has been made, so that people are without excuse. (Rom 1:19–20)

God's first commandment in the Ten Commandments condemns idolatry (Exod 20:1–5). God alone is worthy of worship. Those who worship idols are deluded (Ps 115:4–5; 135:15–16; Hab 2:18). A text worth quoting at length regarding idols is Isaiah 44:9–20:

> All who make idols are nothing,
> and the things they treasure are worthless.
> Those who would speak up for them are blind;
> they are ignorant, to their own shame.
> Who shapes a god and casts an idol,
> which can profit nothing?
> People who do that will be put to shame;
> such craftsmen are only human beings.
> Let them all come together and take their stand;
> they will be brought down to terror and shame.
>
> The blacksmith takes a tool
> and works with it in the coals;
> he shapes an idol with hammers,
> he forges it with the might of his arm.
> He gets hungry and loses his strength;
> he drinks no water and grows faint.
> The carpenter measures with a line
> and makes an outline with a marker;
> he roughs it out with chisels
> and marks it with compasses.
> He shapes it in human form,
> human form in all its glory,
> that it may dwell in a shrine.
> He cut down cedars,
> or perhaps took a cypress or oak.
> He let it grow among the trees of the forest,
> or planted a pine, and the rain made it grow.

> It is used as fuel for burning;
>> some of it he takes and warms himself,
>> he kindles a fire and bakes bread.
> But he also fashions a god and worships it;
>> he makes an idol and bows down to it.
> Half of the wood he burns in the fire;
>> over it he prepares his meal,
>> he roasts his meat and eats his fill.
> He also warms himself and says,
>> "Ah! I am warm; I see the fire."
> From the rest he makes a god, his idol;
>> he bows down to it and worships.
> He prays to it and says,
>> "Save me! You are my god!"
> They know nothing, they understand nothing;
>> their eyes are plastered over so they cannot see,
>> and their minds closed so they cannot understand.
> No one stops to think,
>> no one has the knowledge or understanding to say,
> "Half of it I used for fuel;
>> I even baked bread over its coals,
>> I roasted meat and I ate.
> Shall I make a detestable thing from what is left?
>> Shall I bow down to a block of wood?"
> Such a person feeds on ashes; a deluded heart misleads him;
>> he cannot save himself, or say,
>> *"Is not this thing in my right hand a lie?"* (emphasis added)

Worshipping any created object or being is exchanging the glory of God for a lie. As God says, "I am the LORD; that is my name! I will not yield my glory to another or my praise to idols" (Isa 42:8). And "I, the LORD your God, am a jealous God, punishing the children for the sin of the fathers to the third and fourth generation of those who hate me, but showing love to a thousand generations of those who love me and keep my commandments" (Exod 20:5–6).

2. Overstepping the Boundaries of Human Sexuality

Apart from the worship of inanimate objects and lower creatures like reptiles, people with depraved minds overstep the boundaries of human sexuality. First, they engage in general sexual licentiousness or perversion. "Therefore God gave them over in the sinful desires of their hearts to sexual impurity for the degrading of their bodies with one another" (Rom 1:24). Second, they specifically practice homosexuality, that is, they engage in sexual activity between members of the same sex.

Today support for homosexuality is usually precipitated on the grounds of "new insights" on human sexuality. These "new insights" from modern science and psychology presuppose that some human beings have sexual orientations that are other than heterosexuality which have been misunderstood and therefore suppressed by primitive culture and religion. Therefore, the "enlightened" world believes that to speak against homosexuality is ignorance, "homophobia,"[17] and hate speech. However, Jeffrey Satinover rejects what the "enlightened" world believes regarding homosexuality as flawed because nobody is just "born that way." His conclusion based on modern science and psychology is that homosexuality "is not a true illness, though it may be thought an illness in the spiritual sense of 'soul sickness,' innate to fallen human nature."[18]

What are the consequences of overstepping the boundaries of human sexuality? According to Paul,

> Because of this, God gave them over to shameful lusts. Even their women exchanged natural sexual relations for unnatural ones. In the same way the men also abandoned natural relations with women and were inflamed with lust for one another. Men committed shameful acts with other men, and received in themselves the due penalty for their error. (Rom 1:26-27)

Whatever the "reinterpretation," Paul's clear words are that sexual activity with the same sex is *unnatural*. Like every good gift from God, the sexual drive is manipulated and destroyed.

Some of the key passages of the Bible that clearly speak against homosexuality include Genesis 19:1-11; Leviticus 20:13; Judges 19:22-23; 1 Corinthians 6:9-10; and Jude 9.[19] Given the Genesis 19 account for example, those who support homosexuality claim that God was condemning the *rape*

---

17. Aaron Cooper, "No Longer Invisible: Gay and Lesbian Jews Build a Movement," *Homosexuality and Religion*, ed. Richard Hasbany (New York: Harrington Park, 1989), 90.

18. Jeffrey Satinover, *Homosexuality and the Politics of Truth* (Grand Rapids: Baker, 1996), 246.

19. See also Jesus's description of God's original intention for marriage in Matthew 19:4-6.

of Lot's guests "without consent" and not homosexuality.[20] In other words, pro-homosexuals condemn rape but not homosexuality. Perhaps Afriyie is right in saying that if rape was the issue with the men of Sodom, Lot would not have offered his daughters in place of the men.[21] Another argument advanced by homosexual promoters is that the reason the Old Testament condemns homosexuality is that homosexual behavior was connected with idolatrous worship. But this argument cannot be proven from Scripture. Although homosexual and lesbian acts may have been associated with idolatry, this was not always the case. Finally, advocates of homosexuality believe that "Christ is the end of the Law for the Christian (Rom 10:4),"[22] so Christians are not bound by the morality of ancient culture. But as Afriyie points out, the prohibition against homosexuality is also found in the New Testament.[23]

We conclude that those who do not hold a high view of Scripture as a rule often twist the biblical text to justify aberrant behaviors and practices. If anyone does not believe the Bible to be the inspired word of God, why would they not reject any biblical teaching that counteracts their own opinion? After all, the reason human beings reject God is that he places moral demands on them that they are unwilling to obey. Yusufu Turaki well says, "Pastors and counsellors need to recognize that homosexuality has deep roots in our sinful nature."[24] According to Turaki, sin is not merely what we do. "Because of the fall, sin has affected all aspects of our inner being."[25]

3. Practicing Every Form of Wickedness

People with depraved minds embrace a "detestable lifestyle."[26] Nothing better explains the prevalence of evil in the world than Romans 1:28–32:

---

20. See Ernestina Afriyie, "A Christian Response to Homosexuality," in *West African Journal of Higher Education, God, the Bible and Human Sexuality* 6 (2017): 38.

21. Afriyie, "Christian Response to Homosexuality," 40.

22. Afriyie, 40.

23. Afriyie, 40. For more on this topic, see Hope Amolo, "Paul's View of Same Sex as Sexual Deviation," in *West African Journal of Higher Education, God, the Bible and Human Sexuality* 6 (2017): 80–111; and Francis O. Falako, "Heterosexuality in Traditional African Culture: Peculiarities, Modern Concerns and Implications for the Church," in *West African Journal of Higher Education, God, the Bible and Human Sexuality* 6 (2017): 46–63.

24. Yusufu Turaki, "Homosexuality," in *Africa Bible Commentary*, ed. Tokunboh Adeyemo (Nairobi: WordAlive, 2006), 1355.

25. Turaki, "Homosexuality," 1355.

26. David M. Kasali, "Romans," in *Africa Bible Commentary*, ed. Tokunboh Adeyemo (Nairobi: WordAlive, 2006), 1354.

> Furthermore, just as they did not think it worthwhile to retain the knowledge of God, so God gave them over to a depraved mind, so that they do what ought not to be done. They have become filled with every kind of wickedness, evil, greed and depravity. They are full of envy, murder, strife, deceit and malice. They are gossips, slanderers, God-haters, insolent, arrogant and boastful; they invent ways of doing evil; they disobey their parents; they have no understanding, no fidelity, no love, no mercy. Although they know God's righteous decree that those who do such things deserve death, they not only continue to do these very things but also approve of those who practice them.

When human beings deliberately reject the knowledge of God, he gives them over to a depraved mind, to do what ought not to be done. The result is that they become "filled with every kind of wickedness, evil, greed and depravity" (1:29).

The Righteousness of God

The Greek verb *dikaioō* is prominent in Pauline letters. It means to declare righteous or justify.[27] The noun "righteousness" (*dikaiosynē*) is usually translated "righteousness," "justice," "innocence," or "justification."[28] Paul declares,

> For I am not ashamed of the gospel, because it is the power of God that brings salvation to everyone who believes: first to the Jew, then to the Gentile. For in the gospel the righteousness of God is revealed – a righteousness that is by faith from first to last, just as it is written: "The righteous will live by faith." (Rom 1:16–17)

The righteousness (*dikaiosynē*) of God or from God is one of the dominant themes in Romans (cf. 3:21–22, 25–26; 10:3). But what does righteousness from God mean? John P. T. Hunt well notes that in recent times there are divergent views regarding the phrase "righteousness from God."[29] The ambiguous nature of the Greek genitive (*qeou*) could be responsible for the divergent views.[30] Some think that this righteousness from God "refers to *God's character*, just

---

27. Mounce, "Righteous, righteousness," 594.

28. Mounce, 595.

29. See John P. T. Hunt, *An Introduction to Romans: A Resource for the Nigerian Church* (Kaduna, Nigeria: Prudent Universal, 2020), 26.

30. See John P. T. Hunt's larger commentary on Romans, *Understanding and Applying Romans: A Commentary for the Nigerian Church* (Kaduna, Nigeria: Prudent Universal, 2020), 71–75.

like the wrath of God." Others believe it means "*God's saving activity.*" And some think that righteousness from God "refers to God's *faithfulness to his promises.*" Finally, there are those who hold that righteousness from God means "God's *gift of righteousness,* that is, the gift of right legal standing before God." In the light of Habakkuk 2:4, Hunt rightly concludes that the apostle Paul had the "gift of God" in mind when he spoke about the righteousness from God.[31]

The concept of righteousness from God provides the key to understanding the rest of the book. According to Paul, the gospel is the power of God for salvation because God's righteousness "that is by faith from first to last" (Rom 1:17) is revealed in the gospel. The essential content of the gospel is that "Christ died for our sins according to the Scriptures, that he was buried, that he was raised on the third day according to the Scriptures" (1 Cor 15:3-4). This is of "first importance" (15:3) and is consistent in Pauline theology. As Paul puts it in Romans 10:9-11:

> If you declare with your mouth, "Jesus is Lord," and believe in your heart that God raised him from the dead, you will be saved. For it is with your heart that you believe and are justified, and it is with your mouth that you profess your faith and are saved. As the Scripture says, "Anyone who believes in him will never be put to shame."

Therefore, the righteousness of God or from God is God's imputed righteousness rather than righteousness obtained through observance of the law (Rom 3:21-22, 25-26; 10:3). Paul's thesis is that no one will be justified in God's sight through observance of the law. Rather, through the law comes knowledge of sin. Therefore, God's righteousness is obtained through faith in Christ who died for our sins. This means that instead of the heavy burden of the law's requirements, the gospel is "the good news of God's righteousness."[32]

Justification by Faith in Christ[33]

Romans 3:21–5:21 is Paul's discourse on "the righteousness that comes by faith" in Christ Jesus (4:13). Although the Jews possessed the Scriptures, their

---

31. Hunt, *Introduction to Romans,* 26–27, all emphasis original.
32. Johnson, *Writings of the New Testament,* 346.
33. Justification by faith alone is believed to be *sine qua non* of the Reformation movement. But the new perspective(s) on Paul seems to challenge this. And many scholars have written in support or repudiation. For scholars on either side of the debate, see E. P. Sanders, *Paul and Palestinian Judaism: A Comparison of Patterns of Religion* (London: SCM/Philadelphia Fortress,

advantage over the Gentiles was short lived by the fact that they too failed to keep the law. According to Romans 3:21–26, "There is no distinction between Jews and Gentiles with regard to their status before God as far as their sins are concerned."[34]

Therefore, righteousness comes through God's act of justification. And justification is the act by which "God declares as righteous anyone who places faith in Jesus Christ."[35] The path to righteousness is rooted in the person and works of Christ. The atoning sacrifice of Christ is the means by which a person is justified before God. "God presented Christ as a sacrifice of atonement (Greek *hilastērion*),[36] through faith in his blood – to be received by faith. He did this to demonstrate his righteousness, because in his forbearance he had left the sins committed beforehand unpunished" (Rom 3:25). Just as God chose the blood of animals as the means by which the sins of the people in the Old Testament were atoned for (Lev 17:11), God set apart Jesus as the means of atonement for the sins of the world.

Sanctification of the Justified

Although the book of Romans does not mention the word "sanctification," the concept is pronounced in Romans 6:1–8:39. Lea rightly refers to this section as "the path of holy living."[37] The overriding theme is sanctification of the believer. The Greek word to sanctify, *hagiazō*, occurs infrequently in the New Testament

---

1977); James D. G. Dunn, *The New Perspective on Paul*, rev. ed. (Grand Rapids: Eerdmans, 2008); N. T. Wright, *What Paul Really Said: Was Paul of Tarsus the Real Founder of Christianity?* (Oxford: Lion, 1997); Robert J. Cara, *Cracking the Foundation of the New Perspective on Paul: Covenantal Nomism versus Reformed Covenantal Theology* (Ross-shire: Mentor, 2017); D. A. Carson, Peter T. O'Brien, and Mark A. Seifrid, eds., *Justification and Variegated Nomism*, vol. 1: *The Complexities of Second Temple Judaism* (Tübingen: Mohr Siebeck/Grand Rapids: Baker, 2001); D. A. Carson, Peter T. O'Brien, and Mark A. Seifrid, eds., *Justification and Variegated Nomism*, vol. 2: *The Paradoxes of Paul* (Tübingen: Mohr Siebeck/Grand Rapids: Baker, 2001); Simon J. Gathercole, *Where Is Boasting? Early Jewish Soteriology and Paul's Response in Romans 1–5* (Grand Rapids: Eerdmans, 2002); and Peter Stuhlmacher, *Revisiting Paul's Doctrine of Justification: A Challenge to the New Perspective* (Downers Grove: IVP Academic, 2001).

34. Eckhard J. Schnabel, *Paul the Missionary: Realities, Strategies and Methods* (Downers Grove: IVP Academic, 2008), 217.

35. Lea, *New Testament*, 402.

36. For the possible sources of Paul's theology on the atonement, see Udo Schnelle, *Apostle Paul: His Life and Theology*, trans. M. Eugene Boring (Grand Rapids: Baker Academic, 2005), 447–48. For comprehensive treatment of the concept of atonement, see Frank S. Thielman, "The Atonement," in *Central Themes in Biblical Theology: Mapping Unity in Diversity*, ed. Scott J. Hafemann and Paul R. House (Nottingham: Apollos, 2007), 102–27.

37. Lea, *New Testament*, 403.

(John 17:17, 19; 1 Thess 5:23; Heb 9:13). The word means to consecrate, hallow, dedicate, purify, and set apart. In the Old Testament, objects and persons were consecrated and set apart for special purposes. People who were consecrated to the Lord like the priests, kings, and Nazarites were supposed to give themselves wholly to the Lord.

Paul shows that salvation through God's grace is not a license for unholy living. On the contrary, those who are recipients of God's grace have died to sin (Rom 6:1–7). Sin no longer has mastery over them. Instead, they must continually offer their bodies to God as "instruments of righteousness" (Rom 6:13). This offering is necessary because even believers are constantly dragged by the power of sin (Rom 7:14–25). But the struggle is not fatal because "the law of the Spirit of life" has set the believer "free from the law of sin and death" (Rom 8:2). Similarly, the indwelling Spirit of God is the guarantee of their place as children of God and of seeing the future glory that will be revealed. These assurances are the motivation for holy living.

The Place of Jews and Gentiles in the Redemptive Scheme

Paul treats the complex issues of election and predestination in Romans 9:1–11:36. This section deals with God's plan for the salvation of Jews and Gentiles. But here we also find one of the troublesome waters in theology, namely the concept of predestination in Pauline theology. Any attempt to treat the subject of predestination, like the Trinity, is delving into what the song writer Carl P. Daw, Jr., regards as something, "Deeper than our minds can fathom / Greater than our creeds rehearse."[38] Therefore, my intention is to comment on the biblical data in plain language, as much as possible. According to Johnson,

> Despite the invitation these chapters appear to offer for discussion concerning free will and predestination, Paul's concern here is not with the ultimate fate of any individual before God, still less with philosophical issues of fate versus freedom. Paul rather praises God's work in the history of peoples, as he can trace it in the stories of his own tradition. His engagement with biblical history is governed by the contemporary Jewish rejection of the "good news" about Jesus as Messiah and Lord, and the acceptance of that same proclamation by contemporary Gentiles. These events,

---

38. Carl P. Daw, Jr., "God the Spirit, Guide and Guardian" (1987), in *Sing to the Lord: Church of the Nazarene Hymnal* (Kansas City: Lillenas, 1993), #780.

> in which Paul's mission itself plays the most pivotal role, raise difficult questions: What is the meaning of "God's people"? Has God been faithful to his word? Is Israel as a people rejected, and if so, can God be trusted?[39]

According to Johnson, accent is not placed on free will and predestination as it may seem to be. Rather, Paul is engaged with biblical history in the light of Israel's rejection of the Messiah "and the acceptance of that same proclamation by contemporary Gentiles." This raises the question of the identity of God's people. According to Paul,

> The prophets show God's mercy reaching out to people who were not part of the historical nation; already in Torah, God calls into being a people from among the nations (9:24). The prophets also show that many of the Jews were stubborn, failing to heed God's call to repentance. Israel as a religious reality was both larger and smaller than the nation: it was a remnant defined by faith (9:25–29).[40]

This means that God's people are to be defined by faith rather than ancestral lineage or the historical Israel. For this reason, the Gentiles who demonstrate faith in the Messiah qualify as God's people along with the Jews who believe.

The concepts of predestination and election as exemplified in Isaac's children (Rom 9:6–22) raise questions about God's justice and fairness. But Paul argues that "election has everything to do with God's gift and nothing to do with human accomplishment (9:6–9)."[41] Furthermore, God must not be conceived as a despot who makes arbitrary choices. Human concepts of justice and fairness are merely a demonstration of the expanse between the Creator and the creature, "a distance measurable only in terms of the Creator's mercy, not the creature's standards of justice."[42] This means that the creatures are unable to fully understand the concept of justice from God's standpoint. Similarly, since everything comes from God, "there is no independent standpoint from which the critic can question God (9:19–21)."[43] On the whole, Paul argues that the concept of election, even as it applies to individual cases such as that of

---

39. Johnson, *Writings of the New Testament*, 357.
40. Johnson, 358.
41. Johnson, 358.
42. Johnson, 358.
43. Johnson, 358.

Isaac and Jacob, is to be understood in terms of God's mercy rather than his wrath. Everything depends on God's mercy (9:11, 16).

The next crucial theological issue Paul addresses is the rejection of the Jews and the call of the Gentiles (Rom 9:30–10:21). Drawing from his arguments in chapters 1 through 8, Paul shows that the determining factor for inclusion in the people of God is faith (9:30). Most of Israel rejected the "good news" which the Gentiles embraced (10:16). Therefore, the Gentiles are now part of the people of God. The cross, which is "the power of God that brings salvation to everyone who believes" (1:16), became "a stumbling block to Jews" (1 Cor 1:23). Most Jews rejected God's righteousness that comes by faith and pursued the righteousness that comes through observing the law, not realizing that "no one will be declared righteous in God's sight by the works of the law; rather, through the law we become conscious of our sin" (Rom 3:20; cf. Gal 2:16). The Gentiles who come to Christ by faith are justified, "For we maintain that a person is justified by faith apart from the works of the law" (Rom 3:28).

But the rejection of Israel is not final, and neither has God's word failed (Rom 11:1–32). Rather by their rejection, God is working out his salvific purposes for the entire human race. Similarly, the inclusion of the Gentiles is not based on their merit before God. It is based on his grace and mercy. Therefore, as ingrafted branches, they have no reason to boast, and they must be cautious.

> If some of the branches have been broken off, and you, though a wild olive shoot, have been grafted in among the others and now share in the nourishing sap from the olive root, do not consider yourself to be superior to those other branches. If you do, consider this: You do not support the root, but the root supports you. You will say then, "Branches were broken off so that I could be grafted in." Granted. But they were broken off because of unbelief, and you stand by faith. Do not be arrogant, but tremble. For if God did not spare the natural branches, he will not spare you either. (11:17–21)

Israel's rejection is temporary because God wants all Israel to be saved (11:26), "for God's gifts and his call are irrevocable" (11:29).

Redemption as the Restoration of Creation

Paul's Letter to the Romans shows the anticipation for the final restoration and renewal of the world. The whole creation is longing for rest and wholeness (Rom 8:18–26; cf. 1 Cor 15:20–26). Like the prophet Isaiah (Isa 65:17–25),

Paul believed that the world in which we live will one day be transformed.[44] Therefore in Romans 8:18–25, Paul provides a fundamental understanding of the glorification of believers which will also be the time of liberation for the entire creation. He says,

> I consider that our present sufferings are not worth comparing with the glory that will be revealed in us. The creation waits in eager expectation for the children of God to be revealed. For the creation was subjected to frustration, not by its own choice, but by the will of the one who subjected it, in hope that the creation itself will be liberated from its bondage to decay and brought into the freedom and glory of the children of God. (Rom 8:18–21)

This renewal of all things will take place at Christ's return.

What is not certain, however, is whether this renewal takes us into the eternal state or gives room for the earthly paradise described in Isaiah 11:6–9. According to David Lowery, the Pauline epistles are "indecisive on this point, but if he envisioned such an era before the advent of the eternal state, he has only given a vague indication of it in 1 Corinthians 15:23–24."[45]

Questions for Review and Application

1. What would you consider to be the theme of the book of Romans?
2. What is moral depravity and in what particular ways is moral depravity displayed in your community and in the world today?
3. What are the major theological themes in the book of Romans?
4. What is the meaning of justification, and how does one stand justified before God?
5. How does the book of Romans provide comfort for suffering Christians in Africa and in the world?
6. According to Romans chapters 12–16, in what practical ways can we offer our bodies as living sacrifices?

---

44. David L. Lowery, "A Theology of Paul's Missionary Epistles," in *A Biblical Theology of the New Testament*, ed. Roy B. Zuck (Chicago: Moody, 1994), 296.

45. Lowery, "Theology of Paul's Missionary Epistles," 296.

9

Drums of Redemption in 1 Corinthians

The burning light of divine wisdom illumines a hundred shadows of our human folly. And at the center of the blaze is the mighty cross of Jesus Christ defining the final meaning of everything.

John Piper[1]

For Christ did not send me to baptize, but to preach the gospel – not with wisdom and eloquence, lest the cross of Christ be emptied of its power.

For the message of the cross is foolishness to those who are perishing, but to us who are being saved it is the power of God. For it is written:

"I will destroy the wisdom of the wise;
the intelligence of the intelligent I will frustrate."

Where is the wise person? Where is the teacher of the law? Where is the philosopher of this age? Has not God made foolish the wisdom of the world? For since in the wisdom of God the world through its wisdom did not know him, God was pleased through the foolishness of what was preached to save those who believe. Jews demand signs and Greeks look for wisdom, but we preach Christ crucified: a stumbling block to Jews and foolishness to Gentiles, but to those whom God has called, both Jews and Greeks, Christ the power of God and the wisdom of God. For the

---

1. John Piper, "Praise for *Culture Shift*," in R. Albert Mohler, Jr., *Culture Shift: The Battle for the Moral Heart of America* (Colorado Springs: Multnomah, 2011), i.

foolishness of God is wiser than human wisdom, and the weakness of God is stronger than human strength.

1 Corinthians 1:17–25

Do you not know that in a race all the runners run, but only one gets the prize? Run in such a way as to get the prize. Everyone who competes in the games goes into strict training. They do it to get a crown that will not last, but we do it to get a crown that will last forever. Therefore I do not run like someone running aimlessly; I do not fight like a boxer beating the air. No, I strike a blow to my body and make it my slave so that after I have preached to others, I myself will not be disqualified for the prize.

1 Corinthians 9:24–27

Synopsis of 1 Corinthians

Corinth occupied an important place as the fourth largest city in the Roman Empire after Rome, Alexandria, and Antioch. As capital of the Roman province of Achaia and an important port between two seas – the Aegean and the Adriatic – Corinth served as a commercial center and bridge between the East and West. As a commercial center, Corinth brought together and connected Greeks, Western Europeans, Syrians, Asians, Egyptians, and Jews "rubbing shoulders in daily business."[2] Because Corinth was "situated at such an important crossroads of the ancient world, it became notorious for its sexual vice and immorality."[3] Similarly, religious practices connected with fertility cults also encouraged sexual promiscuity.

Acts 18:1–18 gives us the background of Paul's successful ministry in Corinth. Through Paul, God brought both Jews and Gentiles to the Christian faith. Corinth's strategic geographic location, connecting the East and the West, was important for the rapid spread of the gospel as well. Paul took advantage of this in reaching out to merchants and travelers.

Paul likely wrote 1 Corinthians from Ephesus during his third missionary journey. But it is evident that 1 Corinthians is Paul's second letter to the Corinthians (1 Cor 5:9). His first letter is no longer extant, hence the one we have is named 1 Corinthians. This letter is dated around AD 55 or 56, and this early date is attested by Clement of Rome. It is reported that in

---

2. Derek Prime, *Let's Study 2 Corinthians* (Edinburgh: Banner of Truth Trust, 2000), xi.
3. Prime, *Let's Study 2 Corinthians*, xi.

AD 95, Clement wrote to the church at Corinth regarding their rebellious spirit. In his letter, Clement reminded the Corinthian Christians about Paul's warnings to them with the words, "Take up the epistle of the blessed Apostle Paul. What did he write to you at the time when the Gospel first began to be preached?"[4] Clement was concerned about the persistent contentious spirit of the Corinthian believers.

The early church source above affirms the genuineness of 1 Corinthians. It also confirms that the church in Corinth had many unsettling issues. Paul's letter was occasioned by a report from Chloe's household regarding divisions and disagreements in the church (1 Cor 1:11). Paul had also received a letter from the church with questions regarding some issues (7:1, 25; 8:1; 12:1; 15:1; 16:1).[5] Some of the problems in the church included unhealthy rivalries and factions among the believers (1:10–4:21); pride (4:6–13); sexual immorality (5:1–6:20); confusion on marital issues (7:1–40); confusion about meat offered to idols (8:1–11:1); disorder in public worship (11:2–14:40); and uncertainties regarding the resurrection (15:1–58).

Key Theological Themes in 1 Corinthians

As Paul treats problems in the church at Corinth, some theological themes emerge. These theological concepts present themselves as unavoidable issues that relate to the problems at hand.

Redemption as the Message of Christ Crucified

The divisions in the Corinthian church indicate that they misunderstood the nature of the gospel. Therefore, Paul takes time to explain the central theme of the gospel which is the cross of Christ (1 Cor 1:18–3:4). Instead of boasting about human beings, the Corinthians must remember that it was not Paul nor Apollos nor any of the apostles who was crucified for them. Jesus was crucified for them, which constitutes the central message of the gospel (2:1–2). And as Jeremy Punt says, "The cross of Jesus is an important theme in Paul's letters, identified by him as the focus and content of his message: Christ crucified (e.g. 1 Cor 1:23; 2:5)."[6]

---

4. Clement of Rome, *The First Epistle of Clement*, 47, quoted in Lea, *New Testament*, 413.

5. Lea, *New Testament*, 414.

6. Jeremy Punt, "Cross-Purpose in Paul? Violence of the Cross, Galatians, and Human Dignity," *Scriptura* 102 (2009): 446.

But the Jews and the Gentiles saw the message of the cross as a contradiction, a stumbling block and foolishness:

> Jews demand signs and Greeks look for wisdom, but we preach Christ crucified: a stumbling block to Jews and foolishness to Gentiles, but to those whom God has called, both Jews and Greeks, Christ the power of God and the wisdom of God. For the foolishness of God is wiser than human wisdom, and the weakness of God is stronger than human strength. (1 Cor 1:22–25)

For many of the Jews it was inconceivable that the Messiah could suffer the death of the accursed (Deut 21:22–23). They did not understand that Jesus became a curse for us (Gal 3:13). The message of the cross was foolishness to the unbelieving Gentiles because they could not conceive of a savior dying as a criminal on a cruel cross.

But Christ's death was a sacrificial death for the salvation of human kind. According to James D. G. Dunn,

> One of the most powerful images used by Paul to explicate the significance of Christ's death is that of the cultic sacrifice, or more precisely the "sin offering" which could be offered up by individuals or groups in the Jerusalem temple (Leviticus 4) and the annual Day of Atonement sacrifices (Lev. 16.11–19).[7]

In summary, the central message of the gospel is the cross. The message of the gospel as Christ crucified confronts the false wisdom of the world.[8] But too many people are "turning to a different gospel – which is really no gospel at all" (Gal 1:6–7). These other gospels include prosperity preaching that focuses on the material world and the here and now rather than on Christ and the future life promised in the Bible. But if Christians in Africa are to maintain their cutting age, the central message of the gospel (1 Cor 15:1–6) must not be substituted by other gospels.

Redemption as the Basis for Unity in the Body of Christ

Billy Graham said, "Satan will do everything he can to divide Christians and destroy our witness. Only the Holy Spirit can subdue our old nature and

---

7. James D. G. Dunn, *The Theology of Paul the Apostle* (Grand Rapids: Eerdmans, 1998), 212.

8. Dachollom Datiri, "1 Corinthians," in *Africa Bible Commentary*, ed. Tokunboh Adeyemo (Nairobi: WordAlive, 2006), 1379.

overcome with God's love."⁹ The church at Corinth became divided over personalities (1 Cor 1:10–4:21). The loyalties of the believers were misplaced. They gave their allegiance to some influential human figures rather than to Jesus Christ (1:12). Disappointed, Paul reprimanded them (1:13). The believers in Corinth misunderstood the nature of the gospel (1:18–3:4) and the nature of the ministry (3:5–4:5) and were inflamed by pride (4:6–13).[10] The most important point Paul makes is that Christ is not divided, so the church must not be divided. Division in the church is blatant abuse of the one body of Christ who was crucified for all.

Similarly, the problem of the "outsider" is a critical issue in African society today. Tribal differences often degenerate into conflicts of alarming proportions in the church. Christian communities often take up arms against one another. Lives and properties are destroyed, and churches are demolished by the same Christians – even people of the same church denomination. The result is that Christian testimony is fatally wounded. But African Christians can overcome divisive ethnicity and ancient hostilities by applying the one body concept taught by Paul in 1 Corinthians (cf. Eph 2:11–4:16) and Jesus (cf. John 17:20–23).

Furthermore, believers must keep in mind that unity of the body does not come automatically or naturally. As Paul says elsewhere, the ground rule is: "*Make every effort* to keep the unity of the Spirit through the bond of peace" (Eph 4:3, emphasis added). Unity of the body overrides all social and ideological divides. Instead of promoting division, it is the duty of every believer to discover, nurture, and use their gift(s) for the benefit of all.

Redemption as the Basis of Grace Gifts (Charismata) in the One Body

The apostle Paul provides an extended list of spiritual gifts in 1 Corinthians 12–14. These gifts are the "manifestation" or "demonstration" of the Holy Spirit in the body of Christ, and each gift plays a particular essential role for the mutual benefit of the whole.

> Now to each one the manifestation of the Spirit is given for the common good. To one there is given through the Spirit a message of wisdom, to another a message of knowledge by means of the same Spirit, to another faith by the same Spirit, to another gifts

---

9. Graham, *Billy Graham in Quotes*, 107.
10. Lea, *The New Testament*, 415.

of healing by that one Spirit, to another miraculous powers, to another prophecy, to another distinguishing between spirits, to another speaking in different kinds of tongues, and to still another the interpretation of tongues. All these are the work of one and the same Spirit, and he distributes them to each one, just as he determines. (1 Cor 12:7–11)

The Holy Spirit distributes these diverse spiritual gifts for diverse services. But we serve the same Lord (12:4–5; cf. Rom 12:6–8; Eph 4:4–6, 11–12; 1 Pet 4:10–11). The implication of 1 Corinthians 12:7–11 is that everyone who is born of the Spirit has a spiritual gift. Similarly, every spiritual gift is for the common good of the entire body.

To support his argument, Paul uses the analogy of a physical human body to show that believers belong to the same spiritual body (1 Cor 12:12–26). The body is a unit made up of many parts (cf. Rom 12:4–5; Eph 4:11–16; Col 2:18–19). Jesus is the head of the body. Each part is indispensable, including the unpresentable parts. Each part belongs to the whole. Therefore, collective interest overrides individual interest. No part is insignificant (12:15–25). "If one part suffers, every part suffers with it," and vice versa (1 Cor 12:26). And Paul's rhetorical questions affirm this unity in diversity (12:29–30).

Redemption as Union with Christ: A Theology of the Body[11]

To be a Christian is to be united with Christ. Just as Christ is the head of the church, he is the head of every believer. Collectively and individually, we belong to Christ who is the head. Believers are one with Christ in soul, spirit, and body. This means that even our physical bodies are mystically united with him. It is from this union that Paul draws the conclusions below.

1. Sexual Immorality Is Defilement of Christ's Body and God's Temple
As highlighted in the synopsis, sexual immorality was one of the problems in the church in Corinth (1 Cor 5:1–6:20). There was even incestuous sexual activity – "A man is sleeping with his father's wife." But instead of grieving for the scandalous sin, they were proud! (5:1–2). Their pride reflected a deeply entrenched lifestyle and worldview that was obviously incongruent with the gospel message they had received. The Corinthians totally misunderstood the concept of Christian liberty. They believed they were free to do anything they

---

11. Anthony C. Thiselton, *The First Epistle to the Corinthians: A Commentary on the Greek Text* (Grand Rapids: Eerdmans, 2000), 458.

wanted. They seemed to have bought into the popular maxim, "I have the right to do anything." Paul's response is: "but not everything is beneficial. 'I have the right to do anything' – but I will not be mastered by anything'" (6:12; cf. 10:23).

So after reprimanding the church at Corinth, Paul turns in 1 Corinthians 6:12–20 to what Anthony C. Thiselton rightly calls "union with Christ and the theology of the body."[12] Paul is categorical here.

> Do you not know that your bodies are members of Christ himself? Shall I then take the members of Christ and unite them with a prostitute? Never! Do you not know that he who unites himself with a prostitute is one with her in body? For it is said, "The two will become one flesh." But whoever is united with the Lord is one with him in spirit.
>
> Flee from sexual immorality. All other sins a person commits are outside the body, but whoever sins sexually, sins against their own body. Do you not know that your bodies are temples of the Holy Spirit, who is in you, whom you have received from God? You are not your own; you were bought at a price. Therefore honor God with your bodies. (1 Cor 6:15–20)

Paul says that our "limbs and organs" belong to Christ's body.[13] The Christian who is intimately united with Christ cannot take "the limbs and organs which have been grafted into Christ for un-Christlike purposes that wrench them apart again."[14]

2. If Anyone Destroys God's Temple, God Will Destroy that Person

According to Paul, every believer's body is God's holy temple because the Spirit of the Lord dwells in him or her: "Don't you know that you yourselves are God's temple and that God's Spirit dwells in your midst? If anyone destroys God's temple, God will destroy that person; for God's temple is sacred, and you together are that temple" (1 Cor 3:16–17). Being God's temple is an awesome privilege and responsibility. Therefore, Paul urges the believers in Corinth to be separate from the world in their conduct (2 Cor 6:14–18).

Speaking about the significance of believers as God's temple, Kenneth Boa says,

---

12. Thiselton, *First Epistle to the Corinthians*, 458.
13. Thiselton, 465.
14. Thiselton, 466.

God the Holy Spirit desires to create a community of spiritual beings who will receive and reflect the likeness of God and glorify him forever (Ephesians 2:21–22). The desire is being realized in his plan to create a spiritual temple of living stones into whom he can invest his likeness, and power, competent to serve and glorify him in eternal fulfilment (1 Peter 2:4–5). We are that temple, and Christ is the cornerstone (Ephesians 2:20).[15]

Christians who defile themselves through sexual immorality defile the temple of the living God (1 Cor 6:18–20). Each member is like a building stone. A bad stone does not fit well with the entire building and is likely to weaken and destroy it. Thomas Hale says,

> How can God's temple, or church, be destroyed? If we, the members – the stones – become worldly and unspiritual, our temple will be destroyed. Our temple (church) can be destroyed by the sins, the worldliness, of its members. It is destroyed by false teaching, divisions, quarrels, and slander of one member against another.[16]

Similarly, all Christians must also keep in mind that their body is not their own, contrary to popular opinion. As Paul states, "You are not your own; you were bought at a price" (1 Cor 6:19–20).[17] Christians who believe that their bodies belong to God must flee from everything that is likely to pollute the temple of God.

Wilbur O'Donovan says,

> The church in Africa today needs to take a strong stand on the word of God concerning marriage, sex and the family. The church needs to demand sexual purity and faithfulness of members and leaders before and during marriage. The church needs to speak out plainly about the responsibilities of husbands and wives toward each other. *The church needs to speak out strongly against those practices in the church which undermine the institution of marriage.*

---

15. Kenneth Boa, *Conformed to His Image: Biblical and Practical Approaches to Spiritual Formation* (Grand Rapids: Zondervan, 2001), 112.

16. Thomas Hale, *The Applied New Testament Commentary* (Colorado Springs: Victor, 1996), 635. Hale rightly points out that the universal church cannot be destroyed "but a local church can be destroyed through the sins of its members" (635n8). History has also shown that the church can be destroyed in a particular nation or even continent by the sins of its members.

17. Even those who think that they own their bodies deceive themselves because there must come a time when they cannot keep it.

The church needs to openly and vigorously condemn a godless and evil society which mocks the word of God.[18]

The church in the twenty-first century must be reminded that God is the same yesterday, today and forever. Sexual purity is still a requirement for all those who believe in Christ.

Redemption and the Place of Women in Worship and Ministry

One of the theological conundrums in 1 Corinthians is what Paul says about women in worship (1 Cor 11:1–16; 14:33–35; cf. 1 Tim 2:11–15). Scholars interpret the "distinctions at worship"[19] implied in the texts from their different presuppositions and ideologies. The aim of this section is to raise the theological issues and present viewpoints rather than give final answers. It is important to note that the passages in question are in the context of worship in the local church.

1. Head Coverings for Women in Worship

What are the issues? The first is head covering (1 Cor 11:1–11). Paul tells the women to cover their heads while in worship. He tells the men not to cover their heads. What occasioned this controversial passage? Yamsat says that although it is uncertain, it appears that some people in the church at Corinth wanted the abolition of gender distinctions in worship, while others wanted to maintain the tradition "expressed by the different hairstyles and/or headgear."[20] According to Yamsat, although Paul's instruction would have favored the Jewish women who used veils, "the varying practices among the Greeks, regarding veil, headgear and hairstyle would have been so evident in the church as to make it difficult for Paul to advocate what would have appeared to the majority members, who were Greeks, an imposition of a foreign practice."[21]

But how is the passage understood among theologians? The trajectory of interpretation shows that the passage has been construed in support of the headship of the man over the woman. In recent scholarship, however, the concept of the man as the head having authority over the woman is disputed

---

18. Wilbur O'Donovan, *Biblical Christianity in Modern Africa* (Carlisle: Paternoster, 2000), 85, emphasis added.
19. Pandam Yamsat, *An Exposition of First Corinthians* (Bukuru, Nigeria: Africa Christian Textbooks, 2004), 129.
20. Yamsat, *Exposition of First Corinthians*, 131.
21. Yamsat, 131.

and rejected by many scholars who contend that the head (Greek *kēphale*) in the text is to be rendered "source" rather than headship in terms of authority or hierarchy.[22] This mean that the man is the source from which the woman came, just as in Genesis 2:21–23. This understanding is more pronounced among feminist scholars. For instance, Catherine Clark Kroeger says, "The concept of *head* as 'source' is well documented in both classical and Christian antiquity and has long been accepted by scholars. Some evangelicals, however, have shown reluctance to deal with the data."[23] According to this view, Paul expresses the interdependence between the two sexes by saying, "Nevertheless, in the Lord woman is not independent of man, nor is man independent of woman. For as woman came from man, so also man is born of woman. But everything comes from God" (1 Cor 11:11–12). This means that the man must not capitalize on the headship because there is mutuality and interdependence between the two genders. But most evangelicals would acknowledge the mutuality and interdependence of the two sexes as well.

Similarly, those who reject the normativity of 1 Corinthians 11:1–16 see the text as primarily addressing the church at Corinth and must be interpreted in its cultural setting without universalizing it. For such interpreters, the text is confined to the local community of believers in Corinth and based on the culture of the people at that time and place. Therefore, head covering in worship cannot be applied to all Christian women at all times and places. This understanding implies that the matter is cultural rather than theological. But a careful reading shows that the text is more complex than addressing a mere cultural setting, especially given the varying practices in Corinth as highlighted above. Yamsat thinks that the complexity of the matter made Paul take a flexible position.[24]

Other scholars go to extremes and see Paul as a product of his chauvinistic and male-controlled society. According to these scholars, Paul contradicts himself by swinging to the patriarchal mode of thinking that women are subordinates of men. How can Paul say in one breath that "There is neither Jew nor Gentile, neither slave nor free, nor is there male and female, for you are all one in Christ Jesus" (Gal 3:28), and with the next say that the man is the head of the woman? These scholars advocate for gender equality and the abolition of gender roles. According to them, the concept of the authority

---

22. Catherine Clark Kroeger, "The Classical Concept of *Head* as 'Source,'" in Gretchen G. Hull, *Equal to Serve: Women and Men in the Church and Home* (Westwood: Revell, 1987), 267.

23. Kroeger, "Classical Concept of *Head*," 267.

24. Yamsat, *Exposition of First Corinthians*, 132.

of man over woman is to be rejected as a product of the patriarchal, male-dominated society.

But those of the traditional and conservative persuasion believe that "head" in 1 Corinthians 11:3–16 means authority, and the text has universal relevance. That is, all women at all times are to cover their heads while in public worship. They argue that Paul is stating his case according to the order of things: "But I want you to realize that the head of every man is Christ, and the head of the woman is man, and the head of Christ is God" (11:3). With this logic of headship, "Every man who prays or prophesies with his head covered dishonors his head. But every woman who prays or prophesies with her head uncovered dishonors her head – it is just as though her head were shaved" (11:4–5). Clearly, both men and women can pray and prophesy in public worship. The issue, however, is the distinction between the sexes in matters of head covering. According to Paul,

> A man ought not to cover his head, since he is the image and glory of God; but woman is the glory of man. For man did not come from woman, but woman from man; neither was man created for woman, but woman for man. It is for this reason that a woman ought to have authority over her own head, because of the angels. (1 Cor 11:7–10)

The argument is that if head covering is commanded "because of the angels," what particular culture did the angels favor? Or was Paul using angels in order to intimidate the women? Similarly, Paul says,

> Judge for yourselves: Is it proper for a woman to pray to God with her head uncovered? Does not the very nature of things teach you that if a man has long hair, it is a disgrace to him, but that if a woman has long hair, it is her glory? For long hair is given to her as a covering. (1 Cor 11:13–15)

This text seems to compound the already complex issue. If long hair is given as a covering, was there need for the women to cover their heads again? According to Yamsat, Paul is much more likely using long hair "as an example from nature to prove his case for covering the head on the part of women."[25] Finally, traditional interpretation holds that Paul was not confining the text to the Corinthian church in the light of 11:16, "If anyone wants to be contentious about this, we have no other practice – nor do the churches of God."

---

25. Yamsat, 135.

2. Women Speaking or Teaching in Worship

The second theological puzzle is the issue of women speaking or teaching in the church (1 Cor 14:33–35; cf. 1 Tim 2:11–15). The text raises "a huge question for the church today about the role of women in Christian leadership."[26] Is the text culturally bound, or is it meant for all Christians of every age and place? J. Carl Laney asks what

> Paul meant when he wrote of women "praying and prophesying" in 1 Corinthians 11:5, yet instructed women to "keep silent" and not "to speak" in 1 Corinthians 14:34–35. How does one understand these apparently differing Pauline statements? Is there a reasonable solution to this apparent contradiction? Did Paul intend gathered congregations to observe gender based restrictions in the exercise of church ministry? Is there sufficient evidence to regard the text of 1 Corinthians 14:34–35 [and 1 Timothy 2:11–15] as authentic and thus authoritative for believers?[27]

Similarly, on 1 Timothy 2:11–15, William D. Mounce says,

> Although there are other passages in the PE [Pastoral Epistles] more difficult to interpret, in recent years more has been written on vv 11–12 than on any other passage in PE. Interpretations are so varied that one wonders how much of the exegesis is based on the text and how much on presuppositions and varying methodologies. . . . The historical reading of the text sees Paul limiting the scope of women's ministry and grounding that prohibition in the creation of Adam and Eve before the curse of the fall. If it could be proven that elsewhere Paul allows women to teach overseas (i.e., men) authoritatively within the context of the household of God (1 Tim. 3:15), then it would have to be concluded that Paul is inconsistent or that vv 11–14 have been misunderstood.[28]

Most feminist and egalitarian interpreters believe that the texts in question should be interpreted in their sociocultural contexts. According to these

---

26. Yamsat, 189.

27. J. Carl Laney, "Gender Based Boundaries for Gathered Congregations: An Interpretive History of 1 Corinthians 14:34–35," *Journal for Biblical Manhood and Womanhood* 7, no. 1 (Spring 2002): 4.

28. William D. Mounce, *Pastoral Epistles*, Word Biblical Commentary (Nashville: Thomas Nelson, 2000), 117.

scholars, the women in question were illiterate and not able to teach. They cite the equal endowment of men and women with spiritual gifts (Rom 12:3–8; 1 Cor 12:1–11; Eph 4:11–12) in support of equal opportunities for men and women in ministry. Similarly, it is argued that 1 Corinthians 14:33–35 addresses a particular local church and is not meant to be universally applied. Thus this passage, along with 1 Timothy 2:11–14, must not be regarded as binding on all women at all times and places. For example, Nyambura J. Njoroge says,

> The role of women in the church is a contentious issue, particularly when passages such as 1 Corinthians 13:34 and 1 Timothy 2:11–14 are regarded as laying down absolutes rather than general principles within a particular culture, there can be no denying that women and men are created equal in the image of God. Thus we must not focus on the gender roles that society, church and African cultures have assigned to women. The focus should fall on the biblical call for all human beings to discern what is the will of God in their lives (Romans 12:2). Jesus' radical mission of transformation for liberation (Luke 4:18–27) and fullness of life (John 10:10) means that women and men are equally empowered to participate in the same mission in the church. What men and women can do depends on our obedience to the guidance and empowerment of the Holy Spirit.[29]

According to Njoroge, "Where churches have listened to the voice of the Holy Spirit and have accorded women their rightful place in all the ministries of the church, women have been ordained to the ministry of word and sacrament."[30] The reason is that Galatians 3:26–29 has abolished any differences between males and females.

But what does Galatians 3:26–29 mean? Those who believe that men and women play complementary roles interpret the text differently. According to James Montgomery Boice, Paul presents here the results of the passage from the reign of law to grace through faith in Christ. First, through faith in Christ, all those who believe become sons (daughters) of Christ, that is, "they have passed through spiritual infancy into full maturity as justified persons."[31] They have passed to a new and right relationship to God. Baptism signifies this

---

29. Nyambura J. Njoroge, "The Role of Women in the Church," in *Africa Bible Commentary*, ed. Tokunboh Adeyemo (Nairobi: WordAlive, 2006), 1471.

30. Njoroge, "Role of Women in the Church," 1471.

31. James Montgomery Boice, "Galatians," *The Expositor's Bible Commentary*, abr. ed., ed. Kenneth L. Barker and John R. Kohlenberger III (Grand Rapids: Zondervan, 1994), 727.

new relationship. Therefore, what Paul says in 1 Corinthians 12:12–13 and Ephesians 4:1–8 may apply here. Baptism is the outward sign of this union.

The second result of passing from the reign of law to grace through faith is that all who believe become one with each other so that now "neither Jew or Greek, slave or free, male or female, but all are one in Christ."[32] According to Boice,

> Clearly, it does not mean that differences of nationality, status, and sex cease to exist. A Jew remains a Jew; a Gentile a Gentile. Instead, having become one with God as his sons and daughters, Christians now belong to each other in such a way that distinctions that had divided them lose significance.[33]

Therefore, social divides such as race (Jews versus Gentiles), status (free versus slaves), and sex (male versus female) now lose their significance. According to Boice,

> It is hard to imagine how badly women were treated in antiquity, even in Judaism, and how difficult it is to find any statement about the equality of the sexes, however weak, in any ancient texts except those of Christianity. Paul reverses this. Indeed, in this statement we have one factor in the gradual elevation and honoring of women that has been known in Christian lands. When Paul concludes this breakdown of the distinctions that are superseded by Christianity, he speaks of the fact that all who are in Christ are "one," one unified personality as the living body of Christ. In this body all are truly one with one another. The only possible distinctions are those of functions (cf. 1Co 12).[34]

According to Craig S. Keener,

> Some Greco-Roman cults claimed to ignore social divisions like those Paul mentions here, although they rarely erased them (most cults were expensive enough to exclude all but the well-to-do). But the early Christians were especially distinctive in surmounting such divisions. They formed the only bridge between Jews and

---

32. Boice, "Galatians," 727.
33. Boice, 727.
34. Boice, 727.

Gentiles and had few allies in challenging class (slave versus free) and gender prejudice.[35]

The third result of passing from law to grace "is that all those who believe become one with those who have been saved by faith through the long history of salvation. Thus, by union with Christ, believers become 'Abraham's seed, and heirs according to the promise.'"[36] The entire church now partakes of the promise made to Abraham and to his seed (Gal 3:16, 29)!

To sum up, although women were among the marginalized in society, they played a key role in the ministry of Jesus (Luke 8:1–3; John 12:2). And Paul clearly speaks about the dignity and place of women in ministry.[37] Paul mentions key players in the ministry of the gospel such as Phoebe, Prisca (Priscilla), Mary, Tryphena and Tryphosa, Persis, Junia, Julia, the sister of Nereus, Euodia and Syntyche, Apphia, Lois, and Eunice (Rom 16:3–15; Phil 4:2–3; 2 Tim 1:5; Phlm 1:2; cf. Acts 9:36; 16:14–15, 40; 1 Tim 5:9–10). Some of the women "contended at my side in the cause of the gospel" (Phil 4:3). Therefore, men and women have equal standing before God and share together in the ministry of the gospel. But there is no convincing evidence that Galatians 3:28 abolishes distinctive gender roles. Similarly, it is hard to draw conclusive statements on 1 Corinthians 11:1–16; 14:33–35 and 1 Timothy 2:11–15. But we will do well to never let personal prejudices, agendas, ideologies, or presuppositions determine the meaning of the biblical text. Reverent scholarship demands that we submit to the text through the leading of the Holy Spirit.

Resurrection of the Body as the Consummation of Redemption

What is the significance of the resurrection in the redemption saga?[38] The resurrection of Christ from the dead is the fundamental belief by which the Christian faith stands or falls. The essence of the gospel is that Jesus died and rose again, and these events were attested by many witnesses (1 Cor 15:1–11). According to Paul, the resurrection of Jesus was not just a tradition that was

---

35. Craig S. Keener, *The IVP Bible Background Commentary* (Downers Grove: InterVarsity, 1993), 528.

36. Boice, "Galatians," 727.

37. William Hendricksen and Simon J. Kistemaker, *Exposition of Thessalonians, the Pastorals, and Hebrews*, New Testament Commentary (Grand Rapids: Baker, 1996), 113.

38. See N. T. Wright, *The Resurrection of the Son of God* (London: SPCK, 2003), chs. 6 and 7. Wright examines the Pauline concept of the resurrection in 1 Corinthians 15 and 2 Corinthians.

passed on by the apostles who were before him; he too encountered the risen Lord on the road to Damascus.

Paul's argument in 1 Corinthians 15:12–34 is that resurrection from the dead is "based on Christ's resurrection."[39] Jesus rose from the dead as a pattern for all who believe.

> But Christ has indeed been raised from the dead, the firstfruits of those who have fallen asleep. For since death came through a man, the resurrection of the dead comes also through a man. For as in Adam all die, so in Christ all will be made alive. But each in turn: Christ, the firstfruits; then, when he comes, those who belong to him. (1 Cor 15:20–23)

Therefore, in the words of Isaak, "Jesus' followers were saying that the resurrection had happened to one man, who was now able to include others in the same resurrection at the end of time."[40] But "If there is no resurrection of the dead, then not even Christ has been raised" (15:13). The substance of Christian faith rests on the resurrection of Christ.

The resurrection of believers is the consummation of all things as Christ is

> universally acknowledged and His judgements comprehensively applied. When that is completed, the Son Himself will defer to the Father's authority in whose stead and power He had acted. That submission of the Son will be the last act of history. Then will begin the eternal state that Paul cryptically described as God's being "all in all" (1 Cor 15:28).[41]

Questions for Review and Application

1. What major problems did Paul address in 1 Corinthians? Do we have similar problems today?
2. How did Paul address the issue of divisions in the church in Corinth?

---

39. Yamsat, *Exposition of First Corinthians*, 200.

40. Isaak, *New Testament Theology*, 37. Against the critics who believe that the disciples of Jesus suffered from hallucinations, the response is, "A mass hallucination of over five hundred persons simultaneously is difficult to sustain; Paul cites as witnesses respected church leaders who had suffered for their claims, plus himself (and probably James) as former skeptics." Craig S. Keener, *1–2 Corinthians*, NCBC (Cambridge: Cambridge University Press, 2005), 125.

41. Lowery, *Theology of the Missionary Epistles*, 297.

3. How did Paul address the problem of sexual immorality in the church in Corinth?
4. Why does sexual immorality constitute a serious threat to the body of Christ?
5. Why is the believer's body called the temple of the living God? And what happens to the one who destroys the temple of the living God?
6. What does Paul say about the resurrection of the body?
7. How does 1 Corinthians encourage you to draw closer in your walk with the Lord?

10

Drums of Redemption in 2 Corinthians

Now the Lord is the Spirit, and where the Spirit of the Lord is, there is freedom. And we all, who with unveiled faces reflect the Lord's glory, are being transformed into his image with ever-increasing glory, which comes from the Lord, who is the Spirit.

2 Corinthians 3:17–18

Therefore, since through God's mercy we have this ministry, we do not lose heart. Rather, we have renounced secret and shameful ways; we do not use deception, nor do we distort the word of God. On the contrary, by setting forth the truth plainly we commend ourselves to everyone's conscience in the sight of God. And even if our gospel is veiled, it is veiled to those who are perishing. The god of this age has blinded the minds of unbelievers, so that they cannot see the light of the gospel that displays the glory of Christ, who is the image of God. For what we preach is not ourselves, but Jesus Christ as Lord, and ourselves as your servants for Jesus' sake. For God, who said, "Let light shine out of darkness," made his light shine in our hearts to give us the light of the knowledge of God's glory displayed in the face of Christ.

2 Corinthians 4:1–6

Synopsis of the Letter 2 Corinthians

Second Corinthians is "Paul's most autobiographical letter, in which he opens his heart more than in any other."[1] Paul seems to have written 2 Corinthians not long after he wrote 1 Corinthians. Paul likely wrote following his meeting with Titus (2 Cor 7:4–16), while he was in Macedonia (2 Cor 7:5). The letter was prompted by the glad tidings received from Titus that the erring Corinthian believers had repented (2 Cor 7:8–11). Paul used this occasion to emphasize the collection for the church in Jerusalem (2 Cor 8–9; cf. 1 Cor 16:1–4) and to express some personal concerns. The letter is dated AD 56 or 57.[2]

Key Theological Themes in the Letter 2 Corinthians

There are important theological themes in 2 Corinthians. We will highlight some of themes as follows:

Redemption and God's Purposes in Suffering

After his conventional greetings (2 Cor 1:1–2), Paul launches into one of the perplexing issues in Scripture, namely, the problem of suffering (1:3–11). Paul states his thesis regarding Christian suffering in the form of praise and worship: "Praise be to the God and Father of our Lord Jesus Christ, the Father of compassion and the God of all comfort, who comforts us in all our troubles, so that we can comfort those in any trouble with the comfort we ourselves have received from God" (1:3–4). The thesis is that God comforts us in our troubles so that we can comfort others who are in trouble, using the comfort we received from the Lord. For example at a recent funeral service of a family who lost a beloved daughter, the father counted many in the congregation who had lost their loved ones. Two of the parents had lost their only sons. Others had lost their first born children like he had. Others had lost their wife or husband. And he said these people were his source of comfort. The tragic loss and pain of those other parents and friends brought comfort to a grieving father because he felt he was not alone in his situation. Other "clouds of witnesses" surrounded him at the moment of intense grief.

The entire passage is insightful on the subject of Christian suffering. Paul uses the expressions "troubles" (2 Cor 1:4, 8), "sufferings" (1:5–7), "pressure" (1:8), "despair" (1:8), "the sentence of death" (1:9), and "deadly peril" (1:10)

---

1. Prime, *Let's Study 2 Corinthians*, xiii.
2. Lea, *New Testament*, 425.

"to remind us of the variety of difficulties we may meet."[3] Paul explains that Christian suffering is participation in the sufferings of Christ (cf. 1 Pet 2:21; 4:13). According to Paul, "For just as we share abundantly in the sufferings of Christ, so also our comfort abounds through Christ" (2 Cor 1:5).

The rest of the book illustrates how Paul's personal sufferings accomplish God's purposes. He says, "For our light and momentary troubles are achieving for us an eternal glory that far outweighs them all. So we fix our eyes not on what is seen, but on what is unseen, since what is seen is temporary, but what is unseen is eternal" (2 Cor 4:17–18). Understanding suffering from this perspective, Paul says, "Rather, as servants of God we commend ourselves in every way: in great endurance; in troubles, hardships and distresses; in beatings, imprisonments and riots; in hard work, sleepless nights and hunger" (6:4–5). Paul's sufferings also included a thorn in his flesh, "because of these surpassingly great revelations.... in order to keep me from becoming conceited, I was given a thorn in my flesh, a messenger of Satan, to torment me" (2 Cor 12:7). Other forms of suffering were emotional pain caused by the weakness and failures of fellow believers in Corinth (2 Cor 11:29).

Redemption and the Superiority of the New Covenant

In 2 Corinthians 3:4–18, Paul continues in the defense of his ministry and insists that he received his call and ministry from God (3:5–6). He shows that the new covenant is superior to the one given at the time of Moses because the new covenant is the ministry of the Spirit rather than the one "engraved in letters on stone" (3:7). Although the Mosaic covenant came with glory, that glory was transitory. The new covenant produces righteousness; the old brought condemnation (3:9). Similarly, the new covenant is permanent (3:10–11). According to Paul, the ministry of the new covenant is a ministry of the Spirit.[4] Paul says,

> He has made us competent as ministers of a new covenant – not of the letter but of the Spirit; for the letter kills, but the Spirit gives life.
> Now if the ministry that brought death, which was engraved in letters on stone, came with glory, so that the Israelites could not look steadily at the face of Moses because of its glory, transitory

---

3. Prime, *Let's Study 2 Corinthians*, 5–6.
4. Gordon D. Fee, *God's Empowering Presence: The Holy Spirit in the Letter of Paul* (Peabody: Hendrickson, 1994), 299–302.

though it was, will not the ministry of the Spirit be even more glorious? (3:6–8)

The glory of the ministry of the Holy Spirit lies in permanence and efficacy. Jesus said, "And I will ask the Father, and he will give you another advocate to help you and *be with you forever*" (John 14:16, emphasis added). Not only will the Holy Spirit be with them forever, he is the perfect guide and teacher. Jesus said,

> I have much more to say to you, more than you can now bear. But when he, the Spirit of truth, comes, he will guide you into all truth. He will not speak on his own; he will speak only what he hears, and he will tell you what is yet to come. (John 16:12–13)

Similarly, the apostle John wrote, "As for you, the anointing you received from him remains in you, and you do not need anyone to teach you. But as his anointing teaches you about all things and as that anointing is real, not counterfeit – just as it has taught you, remain in him" (1 John 2:27).

Redemption as Reconciliation of the World to God

Paul speaks about the work of reconciliation in 2 Corinthians 5:11–6:2. Christ is the mediator between God and human kind "who gave himself as a ransom for all people. This has now been witnessed to at the proper time" (1 Tim 2:6). Christ gave his own life, propelled by love. "Greater love has no one than this: to lay down one's life for one's friends" (John 15:13). Therefore, "The deep motivation of Paul's ministry is *Christ's love* (5:14)."[5] Coulibaly explains that this is the love that comes from Christ (Rom 8:35–39; Gal 2:20) as well as the love Paul and believers have for Christ.[6] According to Paul, because Christ died for all, those who live must live for the one who died for them.

Christ's death is God's own initiative of reconciling the world to himself (2 Cor 5:18). Having performed the most difficult task of giving his Son for the reconciliation of the world, God now enlists his followers in the ministry of reconciliation, "not counting people's sins against them" (5:19). Therefore, all believers are "Christ's ambassadors, as though God were making his appeal through us" (5:20).

---

5. Issiaka Coulibaly, "2 Corinthians," in *Africa Bible Commentary*, ed. Tokunboh Adeyemo (Nairobi: WordAlive, 2006), 1404, emphasis original.

6. Coulibaly, "2 Corinthians," 1404.

The reconciled position believers enjoy with God is never cheap. It came at a high cost. It cost God his only begotten Son (John 3:16). The believer's logical reciprocation of the work of reconciliation with God is grateful living to please him and to persuade the unbelievers to receive God's gift of salvation. "Since, then, we know what it is to fear the Lord, we try to persuade others" (2 Cor 5:11).

Redemption as Hope of Heavenly Abode

Eschatological underpinning is not absent in Paul's second letter to the Corinthians. "Paul's ministry radiated with the hope of receiving the resurrected body at Christ's return (5:1–4). His present possession of the Holy Spirit was a deposit assuring him of future victory (5:5)."[7] This is reminiscent of Ephesians 1:13–14: "When you believed, you were marked in him with a seal, the promised Holy Spirit, who is a deposit guaranteeing our inheritance until the redemption of those who are God's possession – to the praise of his glory." This eschatological hope of being at home with the Lord fills the believer with the desire to please the Lord (2 Cor 5:9).

Redemption and the Theology of Giving

The issue of giving is a dicey area especially with the increasing prosperity preaching of some preachers who are ready to squeeze the last penny and the last drop of blood from their members in order to fulfill their dreams of being super apostles. For these "Men of God," their sense of achievement and worth is measured by the chain of exotic jeeps and the jet planes they own. But giving to support these "Gospel hucksters"[8] – "who peddle the word of God for profit" (2 Cor 2:17) – must be distinguished from the grace of giving that Paul encourages the believers in Corinth to exercise.

Paul devotes two chapters (2 Cor 8–9) to the issue of giving, and he outlines four theological principles of giving. First, Christian giving is a spiritual ministry enabled by the grace of God. He therefore urges the believers in Corinth to excel in the grace of giving. He writes, "But since you excel in everything – in faith, in speech, in knowledge, in complete earnestness and in the love we have kindled in you – see that you also excel in this grace of

---

7. Lea, *New Testament*, 429.

8. V. George Shillington, *2 Corinthians*, Believers Church Bible Commentary (Waterloo, ON: Herald, 1998), 67.

giving" (8:7). Such giving must come from the heart. And it does not depend on the abundance of one's possessions or the material condition in which one finds himself or herself but is a demonstration of conviction. Paul refers to the Macedonian believers who were poor but gave generously.

> And now, brothers and sisters, we want you to know about the grace that God has given the Macedonian churches. In the midst of a very severe trial, their overflowing joy and their extreme poverty welled up in rich generosity. For I testify that they gave as much as they were able, and even beyond their ability. Entirely on their own, they urgently pleaded with us for the privilege of sharing in this service to the Lord's people. And they exceeded our expectations: They gave themselves first of all to the Lord, and then by the will of God also to us. (8:1–5)

The Macedonian believers are the best example of the grace of giving. Love for Christ and God's people who are in need propels the believer to give generously.

Second, Christian giving should be in proportion to income (2 Cor 8:10–15). "For if the willingness is there, the gift is acceptable according to what one has, not according to what one does not have" (8:12; cf. 1 Cor 16:2). "It is not the portion but the proportion that God seeks."[9]

Third, gifts must be handled honestly (2 Cor 8:16–24).[10] Paul wanted to ensure that no one accused him or any of his coworkers of financial mismanagement. Titus, along with two others (8:17–19, 22), were appointed for their trustworthiness. Paul said,

> And we are sending along with him the brother who is praised by all the churches for his service to the gospel. What is more, he was chosen by the churches to accompany us as we carry the offering, which we administer in order to honor the Lord himself and to show our eagerness to help. We want to avoid any criticism of the way we administer this liberal gift. For we are taking pains to do what is right, not only in the eyes of the Lord but also in the eyes of man. (2 Cor 8:18–21)

This passage is important for the church in Africa because scandals of financial mismanagement by church leaders are rampant. Some members of the church no longer trust the ministers of the gospel with their money. Therefore, "We

---

9. Warren W. Wiersbe, *Wiersbe's Expository Outlines on the New Testament* (Colorado Springs: David C. Cook, 1992), 657.

10. Wiersbe, *Wiersbe's Expository Outlines*, 658.

must remember that others are watching us, and we dare not give the enemy any opportunity to accuse us of dishonesty."[11] As a remedial,

> No Christian or local church should send money to works that are not financially sound. The fact that "there is a need" is not reason enough for giving; there must be proof that the money is handled honestly and spent wisely. We are not obligated to pay a debt we never incurred.[12]

Fourth, Christian giving brings blessings. This blessing is huge impetus for Christian giving. Paul says,

> Remember this: Whoever sows sparingly will also reap sparingly, and whoever sows generously will also reap generously. Each of you should give what you have decided in your heart to give, not reluctantly or under compulsion, for God loves a cheerful giver. And God is able to bless you abundantly, so that in all things at all times, having all that you need, you will abound in every good work. As it is written:
>
> "They have freely scattered their gifts to the poor;
>   their righteousness endures forever."
>
> Now he who supplies seed to the sower and bread for food will also supply and increase your store of seed and will enlarge the harvest of your righteousness. You will be enriched in every way so that you can be generous on every occasion, and through us your generosity will result in thanksgiving to God. (2 Cor 9:6–11)

Paul concludes the fascinating logic of sowing and reaping by saying that giving causes praise and worship in the hearts of recipients (2 Cor 9:12–13). According to Paul, God himself is the best example of giving through "his indescribable gift" in Christ Jesus (9:15). In other words, "giving is an appropriate response to grace."[13] The enormous grace of God in Christ is motivation for generous giving.

Putting the text into practice, just as Paul urged the churches in Corinth to contribute to the needs of the poor in Jerusalem, Christians must never ignore fellow believers who are in need. Generosity is a Christian virtue. Similarly, wealthy churches have the privilege of contributing more in support of the

---

11. Wiersbe, 658.
12. Wiersbe, 658.
13. Prime, *Let's Study 2 Corinthians*, 83.

poor churches and believers around the world.[14] This is what being the body of Christ means.

Questions for Review and Application

1. Why did Paul write 2 Corinthians?
2. What are the key theological themes in 2 Corinthians?
3. What does Paul say about Christian suffering?
4. Why did Paul devote two chapters (8–9) in 2 Corinthians to talking about giving?
5. What are the four theological principles of giving implied in 2 Corinthians 8–9?
6. What is the relevance of 2 Corinthians 8–9 for the church in Africa with regards to giving?
7. How does 2 Corinthians encourage your walk with the Lord?

---

14. Churches in peaceful countries could give more to victims of terrorism in the rest of the world besides the scanty help that comes from a few Christian non-governmental organizations (NGOs).

11

Drums of Redemption in Galatians

God has laid upon man the duty of being free, of safeguarding freedom of spirit, no matter how difficult that may be or how much sacrifice and suffering it may require.

Nicolai Berdyaev[1]

It is for freedom that Christ has set us free. Stand firm, then, and do not let yourselves be burdened again by a yoke of slavery.

Galatians 5:1

I am astonished that you are so quickly deserting the one who called you to live in the grace of Christ and are turning to a different gospel – which is really no gospel at all. Evidently some people are throwing you into confusion and are trying to pervert the gospel of Christ. But even if we or an angel from heaven should preach a gospel other than the one we preached to you, let them be under God's curse! As we have already said, so now I say again: If anybody is preaching to you a gospel other than what you accepted, let them be under God's curse!

Galatians 1:6–9

Synopsis of the Letter to the Galatians

According to E. P. Sanders, "The best way to comprehend Galatians is to read it out loud, shouting in an angry voice at appropriate points" because "I think that Paul was angry when he wrote the letter, and I picture him as pacing while

---

1. Nicolai Berdyaev, quoted in Brown, *Scandalous Freedom*, 241.

he dictated, sometimes shouting, occasionally pleading."[2] Boice says that Paul's Letter to the Galatians played a significant role in Western civilization and is regarded as the "Magna Carta[3] of Christian liberty" because of its emphasis on the grace of God that provides escape from the curse of sin and the law, leading to a new life of freedom in Christ.[4] Paul wrote Galatians to the early Christians who were struggling about their roots in Christ and the issue of Christian liberty. From the church's early beginning, false teachers were already confusing the believers about the way of salvation by emphasizing that people earn salvation by works or observance of the law. The news of the confusion in the Galatian church came to Paul as a shock (Gal 1:6–7). So he wrote an urgent response to what he considered "another gospel" which the believers in Galatia were prone to receive. This different gospel was no gospel at all and was only leading them into bondage.

In Galatians, Paul warns them about the danger of trying to work out their salvation through observance of the law. He says, "But when the time had fully come, God sent his Son, born of a woman, born under law, to redeem those under law, that we might receive adoption to sonship" (Gal 4:4–5). Paul explains that if they go back to legalism, the death of Christ will not mean anything to them. He tells them that Christ died to set them free and to use this freedom in the service of God. Similarly, Paul battles the ideology and practice of separatism introduced by promoters of "a different gospel." Even the apostle Peter succumbed to the gospel of separatism (2:11–17). As Vincent M. Smiles says, "As a phenomenon of postexilic Judaism, separatism, understood to be Israel's awareness of being socially and religiously distinct from the Gentiles, is well documented, both in Scripture and in apocryphal literature."[5]

Key Theological Themes in the Letter to the Galatians

Like Colossians, Paul wrote to the believers in Galatia in order to correct some errors that were threatening the spiritual health of the church(es). Key theological themes in the letter include:

---

2. E. P. Sanders, *Paul: The Apostle's Life, Letters, and Thought* (Minneapolis: Fortress, 2015), 475.

3. This is a charter or legislative document on the rights of citizens.

4. Boice, "Galatians," 703.

5. Vincent M. Smiles, *The Gospel and the Law in Galatia: Paul's Response to Jewish-Christian Separatism and the Threat of Galatian Apostasy* (Collegeville, MN: Liturgical Press, 1998), 109.

Redemption as Justification by Faith Alone

The trouble with the believers in Galatia was the Judaizing element that crept in secretly and distorted the gospel message Paul had preached among them.[6] The Galatian believers seemed to have quickly deserted "the one who called you to live in the grace of Christ" and were "turning to a different gospel – which is really no gospel at all" (Gal 1:6–7). The false teachers were throwing the believers into confusion by teaching them that believing in Christ is not sufficient; they must also observe the Jewish law. For example, these Judaizers were teaching that the believers must be circumcised: "Those who want to impress people by means of the flesh are trying to compel you to be circumcised." But their only reason for doing this was "to avoid being persecuted for the cross of Christ" (6:12). They also wanted the believers to observe other Jewish rituals such as dietary laws and festivals and other special days.

In Galatians 2:15–4:31, Paul asserts that no one is justified before God by observing the law. Rather, "the righteous will live by faith" (3:11). In full Paul says,

> Clearly no one who relies on the law is justified before God, because "the righteous will live by faith." The law is not based on faith; on the contrary, it says, "The person who does these things will live by them." Christ redeemed us from the curse of the law by becoming a curse for us, for it is written: "Cursed is everyone who is hung on a pole" (Gal 3:11–13)

Paul's argument is,

> We who are Jews by birth and not sinful Gentiles know that a person is not justified by the works of the law, but by faith in Jesus Christ. So we, too, have put our faith in Christ Jesus that we may be justified by faith in Christ and not by the works of the law, because by the works of the law no one will be justified. (Gal 2:15–16)

Using many arguments, Paul proves that justification comes by faith in Christ alone. For example, God's covenant with Abraham is based on a promise and not on observance of the law (Gal 3:18). According to Paul, the law was given to reveal sin, that is, to make human beings more aware of their sins. Similarly, the law was temporary: "It was added because of transgressions until"

---

6. For more on Judaism, see Jay G. Williams, *Judaism* (Wheaton: Theosophical Publishing House, 1980); and Hagner, "How 'New,'" 99–107.

Christ should come (3:19). The law has no power to give life.[7] Paul also uses the relationship between Hagar and Sarah to advance the argument that the law is powerless to save. Hagar and her son Ishmael symbolize the law, while Sarah and Isaac represent the promise which is the free gift of God (4:21–31).

Redemption and Equality in Christ

When we treated redemption and the place of women in worship and ministry (1 Cor 11:3–16; 14:33–35; 1 Tim 2:11–15) in chapter 9, one of the key texts we referred to was Galatians 3:26–29. We understood this text to mean that the entire church now partakes of the promise made "to Abraham and to his seed" (Gal 3:16). The "most profound and obvious differences in the ancient world"[8] such as Jew versus Greek, slave versus free, and male versus female have been abolished in Christ.

This means that every believer in Christ has equal standing before the Lord, regardless of gender, race, color, or societal status. In Christ "there is no longer any place for the traditional distinctions that divide mankind – cultural, linguistic, religious . . . or even sexual."[9] While this text does not eliminate gender roles, it does stress that no one is inferior to any other among God's people. As for distinctive gender roles, the Trinity may serve as example of what it means to be equal in essence and yet have distinctive functions.

Redemption as Freedom and Life by the Spirit

Samuel Ngewa rightly sees Galatians 5:1–6:10 as having "implications of justification by faith."[10] Against the Judaizing elements whose agenda was to enslave the Galatians, Paul teaches that it is for freedom that Christ set them free. They must stand firm and not let themselves "be burdened again by a yoke of slavery," namely the observance of the law (5:1). "Christ will be of no value" to those who subject themselves to circumcision. And those who go back to the law obligate themselves "to obey the whole law," which is alienation

---

7. See Alpha-Omega Ministries, *Galatians: The Teachers' Outline and Study Guide* (Chattanooga: Leadership Ministries Worldwide, 1994), 90–93.

8. James D. G. Dunn, *The Epistle to the Galatians*, Black's New Testament Commentaries (London: A&C Black, 1993), 206.

9. R. Alan Cole, *Galatians*, rev. ed., Tyndale New Testament Commentaries (Grand Rapids: Eerdmans, 1989), 155–56.

10. Samuel Ngewa, "Galatians," in *Africa Bible Commentary*, ed. Tokunboh Adeyemo (Nairobi: WordAlive, 2006), 1423.

from Christ (5:2–4). Rather, the law of the Spirit sets the believer free from the obligations of the ritualistic observance of the law. Therefore, "through the Spirit we eagerly await by faith the righteousness for which we hope. For in Christ Jesus neither circumcision nor uncircumcision has any value. The only thing that counts is faith expressing itself through love" (5:5–6).

But freed Christians are not to live a life that gratifies the flesh or sinful nature. The right freedom is summed up this way: "You, my brothers and sisters, were called to be free. But do not use your freedom to indulge the flesh; rather, serve one another humbly in love. For the entire law is fulfilled in keeping this one command: 'Love your neighbor as yourself'" (Gal 5:13–14). In other words, "It is freedom for a deeper level of self-giving and commitment to holiness from the heart than the Law could empower on its own."[11]

The redeemed in Christ live by the Spirit. The Spirit teaches and enables the believer to obey "God's most fundamental command, namely that we love one another (5:14)."[12] Similarly, overcoming the desires of the sinful nature is possible only through the Holy Spirit's empowering. "So I say, walk by the Spirit, and you will not gratify the desires of the flesh" (Gal 5:16). Living by the Spirit is the antidote for gratifying the flesh. And those who are led by the Spirit "are not under the law" (5:18). "But the fruit of the Spirit is love, joy, peace, forbearance, kindness, goodness, faithfulness, gentleness and self-control. Against such things there is no law. Those who belong to Christ Jesus have crucified the flesh with its passions and desires" (5:22–24). Those who live by the Spirit keep in step with the Spirit. Christians are not lawless people. Rather, the law has lost its grip on them because they obey the law without being coerced. They are free. In a normal world, "rulers hold no terror for those who do right, but for those who do wrong" (Rom 13:3). For example using the African context, if we drive with complete and relevant car documents, we have no reason to worry about the police or vehicle inspection officers (V.I.O.). Similarly, if we do not violate traffic rules, we do not need to fear road safety marshals.

---

11. David A. deSilva, *An Introduction to the New Testament: Contexts, Methods and Ministry Formation* (Downers Grove: IVP Academic, 2004), 883.

12. Ngewa, "Galatians," 1423.

Questions for Review and Application

1. What particular problem(s) did Paul address in the book of Galatians?
2. Why was Paul angry with the Galatians?
3. What does Paul say is the best way to avoid the acts of the flesh?
4. What are the fruit of the Spirit, and how do they manifest in your own life?
5. How does the book of Galatians draw you closer to God?

12

Drums of Redemption in Ephesians

Praise be to the God and Father of our Lord Jesus Christ, who has blessed us in the heavenly realms with every spiritual blessing in Christ. For he chose us in him before the creation of the world to be holy and blameless in his sight. In love he predestined us for adoption to sonship through Jesus Christ, in accordance with his pleasure and will – to the praise of his glorious grace, which he has freely given us in the One he loves.

Ephesians 1:3–6

But now in Christ Jesus you who once were far away have been brought near by the blood of Christ.

    For he himself is our peace, who has made the two groups one and has destroyed the barrier, the dividing wall of hostility, by setting aside in his flesh the law with its commands and regulations. His purpose was to create in himself one new humanity out of the two, thus making peace, and in one body to reconcile both of them to God through the cross, by which he put to death their hostility. He came and preached peace to you who were far away and peace to those who were near. For through him we both have access to the Father by one Spirit.

Ephesians 2:13–18

The Synopsis of the Letter to the Ephesians

Paul founded the church at Ephesus on his third missionary journey (see Acts 19). For three years, Ephesus became Paul's "center of operations."[1] He "spent more time in Ephesus than anywhere else."[2] Paul's work at Ephesus was characterized by extraordinary miracles "so that even handkerchiefs and aprons that had touched him were taken to the sick, and their illnesses were cured and the evil spirits left them" (Acts 19:11–12). But persecution arose on account of Paul's ministry at Ephesus. This persecution was spearheaded by a silversmith named Demetrius whose silver shrines business was threatened as a result of mass conversions. These conversions to the new faith were forcing him and his fellow craftsmen out of business.

Many scholars believe that Ephesians was intended as a "general letter to the churches within the vicinity or cultural influence of Ephesus."[3] This means that the letter was meant for Asian congregations in general.[4] According to Marshall, Travis, and Paul, "the oldest known form of the letter does not mention Ephesus, and the later wording is rather awkward in Greek, as if somebody had made a clumsy interpolation to fill a surprising gap."[5] Because the letter is not explicit about its circular nature like Colossians (Col 4:16), the issue of audience beyond Ephesus remains scholars' conjectures.

Although no clear purpose for writing the letter is mentioned nor any specific conflict stated, the content of the letter suggests that Paul wanted to provide basic teaching about the nature of the church and the purpose of its existence in the world. In Ephesians 1:3–14, Paul tells the believers the deep truth about God's election and his plan for the church. According to David A. deSilva, "the central theme of Ephesians is the celebration of the multidimensional 'mystery' revealed in the gospel (Eph 1:9; 3:3, 4, 9; 5:32; 6:19)."[6] DeSilva sees the horizontal dimension of this "mystery" as the inclusion of Gentiles in the spiritual heritage of Israel. The wall of hostility between the Jews and Gentiles has been broken through the death of Christ (2:11–16).

---

1. George E. Harpur, "Ephesians," in *New International Bible Commentary*, ed. F. F. Bruce, H. L. Ellison, and G. C. D. Howley (Grand Rapids: Zondervan, 1979), 1430.

2. T. D. Proffitt, III, "Ephesians," *Missional and Messianic Bible Commentary*, pre-publication draft, 2018, 809, used by permission of the author.

3. Bryan Chapell, *Ephesians*, Reformed Expository Commentary (Phillipsburg: P&R, 2009), xv.

4. Howard Marshall, Stephen Travis, and Ian Paul, *Exploring the New Testament*, vol. 2, *The Letters and Revelation* (London: SPCK, 2002), 165.

5. Marshall, Travis, and Paul, *Exploring the New Testament*, 164.

6. deSilva, *Introduction to the New Testament*, 723.

Vertically, "the mystery concerns the reconciliation and reunion of human beings with God."[7] Those who are reconciled with one another join the head of the body, Jesus Christ (1:10, 22–23; 5:32).[8]

In Ephesians, God sets standards for Christian living. One standard is unity. "As a reconciled people the church is to maintain unity above all else."[9] Another aspect of the Christian life underlined in the book is walking in the light as children of God (Eph 4:17–6:4). This walk is in accordance with the new self, "created to be like God in true righteousness and holiness" (4:24). In this walk, the believer is to imitate God and Christ (5:1–2). Walking in the light includes individuals as well as Christian households. And this walk is possible in a Spirit-filled life (5:18). On the whole, the Christian life is countercultural. The believer sets the standards for the life that pleases the Lord. Paul concludes by warning the believers that there is war in the spiritual realm; therefore they need to be alert with all the resources God has put at their disposal (6:10–17). Here believers are likened to soldiers enrolled in battle. They must "put on the full armor of God" (6:13).

Key Theological Themes in the Letter to the Ephesians
Redemption and the Elect in Christ

Following the salutation (Eph 1:1–2), Paul eulogizes God for his work of salvation (1:3–14). Paul says, "For *he chose us in him before the creation of the world* to be holy and blameless in his sight. In love *he predestined us* for adoption to sonship through Jesus Christ, in accordance with his pleasure and will" (1:4–5, emphasis added). The rubric of God's choice of the believer in Christ before the foundation of the world according to his good pleasure is indicative of what is done outside of human will.[10] Salvation is purely the act of God (1:4–6). God's election comes through Christ who is the Redeemer (1:7–13). The Holy Spirit seals the believer as the guarantor for the final redemption (1:13–14).

In Ephesians, the roots of the believer's blessings come from God's sovereign choice in Christ (Eph 1:4), "For he chose us in him before the

---

7. deSilva, 725.
8. deSilva, 725.
9. deSilva, 726.
10. See James Montgomery Boice, *Ephesians: An Expositional Commentary* (Grand Rapids: Baker Academic, 1998), 15–19.

creation of the world" – that is, "pre-creation eternity,"[11] or "before time and creation,"[12] – "to be holy and blameless in his sight." As Arnold notes, "The theme of election in Christ occurs just as frequently in Ephesians as it does in Romans (especially Rom 9–11 and in the later part of Rom 8)."[13] The concept of election has polarized Christians, namely Calvinists versus Arminians. In the simplest terms, Calvinists believe that salvation is God's prerogative, and he chooses whom he wills to inherit eternal life according to his eternal purposes in Christ. Some terms used for this concept are "foreordination" and "predestination." Arminians, however, believe that human beings can exercise their will to receive the offer of salvation in Christ or reject it. The offer is open to whoever wills because God our Savior "wants all people to be saved and to come to a knowledge of the truth" (1 Tim 2:3–4). Therefore, to inherit eternal life or to perish in hell is a personal choice. But Calvinists insist that the doctrine of election is divine revelation and "not human speculation." They insist that the doctrine "was not invented by Augustine of Hippo or Calvin of Geneva." As a revelation, therefore, "no biblical Christian can ignore it."[14] Both positions remain incomprehensible to our finite minds. From the Calvinist standpoint, this choice is based on God's sovereign will "who does whatever pleases him" (Ps 135:6).

Redemption and the Grace of God

The concept of grace is prominent in Pauline theology. But what is grace?[15] The dictionary defines it as "unmerited divine assistance given to humans for their regeneration or sanctification" or "a special favor" or "privilege."[16] In both Hebrew (*ḥen*) and Greek (*charis*), the word conveys the idea of "favorable disposition of one person toward another."[17] By grace, kindness is extended to the undeserving or to one who cannot earn it. Grace is one of God's

---

11. John R. W. Stott, *The Message of Ephesians: God's New Society*, The Bible Speaks Today, ed. J. A. Motyer and John R. W. Stott (Downers Grove: InterVarsity, 1979), 38.

12. Peter T. O'Brien, *The Letter to the Ephesians*, Pillar New Testament Commentary (Grand Rapids: Eerdmans, 1999), 100.

13. Clinton E. Arnold, *Power and Magic: The Concept of Power in Ephesians* (Eugene: Wipf & Stock, 1989), 128.

14. Stott, *Message of Ephesians*, 37.

15. See Bitrus A. Sarma, *Worthy of Worship: Beholding the Beauty of the Lord* (Jos, Nigeria: Yakson, 2014), 76–81.

16. "grace," *Merriam-Webster Dictionary Online*, https://www.merriam-webster.com/dictionary/grace.

17. Mounce, "Grace," 303.

communicable attributes in which he extends goodness, mercy, and patience toward those "who deserve only punishment."[18]

Paul shows that the salvific power of the resurrected Christ (Eph 1:15–23) transforms "believers from spiritual death to heavenly life" (2:1–10).[19] Salvation is purely a gift of God. Grace is a carrier, an agent, or an instrument through which salvation is conveyed to humanity. Paul contrasts the pre-Christian state of the Ephesians with their Christian state. The "ruler of the kingdom of the air, the spirit who is now at work in those who are disobedient" (2:2) had dominated them. Therefore, they were "by nature deserving of wrath" (2:3). But motivated by his mercy and love, God graciously came to their rescue (2:4–10). Therefore, saving grace is the unmerited offer of salvation to the dying sinner. This offer is received by faith: "For it is by grace you have been saved, through faith – and this not from yourselves, it is the gift of God – not by works, so that no one can boast" (2:8–9). This is the grace that saves a sinner from eternal condemnation. Elsewhere Paul speaks extensively about this saving grace, especially as he experienced it firsthand:

> I thank Christ Jesus our Lord, who has given me strength, that he considered me trustworthy, appointing me to his service. Even though I was once a blasphemer and a persecutor and a violent man, I was shown mercy because I acted in ignorance and unbelief. The grace of our Lord was poured out on me abundantly, along with the faith and love that are in Christ Jesus.
>
> Here is a trustworthy saying that deserves full acceptance: Christ Jesus came into the world to save sinners – of whom I am the worst. But for that very reason I was shown mercy so that in me, the worst of sinners, Christ Jesus might display his immense patience as an example for those who would believe in him and receive eternal life. (1 Tim 1:12–16)

But because most Christians understand grace as saving grace only, it is important to see other manifestations of grace in the light of Scripture.[20]

1. **Grace is God's enabling power to run the race "marked out for us" successfully (Heb 12:1).** We may call this persevering grace (Heb 10:35–36). This enabling grace is also well illustrated by the

---

18. Wayne Grudem, *Systematic Theology: An Introduction to Biblical Doctrine* (Leicester: Inter-Varsity/Grand Rapids: Zondervan, 1994), 200.

19. Lea, *New Testament*, 446.

20. I outlined a similar list in Sarma, *Blessed New Humanity in Christ*, 194–95.

fourth stanza of John Newton's song "Amazing Grace": "Thro' many dangers, toils, and snares I have already come. 'Tis grace that brought me safe thus far, and grace will lead me home." This is the grace to resist the evil world, to say "No" to sin and "Yes" to godliness and righteousness. This grace enables us to persevere in following and serving the Lord no matter the cost. This grace manifests itself in our preparedness to carry the cross daily and follow Christ (Luke 9:23). This grace also enables the believer to resist sin (Titus 2:11–14).

2. **Grace is the enabling power to excel in the service of the Lord.** Paul said,

> For I am the least of the apostles and do not even deserve to be called an apostle, because I persecuted the church of God. But by the grace of God I am what I am, and his grace to me was not without effect. No, I worked harder than all of them – yet not I, but the grace of God that was with me. (1 Cor 15:9–10)

3. **Grace is the enabling power of God to withstand adverse circumstances.** When Paul pleaded with the Lord three times to remove the thorn in his flesh, the Lord replied, "My grace is sufficient for you, for my power is made perfect in weakness" (2 Cor 12:9).

4. **Grace is the divine favor resting upon believers because of their knowledge of God and Jesus Christ.** Peter prayed, "Grace and peace be yours in abundance through the knowledge of God and of Jesus our Lord" (2 Pet 1:2). This favor sets the believer apart from the unbeliever.

5. **Grace is the manifestation of the different gifts given by the Holy Spirit**. Paul said, "We have different gifts, according to the grace given to us" (Rom 12:6a; cf. 1 Cor 12:1–11). We may call these grace gifts.

6. **Grace is the favor to receive good gifts, not excluding material things, from the Lord.** In 1 Corinthians 4:7, Paul writes, "For who makes you different from anyone else? What do you have that you did not receive? And if you did receive it, why do you boast as though you did not?" Whatever gift we receive from the Lord is unmerited. He graciously gives all things.

7. **Grace in ordinary language can mean "a controlled, polite, and pleasant way of behaving" or "way of moving that is smooth and attractive."**[21] One can walk or talk graciously or ungracefully. Paul says in Colossians 4:6, "Let your conversation be always full of grace, seasoned with salt, so that you may know how to answer everyone." As God's children, believers are to be gracious in their conduct.

8. **Grace is forgiveness to the undeserving.** The word of the Lord says, "The LORD is gracious and compassionate, slow to anger and rich in love" (Ps 145:8), and, "If you, LORD, kept a record of sins, LORD, who could stand? But with you there is forgiveness, so that we can, with reverence, serve you" (Ps 130:3–4). Similarly, "he does not treat us as our sins deserve or repay us according to our iniquities" (Ps 103:10). This forgiveness differs from the first, namely the offer of salvation through saving grace, and refers to God's mercy in pardoning our sins.

The concept of saving grace resonates in the Pauline letters (Rom 4:16; 5:1–2, 15, 17; Gal 1:6; 2:21; Eph 1:6–7; Titus 2:11). According to 1 Timothy 1:12–16 quoted above, Paul had also been held captive in the "cosmic forces that have enslaved humans to captivity."[22] But the Lord poured out his grace on Paul abundantly. This amazing grace that saves a wretched and lost sinner reverberates in the words of John Newton's song, "Amazing grace! how sweet the sound that saved a wretched like me! I once was lost, but now am found; was blind, but now I see."

Redemption and the New Humanity in Christ

The book of Ephesians celebrates the church.[23] Brown is right that "the church is the concern of God."[24] He tells an interesting story of his friend who went to Jesus to complain about the church. His friend said to Jesus: "They are a mess. They are uncommitted, mean, and lazy. They don't care what you say or even about you and your honor. They are stiff-necked people, and they don't deserve your love."

---

21. "grace," *Merriam-Webster Dictionary Online*.
22. Johnson, *Writings of the New Testament*, 413.
23. Chapell, *Ephesians*, xi.
24. Brown, *Scandalous Freedom*, 81.

"Mike," Jesus answered, "be careful . . . she's my wife!"[25]

As the bride of Christ (Rev 19:7), the church is strategic in "God's universal plan of salvation."[26] Christ is the head of the church (Eph 5:23; cf. Col 1:18). The church is God's new humanity made up of Jews and Gentiles. "His purpose was to create in himself one new humanity out of the two, thus making peace, and in one body to reconcile both of them to God through the cross, by which he put to death their hostility" (Eph 2:15–16). According to Paul, the church is a mystery that was not known by generations past (Eph 3:4–5). It is a mystery because it is comprised of both Jews and Gentiles. The cross has broken the wall of hostility separating the two. A new humanity has emerged.

> For he himself is our peace, who has made the two groups one and has destroyed the barrier, the dividing wall of hostility, by setting aside in his flesh the law with its commands and regulations. His purpose was to create in himself one new humanity out of the two, thus making peace, and in one body to reconcile both of them to God through the cross, by which he put to death their hostility. He came and preached peace to you who were far away and peace to those who were near. For through him we both have access to the Father by one Spirit. (Eph 2:14–18)

As Paul similarly states in Galatians, "There is neither Jew nor Gentile, neither slave nor free, nor is there male and female, for you are all one in Christ Jesus. If you belong to Christ, then you are Abraham's seed, and heirs according to the promise" (Gal 3:28–29; cf. Col 3:11).

But what is God's purpose for the church? "His intent was that now, through the church, the manifold wisdom of God should be made known to the rulers and authorities in the heavenly realms, according to his eternal purpose which he accomplished in Christ Jesus our Lord" (Eph 3:10–11). According to Strecker, the church is the goal of the Christ event.[27] The church is celebrated as a "*cosmic reality*," and its existence "is presented as a *universal, interethnic reality* (2:13)."[28] Consequently, "God placed all things under his feet and appointed him to be head over everything for the church, which is his body, the fullness of him who fills everything in every way" (1:22–23).

---

25. Brown, 81.

26. Yusufu Turaki, "Ephesians," in *Africa Bible Commentary*, ed. Tokunboh Adeyemo (Nairobi: WordAlive, 2006), 1425.

27. Strecker, *Theology of the New Testament*, 568.

28. Strecker, 569, emphasis original.

The church is also God's mystery. This mystery is what the cross accomplished and is the mystery which God gave Paul to preach (Eph 3:1–13). "This mystery is that through the gospel the Gentiles are heirs together with Israel, members together of one body, and sharers together in the promise in Christ Jesus" (3:6). Both Jews and Gentiles have been redeemed by the same blood of Christ. Both Jews and Gentiles can now call God "*Abba*, Father" (Rom 8:15). The point is that Jews and Gentiles are equal in Christ (cf. Gal 3:28). This is a mystery that was not made known in other generations. But God has made it known through his Spirit.

Redemption and the Christian Family

From the Christian perspective, the family is the most important institution established by God. The family provides the nucleus of the community and society. Therefore, good families are essential for healthy communities and society in general. When families thrive, communities flourish as well. When families disintegrate, the society degenerates. There is simply no middle ground here. According to Everett F. Harrison, "Since the family is the basic unit of society, the application of the gospel in this realm is bound to make Christianity a powerful force in the community. By its stability, the family is a means of evangelizing those who are impressed by daily examples of gentleness, love, and sobriety."[29] It is not surprising, therefore, that Paul devotes a long portion of his epistle to the Ephesians giving the appropriate code of conduct for all roles in Christian households – husbands and wives, children, parents – and similarly slaves or servants and masters (Eph 5:22–6:9; cf. Col 3:18–4:1).

The point is that redemption affects the believers' worldview and relationships. Because God sets the standards for them, Christians see life from God's perspective rather than their own human philosophies, cultural ethos, or mere personal convictions or preferences. Christians treat people according to God's principles. Therefore, Paul outlines the principles of how Christian couples, children, parents, slaves, and masters ought to relate to one another according to God's standards for living.

Because the husband and wife play key roles in maintaining a healthy family, Paul begins with them and gives instruction to each (Eph 5:22–33). Paul calls them to submission and love. The wife is called to submit to her husband as she does to the Lord. "For the husband is the head of the wife as Christ is the head of the church, his body, of which he is the Savior. Now as

---

29. Everett F. Harrison, *Colossians: Christ-All Sufficient* (Chicago: Moody, 1971), 96.

the church submits to Christ, so also wives should submit to their husbands in everything" (5:23–24). This submission must not be understood from the African culture and stereotype in which the man is a boss and the woman is a doormat. Christian wives submit to their husbands as to the Lord. The woman is not a second-class citizen. Both man and woman share the same standing, dignity, and worth in the eyes of God (Gal 3:28). As Harold W. Hoehner says, Ephesians 5:21 "contains the controlling thought of mutual submission and, therefore, the rest of the passage (vv. 22–33) should be seen as mutual submission of husband and wives rather than the submission of wives only."[30] Older women are to train younger ones to love their husbands and children (Titus 2:3–4). As love is mutual, we can argue that submission is mutual as well.

But the heavier responsibility lies on the husband. "Husbands, love your wives, just as Christ loved the church and gave himself up for her" (Eph 5:25). The husband must practice Christ's sacrificial love in relation to his wife. The husband must love his wife as he loves himself. Paul was countercultural at a time when women were among the downtrodden in society. This is one of the revolutionary powers of the gospel of Christ. Where Christian men each love their wife like Christ loved the church, the Christian home will be a means of evangelizing as the world sees "daily examples of gentleness, love, and sobriety."[31]

The rest of the instructions include obedience to parents. "Children, obey your parents in the Lord, for this is right. 'Honor your father and mother' – which is the first commandment with a promise – 'so that it may go well with you and that you may enjoy long life on the earth'" (Eph 6:1–3). Paul reminds children of God's fifth commandment, "Honor your father and your mother, so that you may live long in the land the LORD your God is giving you" (Exod 20:12). Similarly, fathers must not embitter their children "instead, bring them up in the training and instruction of the Lord" (Eph 6:4). Slaves are to obey their masters and "Serve wholeheartedly, as if you were serving the Lord, not people, because you know that the Lord will reward each one for whatever good they do, whether they are slave or free" (6:7–8). Masters are to "treat your slaves in the same way. Do not threaten them, since you know that he who is both their Master and yours is in heaven, and there is no favoritism with him" (6:9).

---

30. Harold W. Hoehner, *Ephesians: An Exegetical Commentary* (Grand Rapids: Baker Academic, 2002), 732.

31. Hoehner, *Ephesians*, 732.

Redemption and Spiritual Warfare

Paul punctuates his epistle with the concept of spiritual warfare (Eph 6:10–24). All true believers in Christ are engaged in a fight "against the spiritual forces of evil in the heavenly realms" (Eph 6:12), whether they are aware of it or not.[32] The believer in Christ lives in the world embattled by forces of evil. This reality is not strange for an African Christian who understands the African worldview of the evil forces of demons and witchcraft. Chapell well says, "The realities of our spiritual warfare remain in every spiritual condition."[33] In recent scholarship, however, the concept of battle as depicted in this section of Ephesians is questioned in the light of the peaceful orientation of the rest of the book. As Arnold rightly says, "This is the only place in the Pauline corpus where believers are explicitly called upon to struggle against 'principalities and powers.'"[34] But believers are not hopeless. They derive their strength and victory from the Lord (6:10). Lea shows that "Christians were engaged in an unending struggle against Satan's deceit and treachery (6:10–20)."[35] Therefore, they must put on the whole armor of God and be watchful in prayer.

Redemption and the Ministry of Prayer

Why a theology of prayer? According to Bounds, "When prayer fails, the world prevails. When prayer fails, the church loses its divine characteristics, its divine power; the church is swallowed up by a proud ecclesiasticism, and the world scoffs at its obvious impotence."[36] As we saw, prayer is a prominent feature in the Synoptic Gospels. Jesus is our model in prayer. And as we read the letters of Paul, we see a man who epitomizes the life of prayer. But here we are limiting ourselves to the book of Ephesians. According to Paul, prayer serves the following purposes:

---

32. For a comprehensive treatment of the concept of heavenly realms in Ephesians, see M. Jeff Brannon, *The Heavenlies in Ephesians: A Lexical, Exegetical and Conceptual Analysis* (New York: T&T Clark International, 2011). The sum of it is that evil powers gain access to heaven as we read in the book of Job as well as in the book of Daniel. For "when the evil powers are portrayed as having access to the presence of God, their typical functions are to tempt, deceive, lead astray, or accuse God's people. The New Testament alludes to all of these themes and demonstrates that because of Christ and his authority over the evil powers, they can no longer accuse (Rev 12.7–13) and can no longer completely deceive the nations or prevent the nations from taking part in God's salvation in Christ." Brannon, *Heavenlies in Ephesians*, 198.
33. Chapell, *Ephesians*, 328.
34. Arnold, *Power and Magic*, 103.
35. Lea, *New Testament*, 447.
36. Bounds, *E. M. Bounds on Prayer*, 68.

1. Prayer is a means of giving thanks to God. Paul said, "For this reason, ever since I heard about your faith in the Lord Jesus and your love for all God's people, I have not stopped giving thanks for you, remembering you in my prayers" (Eph 1:15–16).

2. Prayer endows the believer with the Spirit of wisdom and revelation as well as spiritual enlightenment. Paul said,

   > I keep asking that the God of our Lord Jesus Christ, the glorious Father, may give you the Spirit of wisdom and revelation, so that you may know him better. I pray also that the eyes of your heart may be enlightened in order that you may know the hope to which he has called you, the riches of his glorious inheritance in his holy people. (Eph 1:17–18)

3. Prayer strengthens the believer with the power and the knowledge of God. Paul wrote,

   > For this reason I kneel before the Father, from whom every family in heaven and on earth derives its name. I pray that out of his glorious riches he may strengthen you with power through his Spirit in your inner being, so that Christ may dwell in your hearts through faith. And I pray that you, being rooted and established in love, may have power, together with all the Lord's holy people, to grasp how wide and long and high and deep is the love of Christ, and to know this love that surpasses knowledge – that you may be filled to the measure of all the fullness of God.
   >
   > Now to him who is able to do immeasurably more than all we ask or imagine, according to his power that is at work within us, to him be glory in the church and in Christ Jesus throughout all generations, for ever and ever! Amen. (Eph 3:14–21; cf. Phil 1:9–11)

4. Prayer is a means of asking and receiving from the Lord. "And pray in the Spirit on all occasions with all kinds of prayers and requests. With this in mind, be alert and always keep on praying for all the Lord's people" (Eph 6:18).

5. Prayer is a means of staying alert: "be alert and always keep on praying" (Eph 6:18). Alertness is necessary because of our struggle "against the rulers, against the authorities, against the powers of this dark world and against the spiritual forces of evil in the heavenly realms" (6:12). Paul also said to the Colossian believers, "Devote yourselves to prayer, being watchful and thankful" (Col 4:2).

6. Prayer advances the cause of the gospel of Christ. Therefore, Paul asked the believers at Ephesus, "Pray also for me, that whenever I speak, words may be given me so that I will fearlessly make known the mystery of the gospel, for which I am an ambassador in chains. Pray that I may declare it fearlessly, as I should" (Eph 6:19–20). Using similar wordings, Paul wrote in Colossians 4:3–4, "And pray for us, too, that God may open a door for our message, so that we may proclaim the mystery of Christ, for which I am in chains. Pray that I may proclaim it clearly, as I should."

Redemption and the Age to Come

According Ephesians 1:21, God placed Jesus "far above all rule and authority, power and dominion, and every name that is invoked, *not only in the present age but also in the one to come*" (emphasis added). The "age to come" contrasts with this age (cf. Matt 12:32; Mark 10:29–30; Luke 18:29–30; 20:35; 1 Cor 2:6–8; 2 Cor 4:4; 1 Tim 6:19; Titus 2:12–13). The "age to come" is eschatological.

Pointing to eschatology in Ephesians, Strecker observes that in Ephesians 2:21–22 and 4:16, "the church is in the process of growth and reconstruction."[37] Similarly he says "one must ask also whether the 'day of redemption' (Eph 4:30) is not after all best regarded as evidence of Ephesians' having preserved some elements of futuristic eschatology."[38] According to Strecker, even the challenge to make "the most of every opportunity, because the days are evil" (Eph 5:16) has eschatological undertones, "since the characterization of the last period before the Parousia as a time of special threat was a *topos* of apocalyptic thought (2 Thess 2:3–12; Matt 24:15–22)."[39] The point is that the redeemed await their final redemption. As Paul put it, "we ourselves, who have the firstfruits of

---

37. Strecker, *Theology of the New Testament*, 576.
38. Strecker, 576.
39. Strecker, 576.

the Spirit, groan inwardly as we wait eagerly for our adoption to sonship, the redemption of our bodies" (Rom 8:23).

Questions for Review and Application

1. What does the book of Ephesians teach about the church?
2. What is grace? What are the various dimensions of grace?
3. Why is the Christian family important, and what is the obligation of each member?
4. Why is every Christian involved in spiritual warfare?
5. What spiritual battle do you see yourself engaged in?
6. Why is prayer important in the life of every believer?
7. According to E. M. Bounds, what happens when prayer fails?
8. How does the book of Ephesians draw you closer to God?

13

Drums of Redemption in Philippians

Do nothing out of selfish ambition or vain conceit. Rather, in humility value others above yourselves, not looking to your own interests but each of you to the interests of the others.

In your relationships with one another, have the same mindset as Christ Jesus:

> Who, being in very nature God,
>   did not consider equality with God something to be used
>   to his own advantage;
> rather, he made himself nothing
>   by taking the very nature of a servant,
>   being made in human likeness.
> And being found in appearance as a man,
>   he humbled himself
>   by becoming obedient to death –
>   even death on a cross!
>
> Therefore God exalted him to the highest place
>   and gave him the name that is above every name,
> that at the name of Jesus every knee should bow,
>   in heaven and on earth and under the earth,
> and every tongue acknowledge that Jesus Christ is Lord,
>   to the glory of God the Father.

Philippians 2:3–11

Synopsis of the Letter to the Philippians

Paul's letter to the Philippians is well-loved by many. Some of the outstanding passages that have encouraged, rebuked, motivated, and strengthened the faith of Christians through the centuries include these:

- Philippians 1:21: "For to me, to live is Christ and to die is gain."
- Philippians 2:3: "Do nothing out of selfish ambition or vain conceit. Rather, in humility value others above yourselves."
- Philippians 3:10–11: "I want to know Christ – yes, to know the power of his resurrection and participation in his sufferings, becoming like him in his death, and so, somehow, attaining to the resurrection from the dead."
- Philippians 3:14: "I press on toward the goal to win the prize for which God has called me heavenward in Christ Jesus."
- Philippians 4:4–7: "Rejoice in the Lord always. I will say it again: Rejoice! Let your gentleness be evident to all. The Lord is near. Do not be anxious about anything, but in every situation, by prayer and petition, with thanksgiving, present your requests to God. And the peace of God, which transcends all understanding, will guard your hearts and your minds in Christ Jesus."
- Philippians 4:13: "I can do all this through him who gives me strength."
- Philippians 4:19: "And my God will meet all your needs according to the riches of his glory in Christ Jesus."

It is apparent that Paul had a good relationship with the church at Philippi. Paul's preliminaries include greetings, thanksgiving, and prayer (Phil 1:1–11). After this he gives a "missionary report" (1:12–26).[1] The letter contains some practical concerns such as a call for unity (2:1–4) and reconciliation between two sisters (4:2–3) and the exhortation to rejoice in the Lord and shun anxiety (4:4–7).

The place of writing is debated among scholars. Conjectures include Ephesus, Rome, and Caesarea. But Rome is the favored location and attested as early as the second century.[2] In prison, Paul wrote a thank you letter to the church at Philippi for their gift through Epaphroditus (Phil 2:25; 4:10, 14). This church was consistent in supporting Paul in the ministry (4:15–16). The letter

---

1. Moisés Silva, *Philippians*, BECNT, 2nd ed. (Grand Rapids: Baker Academic, 2005), 59.
2. Jerry L. Sumney, *Philippians: A Greek Student's Intermediate Reader* (Peabody: Hendrickson, 2007), xxi.

had a second purpose, namely, to assure and encourage the church regarding the health of Epaphroditus. Finally, Paul wanted to give a word of assurance by explaining to the church at Philippi that his imprisonment was God's plan (1:14). In addition, he wanted to encourage the believers to live in unity and humility, following the example of Christ.[3] It is not certain whether or not those who preached Christ "out of selfish ambition, not sincerely, supposing that they can stir up trouble for me while I am in chains" (1:17) undermined Paul's apostleship among the Philippian believers. But if so, this letter would have been part of Paul's response to these detractors.

Key Theological Themes in the Letter to the Philippians

The key theological themes in Philippians include:

The Sanctification of the Redeemed

The goal of the Christian pilgrim is being conformed to the image of Christ by putting on "the new self, created to be like God in true righteousness and holiness" (Eph 4:24). One of the theological discourses in Paul's Letter to the Philippians is "a call to sanctification" (Phil 1:27–2:30).[4] This call to sanctification includes the need for perseverance and endurance in suffering. Similarly, Paul shows that obedience is part of sanctification (2:12–18). Through obedience, believers must work out their salvation "with fear and trembling, for it is God who works in you to will and to act in order to fulfill his good purpose" (2:12–13).

The Imitation of Christ's Humility by the Redeemed[5]

Christ is the perfect model for Christian living. Therefore, Paul urged the believers in Philippi to imitate Christ's attitude (*Geistesbeschäftigung*), namely, his humility (Phil 2:5–8). Christ's humility is the standard by which the believers gauge their relationship with one another. They must avoid selfish ambition and put the interests of others above their own (2:3–4). Modern scholars think that

---

3. Sumney, *Philippians*, xxii–xxiii. From the surface it appears that the church at Philippi had no problems. But Phil 2:1–11 and 4:1–3 show that leadership tensions and personality clashes existed.

4. Silva, *Philippians*, 79.

5. See Bitrus A. Sarma, *Pursuing the Ultimate Goal: An Exposition of Philippians for Today* (Jos, Nigeria: Yakson, 2015), 59–60.

2:6–11 is a hymn of the early church. Although they generally agree that Paul used this hymn to urge believers to a life of humility, the number of verses in the hymn, "the original source of the words, and the theological meaning of its content" remain controversial.[6]

According to Paul, Christian humility is emulating Christ (Phil 2:5–8). Christ who is the exact image (Greek *morphe*) of God emptied (Greek *ekenōsen*) himself, which is the incarnation of Christ: "The Word became flesh and made his dwelling among us" (John 1:14). But Christ's self-emptying (Greek *kenōsis*) goes beyond coming in the flesh.

> Who, being in very nature God,
>   did not consider equality with God something to be used
>   to his own advantage;
> rather, he made himself nothing
>   by taking the very nature of a servant,
>   being made in human likeness.
> And being found in appearance as a man,
>   he humbled himself
>   by becoming obedient to death –
>   even death on a cross! (Phil 2:6–8)

As a humble servant, Christ paid the ultimate price of his humility – he "became obedient to death – even death on a cross."

Christ's exaltation came only after he emptied himself:

> Therefore God exalted him to the highest place
>   and gave him the name that is above every name,
> that at the name of Jesus every knee should bow,
>   in heaven and on earth and under the earth,
> and every tongue acknowledge that Jesus Christ is Lord,
>   to the glory of God the Father. (Phil 2:9–11)

The Ultimate Pursuit of the Redeemed

The problem of "spiritual bankruptcy (3:7–8)"[7] is putting confidence in the flesh. Paul urged the Philippian believers to "Watch out for those dogs, those evildoers, those mutilators of the flesh" (Phil 3:2). They were "evildoers" because they concerned themselves with outward, legalistic righteousness

---

6. Lea, *New Testament*, 450.
7. Silva, *Philippians*, 156.

at the expense of a right relationship with the Lord. Jesus condemned the teachers of the law and the Pharisees for their outward religiosity while living with unclean hearts,

> Woe to you, teachers of the law and Pharisees, you hypocrites! You clean the outside of the cup and dish, but inside they are full of greed and self-indulgence. Blind Pharisee! First clean the inside of the cup and dish, and then the outside also will be clean.
>
> Woe to you, teachers of the law and Pharisees, you hypocrites! You are like whitewashed tombs, which look beautiful on the outside but on the inside are full of the bones of the dead and everything unclean. In the same way, on the outside you appear to people as righteous but on the inside you are full of hypocrisy and wickedness. (Matt 23:25–28)

Instead of putting confidence in the flesh, one must press forward for better knowledge of and intimacy with Christ. Paul illustrates this pressing forward by his own aspiration to know Christ better.

> I want to know Christ – yes, to know the power of his resurrection and participation in his sufferings, becoming like him in his death, and so, somehow, attaining to the resurrection from the dead.
>
> Not that I have already obtained all this, or have already arrived at my goal, but I press on to take hold of that for which Christ Jesus took hold of me. Brothers and sisters, I do not consider myself yet to have taken hold of it. But one thing I do: Forgetting what is behind and straining toward what is ahead, I press on toward the goal to win the prize for which God has called me heavenward in Christ Jesus. (Phil 3:10–14)

The ultimate pursuit of the believer, therefore, is to know Christ better and to win the prize. Toward the end of his earthly journey, Paul could say,

> I have fought the good fight, I have finished the race, I have kept the faith. Now there is in store for me the crown of righteousness, which the Lord, the righteous Judge, will award to me on that day – and not only to me, but also to all who have longed for his appearing. (2 Tim 4:7–8)

Such is the ambition of the redeemed.

The Exemplary Generosity of the Redeemed

Philippians 4:10–19 is Paul's expression of thanksgiving to the church at Philippi. Paul had received a gift from Epaphroditus, the messenger whom the Philippian believers had sent to Paul while he was in prison, probably in Rome. This gift was so precious, like an unexpected credit alert. Paul described it as "a fragrant offering, an acceptable sacrifice, pleasing to God" (Phil 4:18). Full of gratitude, Paul thanked them for their renewed concern for his physical needs.

The Philippian believers loved the Lord and his servant Paul. And because they loved the Lord and the Lord's work through Paul, they were happy to share their resources with the Lord's servant. Those who love the Lord also love the ministers of the gospel. And because their gifts are pleasing to the Lord, they are like fragrant offerings, using the imagery of temple sacrifices such as fellowship offerings, sin offerings, guilt offerings, burnt offerings, and grain offerings. The burnt offerings and fellowship offerings were made by fire, creating "an aroma pleasing to the LORD" (Lev 1:9; 3:5). The result of their generosity is that "my God will meet all your needs according to the riches of his glory in Christ Jesus" (Phil 4:19).

The biblical principle of giving is that "It is more blessed to give than to receive" (Acts 20:35). Similarly, Jesus declared, "Give, and it will be given to you. A good measure, pressed down, shaken together and running over, will be poured into your lap. For with the measure you use, it will be measured to you" (Luke 6:38). What this means for the church in Africa is that we need to give more and depend less on handouts from abroad because it is more blessed to give than to receive. If we expect credit alerts from heaven, we must learn from the Philippians' exemplary generosity.

Questions for Review and Application

1. What was Paul's purpose for writing the Letter to the Philippians?
2. What exactly does Paul tell the Philippians to imitate from Christ?
3. How did Paul regard his accomplishments in the light of knowing Christ?
4. How can African Christians imitate the life of Christ today?
5. In what ways can Christians in Africa imitate the Philippian believers in the area of giving?
6. How does the book of Philippians encourage you to draw closer to the Lord?

14

Drums of Redemption in Colossians

For he has rescued us from the dominion of darkness and brought us into the kingdom of the Son he loves, in whom we have redemption, the forgiveness of sins.

The Son is the image of the invisible God, the firstborn over all creation. For in him all things were created: things in heaven and on earth, visible and invisible, whether thrones or powers or rulers or authorities; all things have been created through him and for him. He is before all things, and in him all things hold together. And he is the head of the body, the church; he is the beginning and the firstborn from among the dead, so that in everything he might have the supremacy. For God was pleased to have all his fullness dwell in him, and through him to reconcile to himself all things, whether things on earth or things in heaven, by making peace through his blood, shed on the cross.

Colossians 1:13–20

Whatever you do, work at it with all your heart, as working for the Lord, not for human masters, since you know that you will receive an inheritance from the Lord as a reward. It is the Lord Christ you are serving.

Colossians 3:23–24

Synopsis of the Letter to the Colossians

Colossae was located in the region of Phrygia, "a region renowned in the ancient world for its fascination with all things magical and mysterious."[1] Colossians is one of the letters Paul wrote while he was in prison in Rome.[2] He wrote out of his growing concern for all of the churches, and especially because there appeared to be a serious threat to the growth of this church as a result of false teachings (Col 2:8–3:4). Paul responded by pointing the Colossian believers to the supremacy and sufficiency of Christ for salvation.

But apart from responding to errors that were capable of shipwrecking the faith of many, Paul also gives practical guidelines for Christian living. He instructs husbands and wives, children and parents, and servants and masters regarding the right conduct for Christian households.

There are remarkable similarities between Colossians and Ephesians.[3] C. Leslie Mitton juxtaposes the similarities as follows:[4]

3:2	1:25
3:3	1:27
3:4	2:2
3:8	1:27
3:9	1:26

A helpful explanation for these similarities is that Tychicus is the bearer of the two letters according to Colossians 4:7 and Ephesians 6:21, which implies that the composition of the two letters took place at the same time and place.[5]

Key Theological Themes in the Letter to the Colossians

In this letter written to correct some errors in the church, some theological themes stand out. These include:

---

1. Johnson, *Writings of the New Testament*, 395.
2. Scholars debate about the authorship of Colossians.
3. See "Authorship of Ephesians" in Bitrus A. Sarma, *Blessed New Humanity in Christ: A Theology of Hope for African Christianity from the Book of Ephesians* (Nairobi: HippoBooks, 2021), 12–15.
4. C. Leslie Mitton, *Ephesians*, The New Century Bible Commentary (Grand Rapids: Eerdmans, 1973: repr. London: Marshall, Morgan & Scott, 1989), 118.
5. Harrison, *Introduction to the New Testament*, 314.

Faith in the Supremacy of Christ Our Redeemer[6]

Some commentators think that Colossians 1:15–20 is an "early Christian hymn that Paul chose to include in the letter."[7] Others object to the idea of Paul borrowing a hymn in writing his letter. "But the pattern of the ideas, sometimes symmetrical and sometimes parallel, and the rhythm that emerges clearly in the original Greek do indeed seem hymn-like."[8] Whatever is one's take on this, Paul's Christology is most prominent in the text. "The Son is the image of the invisible God" (1:15). This means that Christ is "the very embodiment of God."[9] As John Daille says,

> For however weak and despicable was that form under which he appeared here below, yet he is in reality the true Son of God; his wisdom, his word, and his power; the perfect portrait of his person, his living and essential image, the sovereign Lord and Creator of the universe.[10]

Such is the "dignity and excellency of the Lord Jesus."[11] These characteristics are clearly portrayed in Hebrews 1:3: "The Son is the radiance of God's glory and the exact representation of his being, sustaining all things by his powerful word. After he had provided purification for sins, he sat down at the right hand of the Majesty in heaven." All of this is the "basis for Christ's supremacy."[12]

Christ Is Above All Things

Jesus created all things. He is not one with the work of his creation like the Jesus of the New Age movement who is inseparable from creation. Paul said, "For by him all things were created: things in heaven and on earth, visible and invisible, whether thrones or powers or rulers or authorities; all things have been created through him and for him" (Col 1:16). This verse is an echo of

---

6. This and the following sections are abridged from Bitrus A. Sarma's *Jesus is Lord: Proclaiming the Supremacy of Christ in Africa from the Book of Colossians* (Jos, Nigeria: Yakson, 2014), 64–101.

7. Solomon Andria, "Colossians," in *Africa Bible Commentary*, ed. Tokunboh Adeyemo (Nairobi: WordAlive, 2006), 1451. See also Paul J. Achtemeier, Joel B. Green, and Marianne Meye Thompson, *Introducing the New Testament: Its Literature and Theology* (Grand Rapids: Eerdmans, 2001), 409.

8. Andria, "Colossians," 1451.

9. Achtemeier, Green, and Thompson, *Introducing the New Testament*, 410.

10. John Daille, *An Exposition of the Epistle to the Colossians* (Marshallton, DE: National Foundation for Christian Education, 1972), 90–91.

11. Daille, *Exposition of the Epistle to the Colossians*, 91.

12. Curtis Vaughan, "Colossians," in *The Expositor's Bible Commentary*, abrid., ed. Kenneth L. Barker and John R. Kohlenberger, III (Grand Rapids: Zondervan, 1994), 821.

John 1:1–3. Therefore, in Jesus all things hold together, and he is the Lord of all. Jesus "is before all things, and in him all things hold together" (Col 1:17). This means he is also Lord of all.

Christ Is the Head of the Church

Scripture says of Christ, "And he is the head of the body, the church; he is the beginning and the *firstborn* from among the dead, so that in everything he might have the supremacy" (Col 1:18, emphasis added). What is the meaning of "firstborn" with regard to Christ? Is he to be associated with created beings like the Arians taught and the Jehovah's Witnesses still teach?[13] Firstborn for Paul means "supreme in rank."[14] According to Trevethan,

> The term firstborn is commonly used to mean "supreme" or "sovereign," that is, "having the rights of the firstborn." The best illustration of this usage is Psalm 89:27, where God says of the Davidic king, "And I will make him the firstborn, the highest of the kings of the earth." The king is not the first king ever to exist. "Firstborn" is a synonym for "highest of the kings of the earth."[15]

This means Jesus is "the agent of all creation" who "exists before all things" (Col 1:16–17).[16] In Ephesians 1:22–23, Paul says, "And God placed all things under his feet and appointed him to be head over everything for the church, which is his body, the fullness of him who fills everything in every way."

The Father Is the Source of Christ's Supremacy

Christ is filled with all the fullness of God: "For God was pleased to have all his fullness dwell in him" (Col 1:19). Paul explains that "in Christ all the fullness of the Deity lives in bodily form, and in Christ you have been brought to fullness. He is the head over every power and authority" (2:9–10). But how do we understand this "fullness"? According to D. S. Lim, Paul uses the term "fullness" in five ways: "totality of space" (1 Cor 10:26; cf. Ps 24:1); "totality of quantity" (Rom 11:12); "totality of the law" (Rom 13:8–10); "fulfillment

---

13. R. P. C. Hanson, *The Search for the Christian Doctrine: The Arian Controversy, 318–381* (Edinburgh: T&T Clark, 1988); Harry Boer, *A Short History of the Early Church* (Ibadan, Nigeria: Daystar, 1976), 113–14.

14. Thomas L. Trevethan, *Our Joyful Confidence: The Lordship of Jesus in Colossians* (Downers Grove: InterVarsity, 1981), 37.

15. Trevethan, *Our Joyful Confidence*, 37.

16. Trevethan, 37.

of time" (Gal 4:4); and "fullness of essence" (Col 1:19; 2:9).[17] Paul is talking about the "fullness of essence" in Colossians 1:19 as the source of Christ's supremacy, which means that "the whole total of the Godhead was pleased to dwell in Christ."[18]

And God caused his fullness to dwell in Christ for a purpose: "and through him to reconcile to himself all things, whether things on earth or things in heaven, by making peace through his blood, shed on the cross" (Col 1:20). This means that only he who has all the fullness of God can "reconcile to himself all things." This "image of reconciliation" is a "model by which the salvation mediated by Christ and its results may be visualized" (Rom 5:11; 11:15; 2 Cor 5:18–19).[19] Some scholars believe that "Paul adopted essential elements of his statements about reconciliation from the language and thought world of Hellenistic diplomacy."[20]

The object of reconciliation is obviously the alienated human race: "Once you were alienated from God and were enemies in your minds because of your evil behavior" (Col 1:21). The idea of reconciling the alienated echoes the words of Ephesians 2:1–5:

> As for you, you were dead in your transgressions and sins, in which you used to live when you followed the ways of this world and of the ruler of the kingdom of the air, the spirit who is now at work in those who are disobedient. All of us also lived among them at one time, gratifying the cravings of our flesh and following its desires and thoughts. Like the rest, we were by nature deserving of wrath. But because of his great love for us, God, who is rich in mercy, made us alive with Christ even when we were dead in transgressions – it is by grace you have been saved.

The purpose of this reconciliation is also stated in Colossians 1:22: "But now he has reconciled you by Christ's physical body through death to present you holy in his sight, without blemish and free from accusation."

---

17. D. S. Lim, "Fullness," in *Dictionary of Paul and His Letters*, ed. Gerald F. Hawthorne, Ralph P. Martin, and Daniel G. Reid (Downers Grove: InterVarsity, 1993), 319–20.

18. Lim, "Fullness," 320.

19. Schnelle, *Apostle Paul*, 451.

20. Schnelle, 251; citing Cilliers Breytenbach, *Vershnung: Eine Studie zur paulinischen Soteriologie*, Wissenschaftliche Monographien zum Alten und Neuen Testament 60 (Neukirchen-Vluyn: Neukirchener Verlag, 1989), 221.

Faith in Christ Overrules the Errors of False Philosophy and Religion

According to Vaughan, there are six important keys to understanding Paul's argument regarding the supremacy of Christ in Colossians.[21]

First, one of the heresies in Colossae was emphasis on the worship of angels, called "thrones," "rulers," "powers," and "authorities" (Col 1:13, 15–17; 2:9–10, 15, 18–19). But Paul's argument is that "Christ created these powers and he rules over them; believers are delivered from their power."[22]

Second, many believed that angels serve as intermediaries between God and human beings. But Paul's answer is that Christ is the only mediator between God and humankind (Col 1:3–23; 2:6, 9–10).[23]

Third was "endorsed submission" to the basic principles of the world (Col 2:8, 10). But Paul argues that "Christ rules over these principles, and Christians have died to them in Christ."[24]

Fourth, circumcision of the flesh was considered a necessary requirement for true religion (Col 2:11–13). But Paul shows that dying with Christ is a better circumcision.

Fifth, the heretics were teaching people to observe special religious days and food rules (Col 2:14, 16–17, 20–23). Paul argues, however, that the power of these rules has been canceled in Christ Jesus.

Sixth, these heretics laid emphasis on special, secret knowledge (Col 1:9–10, 28; 2:2–4, 22). But according to Paul, "God fills all believers with wisdom, knowledge, and understanding."[25]

With all these, Paul encourages the believers to persevere in the faith and be rooted and built upon Christ. He says, "So then, just as you received Christ Jesus as Lord, continue to live your lives in him, rooted and built up in him, strengthened in the faith as you were taught, and overflowing with thankfulness" (Col 2:6–7). Abiding in Christ or walking with him is the key to being "rooted and built up in him" and the remedy against the deception of the enemy. The believers in Colossae were in danger. So Paul warned, "See to it that no one takes you captive through hollow and deceptive philosophy, which depends on human tradition and the elemental spiritual forces of this world rather than on Christ" (2:8). "See to it" means "watch out," or "be alert." Alertness is the mark of wise Christians, lest the enemy finds them sleeping (cf.

---

21. Vaughan, "Colossians," 823.
22. Vaughan, 823.
23. Vaughan, 823.
24. Vaughan, 823.
25. Vaughan, 823.

Matt 26:41 // Mark 14:38; Luke 21:36; Eph 6:18). Here, the enemy came through "hollow and deceptive philosophy." According to Donald Guthrie, "It cannot be determined with certainty what sense Paul uses the word 'philosophy,' but it is generally supposed to point to Hellenistic elements."[26] Guthrie states that the Greek terms translated "fullness" (Col 1:19), "knowledge" (2:3) and "neglect of the body" (2:23) "may be also drawn from the same general background. All these terms were in use in second-century Gnosticism."[27]

But we must mention that Paul is not speaking against philosophy as an academic discipline but as a religious system. On the contrary, an important discipline for all Christians is philosophy because it is "the most important intellectual domain" and "because it is the most foundational of the disciplines, since it examines the presuppositions and ramifications of every discipline at the university – including itself!"[28]

Because ideas rule the world, Christians must be prepared to examine the presuppositions of every idea. After all, Scripture says, "But in your hearts set apart Christ as Lord. Always be prepared to give an answer to everyone who asks you to give the reason for the hope that you have" (1 Pet 3:15). To do all of this, we must learn "right thinking."[29] Permit the long quote below from Moreland and Craig on the dangers of wasting away our minds as Christians.

> Our churches are unfortunately overpopulated with people whose minds, as Christians, are going to waste. . . . They may be spiritually regenerate, but their minds have not been converted; they still think like unbelievers. Despite their Christian commitment, they remain largely empty selves. . . . An empty self is a person who is passive, sensate, busy and hurried, incapable of developing an interior life. Such a person is . . . individualistic, infantile and narcissistic.
>
> Imagine now a church filled with such people. What will be the theological understanding . . . of such a church? If the interior life does not really matter all that much, why should one spend the time trying to develop an intellectual, spiritually mature life? If someone is basically passive, he will just not make the effort to read, preferring instead to be entertained. . . . If one is hurried and

---

26. Donald Guthrie, *New Testament Introduction* (Leicester: Apollos, 1990), 566.

27. Guthrie, *New Testament Introduction*, 566–67.

28. J. P. Moreland and William Lane Craig, *Philosophical Foundations for a Christian Worldview* (Downers Grove: IVP Academic, 2003), 3.

29. See Sarma, *Pursuing the Ultimate Goal*, ch. 12.

> distracted, one will have little patience for theoretical knowledge and too short an attention span to stay with an idea while it is being carefully developed. If someone is overly individualistic, infantile and narcissistic, what *will* that person read, if he reads at all? . . . Christian self-help books filled with slogans, simplistic moralizing, . . . and inadequate diagnosis of the problems facing the reader. What will *not* be read are books that equip people to develop a well-reasoned, theological understanding of the Christian faith and assume their role in the broader work of the kingdom of God. Such a church will become impotent to stand against the powerful forces of secularism that threaten to wash away Christian ideas. . . .[30]

This quote is food for thought. Is not the church already "impotent to stand against the power of secularism" today? To say it again, Paul is not against philosophy per se. Rather, his argument is that "Religious practices based on human traditions can be very alluring."[31] That is unprofitable human philosophy and "would be traps for the Colossians."[32] We must think biblically.

The hollow philosophy propagated at Colossae was aimed at changing the simple message of salvation through the cross of Christ (Col 1:9–10). This philosophy presupposes that there is a fuller knowledge to acquire apart from or in addition to Christ. But this thinking is the error of false religion and philosophy. According to 1 Corinthians 1:18–25,

> For the message of the cross is foolishness to those who are perishing, but to us who are being saved it is the power of God. For it is written:
>
> "I will destroy the wisdom of the wise;
>   the intelligence of the intelligent I will frustrate."
>
> Where is the wise person? Where is the teacher of the law? Where is the philosopher of this age? Has not God made foolish the wisdom of the world? For since in the wisdom of God the world through its wisdom did not know him, God was pleased through the foolishness of what was preached to save those who believe. Jews demand signs and Greeks look for wisdom, but we

---

30. Moreland and Craig, *Philosophical Foundations*, 5, emphasis original.
31. Andria, "Colossians," 1453.
32. Andria, 1453.

preach Christ crucified: a stumbling block to Jews and foolishness to Gentiles, but to those whom God has called, both Jews and Greeks, Christ the power of God and the wisdom of God. For the foolishness of God is wiser than human wisdom, and the weakness of God is stronger than human strength.

Therefore, Paul declares that "in Christ all the fullness of the Deity lives in bodily form" (Col 2:9). Christians "have been brought to fullness. He is the head over every power and authority" (2:10). These verses mean that Jesus is the only source of reality and truth.[33]

In Colossae people who were promoting this human philosophy, based on human tradition, were emphasizing circumcision, which was legalistic Judaism. But Paul says that the better circumcision is the one done in the heart. The circumcision of the flesh is unable to deal with the problem of sin. However, the circumcision of the heart or spiritual circumcision is able to help believers overcome sin because they have been buried and raised with Christ (Col 2:11–13).

All believers have been made alive in Christ and have overcome the power of the evil one.

> When you were dead in your sins and in the uncircumcision of your flesh, God made you alive with Christ. He forgave us all our sins, having canceled the charge of our legal indebtedness, which stood against us and condemned us; he has taken it away, nailing it to the cross. (Col 2:13–14)

Paul uses a legal term to describe what God has done for believers in Christ on the cross. Through the cross God forgave their sins. The word picture is that their debt of sin has been canceled. Andria puts it beautifully:

> Paul describes what happened there in terms of a legal obligation or a debt being annulled. There is a legal document, *the written code, with its regulations*, that indicates that we were hopelessly in the wrong with no possibility of setting things right. It is as if we had accumulated a debt we could never possibly pay. This document is our accuser, and we cannot argue with it. We are clearly in the wrong. But when Christ was nailed to the cross, it

---

33. Alpha-Omega Ministries, *Colossians: The Teachers' Outline and Study Guide* (Chattanooga: Leadership Ministries Worldwide, 1994), 100.

was as if God was nailing the document to the cross with Christ. He was cancelling our obligation or debt so that we could go free.[34]

In Colossians 2:15, Paul changes the metaphor "from a courtroom to a military parade":[35] "And having disarmed the powers and authorities, he made a public spectacle of them, triumphing over them by the cross." It is like an army general who has conquered a city and now displays the "conquered enemies and all the goods they had plundered."[36] The devil and all of his allies have been defeated by the cross and are there for all to see "in Christ's parade."[37] This verse is probably "the most important text on Christ's victory over evil powers."[38] Christ has subjugated all his enemies through the cross, and "Believers share in Christ's triumph because their sins have been forgiven, their certificate of debt has been erased, and their sins have been decisively and finally nailed to the cross."[39] This means that the cross and the resurrection brought final triumph over the demonic powers. At the cross, "God stripped the rulers and their authorities of their power."[40] This is good news for African Christians who live in constant fear of evil forces.

Faith in Christ Overrules the Error of Legalism

Paul counteracts legalism in Colossians 2:16–17 when he says, "Therefore do not let anyone judge you by what you eat or drink, or with regard to a religious festival, a New Moon celebration or a Sabbath day. These are a shadow of the things that were to come; the reality, however, is found in Christ." According to Keener, "Asceticism was growing in paganism and many viewed it as a means of achieving spiritual power or revelatory experiences."[41] According to Keener, the text refers to Jewish customs.[42] But there is need to think more broadly in the light of the fact that "Asceticism was growing in paganism." Paul is speaking about Christian freedom versus legalism, whether pagan or Jewish

---

34. Andria, "Colossians," 1453, emphasis original.
35. Andria, 1453.
36. Andria, 1453.
37. Andria, 1453.
38. Schreiner, *New Testament Theology*, 370.
39. Schreiner, 370.
40. Schreiner, 371.
41. Craig S. Keener, *The IVP Bible Background Commentary: New Testament* (Downers Grove: InterVarsity, 1993), 576.
42. Keener, *IVP Bible Background Commentary*, 576.

legalism. Paul had once considered himself righteous according to legalistic righteousness. He says in Philippians 3:4-6,

> If someone else thinks they have reasons to put confidence in the flesh, I have more: circumcised on the eighth day, of the people of Israel, of the tribe of Benjamin, a Hebrew of Hebrews; in regard to the law, a Pharisee; as for zeal, persecuting the church; as for righteousness based on the law, faultless.

But Paul found a better way of righteousness in Christ.

> But whatever were gains to me I now consider loss for the sake of Christ. What is more, I consider everything a loss because of the surpassing worth of knowing Christ Jesus my Lord, for whose sake I have lost all things. I consider them garbage, that I may gain Christ and be found in him, not having a righteousness of my own that comes from the law, but that which is through faith in Christ – the righteousness that comes from God on the basis of faith. (Phil 3:7-9)

The false teachers were emphasizing abstinence from certain foods or drinks and the observance of certain festivals and special days. Perhaps this was enforcing Levitical law on certain foods and observance of certain days. "But Christ by His death has abrogated these legal demands, and to look to these is to prefer the shadow to the substance which is Christ Himself."[43]

The legalists were judging people according to their observance of these laws. But Paul teaches that Levitical regulations with their ritual observances are a shadow of the things to come. "These are a shadow of the things that were to come; the reality, however, is found in Christ" (Col 2:17).

According to Galatians 5:1, Christians are free from legalism: "It is for freedom that Christ has set us free. Stand firm, then, and do not let yourselves be burdened again by a yoke of slavery." But we need to guard against the false concepts of freedom that many people advocate, that is, freedom to do *anything* we want to do. The Bible tells us what is the right kind of freedom. According to Galatians 5:13, "You, my brothers and sisters, were called to be free. But do not use your freedom to indulge the flesh; rather, serve one another humbly in love." We Christians must run away from the errors of legalism and postmodernism. We are not religious legalists. We are free. But our freedom is not the freedom to do what is right in our own eyes. We are free to do what

---

43. Ernest G. Ashby, "Colossians," in *New International Bible Commentary*, ed. F. F. Bruce, H. L. Ellison, and G. C. D. Howley (Grand Rapids: Zondervan, 1979), 1457.

is best in the eyes of God. That is true freedom. Jesus says in John 8:32, "Then you will know the truth, and the truth will set you free."

Faith in Christ Overrules the Worship of Angels

In Colossians 2:18–19, Paul rebukes the error of the worship of angels. The book of Hebrews tells us that Christ is superior to angels. Hebrews 1:3–14 says,

> The Son is the radiance of God's glory and the exact representation of his being, sustaining all things by his powerful word. After he had provided purification for sins, he sat down at the right hand of the Majesty in heaven. So he became as much superior to the angels as the name he has inherited is superior to theirs.
>
> For to which of the angels did God ever say,
>
> "You are my Son;
> today I have become your Father"?
>
> Or again,
>
> "I will be his Father,
> and he will be my Son"?
>
> And again, when God brings his firstborn into the world, he says,
>
> "Let all God's angels worship him."
>
> In speaking of the angels he says,
>
> "He makes his angels spirits,
> and his servants flames of fire."
>
> But about the Son he says,
>
> "Your throne, O God, will last for ever and ever;
> a scepter of justice will be the scepter of your kingdom.
> You have loved righteousness and hated wickedness;
> therefore God, your God, has set you above your companions
> by anointing you with the oil of joy."
>
> He also says,
>
> "In the beginning, Lord, you laid the foundations of the earth,
> and the heavens are the work of your hands.

> They will perish, but you remain;
> > they will all wear out like a garment.
> You will roll them up like a robe;
> > like a garment they will be changed.
> But you remain the same,
> > and your years will never end."
>
> To which of the angels did God ever say,
>
> > "Sit at my right hand
> > > until I make your enemies
> > > a footstool for your feet"?
>
> Are not all angels ministering spirits sent to serve those who will inherit salvation?

This text clearly tells us that Jesus is superior to the angels.

- Jesus is "the radiance of God's glory and the exact representation of his being, sustaining all things by his powerful word" (Heb 1:3).
- Jesus provided purification for sins. No angel did that.
- Jesus is the Son of God.
- Angels worship Jesus.
- Jesus is God and he rules forever. "But about the Son he says, 'Your throne, O God, will last for ever and ever; a scepter of justice will be the scepter of your kingdom'" (Heb 3:8).
- Jesus made the world. "He also says, 'In the beginning, Lord, you laid the foundations of the earth, and the heavens are the work of your hands'" (Heb 3:10).

Angels are powerful beings. Human beings are made "a little lower than the angels" (Ps 8:5). But angels are ministering spirits. This means that they run errands for God and serve God's people (cf. Acts 27:23–24).

Believers must be grateful to God for his ministering spirits that serve him and minister to them. But angels must not be regarded as mediators. "For there is one God and one mediator between God and mankind, the man Christ Jesus, who gave himself as a ransom for all people. This has now been witnessed to at the proper time" (1 Tim 2:5–6). But there are some who venerate angels today. This practice is clearly unscriptural. Worshiping anything God created is idolatry, and the consequences are deadly.

Faith in Christ Overrules the Error of Asceticism

In Colossians 2:20–23, Paul says,

> Since you died with Christ to the elemental spiritual forces of this world, why, as though you still belonged to the world, do you submit to its rules: "Do not handle! Do not taste! Do not touch!"? These rules, which have to do with things that are all destined to perish with use, are based on merely human commands and teachings. Such regulations indeed have an appearance of wisdom, with their self-imposed worship, their false humility and their harsh treatment of the body, but they lack any value in restraining sensual indulgence.

It appears that the Greek religious and philosophical movement called Gnosticism was gaining ground in the city of Colossae.[44] The basic quest of Gnosticism was "the true nature of reality."[45] Gnostics believed there are two realities, namely, the spiritual and the material. "The spiritual was presided over by a panoply of deities, with proportionately less divinity from the highest deity to the lowest."[46] The material world is evil because it was created by "a cosmic accident" through "a lesser deity."[47] According to the Gnostics, "Humans were originally spiritual beings, or at least those capable of salvation were. But creation trapped them in physical bodies."[48]

How did Gnostics believe salvation was obtained?

> Only possession of knowledge of the nature of reality and of human existence can, the Gnostics held, free a person from slavery to the material in order to emphasize the better part of his or her nature, the spiritual part. This secret knowledge came, many

---

44. The Gnostic movement is said to have developed in the second century. See Nicolas Denzey Lewis, "A New Gnosticism: Why Simon Gathercole and Mark Goodacre on the *Gospel of Thomas* Change the Field," *JSNT* 36, no. 3 (March 2014): 240–50. But there is no doubt that elements of Gnosticism were present in the Colossian church. Eduard Schweizer says,

> the strong emphasis on spiritual knowledge is particularly reminiscent of Gnostic thought; so also is the remarkable accumulation of expressions intended to hint at God's being which transcends the world, and for which every concept is inadequate. However, the idea of this knowledge being knowledge of the will of God is completely different to anything found in Gnosticism.

Eduard Schweizer, *The Letter to the Colossians*, trans. Andrew Chester (London: SPCK, 1982), 44.

45. Achtemeier, Green, and Thompson, *Introducing the New Testament*, 412.
46. Achtemeier, Green, and Thompson, 412.
47. Achtemeier, Green, and Thompson, 412.
48. Achtemeier, Green, and Thompson, 412.

Gnostics believed, from a revealer figure sent by the highest deity. The Gnostics taught this secret knowledge to their followers and thus enabled them to return to the heavenly realm from which they had originally come. Salvation thus had to do not with forgiveness of sin but with removal of ignorance.[49]

Therefore, advocates of asceticism believed that abstinence is the best way to avoid engagement with the material world. But Paul says that believers have died to the basic principles of this world and need not submit to the rules: "Do not handle! Do not taste! Do not touch!" (Col 2:22). According to Paul, these rules are based on merely human commands and teaching and lack any value in restraining sensual indulgence.

As Paul says in 1 Timothy 4:1–5:

> The Spirit clearly says that in later times some will abandon the faith and follow deceiving spirits and things taught by demons. Such teachings come through hypocritical liars, whose consciences have been seared as with a hot iron. They forbid people to marry and order them to abstain from certain foods, which God created to be received with thanksgiving by those who believe and who know the truth. For everything God created is good, and nothing is to be rejected if it is received with thanksgiving, because it is consecrated by the word of God and prayer.

Christians are free, not for self-indulgence, but to serve the Lord and enjoy every gift of God according to his will. Similarly, Christians must recognize Jesus's supremacy over false religions and philosophies. We must also know the freedom we have in Christ and not be bound by legalism and asceticism. And when tempted to worship angels or anything else, we must remember the words of Jesus and imitate him: "Away from me, Satan! For it is written: 'Worship the Lord your God, and serve him only'" (Matt 4:10).

---

49. Achtemeier, Green, and Thompson, 412.

Questions for Review and Application

1. Why and how is Christ supreme over all?
2. If Jesus defeated the devil and his demons on the cross, why do many African Christians still live with excessive fear of demons and evil forces?
3. In what particular ways should Christians in Africa appropriate the supremacy of Christ in their daily lives?
4. How does Colossians draw you closer to Jesus?

15

Drums of Redemption in 1 and 2 Thessalonians

> For the appeal we make does not spring from error or impure motives, nor are we trying to trick you. On the contrary, we speak as those approved by God to be entrusted with the gospel. We are not trying to please people but God, who tests our hearts. You know we never used flattery, nor did we put on a mask to cover up greed – God is our witness.
>
> 1 Thessalonians 2:3–5

> Don't let anyone deceive you in any way, for that day will not come until the rebellion occurs and the man of lawlessness is revealed, the man doomed to destruction. He will oppose and will exalt himself over everything that is called God or is worshiped, so that he sets himself up in God's temple, proclaiming himself to be God.
>
> Don't you remember that when I was with you I used to tell you these things? And now you know what is holding him back, so that he may be revealed at the proper time. For the secret power of lawlessness is already at work; but the one who now holds it back will continue to do so till he is taken out of the way.
>
> 2 Thessalonians 2:3–7

Synopsis of the Letters 1 and 2 Thessalonians

Thessalonica was the capital and largest city of Macedonia. We recall Paul's Macedonian call in Acts 16:6–10. According to Acts 17:1–4, Paul planted the church in Thessalonica on his second missionary journey. Paul's mission work in Thessalonica lasted for only three weeks. With the growing opposition of the Jews, Paul had to leave the city. But his ministry bore much fruit. While Paul was in Corinth, Timothy reported to him the condition of the church in Thessalonica. Therefore, Paul wrote to encourage the believers and to teach them more about the Christian faith.

In 1 Thessalonians, Paul praises the believers for their braveness and growing faith in spite of increasing persecution (1 Thess 1:6). The thrust of the letter is "how to live in order to please God" (4:1). Paul urges the believers to please the Lord more and more and live sanctified lives by avoiding sexual immorality and exercising self-control. Other practical matters of the Christian faith that Paul discusses include love for one another and minding one's business by working hard to provide for daily necessities as a testimony to those outside the Christian faith (4:9–12). The major theological concerns raised pertain to believers who have died before the day of the Lord (4:13–5:11).

Paul was still in Corinth when he wrote 2 Thessalonians, a few months after he sent the first letter. Paul begins with encouraging the believers in their suffering and endurance for the sake of the kingdom of God. They were growing in love and faith. Paul says, "We ought always to thank God for you, brothers and sisters, and rightly so, because your faith is growing more and more, and the love all of you have for one another is increasing" (2 Thess 1:3). But it appears that some of the believers in Thessalonica misunderstood Paul's treatise about the second coming of Jesus Christ. They thought that his return would be so soon that they had stopped working in order to wait. Paul had to correct that misconception and to encourage them to work hard rather than live in idleness (3:6–15).

Key Theological Themes in the Letters 1 and 2 Thessalonians

Within 1 and 2 Thessalonians, we find some important theological themes which include the dead in Christ, the Day of the Lord and the Man of Lawlessness.

Redemption and the Dead in Christ

It is apparent that the believers in Thessalonica were troubled by those who had died before the *parousia*. Many of them expressed excessive grief, fearing that their loved ones were now lost since Jesus had not yet come.

> This raises the question of whether or not they have missed out on the full realization of the kingdom. It would seem so, especially

if the revelation of God's power was for the future only, and not already revealed in the present. Because those who died apparently missed out on the "not yet," the members of the community mourned, forgetting their more significant participation in the "already" of God.[1]

Paul teaches the believers that the dead in Christ are not lost. On the contrary, "According to the Lord's word, we tell you that we who are still alive, who are left until the coming of the Lord, will certainly not precede those who have fallen asleep" (1 Thess 4:15). For at the announcement of the coming of the Lord "with the voice of the archangel and with the trumpet call of God . . . the dead in Christ will rise first" (4:16). Then the living saints "will be caught up together with them in the clouds" (4:17).

Redemption and the Day of the Lord (Parousia)[2]

In the Old Testament, the "day of the Lord is essentially a day of judgement, and that day is evoked 'to awaken the people from their moral slumber.'"[3] The prophet Amos asked, 'Will not the day of the LORD be darkness, not light – pitch-dark, without a ray of brightness?" (Amos 5:20). According to House,

> Paul's usage of the day of the Lord continues to reflect ideas found in the Old Testament and in the Gospels, yet he also fits Jesus into the patterns in distinctive ways. Most of his direct references to the "day" indicate his interest in the vindication of his ministry and of his people on the final "day" of judgement.[4]

The day of the Lord in 1 and 2 Thessalonians is the *parousia*, the second coming of Christ. Paul hints about the *parousia* in 1 Thessalonians 2:19: "For what is our hope, our joy, or the crown in which we will glory in the presence of our Lord Jesus when he comes? Is it not you?" The expression "The presence of the Lord when he comes" describes the hope of the believers. Perhaps many of the Christians in Thessalonica were wondering about when the *parousia* would take place. "Some of the Thessalonians had evidently understood Paul

---

1. Johnson, *Writings of the New Testament*, 285.

2. For a good treatment of the concept of the day of the Lord, see Paul R. House, "The Day of the Lord," in *Central Themes in Biblical Theology: Mapping Unity in Diversity*, ed. Scott J. Hafemann and Paul R. House (Nottingham: Apollos, 2007), 179–224.

3. House, "Day of the Lord," 195.

4. House, 214.

to say that all who believed would see the Parousia. Some believers had died. Did this mean they would be at a disadvantage when the Lord came? Had they forfeited their share in the wonderful happenings in the End?"[5] Paul responds to the speculations in 1 Thessalonians 5:1–11. Basically, the time of Jesus's coming is unknown. There is no timetable for believers to observe. It is a secret and likened to "a thief in the night" (1 Thess 5:2). The day will come when the world is shouting "peace and safety" (5:3). Paul here is echoing Jesus (Luke 17:26–27).[6]

While the day of the Lord comes like a thief in the night, the believers are "not in darkness," and the day will not surprise them (1 Thess 5:4). For as children of the light, believers live prepared "like servants waiting for their master to return from a wedding banquet, so that when he comes and knocks they can immediately open the door for him" (Luke 12:36). This means that the "uncertainty on our part of the day and the hour of Christ's return is a reason for watchfulness (Matt 24:42; 25:13; Mark 13:35, 37)."[7]

The Redeemed and the Man of Lawlessness

In 2 Thessalonians 2:1–12, Paul sets forth the conditions for the coming of the Lord, which was necessary in the light of the unsettling "false eschatological teachers."[8] While in 1 Thessalonians, Paul addressed the fear that many of the brothers and sisters had died before the coming of the Lord, in 2 Thessalonians he addresses the opposite concern. The "false eschatological teachers" claimed that the *parousia* had already taken place. And this teaching was supposedly from Paul and his associates – "allegedly from us" (2:2).

For this reason, Paul takes time to teach that the day of the Lord had not yet taken place, "for that day will not come until the rebellion occurs and the man of lawlessness is revealed, the man doomed to destruction" (2 Thess 2:3). This man of lawlessness "will oppose and will exalt himself over everything that is called God or is worshipped, so that he sets himself up in God's temple, proclaiming himself to be God" (2:4). According to Paul, this lawless one or man of rebellion had not yet come. But there were some manifestations of

---

5. Leon Morris, *1 and 2 Thessalonians*, Tyndale New Testament Commentaries, rev. ed. (Grand Rapids: Eerdmans, 1984), 89.

6. Ray C. Stedman, *Waiting for the Second Coming: Studies in Thessalonians* (Grand Rapids: Discovery House, 1990), 85.

7. William Hendriksen, *1 & 2 Thessalonians, 1 & 2 Timothy, Titus* (Banner of Truth Trust, 1972, repr. 2001), 125.

8. Strecker, *Theology of the New Testament*, 594.

his presence, "For the secret power of lawlessness is already at work" (2:7). Therefore, "the congregation should consider itself as being in the general period of the end-time. It is not, however, at its climax."[9] Yet this secret power of lawlessness is being restrained. The full revelation of the lawless one will be characterized by Satan's display of power "through signs and wonders that serve the lie, and all the ways that wickedness deceives those who are perishing" (2:9–10).

Today anti-religious sentiments are growing in the world. The illusion is that if religion is removed, the world will be a safer and freer place to live. Religion is targeted as the number one culprit in restricting human freedom and promoting religious acrimony and hatred in the world. Terrorism and other forms of religious bigotry and violence are cited as proofs for the characterization of religion as an undesirable element in a civilized world. Christianity is the number one victim of this philosophy. The stage is being set for the manifestation of the man of lawlessness, one who "will oppose and will exalt himself over everything that is called God or is worshiped" (2 Thess 2:4).

Questions for Review and Application

1. What were Paul's instructions to the Thessalonians? In what ways do we live to please God?
2. What is the most important preparation for the day of the Lord?
3. Paul says that the "the man of lawlessness" will oppose "everything that is called God or is worshiped." How is this behavior manifested in the world today?
4. What indicators are there that "the man of lawlessness" is already at work in our times?
5. How do 1 and 2 Thessalonians encourage your walk with the Lord?

---

9. Johnson, *Writings of the New Testament*, 290.

16

Drums of Redemption in the Pastoral Epistles

Although I hope to come to you soon, I am writing you these instructions so that, if I am delayed, you will know how people ought to conduct themselves in God's household, which is the church of the living God, the pillar and foundation of the truth. Beyond all question, the mystery from which true godliness springs is great:

He appeared in the flesh,
>was vindicated by the Spirit,

was seen by angels,
>was preached among the nations,

was believed on in the world,
>was taken up in glory.

1 Timothy 3:14–16

The Spirit clearly says that in later times some will abandon the faith and follow deceiving spirits and things taught by demons. Such teachings come through hypocritical liars, whose consciences have been seared as with a hot iron.

1 Timothy 4:1–2

Synopsis of the Pastoral Epistles

Three of Paul's letters are called the "Pastoral Epistles." They are 1 and 2 Timothy and Titus. As the name "Pastoral" implies, Paul wrote these letters to Timothy and Titus, two of his spiritual sons who were working as pastors at Ephesus and Crete respectively. The purpose of the letters is to give these pastors personal advice on church matters such as leadership, Christian conduct, false teaching, worship, and interpersonal relationships among believers.

The thrust of the Pastoral letters is "trustworthy management of God's household."[1] In these letters, Paul stresses that those who lead the church must do so from their good lifestyle. Likewise, believers must conduct themselves in a manner worthy of their calling so that the gospel message will be attractive to the unbelievers. Four overarching theological concerns dominate the Pastoral Epistles: sound doctrine, the church, the person and work of Christ, and suffering for the gospel of Christ. We will treat sound doctrine along with the nature of the church.

Key Theological Themes in the Pastoral Epistles

Although we do not have many theological themes in the Pastoral Epistles, three are worth mentioning.

Redemption and the Person of Christ

The Christology in the Pastoral Epistles is not limited to what is regarded as the "Christ Hymn" in 1 Timothy 3:16.[2] According to Willard M. Swartley,

> While the pastorals have often been viewed as accommodating to the prevailing cultural ethic on such matters as the role of women, submission of slaves, and subordination to government, they nevertheless present Jesus with Christological titles that suggest the Pastorals functioned to strengthen believers in their stance against the imperial cult.[3]

According to Swartley, the eastern emperors of the Roman Empire were addressed with the titles "Lord" (Greek *kyrios*) and "King of kings and Lord of lords." Even "Savior" or "Savior of the world" was bestowed upon Julius Caesar, Augustus, Claudius, Vespasian, Titus, and Hadrian. Therefore, addressing Jesus with the same titles was "a counter claim to Caesar's authority over their lives."[4]

---

1. deSilva, *Introducing the New Testament*, 732.
2. Strecker, *Theology of the New Testament*, 580.
3. Willard Swartley, *Covenant of Peace: The Missing Peace in New Testament Theology and Ethics* (Grand Rapids/Cambridge: Eerdmans, 2006), 251.
4. Swartley, *Covenant of Peace*, 252.

It follows that by acknowledging Jesus as Lord and Savior, the Christian believers who lived faithfully in the empire recognized "the rightful limited role of earthly kings and all those in high position, and also to be clear about who is the King of kings and Lord of lords."[5] Although the believers were urged to obey the earthly rulers and be good to all, they must have in mind that they function

> under the sovereignty of the true Savior (God/Jesus Christ) of all, performing their roles so that believers may live faithfully the Christian moral life and proclaim the gospel so that all may come to worship God, the king of all ages, and Jesus Christ, King of kings and Lord of lords. Hence, believers "wait for the blessed hope and the manifestation of the glory of our great God and Savior, Jesus Christ" (Tit. 2:13).[6]

Therefore, the Christology of the Pastoral Epistles is that Christ is "unique in relation to 'other Lords,'" in the words of Kwame Bediako.[7]

Redemption and the Nature of the Church

According to Paul, the church is the household of God (1 Tim 3:15). Therefore, all the instructions in the pastoral letters deal with matters that are pertinent to the household of God. Paul is strongly concerned about order as he mentions the various officers of the church and the conduct appropriate to those who hold those offices as well as members of the church community (1 Tim 3:1–12; Titus 1:5–9; 2:1–10). Because it is "the pillar and foundation of the truth" (1 Tim 3:15), the church must be led by credible leaders whose lives are above reproach (1 Tim 3:1–12). It is for this reason that the "most extended attention is given to the officers of the Ephesian church,"[8] namely the bishops (Greek *episkopos*), deacons (Greek *diakonos*), and elders (Greek *presbyteros*). By emphasizing the character qualities of leaders, Paul shows that integrity is more important than professional competence.

---

5. Swartley, 253.

6. Swartley, 253.

7. Kwame Bediako, *Jesus in Africa: The Christian Gospel in African History and Experience* (Akroppong-Akuapem, Ghana: Regnum Africa, 2000), 37. Bediako is speaking in the context of Jesus as Lord in evangelical Christian apologetics amid African religious pluralism.

8. Johnson, *Writings of the New Testament*, 442.

> Now the overseer is to be above reproach, faithful to his wife, temperate, self-controlled, respectable, hospitable, able to teach, not given to drunkenness, not violent but gentle, not quarrelsome, not a lover of money. He must manage his own family well and see that his children obey him, and he must do so in a manner worthy of full respect. (1 Tim 3:2–4)

Profession is mentioned once, that is "able to teach," while the rest of the qualifications have to do with credibility and character. Church leadership is about character. The Christian leader must be above reproach.

Similarly, Paul is also concerned about sound doctrine in the light of false teachers. According to James Nkansah-Obrempong,

> Theological heresy was seen by the apostles and the early church fathers as a serious and rebellious departure from established doctrine. In the Pastoral Epistles, the elders are instructed to teach sound doctrine and oppose false teaching (1 Tim 3:11–11; 4:1–16; 2 Tim 1:13–14; 4:1–5; Titus 1:9–2:1).[9]

That is why Paul tells Timothy, "As I urged you when I went into Macedonia, stay there in Ephesus so that you may command certain people not to teach false doctrines any longer or to devote themselves to myths and endless genealogies. Such things promote controversial speculations rather than advancing God's work – which is by faith" (1 Tim 1:3–4). The church must guard against the hypocritical false teachers whose goal is to seduce and lead astray by their doctrines taught by demons.[10] It is in the Pastoral Epistles that the term "knowledge" (*gnosis*) "is used as a heresiological term (1 Tim 6:20)."[11]

Paul places strong accent on good conduct and sound doctrine because the church is "the pillar and foundation of the truth" (1 Tim 3:15). The means of teaching sound doctrine and building character is the Scriptures. According to Paul, "All Scripture is God-breathed and is useful for teaching, rebuking, correcting and training in righteousness, so that the servant of God may be thoroughly equipped for every good work" (2 Tim 3:16–17). Sound doctrine is possible only by upholding the word of God as God-breathed. What guides the conduct of the members of the church is the word of God that is "useful for teaching, rebuking, correcting and training in righteousness." And the

---

9. James Nkansah-Obrempong, "Theological Heresy," in *Africa Bible Commentary*, ed. Tokunboh Adeyemo (Nairobi: WordAlive, 2006), 1553.

10. Hendriksen, *1 & 2 Thessalonians, 1 & 2 Timothy, Titus*, 146.

11. Strecker, *Theology of the New Testament*, 591.

leaders of the church, according to Paul, serve as the model of the Christian life (1 Tim 3:1–13; Titus 1:5–9).

Redemption and Suffering for the Gospel

The dominant theme in Paul's second letter to Timothy is Christian suffering. Paul shows that suffering is embedded in the Christian life. What he says to Timothy applies to the entire body of Christ. He tells Timothy, "So do not be ashamed of the testimony about our Lord or of me his prisoner. Rather, join with me in suffering for the gospel, by the power of God" (2 Tim 1:8). Paul uses his personal example of suffering for the gospel (1:12). He is a "model of suffering in hope."[12] He suffered unjust incarceration, bound with chains "like a criminal," and endured "everything for the sake of the elect, that they too may obtain the salvation that is in Christ Jesus" (2:9–10). Therefore, Timothy must also endure hardship like a good soldier, a good athlete, and a hardworking farmer (2:3–7). Again, Timothy is to learn from Paul's example of suffering for the gospel,

> You, however, know all about my teaching, my way of life, my purpose, faith, patience, love, endurance, persecutions, sufferings – what kinds of things happened to me in Antioch, Iconium and Lystra, the persecutions I endured. Yet the Lord rescued me from all of them. In fact, everyone who wants to live a godly life in Christ Jesus will be persecuted, while evildoers and impostors will go from bad to worse, deceiving and being deceived. (2 Tim 3:10–13)

Paul continued urging Timothy to endure hardship (4:5), and he names some of those who became the reason for his suffering for the gospel (4:14–18).

But because suffering is part of Christian experience, the believer is to respond in faith, trusting the grace and the power of God to persevere to the end. First, Paul told Timothy that he must not be ashamed to suffer for the sake of the gospel (2 Tim 1:8). Second, Timothy is to "be strong in the grace that is in Christ Jesus" (2:1, cf. 11–13). Third, Timothy must "Preach the word; be prepared in season and out of season; correct, rebuke and encourage – with great patience and careful instruction" (4:2). He must endure hardship as he does his work faithfully. But the incentive is that his "labor in the Lord is not in vain" (1 Cor 15:58). Paul said, "Now there is in store for me the crown of

---

12. Johnson, *Writings of the New Testament*, 438.

righteousness, which the Lord, the righteous Judge, will award to me on that day – and not only to me, but also to all who have longed for his appearing" (2 Tim 4:8). Therefore, "the point for Timothy is clear. He should not be cowardly but imitate the perseverance of Paul and 'take his share of suffering for the gospel.'"[13]

Questions for Review and Application

1. Why did Paul write the Pastoral Epistles?
2. What particular issues was Paul confronting in the Pastoral Epistles?
3. How do the Pastoral Epistles address the church in Africa with regards to sound doctrine and good conduct?
4. What are the qualities of a good church leader?
5. How do the Pastoral Epistles encourage your walk with the Lord?

---

13. Johnson, *Writings of the New Testament*, 438.

17

Drums of Redemption in Philemon

> I appeal to you for my son Onesimus, who became my son while I was in chains. Formerly he was useless to you, but now he has become useful both to you and to me.
> I am sending him – who is my very heart – back to you.
>
> Philemon 10–12

Synopsis of the Letter to Philemon

The Letter to Philemon is the shortest of Paul's letters. D. A. Carson and Douglas J. Moo state that the brevity of the letter and its personal nature cause many to question its place in the canon.[1] Philemon is Paul's private letter to a "dear friend and fellow worker" (Phlm 1). It is one of Paul's prison epistles and was written to a beloved friend whose commitment to church work was outstanding. The place of writing is associated with the Letter to the Colossians as both letters indicate that Timothy was the co-sender, and both letters mention Epaphras (Col 1:7; Phlm 23) and Archippus (Col 4:17; Phlm 2). Similarly, the two letters mention Mark, Aristarchus, Demas, and Luke as Paul's coworkers (Col 4:10, 14; Phlm 24). Moreover, mention is made of Onesimus in Colossians 4:9. "And since Onesimus is a resident of Colossae (Col. 4:9), we are safe in assuming that Philemon was also."[2] The assumption is that both letters were written at the same time, between AD 55–62.

---

1. D. A. Carson and Douglas J. Moo, *An Introduction to the New Testament*, 2nd ed. (Leicester: Apollos, 2005), 593.
2. Carson and Moo, *Introduction*, 592.

Onesimus, a slave of Philemon, appears to have run away from his master and headed for Rome. We are not sure how Onesimus wronged his master (Phlm 18–19). Similarly, the details of his encounter with Paul remain vague. What is certain is that in Rome, Onesimus met Paul who preached to him the good news of the gospel of salvation through Jesus Christ (10). Onesimus turned his life over to Jesus. With his life transformed, Onesimus became a faithful disciple of Paul. But knowing Onesimus' story, Paul did not want to keep him. He wanted to have Onesimus return to his master who was also a Christian. Paul now sends Onesimus back to Philemon, urging Philemon to accept his former slave not as a slave but as a brother. In this letter, Paul diplomatically encourages Christian brotherhood and forgiveness. The letter "is a carefully crafted witness to an emerging Christian ethos, showing both its power to transform symbols and attitudes and its struggle to transcend social forms."[3]

In Philemon, Paul's customary greetings appear in verses 1–3, followed by showers of gratitude to Philemon (4–7). Verses 8–21 are a summary of the circumstances surrounding Onesimus and his conversion. Verse 22 is Paul's personal request to Philemon. The final verses (23–25) are the greetings and a benediction. But are there theological concepts in this letter?

Key Theological Themes in the Letter to Philemon

Within this short letter, key theological themes emerge as follows:

Redemptive Love Subjugating Inhuman Institutions

Today many people question why the New Testament seems to be silent about the obnoxious practice of slavery. Does this appearance of silence mean that the New Testament writers condone or even affirm slavery? But the New Testament documents are not totally silent. Tucked within the body of the Letter to Philemon is Paul's subtle attack on the institution of slavery. Slavery was universally accepted in the Roman world. It was "an integral part of the ancient world; the whole society was built on it. Aristotle held that it was in the nature of things that certain men should be slaves, hewers of wood and drawers of water, to serve the higher classes of men."[4] However the society

---

3. Johnson, *Writings of the New Testament*, 387.

4. William Barclay, *The Letter to Timothy, Titus, and Philemon*, rev. ed. (Philadelphia: Westminster, 1975), 271.

viewed it, slavery remained a social problem because of its inhuman nature. Slavery's inhuman nature can be deduced from Paul's instructions to the church at Ephesus, "And masters, treat your slaves in the same way. Do not threaten them, since you know that he who is both their Master and yours is in heaven, and there is no favoritism with him" (Eph 6:9; cf. Col 4:1). Marshall, Travis, and Paul are right that "Paul issues guidance for the better running of the institution, but at the same time his stress on the kinship of masters and slaves *both in the Lord and in the flesh* (Gal 3:28; Phlm 16), in effect undermines the institution."[5] They also rightly observed that "Paul himself does not yet take that step of affirming that slavery is incompatible with this kinship [of masters and slaves], but that is the logical issue of his basic Christian understanding of humanity."[6] Meanwhile, Paul's perspective is stated in 1 Corinthians 7:21, "Were you a slave when you were called? Don't let it trouble you – although if you can gain your freedom, do so." This verse means that emancipation from slavery is the right thing, and those who can gain their freedom should do so.

The point is that Paul appeals to Philemon to forgive his errant slave and to accept him no longer as a bond servant but as a brother.[7] According to Carson and Moo, "the letter gives us a beautiful picture of the mutual love and respect that is to characterize the body of Christ at work."[8] Brotherly love overthrows the inhuman institution of slavery. Not only does Paul urge Philemon to pardon the wayward Onesimus, he urges Philemon to accept him as a brother. Redemptive love of God (Greek *agape*) flows through the veins of the redeemed. "We love because he first loved us" (1 John 4:19). The Pauline epistles are replete with the concept of the love of God that characterizes the life of his children (Rom 12:9–10; 13:8–10; 1 Cor 13:1–13; 16:14). In Philemon, redemptive love levels humanity and brings both slave and master under the cross of Calvary. Therefore, we see in the Letter to Philemon the subjugation of human institution of slavery.

---

5. Marshall, Travis, and Paul, *Exploring the New Testament*, 209, emphasis original.

6. Marshall, Travis, and Paul, 209.

7. In the ancient world people became slaves for various reasons, sometimes for set times and sometimes for life. People could become slaves if they were not able to pay off a debt or because of a crime they committed. A slave could also be a bond servant. Bond servants served their masters for a specific period of time and could regain their freedom after the period had elapsed.

8. Carson and Moo, *Introduction*, 593.

Redemptive Love as a Basis for Compassion and Reconciliation

Forgiveness and reconciliation are key themes in Paul's Letter to Philemon. Paul wanted to reconcile Philemon to his slave Onesimus. Reconciliation is a language of diplomacy "which was used extensively in Greek thought to refer to establishing peace between waring persons."[9] In this case the "waring persons" are Philemon and his slave. While one side may take the initiative for reconciliation, Paul assumes the role of a mediator and appeals to Philemon to forgive Onesimus. Philemon is acknowledged for his love for the brethren (Phlm 5). Therefore, Paul appeals to Philemon on the basis of love (9) to accept Onesimus as a Christian brother (16).

Questions for Review and Application

1. Why did Paul write the Letter to Philemon?
2. How does the letter address the practice of slavery in the first century?
3. How does the letter address human trafficking in Africa?
4. On what basis does Paul ask for reconciliation between Onesimus and Philemon?
5. How does the Letter to Philemon encourage you to practice God's love?

---

9. Marshall, Travis, and Paul, *Exploring the New Testament*, 198.

18

Drums of Redemption in Hebrews

In the past God spoke to our ancestors through the prophets at many times and in various ways, but in these last days he has spoken to us by his Son, whom he appointed heir of all things, and through whom also he made the universe. The Son is the radiance of God's glory and the exact representation of his being, sustaining all things by his powerful word. After he had provided purification for sins, he sat down at the right hand of the Majesty in heaven. So he became as much superior to the angels as the name he has inherited is superior to theirs.

Hebrews 1:1–4

Since the children have flesh and blood, he too shared in their humanity so that by his death he might break the power of him who holds the power of death – that is, the devil – and free those who all their lives were held in slavery by their fear of death. For surely it is not angels he helps, but Abraham's descendants. For this reason he had to be made like them, fully human in every way, in order that he might become a merciful and faithful high priest in service to God, and that he might make atonement for the sins of the people. Because he himself suffered when he was tempted, he is able to help those who are being tempted.

Hebrews 2:14–18

Synopsis of the Book of Hebrews

Three issues associated with the book of Hebrews include authorship, recipients, and literary composition. First, the author of the book of Hebrews is unknown to us. Similarly, "the second riddle centers on questions like, who were the addressees, and what were the occasioning circumstances?"[1] Third, scholars are concerned about the literary form of Hebrews since its genre as a letter is challenged. But as Isaak points out, "No explanation for its strange form has achieved consensus."[2] While Johnson calls Hebrews a "sermon,"[3] Isaak argues that, "it would not be unusual to situate Hebrews as a persuasive literary effort written by a gifted exegete and aimed at a general Christian audience."[4] But we will not dig into these matters.

The book of Hebrews is replete with concepts of continuity and discontinuity. For example, "In the past God spoke to our ancestors through the prophets at many times and in various ways, but in these last days he has spoken to us by his Son, whom he appointed heir of all things, and through whom also he made the universe" (Heb 1:1–2). God who spoke in the past continues to speak in the present.[5] Several passages allude to this fact (2:1–4; 3:5–8; 4:12–13).[6] But "the element of discontinuity is the agent that brings the word."[7] Prophets, angels, Moses, and the Torah as mediators of the word are contrasted with Christ. Jesus is superior to them all. It is obvious that "the word spoken through the Son holds a greater promise and a more certain fulfillment than that spoken of old (12:22–24)."[8]

Hebrews contains warnings and appeals to those in the audience who might be contemplating turning back from the faith which they once professed and returning to Judaism.[9] By way of analogical arguments, the author calls

---

1. Isaak, *New Testament Theology*, 194.
2. Isaak, 194.
3. Johnson, *Writings of the New Testament*, 463.
4. Isaak, *New Testament Theology*, 195.
5. Johnson, *Writings of the New Testament*, 463.
6. Johnson, 463.
7. Johnson, 464.
8. Johnson, 464.
9. Warning passages in the book include Heb 6:4–8; 10:26–31. Ray C. Stedman says, "Here the clashing proponents of Calvinism and Arminianism have wheeled and charged, unleashing thunderous volleys of acrimony against one another, only to generate much heat and little profit." Ray C. Stedman, *Hebrews*, The IVP New Testament Commentary Series, ed. Grant R. Osborne (Downers Grove: InterVarsity, 1992), 71. The key issue is whether "those who have once been enlightened, who have tasted the heavenly gift, who have shared in the Holy Spirit, who have tasted the goodness of the word of God and the powers of the coming age" and have still "fallen

upon the audience to consider the superiority of the person of Christ (Heb 1:1–2:18). The writer shows that Jesus is superior as the Son of God as well as superior in his ministry as the Son of Man. The author also demonstrates that Jesus is a better savior because of his preeminence and priesthood (3:1–8:5). In Christ we have a better security, a better sanctuary, and a better sacrifice. The author then concludes by the "superior principles" for Christian living which are by faith (11:1–40), the "wisdom of hope" (12:1–29), and the way of love (13:1–7).[10]

The writer of the book of Hebrews draws heavily from the Old Testament to support his arguments that Jesus "fulfills the OT intentions."[11] This means that the Old Testament is the primary source of the writer's understanding of the person and work of Christ.

Key Theological Themes in the Book of Hebrews

The subject of the book of Hebrews is Christ whom God appointed "heir of all things" (Heb 1:2). Therefore, the author's theological themes are structured around the figure of Christ, using the Old Testament as a framework "to show that what God spoke in fragmentary ways through the prophets (1:1), has now been fully revealed in Jesus, the Son who achieves God's purposes for humanity."[12] The writer of Hebrews cites four Old Testament texts – Psalm 8; 95; 110; and Jeremiah 31 – regarding the perfect humanity of Christ, God's promised rest,[13] the "new and eternal priesthood, and a new covenant which have been all fulfilled in the coming of Jesus Christ."[14] It is on the basis of the above that the writer exhorts his "fellow pilgrims" to commit themselves to a life of faith, obedience, and perseverance.

---

away" (Heb 6:4–6) are indeed real Christians or those who merely "tasted" what was offered to them. Some argue that true Christians can fall away from the faith, while others believe that those who fall away from the faith were never true Christians in the first place. However, a problem of the warning passages is reconciling them with other passages of Scripture that clearly teach perseverance of the saints, such as John 6:37–39, 65 and Rom 8:28–30. For more discussion on this topic, see D. H. Tongue, "The Concept of Apostasy in the Book of Hebrews," *Tyndale Bulletin* 5–6 (April 1960): 19–27.

10. See John Philips's detailed outline in *Exploring Hebrews: An Expository Commentary*, The John Philips Commentary Series (Grand Rapids: Kregel, 2002), table of contents.

11. Isaak, *New Testament Theology*, 195.

12. Isaak, 195.

13. A key promise in Hebrews is rest. For Israel, the promise of rest is Canaan. For the church, the promise of rest is heaven. And just as the wilderness journey was full of obstacles, the Christian pilgrimage is marked by strong constraints, hence the urge to persevere.

14. Isaak, *New Testament Theology*, 195–96.

The Redeemed and the Incomparable Christ

According to the author of Hebrews, Jesus the Son of God "is the radiance of God's glory and the exact representation of his being, sustaining all things by his powerful word. After he had provided purification for sins, he sat down at the right hand of the Majesty in heaven" (Heb 1:3). This exalted position makes him "as much superior to the angels as the name he has inherited is superior to theirs" (1:4). In Hebrews 1:5-2:18, the author contrasts Jesus with angels, using convincing proofs that the Son is superior to the angels. He is the Son of God. The angels worship the Son. The Son is the creator of the world. The Son sits at the right hand of God. Angels are ministering spirits. And "It is not to angels that he has subjected the world to come" (2:5). Finally, Jesus shared in the fate of humanity by suffering death on the cross in order to "break the power of him who holds the power of death – that is, the devil – and free those who all their lives were held in slavery by their fear of death" (2:14-15).

But the Son is also greater than Moses and Joshua, Israel's iconic leaders (Heb 3:1-4:13). Jesus was faithful to God who appointed him, "just as Moses was faithful in all God's house" (3:2). But Jesus "has been found worthy of greater honor than Moses, just as the builder of a house has greater honor than the house itself" (3:3). The comparison is between the faithfulness of a servant and that of a son. Moses was a servant in the house of God. "But Christ is faithful as the Son over God's house" (3:6a). And the house here refers to the believers in Christ, "if indeed we hold firmly to our confidence and the hope in which we glory" (3:6b).

The writer of Hebrews also contrasts Jesus with Joshua (Heb 4:1-10). Joshua led the people into the promised land. But Canaan is not the place of final and permanent rest for God's people. "For if Joshua had given them rest, God would not have spoken later about another day. There remains, then, a Sabbath-rest for the people of God" (4:8-9). Although Israel entered in the promised land, they persisted in disobedience. This final rest is obtained through Christ. "Let us, therefore, make every effort to enter that rest, so that no one will perish by following their example of disobedience" (4:11). As Richard D. Phillips well says, "It is ultimately heaven that is on the mind of the writer of Hebrews as he urges his readers to enter into the rest of God through faith in Christ."[15]

But Jesus is not only greater than Moses and Joshua; he also assumes a superior priesthood (Heb 4:14-7:28). His priesthood is in the order of

---

15. Richard D. Phillips, *Hebrews*, Reformed Expository Commentary (Phillipsburg: P&R, 2006), 124.

Melchizedek. Jesus is the great high priest who "ascended into heaven" (4:14), namely, the very presence of God. "Jesus offers an unrestricted supply of grace to anyone who will acknowledge a need for it and claim it (4:15–16)."[16] For this reason, the writer warns against turning away from Christ (5:11–6:20).

Moreover, Jesus doubles as royal high priest (8:1–6). "He is not only a priest but a king, and he sits on the throne of universal authority."[17] According to Psalm 110:1–4,

> The LORD says to my lord:
>
> "Sit at my right hand
> until I make your enemies
> a footstool for your feet."
>
> The LORD will extend your mighty scepter from Zion, saying,
> *"Rule in the midst of your enemies!"*
> Your troops will be willing
> on your day of battle.
> Arrayed in holy splendor,
> your young men will come to you
> like dew from the morning's womb.
>
> The LORD has sworn
> and will not change his mind:
> *"You are a priest forever,*
> in the order of Melchizedek. (emphasis added)

In addition to being a priestly king, Christ provided a superior covenant (Heb 8:1–13). As Lea rightly states,

> "1. The new covenant offered an internalization of the law. God wrote the law in the hearts and minds of his people (8:10).
>
> "2. Christ's covenant provided a new, direct knowledge of God (8:12).
>
> "3. The new covenant promised complete forgiveness of sin (8:12)."[18]

Finally, the author of Hebrews shows that Christ offered a superior sacrifice (Heb 9:1–10:18). Christ offered himself, which is far greater than the blood of animals offered by the Aaronic priesthood. The writer says,

---

16. Lea, *New Testament*, 511.
17. Stedman, *Hebrews*, 87.
18. Lea, *New Testament*, 512.

> But when Christ came as high priest of the good things that are now already here, he went through the greater and more perfect tabernacle that is not made with human hands, that is to say, is not a part of this creation. He did not enter by means of the blood of goats and calves; but he entered the Most Holy Place once for all by his own blood, thus obtaining eternal redemption. The blood of goats and bulls and the ashes of a heifer sprinkled on those who are ceremonially unclean sanctify them so that they are outwardly clean. How much more, then, will the blood of Christ, who through the eternal Spirit offered himself unblemished to God, cleanse our consciences from acts that lead to death, so that we may serve the living God! (Heb 9:11–14)

This passage means that Jesus's "mediation of salvation is once and for all an acceptable offering to God."[19] We see, then, that the author of Hebrews is convincing his readers that the key elements of Judaism such as prophets, angels, Moses, and the priesthood, among others, merely foreshadowed the coming of Christ, "the pioneer and perfecter of our faith" (Heb 12:2). But as the people of God failed to enter the rest through unbelief and disobedience, the same could happen to everyone who refuses to believe. Hence the call for perseverance.

The Redeemed and Steadfastness in the Pilgrimage

Interspersed in the book of Hebrews are a warning to pay attention (Heb 2:1–4); a warning against unbelief (3:7–19); a warning against apostasy or falling away (5:11–6:12); and calls to persevere in faith (10:19–39; 12:14–28). The audience is urged to "pay the most careful attention" to all they have heard and are cautioned against drifting away (2:1). They are particularly warned against unbelief, the greatest hindrance to entering the rest God promised his people. This warning is followed by a more severe warning against falling away (6:4–8). But what is the essence of these warning passages? According to Isaak,

> Hebrews narrates the journey of discipleship as one of gradual learning and becoming the one whom God always intended, through a series of educational choices and decisions. Hebrews's Christology develops the exhortation to Christian discipleship. The human experience of learning, suffering, and growing shapes

---

19. Johnson, *Writings of the New Testament*, 471.

Christians in the pattern of Jesus, the one who confirmed his identity as God's Son, the Messiah, by faithfully reaching out to others – by being made "perfect" in the sense of completing or filling out what was his identity from the start (5:8–9).[20]

According to Isaak, Jesus's faithfulness provides encouragement for others to be faithful. On the whole, what characterizes the pilgrimage journey is a life of perseverance in faith and obedience. The disciples of Jesus respond to his saving work by faith and perseverance in the face of all sorts of dangers and attractions and distractions of sin. Therefore, "Hebrews stresses the urgent call to faithful obedience and endurance, even through testing; and this remains the identifying characteristic of God's people from the beginning."[21] This obedience and endurance is attested by the long catalog of heroes and heroines of faith in 11:1–40.

The Redeemed and Steadfastness in Faith

The writer of Hebrews contrasts the life of unbelief and the life of faith. Unbelief is refusing to trust God. Faith is believing or trusting God. But what is the nature of faith? It is important that we understand the nature of faith in a broader sense. Generally speaking, there are three dimensions of faith in the New Testament:

1. Saving faith (John 3:16; Rom 10:9–11; Eph 2:8–9). Saving faith is trusting the Lord Jesus for the salvation of one's soul. The apostle Paul put it this way:

   > If you declare with your mouth, "Jesus is Lord," and believe in your heart that God raised him from the dead, you will be saved. For it is with your heart that you believe and are justified, and it is with your mouth that you profess your faith and are saved. As Scripture says, "Anyone who believes in him will never be put to shame." (Rom 10:9–11)

2. Doctrinal faith (1 Tim 3:9; 2 Pet 1:1; Jude 3). Doctrinal faith is the body of truths or belief system that is embraced by a person or group of people. Therefore, the writer of Jude says, "Dear friends,

---

20. Isaak, *New Testament Theology*, 199.
21. Isaak, 199.

although I was very eager to write to you about the salvation we share, I felt compelled to write and urge you to contend for the faith that was once for all entrusted to God's holy people" (3). Similarly, Paul wrote concerning deacons, "They must keep hold of the deep truths of the faith with a clear conscience" (1 Tim 3:9). The "deep truths of the faith" here are the body of doctrines or beliefs held by the church. There are different kinds of belief systems or faiths in the world. They include the Christian faith; the Islamic faith; the Buddhist faith; and the Hindu faith.

3. Receiving faith (Matt 8:5–13; 17:20; Mark 11:22–24; Luke 17:19; John 14:12). This kind of faith receives both temporal and permanent blessings from the Lord. It is believing God to do even what is seemingly impossible. This is the faith that moves mountains.

Hebrews chapter 11 is called the hallmark of faith or "faith made visible."[22] Here the writer of Hebrews defines faith broadly, "Now faith is confidence in what we hope for and assurance about what we do not see" (Heb 11:1). Similarly, the writer says that "without faith it is impossible to please God, because anyone who comes to him must believe that he exists and that he rewards those who earnestly seek him" (11:6). This means that faith embraces realities beyond the visible. God is not visible; but we believe that he exists. And the catalog of heroes and heroines of faith in the entire chapter proves that walking by faith is crucial for receiving what God has promised. Some of the heroes and heroines of faith are Abel, Enoch, Noah, Abraham, Isaac, Jacob, Joseph, Moses, Rahab, Barak, Samson, Jephthah, David, Samuel, and the prophets. All of these "ancients" were commended for their faith. By faith some of them "shut the mouths of lions, quenched the fury of the flames, and escaped the edge of the sword; whose weakness was turned to strength; and who became powerful in battle and routed foreign armies. Women received back their dead, raised to life again" (Heb 11:33–35a).

But the complexity of faith is imbedded in the narratives as well.

> There were others who were tortured, refusing to be released so that they might gain an even better resurrection. Some faced jeers and flogging, and even chains and imprisonment. They were put to death by stoning; they were sawed in two; they were killed by the sword. They went about in sheepskins and goatskins, destitute, persecuted and mistreated – the world was not worthy of them.

---

22. Stedman, *Hebrews*, 116.

> They wandered in deserts and mountains, living in caves and in holes in the ground.
> These were all commended for their faith, yet none of them received what had been promised, since God had planned something better for us so that only together with us would they be made perfect. (Heb 11:35b–40)

Contrary to popular theology, faith is not a guarantee that things will always go well with us and according to our own terms. The heroes of faith trusted the Lord in adversity as well. Like Paul, they believed that their "light and momentary troubles" were achieving for them "an eternal glory that far outweighs them all." Therefore, they fixed their eyes "not on what is seen, but on what is unseen, since what is seen is temporary, but what is unseen is eternal" (2 Cor 4:17–18). Some of these heroes and heroines of faith in Hebrews 11 "were still living by faith when they died. They did not receive the things promised; they only saw them and welcomed them from a distance, admitting that they were foreigners and strangers on earth" (Heb 11:13). But God commended them for their faith.

Christians walk by faith, not by sight (2 Cor 5:7). They "know that in all things God works for the good of those who love him, who have been called according to his purpose" (Rom 8:28). Therefore, they radiate faith in God even when life does not go their own way. That is biblical faith as exemplified by the heroes and heroines of faith.

Questions for Review and Application

1. What arguments does the writer of Hebrews advance to show that Jesus is superior to the angels?
2. How is Jesus greater than Moses and Joshua?
3. How is Jesus's priesthood superior to the Aaronic priesthood?
4. How would you explain Hebrews 6:4–8? Does this passage teach the doctrine that Christians can lose their salvation? Please explain.
5. How does the book of Hebrews address the issues of Christians who are returning to African traditional religions in some parts of Africa or are deserting the Christian faith altogether as a result of terrorism or other forms of persecution?
6. How does the book of Hebrews encourage your walk with the Lord?

19

Drums of Redemption in James

> If any of you lacks wisdom, you should ask God, who gives generously to all without finding fault, and it will be given to you. But when you ask, you must believe and not doubt, because the one who doubts is like a wave of the sea, blown and tossed by the wind. That person should not expect to receive anything from the Lord. Such a person is double-minded and unstable in all they do.
>
> James 1:5–8

> Do not merely listen to the word, and so deceive yourselves. Do what it says. Anyone who listens to the word but does not do what it says is like someone who looks at his face in a mirror and, after looking at himself, goes away and immediately forgets what he looks like. But whoever looks intently into the perfect law that gives freedom, and continues in it – not forgetting what they have heard, but doing it – they will be blessed in what they do.
>
> James 1:22–25

Synopsis of the Epistle of James

The writer of James identifies himself as "a servant of God and of the Lord Jesus Christ" (Jas 1:1). It is believed that this James is the brother of Jesus who came to faith after the death and resurrection of Christ (cf. Acts 12:17; 15:13; 21:18; Gal 1:19; Jude 1:1). The letter is a catholic epistle sent to the "twelve tribes scattered among the nations" (Jas 1:1).

The Epistle of James was called a "right straw epistle" by the Reformer Martin Luther who believed that the book contradicted the gospel of salvation by faith alone. For Luther, the Epistle of James lacked "gospel character," or did not point people to Christ.¹ But we must realize that Luther was not echoing the views of the early church because the early church saw the book of James as "a powerful moral exhortation."² Luther's views had to do with his personal experience as a religious monk in the Roman Catholic church and his new understanding of faith and righteousness taught in the book of Romans. Because of "a few misunderstood verses" such as James 2:14–26, Luther concluded that James taught the theology of salvation by works rather than by grace through faith.³

In this epistle, James instructs his readers on "practical obedience"⁴ such as how to respond to trials (Jas 1:2–18); self-control (1:19–21); responding to the word of God (1:22–27); avoiding partiality (2:1–13); producing good works (2:14–26); controlling the tongue (3:1–12); renouncing false wisdom and embracing true wisdom (3:13–18); renouncing worldly behavior (4:1–12); renouncing arrogance and the lure of wealth (4:13–5:6); and demonstrating endurance (5:7–20).⁵ Looking at the content above, James appears to be like a commentary on the Beatitudes in Matthew 5:1–12.

Key Theological Themes in the Epistle of James

James is a book of moral exhortation "to sound faith and practice for God's people everywhere (i.e., 'the twelve tribes')."⁶ The dominant mood of the epistle is the imperative.⁷ Like Israel's wisdom literature (Proverbs, Ecclesiastes, Sirach), "James is not driven by a particular logic or by a sustained argument or a rhetorical device."⁸ Instead, like wisdom literature, the author is driven by "short, pithy sayings offering practical, ethical instructions dealing with the observable realities of life."⁹ But is there also a theology in the book of James? According to Johnson, the ethic in James is "in the strictest sense a theological ethic."¹⁰ Interwoven in the moral and ethical exhortations are the

---

1. Johnson, *Writings of the New Testament*, 507.
2. Johnson, 507.
3. Johnson, 507.
4. Stott, *Men with a Message*, 122.
5. Lea, *New Testament*, 526–31.
6. Isaak, *New Testament Theology*, 204.
7. Johnson, *Writings of the New Testament*, 507.
8. Isaak, *New Testament Theology*, 205.
9. Isaak, 205.
10. Johnson, *Writings of the New Testament*, 507.

theological propositions of the book of James. Peter H. Davids extracts eight areas on which James speaks.[11] These include suffering or testing, eschatology, Christology, poverty-piety, law, grace and faith, wisdom, and prayer. According to Davids, "the Christology of James is an assumed Christology."[12] We will examine some of these theological propositions.

Christian Trials and Temptations

James opens by instructing believers on how to handle trials and temptations. According to him, faith is demonstrated when it is put to the test. In other words, patient endurance in times of trials prove that our faith is genuine. Therefore, rather than mourning, believers are to "Consider it pure joy, my brothers and sisters, whenever you face trials of many kinds" (Jas 1:2). Trials and temptations are designed to produce perseverance "so that you may be mature and complete, not lacking anything" (1:4). These verses mean that trials, which come in diverse forms, accomplish God's purposes in the life of the believer. Trials are part of the testing of faith. God permits them for the maturing of the believer.

However, the believer must not conclude that God is the author of temptations. "For God cannot be tempted by evil, nor does he tempt anyone" (Jas 1:13). Rather, people are tempted by their human desires which drag them into sin. God, the giver of "Every good and perfect gift" (1:17) cannot be responsible for tempting his children.

Christian Faith in Practice

Similarly, Christian faith must be practical. The Christian community is one that practices what they believe. One aspect in which Christian faith must be seen in practice is avoiding partiality or favoritism in the community of believers (Jas 2:1–13). Partiality dehumanizes the one who is belittled in the eyes of the congregation.

James also expounds the theology of good works. Good works are demonstrations of faith (Jas 2:14–26). They are the proof that one has a living faith because "faith by itself, if it is not accompanied by action, is dead" (2:17). In other words, faith produces good works. This idea is not incongruent with

---

11. Peter H. Davids, *The Epistle of James: A Commentary on the Greek Text* (Grand Rapids: Eerdmans, 1982), 35.

12. Davids, 39.

the rest of Scripture. For example, Paul commended the Thessalonian believers by saying, "We remember before our God and Father *your work produced by faith*, your labor prompted by love, and your endurance inspired by hope in our Lord Jesus Christ" (1 Thess 1:3, emphasis added).

The practicality of Christian faith includes listening and responding to God's word (Jas 1:19–27). Listening to the word of the Lord and not putting it into practice is self-deception. Jesus likens such a hearer to a foolish builder who built his house upon the sand (Matt 7:26–27). Such a house cannot endure wind and rain. Likewise, people who do not put the word of God into practice cannot endure the trials and temptations that come their way because they lack the foundation upon which to rest their lives.

James 1:26–27 is referred to as "the three pillars of the Christian life."[13] As a summary of his message, James outlines the heart of true religion as keeping "a tight rein" on the tongue; looking after widows and orphans; and keeping "oneself from being polluted by the world." James picks up taming the tongue again in 3:1–12 and elaborates on it. According to James, the untamed tongue is a destructive fire, setting others and oneself ablaze (3:5–6). Regrettably, the same tongue is used for praise and worship of God as well as cursing (3:9–10). This is not acceptable before the Lord.

Christians and True Wisdom in Practice

Wisdom involves good sense and wise decisions. But the world's wisdom usually involves outsmarting others for personal advantage. In James 3:13–5:12, "the wisdom that comes from heaven is first of all pure; then peace-loving, considerate, submissive, full of mercy and good fruit, impartial and sincere" (3:17). True wisdom is submission to God rather than quarreling and fighting driven by covetousness (4:1–3). The life of covetousness is human wisdom, and at worst friendship with the world. The severe warning from James is, "You adulterous people, don't you know that friendship with the world means enmity against God? Therefore, anyone who chooses to be a friend of the world becomes an enemy of God" (4:4).

The wise come near to God in submission. And those who submit to God can resist the devil (Jas 4:7). Submission to God means getting rid of sins in one's life. James urges the reader, "Come near to God and he will come near to you. Wash your hands, you sinners, and purify your hearts, you double-minded. Grieve, mourn and wail. Change your laughter to mourning and

---

13. Stott, *Men with a Message*, 125.

your joy to gloom. Humble yourselves before the Lord, and he will lift you up" (4:8–10).

True wisdom, says James, avoids slandering one another (Jas 4:11–12), shuns boasting about tomorrow and leaving God's will out of one's plans (4:13–17), eschews putting hope in material wealth, and refuses to oppress the poor and needy (5:1–6).

Christians and Patience in Suffering in Light of Future Hope

James encourages believers to be patient in suffering in view of their eschatological hope.

> Be patient, then, brothers and sisters, until the Lord's coming. See how the farmer waits for the land to yield its valuable crop, patiently waiting for the autumn and spring rains. You too, be patient and stand firm, because the Lord's coming is near. Don't grumble against one other, brothers and sisters, or you will be judged. The Judge is standing at the door! (Jas 5:7–9)

The hope of the Lord's coming outweighs the pain of trials and temptation. They are temporary. Like the apostle Paul said, "For our light and momentary troubles are achieving for us an eternal glory that far outweighs them all. So we fix our eyes not on what is seen, but on what is unseen, since what is seen is temporary, but what is unseen is eternal" (2 Cor 4:17–18).

Therefore in the light of the imminent coming of Jesus, the Judge, the believer is to be patient in suffering, like a farmer waiting for the land to yield its crops. Every trouble with an imminent expiry date is endurable. The believer's examples are the prophets "who spoke in the name of the Lord" (Jas 5:10) and "Job's perseverance" (5:11). They are part of the "great cloud of witnesses" (Heb 12:1) in suffering for the Lord.

Questions for Review and Application

1. What are the key theological issues addressed in James? Which among them are relevant for the church in Africa?
2. What trials and temptations are Christians facing in your country today?
3. What is dead faith?
4. What is the place of good works in the life of a Christian?

5. Why is favoritism forbidden? How does favoritism destroy the church?
6. What does James say about the use of the tongue?
7. How does the Epistle of James encourage your walk with the Lord?

20

Drums of Redemption in 1 Peter

> Praise be to the God and Father of our Lord Jesus Christ! In his great mercy he has given us new birth into a living hope through the resurrection of Jesus Christ from the dead, and into an inheritance that can never perish, spoil or fade. This inheritance is kept in heaven for you, who through faith are shielded by God's power until the coming of the salvation that is ready to be revealed in the last time. In all this you greatly rejoice, though now for a little while you may have had to suffer grief in all kinds of trials. These have come so that the proven genuineness of your faith – of greater worth than gold, which perishes even though refined by fire – may result in praise, glory and honor when Jesus Christ is revealed.
>
> 1 Peter 1:3–7

The Synopsis of the Letter 1 Peter

Peter is one of the twelve disciples of Jesus. He wrote to Christians in the northern parts of Asia Minor – Pontus, Galatia, Cappadocia, Asia, and Bithynia. These Christians were experiencing persecution because of their faith. Therefore, the overarching message of the book is perseverance in suffering.[1] Peter emphasizes joy and hope in suffering. Key points in the book include the believer's living hope, holiness, following the example of Christ in suffering, and living as the unique people of God in a pagan culture.

---

1. Sean Christensen, "Reborn Participants in Christ: Recovering the Importance of Union with Christ in 1 Peter," *JETS* 61, no. 2 (2018): 339–54.

Key Theological Themes of the Letter 1 Peter

Although 1 Peter resonates with many theological themes, three stand out: the elect people of God, participation in the suffering of Christ, and Christ's victory over evil.

Redemption as the Elect People of God[2]

As Christopher J. H. Wright rightly points out, "Peter connects his Christian readers with the whole heritage of Old Testament Israel."[3] And throughout the epistle, Peter sees the church as a distinct community in relation to the surrounding pagan culture, just like Israel is a distinct community. It is in this context that we may understand Peter's use of the words "foreigners and exiles" (1 Pet 2:11).

Peter opens with the believers' identity as "God's elect . . . who have been chosen according to the foreknowledge of God the Father" (1 Pet 1:1–2). This choice, according to verse 3, is based solely on God's mercy: "In his great mercy he has given us new birth into a living hope through the resurrection of Jesus Christ from the dead."

Christian identity as the people of God is cast using two images. The first is "the living Stone." Jesus is the foundation stone of the house of God. He was "rejected by humans but chosen by God" (1 Pet 2:4). He is the living Stone because he rose from the grave and now lives forever. As their head is a living Stone, Christians are also living stones (2:5). J. De Wa Al Dryden says, "That Christians are called 'living stones' shows that their life and identity are drawn from connection with Christ."[4]

The second image is a house. It is a "spiritual house" because this holy household is comprised of the elect of God (1 Pet 2:5). All the members of this household are bound together, not by the physical blood of human beings or relatives, but by the Spirit of the Lord. As it says in Hebrews 3:1–2, "Therefore, holy brothers and sisters, who share in the heavenly calling, fix your thoughts

---

2. The church as the elect people of God raises the theological question of the place of Israel. Does the church replace ethnic Israel (replacement theology)? Are there two covenants or one? Is Christianity a separate religion from Judaism? As Marshall, Travis, and Paul well say, "Christians must think about this sensitively in the light of a long history of anti-Semitism." *Exploring the New Testament*, 267.

3. Christopher J. H. Wright, *The Mission of God: Unlocking the Bible's Grand Narrative* (Nottingham: Inter-Varsity, 2006), 387.

4. J. De Wa Al Dryden, *Theology and Ethics in 1 Peter: Strategies for Christian Character Formation* (Tübingen: Mohr Siebeck, 2006), 120.

on Jesus, whom we acknowledge as our apostle and high priest. He was faithful to the one who appointed him, *just as Moses was faithful in all God's house*" (emphasis added). All those who are in Christ belong to the family of God, the house of God. For they have become one body with "one Lord, one faith, one baptism; one God and Father of all, who is over all and through all and in all" (Eph 4:4–5). Dryden says, "The spiritual house constitutes the root metaphor for Christian community in 1 Peter, the fundamental concept that identifies the collective identity of the Christians, their relation to God and to one another, and the basis of their behavior as a family or brotherhood."[5]

Again, in Christ Jesus God chose a new family, a spiritual family that is called "a holy priesthood" and "a royal priesthood, a holy nation, God's special possession" (1 Pet 2:5, 9). This imagery is taken from Exodus 19:5–6, "Although the whole earth is mine, you will be for me a kingdom of priests and a holy nation." Israel is the nation set apart by God as his elect people. And now the title given by God to Israel is transferred to the church. This means that there is now a reconfigured Israel made up of Jews and Gentiles.

The purpose or vocation of the church as "a holy priesthood" is to offer "spiritual sacrifices acceptable to God" (1 Pet 2:5). As the literal sacrifices were acts of worship to God, so are the spiritual sacrifices. Believers' sacrifices are no longer animal and ceremonial sacrifices. As Paul says, "Therefore, I urge you, brothers and sisters, in view of God's mercy, to offer your bodies as living sacrifices, holy and pleasing to God – this is your spiritual act of worship" (Rom 12:1). The church is to offer praise to God and proclaim his deeds.

As the elect people of God, believers must

> not grow too comfortable within the structures of our particular cultures but orient ourselves by our primary identification as a "royal priesthood" of God. However, life as resident aliens does not mean becoming dangerous or a threat to the social fabric, but living as a sign of authentic life in contrast to the culture of death, dysfunction, and destruction, wherever it may be found.[6]

Hence Peter says, "Live such good lives among the pagans that, though they accuse you of doing wrong, they may see your good deeds and glorify God on the day he visits us" (1 Pet 2:12). Living this good life includes submission to constituted governing authorities; using one's freedom to please the Lord rather

---

5. Dryden, *Theology and Ethics in 1 Peter*, 123.
6. Isaak, *New Testament Theology*, 212.

than "as a cover up for evil"; showing "proper respect to everyone"; loving "the family of the believers"; fearing God; and "honoring the emperor" (2:13–17).

Redemption as Joyful Participation in the Suffering of Christ

The theme of Christian suffering is expressed in 1 Peter 2:21, "To this you were called, because Christ suffered for you, leaving you an example, that you should follow in his steps." Stuart Briscoe says, "Christians have a unique approach to suffering. We recognize that we don't understand many aspects of suffering, but we do understand that God identified himself with humanity in its suffering."[7] The imitation of Christ marks the life of the believer. According to Howard, Travis, and Paul, "Peter writes vividly of the significance of the suffering of Christ" as part of his "strategy for encouraging his readers to face suffering."[8] The key passages that allude to the suffering of Christ include 1 Peter 1:18–19; 2:21–24; 3:18. According to Peter, "Jesus' death was not a ghastly accident."[9] Instead, the Righteous One died for the unrighteous in order to bring these unrighteous to God. His suffering and death also serve as an example for the believers to follow. Therefore, Peter shows that suffering can be God's will for the believer as God works out his own purposes (3:17–18).

In 1 Peter 3:13–4:19, the apostle appeals to the persecuted believers to be patient in suffering. But this section also poses a theological conundrum regarding Christ's descent into Hades, which is treated below. Peter also assures faithful servants of the Lord that they will receive their reward when the Chief Shepherd appears (5:1–4).

Redemption as Christ's Descent into Hades and Victory over Evil

A theological riddle in 1 Peter is found in 3:18–20. The apostle wrote,

> For Christ also suffered once for sins, the righteous for the unrighteous, to bring you to God. He was put to death in the body but made alive in the Spirit. After being made alive, *he went and made proclamation to the imprisoned spirits* – to those who were disobedient long ago when God waited patiently in the days of Noah while the ark was being built. (emphasis added)

---

7. Stuart Briscoe, *1 Peter: Holy Living in a Hostile World*, Understanding the Books Series (Chicago: Harold Shaw, 1993), 145.

8. Marshall, Travis, and Paul, *Exploring the New Testament*, 266.

9. Stott, *Men with a Message*, 135.

What is the identity of these "imprisoned spirits"? And in 1 Peter 4:6 we find that "the gospel was preached even to those who are now dead." What was the essence of this preaching? Does not the Bible say "people are destined to die once, and after that to face judgment" in Hebrews 9:27?

According to Marshall, Travis, and Paul, the "imprisoned spirits" refer to supernatural powers who are imprisoned, "held captive to await the final judgement."[10] This view follows the Jewish tradition that equates the "fallen angels" with "sons of God" (Gen 6:1–4) "who seduced women on earth in the period before the Flood."[11] This tradition of fallen angels being in prison, already familiar in New Testament times, is reflected in 2 Peter 2:4 and Jude 6. The problem in these 1 Peter texts can be understood partly by considering the nuances in which the Greek word translated "made proclamation" and "preached" is used in the original text. The verb can mean "proclaim," "announce," "mention publicly," and "preach." When preaching is meant, it is in reference to God's saving work. But proclamation can also mean an announcement of victory or simply proclamation as in Revelation 5:2: "And I saw a mighty angel proclaiming in a loud voice, 'Who is worthy to break the seals and open the scroll?'" In both 1 Peter 3:19 and Revelation 5:2, the same Greek word *kerussō* is employed. In the light of this use, Marshall, Travis, and Paul conclude,

> It seems best here to translate "proclaim victory," in view of the emphasis in v. 22 [1 Pet 3:22] that the ascended Christ is victorious over "angels, authorities, and powers." Through this vivid – but difficult – imagery or mythology Peter is assuring his readers that they have nothing to fear from those who threaten and oppress them. Christ has defeated the forces of evil, both supernatural and human, and will ultimately bring them to judgement.[12]

Similarly, Ladd points out that this preaching may not have involved the offer of salvation, "but the triumphant announcement that through his death and resurrection, Christ had broken the power of the spirit world."[13]

Related to the above is 1 Peter 4:6 where the apostle categorically wrote, "For this is the reason the gospel was preached even to those who are now dead, so that they might be judged according to human standards in regard

---

10. Marshall, Travis, and Paul, *Exploring the New Testament*, 268.
11. Marshall, Travis, and Paul, 268.
12. Marshall, Travis, and Paul, *Exploring the New Testament*, 268.
13. Ladd, *Theology of the New Testament*, 648.

to the body, but live according to God in regard to the spirit." But this verse is to be understood as those who had not heard the gospel while they were alive and are now dead.[14]

Questions for Review and Application

1. Do you perceive a moral demarcation between believers and unbelievers in your community? Please explain.
2. How does Peter encourage Christian unity? What concept clearly brings this encouragement?
3. The apostle Peter says that Christian suffering is an imitation of Christ's suffering. In what ways is this true of the suffering of Christians in Africa, specifically Nigeria, and in other parts of the world?
4. How does 1 Peter encourage your walk with the Lord?

---

14. Marshall, Travis, and Paul, *Exploring the New Testament*, 268.

21

Drums of Redemption in 2 Peter and Jude

Truth is incontrovertible. Panic may resent it; ignorance may deride it; malice may distort it; but there it is.

Winston Churchill[1]

His divine power has given us everything we need for a godly life through our knowledge of him who called us by his own glory and goodness. Through these he has given us his very great and precious promises, so that through them you may participate in the divine nature, having escaped the corruption in the world caused by evil desires.

2 Peter 1:3–4

Dear friends, although I was very eager to write to you about the salvation we share, I felt compelled to write and urge you to contend for the faith that was once for all entrusted to God's holy people. For certain individuals whose condemnation was written about long ago have secretly slipped in among you. They are ungodly people, who pervert the grace of our God into a license for immorality and deny Jesus Christ our only Sovereign and Lord.

Jude 1:3–4

---

1. Winston Churchill quoted in Brown, *Scandalous Freedom*, 180.

The Synopsis of the Letters 2 Peter and Jude

According to the opening (2 Pet 1:1–2), the author of 2 Peter is Simon Peter, one of the apostles of Jesus Christ.[2] The audience had already received a letter from him (3:1) as well as a letter from Paul (3:15). The author was also an eyewitness of the transfiguration of Jesus (1:16–18; cf. Matt 17:1–8).

The similarities between 2 Peter and Jude have caused much theological discussion among scholars. What is responsible for the "substantial overlap of material between them"?[3] Are both drawing from a common source (oral or written), or is one copying from the other? Our purpose is not to pursue these arguments by modern scholars. Rather, this discussion is mentioned to stimulate the reader to pursue further study of the parallels in the two letters.

Second Peter and Jude beat the drums of war against false teachers. According to the two letters, the deceit of false teachers is a spiritual disaster. These "ignorant" and "unstable" (2 Pet 3:16) deceivers peddle "cleverly devised stories" (2 Pet 1:16) capable of shipwrecking the faith of many in the Christian community. And it is for this reason that "growth in grace and knowledge of our Lord and Savior Jesus Christ" (2 Pet 3:18) is "indispensable" in order to "rescue the young believers from spiritual disaster."[4] Both 2 Peter and Jude were written "to motivate believers to adhere to the integrity of their Christian identity and not to be sidetracked by distracting behaviors and practices."[5] And both authors warn against sin and the judgment to come and call the true believers to persevere in the faith. Unfortunately, though, "2 Peter and Jude could lay claim to being the two least valued and noticed books of the New Testament. Their special contribution to Christian living lies unrecognized and unread at the back of most Bibles."[6]

---

2. Many modern scholars reject Peter's authorship of 2 Peter on the grounds of style, claiming that the style is different from 1 Peter. Many words found in 2 Peter are absent in 1 Peter. Similarly, some reason that Peter, a Galilean fisherman, could not have exhibited sophisticated knowledge of Hellenistic religious and philosophical culture. Other reasons for rejecting Peter's authorship are that the letter reflects a late date, placing it around AD 80–120, and the fact that the early church was slow to include the letter in the canonical writings. See Marshall, Travis, and Paul, *Exploring the New Testament*, 282. The evangelical position is that the early church did not classify this book outside the canon among the books with false names and titles (the New Testament Pseudepigrapha). They believed that 2 Peter was written by Peter, and their view has been the evangelical position on the authorship of this book.

3. Marshall, Travis, and Paul, *Exploring the New Testament*, 268.

4. Dick Lucas and Christopher Green, *The Message of 2 Peter and Jude*, The Bible Speaks Today (Leicester: Inter-Varsity, 1995), 17.

5. Isaak, *New Testament Theology*, 219.

6. Lucas and Green, *Message of 2 Peter and Jude*, 9. See also Marshall, Travis, and Paul, *Exploring the New Testament*, 275.

Jude is known as "a brother of James" (Jude 1). His audience is uncertain. But the theme of his letter is *contending for the faith* (3). The writer confronts the error of false teachers who were distorting the grace of God and turning it "into a license for immorality" and denying "Jesus Christ, our only Sovereign and Lord" (4). They distorted the message of grace to mean that Christians are now free to live the way they please. Theological words for this thinking are "antinomianism" or "lawless libertinism."

Key Theological Themes in the Letters 2 Peter and Jude

The letters to second Peter and Jude address similar theological issues. They include:

The Inspiration and Trustworthiness of Scripture

According to Ladd, 2 Peter holds a distinctive place of significance because of its teaching about Scripture. Ladd states, "2 Peter has one of the classic statements about inspiration in the entire Bible."[7] In defense of Scripture, Peter wrote, "Above all, you must understand that no prophecy of Scripture came about by the prophet's own interpretation of things. For prophecy never had its origin in the human will, but prophets, though human, spoke from God as they were carried along by the Holy Spirit" (2 Pet 1:20–21). Ladd believes that the first part of the text was probably a counteraction against the "gnostic enthusiasts who claimed to have a new word from God that supplemented the received gospel."[8] Since the New Testament canon was not yet collected when Peter wrote, it is understood that he meant the Old Testament Scriptures.

But even in Peter's time, the Pauline writings were viewed as Scripture and equally trustworthy. Peter says,

> Bear in mind that our Lord's patience means salvation, just as our dear brother Paul also wrote you with the wisdom that God gave him. He writes the same way in all his letters, speaking in them of these matters. His letters contain some things that are hard to understand, which ignorant and unstable people distort, as they do the other Scriptures, to their own destruction. (2 Pet 3:15–16)

---

7. Ladd, *Theology of the New Testament*, 652.
8. Ladd, 652.

Inspiration means that the word of God is infallible and totally trustworthy because those who received it were moved by the Spirit of God.

Sin and the Doom of the Ungodly

What methods do the false teachers use when infiltrating God's people? According to 2 Peter and Jude, the ungodly secretly and deceptively worm their way in and introduce their destructive teachings among God's people (2 Pet 2:1–4; Jude 4–5). These techniques are better seen when tabulated as below:

2 Peter 2:1–2	Jude 4
[1]But there were also false prophets among the people, just as there will be false teachers among you. They will secretly introduce destructive heresies, even denying the sovereign Lord who bought them – bringing swift destruction on themselves. [2]Many will follow their depraved conduct and will bring the way of truth into disrepute.	[4]For certain individuals whose condemnation was written about long ago have secretly slipped in among you. They are ungodly people, who pervert the grace of our God into a license for immorality and deny Jesus Christ our only Sovereign and Lord.

Secrecy is the key. In the animal world, camouflage is not only for self-defense. It is one of the best ways of misleading the prey. For example, the weaver ant is a ferocious soldier. He would rather die than to relinquish his territory. My knowledge of the weaver ant goes back to my childhood of growing up in the village. The brown weaver ants make their home in the trees by weaving several leaves together into a beautiful nest. There are usually several of those nests clustered on a single branch. Their architectural design is marvelous. The ants lay their eggs inside the ball-shaped nest, and there are always soldiers on guard at the entrance of the nest. No animal or human being is able to penetrate into the camp of the weaver ant without being attacked. As children looking for fruits, we always avoided any branch that had weaver ants.

But recently I discovered by watching Wildlife, one of my favorite TV channels, that the weaver ant has a match! It is the brown spider. The small brown spider looks very much like the weaver ant in size, shape, and color! This brown spider enters the territory of the weaver ant unnoticed. It is camouflaged and even walks like the weaver ant. So the brown spider is welcomed as one of the members of the weaver ant family. It goes straight to the nest and enters while the guards watch, believing they are seeing one of their own. The spider goes in and steals the eggs undetected! That is the power of camouflage. Therefore Jesus warned, "Watch out for false prophets. They come to you in sheep's clothing, but inwardly they are ferocious wolves" (Matt 7:15).

But just as Jesus said that these false prophets can be recognized by their fruit (Matt 7:16), Peter and Jude tell us that these ungodly people can be recognized by their fruit, for these false prophets follow the corrupt desires of the flesh.

2 Peter 2:12-19	Jude 11-13, 16
[12] But these people blaspheme in matters they do not understand. They are like unreasoning animals, creatures of instinct, born only to be caught and destroyed, and like animals they too will perish. [13] They will be paid back with harm for the harm they have done. Their idea of pleasure is to carouse in broad daylight. They are blots and blemishes, reveling in their pleasures while they feast with you. [14] With eyes full of adultery, they never stop sinning; they seduce the unstable; they are experts in greed – an accursed brood! [15] They have left the straight way and wandered off to follow the way of Balaam son of Bezer, who loved the wages of wickedness. [16] But he was rebuked for his wrongdoing by a donkey – an animal without speech – who spoke with a human voice and restrained the prophet's madness. [17] These people are springs without water and mists driven by a storm. Blackest darkness is reserved for them. [18] For they mouth empty, boastful words and, by appealing to the lustful desires of the flesh, they entice people who are just escaping from those who live in error. [19] They promise them freedom, while they themselves are slaves of depravity – for "people are slaves to whatever has mastered them."	[11] Woe to them! They have taken the way of Cain; they have rushed for profit into Balaam's error; they have been destroyed in Korah's rebellion. [12] These people are blemishes at your love feasts, eating with you without the slightest qualm – shepherds who feed only themselves. They are clouds without rain, blown along by the wind; autumn trees, without fruit and uprooted – twice dead. [13] They are wild waves of the sea, foaming up their shame; wandering stars, for whom blackest darkness has been reserved forever. . . . [16] These people are grumblers and faultfinders; they follow their own evil desires; they boast about themselves and flatter others for their own advantage.

In their arrogance, these ungodly scoff at the righteous and biblical prophecies (2 Pet 3:3; Jude 17–19). They challenge the promise of the coming of the day of the Lord. "They will say, 'Where is this "coming" he promised? Ever since our ancestors died, everything goes on as it has since the beginning of creation'" (2 Pet 3:4). The reason they scoff the day of the Lord is so they can follow their evil desires. And Jude reminds readers of what the apostles of our Lord Jesus Christ foretold, "They said to you, 'In the last times there will be scoffers who will follow their own ungodly desires'" (Jude 18). When "The fool says in his heart 'There is no God,'" the next comment about them is, "They are corrupt, their deeds are vile; there is no one who does good" (Pss 14:1 // 53:1). They deliberately dismiss God from their heart in order to follow their own fleshly instincts.

The ungodly teachers despise authority and insult celestial beings as well (2 Pet 2:10–12; Jude 8–10). Because they constitute themselves as authorities, they are not afraid to despise the true servants of the Lord and celestial beings.

But because God is a just God, these ungodly cannot go free. Judgment awaits them. Past judgments of the ungodly serve as example. Even angels that sinned were judged (2 Pet 2:4; Jude 6). Peter says,

> For if God did not spare angels when they sinned, but sent them to hell, putting them in chains of darkness to be held for judgment; if he did not spare the ancient world when he brought the flood on its ungodly people, but protected Noah, a preacher of righteousness, and seven others; if he condemned the cities of Sodom and Gomorrah by burning them to ashes, and made them an example of what is going to happen to the ungodly; and if he rescued Lot, a righteous man, who was distressed by the depraved conduct of the lawless (for that righteous man, living among them day after day, was tormented in his righteous soul by the lawless deeds he saw and heard) – if this is so, then the Lord knows how to rescue the godly from trials and to hold the unrighteous for punishment on the day of judgment. This is especially true of those who follow the corrupt desire of the flesh and despise authority. (2 Pet 2:4–10a)

Similarly, Jude said,

> And the angels who did not keep their positions of authority but abandoned their proper dwelling – these he has kept in darkness, bound with everlasting chains for judgment on the great Day. In a similar way, Sodom and Gomorrah and the surrounding towns

gave themselves up to sexual immorality and perversion. They serve as an example of those who suffer the punishment of eternal fire. (Jude 6–7)

Evil doers "will be paid back with harm for the harm they have done" (2 Pet 2:13; cf. Jude 13).

Perseverance and Salvation of the Godly

The theme of perseverance is obvious in both 2 Peter and Jude. The scoffers were discouraging the believers and persuading them to abandon their faith in the Lord and in the promise of his coming back again. But Peter wrote,

> But do not forget this one thing, dear friends: With the Lord a day is like a thousand years, and a thousand years are like a day. The Lord is not slow in keeping his promise, as some understand slowness. Instead he is patient with you, not wanting anyone to perish, but everyone to come to repentance.
>
> But the day of the Lord will come like a thief. The heavens will disappear with a roar; the elements will be destroyed by fire, and the earth and everything done in it will be laid bare. (2 Pet 3:8–10)

And Jude says,

> But you, dear friends, by building yourselves up in your most holy faith and praying in the Holy Spirit, keep yourselves in God's love as you wait for the mercy of our Lord Jesus Christ to bring you to eternal life.
>
> Be merciful to those who doubt; save others by snatching them from the fire; to others show mercy, mixed with fear – hating even the clothing stained by corrupted flesh.
>
> To him who is able to keep you from stumbling and to present you before his glorious presence without fault and with great joy – to the only God our Savior be glory, majesty, power and authority, through Jesus Christ our Lord, before all ages, now and forevermore! Amen. (Jude 20–25)

Perseverance is particularly important in the light of the false teachers who "bring the way of truth into disrepute" (2 Pet 2:2) and the prevailing pollution and wickedness.

But God is a just God. He will not let the godly suffer endlessly in the hands of the ungodly. A final day of redemption is coming. While the day of the Lord is a day of judgment for the ungodly, it marks the final victory for the godly.

Both Peter and Jude teach that preparation for the day of the Lord and our eternal dwelling is through holy living (2 Pet 3:9–13; Jude 20–25). As Peter says,

> Since everything will be destroyed in this way, what kind of people ought you to be? You ought to live holy and godly lives as you look forward to the day of God and speed its coming. That day will bring about the destruction of the heavens by fire, and the elements will melt in the heat. But in keeping with his promise we are looking forward to a new heaven and a new earth, where righteousness dwells. (2 Pet 3:11–13)

Every trouble with an expiry date is endurable.

Questions for Review and Application

1. What is the inspiration of Scripture?
2. What happens when the inspiration of the Bible is rejected?
3. How do we recognize false teachers today?
4. How is the church to deal with false teachers who promote doctrines that are contrary to Scripture?
5. What is it that makes false teaching attractive?
6. In what areas can we apply the messages of 2 Peter and Jude as African Christians?

22

Drums of Redemption in 1, 2, and 3 John

This is the message we have heard from him and declare to you: God is light; in him there is no darkness at all. If we claim to have fellowship with him and yet walk in the darkness, we lie and do not live out the truth. But if we walk in the light, as he is in the light, we have fellowship with one another, and the blood of Jesus, his Son, purifies us from all sin.

1 John 1:5–7

See what great love the Father has lavished on us, that we should be called children of God! And that is what we are! The reason the world does not know us is that it did not know him. Dear friends, now we are children of God, and what we will be has not yet been made known. But we know that when Christ appears, we shall be like him, for we shall see him as he is. All who have this hope in him purify themselves, just as he is pure.

1 John 3:1–3

Dear friend, do not imitate what is evil but what is good. Anyone who does what is good is from God. Anyone who does what is evil has not seen God.

3 John 11

Synopsis of the Letters 1, 2, and 3 John

The Johannine letters share common themes. But the overall orientation of the three letters is to call the believers to walk in fellowship with God and with one another. The practicality of the Christian life situates these three letters with the practical theology of the Epistle of James.

According to 1 John, God is light, therefore his children must walk in the light (1:5–2:2). God's children are to emulate him as they walk in love. They must also avoid living by the false values and attractions of the world (2:12–17). But the apostle also confronts some heretical teachers who were seeking to wreck the life of the believers. The error concerns Christ (1 John 2:22; 2 John 7). The believers must renounce the lies of the false teachers because they know the truth (1 John 2:18–27). God's children must follow the voice of the Holy Spirit and watch out for false prophets (4:1–6). And God's children must walk in love because God is love (3:11–24; 4:7–21).[1]

There are striking similarities between the Gospel of John and 1 John. Some include the use of words and theological concepts such as "life," "eternal life," "death," "truth," "light," Jesus as God's Son, Jesus laying down his life, salvation as knowing God, abiding or remaining in Christ, the new commandment, and the world, among others.[2] The emphasis is that God's children are to walk in the light because God is light.

The letter 1 John is the apostle's response to the false teaching known as Gnosticism which denies Jesus's coming in the flesh. John wrote,

> This is how you can recognize the Spirit of God: Every spirit that acknowledges that Jesus Christ has come in the flesh is from God, but every spirit that does not acknowledge Jesus is not from God. This is the spirit of the antichrist, which you have heard is coming and even now is already in the world. (1 John 4:2–3)

John also emphasizes Jesus's redemptive atonement. "He is the atoning sacrifice for our sins, and not only for ours but also for the sins of the whole world" (1 John 2:2). Similarly, "This is love: not that we loved God, but that he loved us and sent his Son as an atoning sacrifice for our sins" (1 John 4:10). As Christopher Holmes states, "Both 1 John and Hebrews present Jesus as God's definitive means of dealing with human sinfulness."[3]

The letter 2 John was written to "the lady chosen by God and to her children" (1).[4] The letter encourages hospitality to missionaries and warns against the

---

1. Marshall, Travis, and Paul, *Exploring the New Testament*, 295–96.

2. Marshall, Travis, and Paul, 290.

3. Christopher T. Holmes, "Gestures to the priesthood: Exploring Jesus' priestly function in 1 John," *R&E* 114, no. 4 (2017): 567.

4. The identity of the chosen lady is debatable among scholars. Does this refer to a human figure or the church?

error of distorted views of Christ. Association with people of questionable doctrines contaminates a healthy church, hence the strong warning.

The letter 3 John is a commendation for Gaius because of his Christian testimony and a condemnation of Diotrephes "who loves to be first" (9). Diotrephes' quest for power would not let him acknowledge the authority of the apostle John. Not only that, he also refused to welcome the brothers. These rejected brothers were itinerant evangelists. Gaius, and the entire church, must not imitate people like Diotrephes.

Key Theological Themes in the Letters 1, 2, and 3 John
Christ Is the Atoning Sacrifice for Sin

According to Keener, John's view of sin is different from the prevailing Greek concept of sin as imperfection. In the Old Testament and Judaism, sin is transgression. "John wants everyone to understand that he means sins in the biblical sense."[5] New Testament writers see Jesus's death as the demonstration of God's love for humankind (Matt 20:28; John 3:16; Rom 5:8–10; 2 Cor 5:21; 1 Pet 3:18). John wrote, "My dear children, I write this to you so that you will not sin. But if anybody does sin, we have an advocate with the Father – Jesus Christ, the Righteous One" (1 John 2:1). An advocate is an intercessor or "defending attorney."[6] Jesus's qualification as "the Righteous One" makes him the right advocate for his people.

> For we do not have a high priest who is unable to empathize with our weaknesses, but we have one who has been tempted in every way, just as we are – *yet he did not sin.* Let us then approach God's throne of grace with confidence, so that we may receive mercy and find grace to help us in our time of need. (Heb 4:15–16, emphasis added)

Jesus is "the atoning sacrifice for our sins, and not only for ours but also for the sins of the whole world" (1 John 2:2). Rather than those who might claim to be without sin (perhaps the Gnostics), believers who peradventure stumble can still find forgiveness because of Jesus, their Advocate (2:1). Jesus is the atoning sacrifice for sin for them and the entire world. This means that

---

5. Keener, *IVP Bible Background Commentary*, 741.
6. Keener, 743.

Christ's atoning sacrifice is efficacious in freeing the human race from the bondage of sin and restoring them to a right relationship with God.[7]

But that Jesus is the atoning sacrifice for sin is not a license for believers to live a sinful life. Therefore, sprinkled in 1 John are several warnings against sinning, because sin contradicts the nature of the children of God (2:1; 3:4–9; 5:14–21). John is emphatic that "No one who is born of God will continue to sin, because God's seed remains in them; they cannot go on sinning, because they have been born of God" (3:9). And persistence in sin leads to a point of no return (5:16–17). What kinds of sins lead to death? "The two sins that John would likely have in mind would be hating the brothers and sisters (the secessionists rejection of the Christian community) and failing to believe in Jesus rightly (their false doctrine about his identity as the divine Lord and Christ in the flesh)."[8]

Christians Confront the Error of the Antichrist

The challenge facing the church is "the error of the opponents."[9] Keener calls this challenge "the theological test."[10] These opponents or false prophets (1 John 4:1) "appeared to have initiated a schismatic movement in the church (2:19)."[11] False members specialize in dividing the community of believers for their selfish interests. Paul wrote to the believers in Rome,

> I urge you, brothers and sisters, to watch out for those who cause divisions and put obstacles in your way that are contrary to the teaching you have learned. Keep away from them. For such people are not serving our Lord Christ, but their own appetites. By smooth talk and flattery they deceive the minds of naive people. (Rom 16:17–18)

And these false members are of the worse type: they claimed a special knowledge from the Spirit (1 John 2:20, 27). John calls them antichrists, and antichrists deny Jesus (2:22–23; cf. 2 John 7). The antichrists had been part of the community, but separated themselves from the community. John wrote,

> Dear children, this is the last hour; and as you have heard that the antichrist is coming, even now many antichrists have come. This

---

7. Isaak, *New Testament Theology*, 244.
8. Keener, *IVP Bible Background Commentary*, 745.
9. Ladd, *Theology of the New Testament*, 657.
10. Keener, *IVP Bible Background Commentary*, 739.
11. Ladd, *Theology of the New Testament*, 657.

is how we know it is the last hour. They went out from us, but they did not really belong to us. For if they had belonged to us, they would have remained with us; but their going showed that none of them belonged to us. (1 John 2:18–19)

These secessionists do not mean the church well. They withdraw from Christian fellowship and cause damage to the flock.

The theological propaganda of antichrists calls for testing the spirits. In Judaism, the Spirit of God is associated with prophecy.[12] But the opponents of the truth are moved by other spirits. They operate in the spirit of the antichrist: "every spirit that does not acknowledge Jesus is not from God. This is the spirit of the antichrist, which you have heard is coming and even now is already in the world" (1 John 4:3). They do not acknowledge that Jesus came in the flesh (1 John 4:1–3). Their agenda is to ruin the fellowship of the body of Christ by introducing doctrines that were inimical to the life and truth the believers received from the Lord.

Christians Walk in the Love of God

A dominant theme in 1, 2, and 3 John is love. This love is expressed as God's love for us, our love for God, and our love for one another. God's love for us is expressed in 1 John 3:1: "See what great love the Father has lavished on us, that we should be called children of God! And that is what we are! The reason the world does not know us is that it did not know him." This verse echoes John 1:12–13: "Yet to all who did receive him, to those who believed in his name, he gave the right to become children of God – children born not of natural descent, nor of human decision or a husband's will, but born of God."

Our love for God and for one another is a reciprocation of God's love for us. Those who love God demonstrate it by their obedience to him. "But if anyone obeys his word, love for God is truly made complete in them" (1 John 2:5; cf. John 15:10). John also explains why and how loving one another is a response to God's love.

> This is how God showed his love among us: He sent his one and only Son into the world that we might live through him. This is love: not that we loved God, but that he loved us and sent his Son as an atoning sacrifice for our sins. Dear friends, since God so loved us, we also ought to love one another. (1 John 4:9–11)

---

12. Keener, *IVP Bible Background Commentary*, 743.

John had already reminded his readers, "For this is the message you heard from the beginning: We should love one another" (1 John 3:11). And he warns his readers not to be like Cain who belonged to the evil one and murdered his brother. John interjects this warning with "Do not be surprised, my brothers and sisters, if the world hates you" (3:13). According to John, "We know that we have passed from death to life, because we love each other. Anyone who does not love remains in death" (3:14). The believer's example of love is Christ: "This is how we know what love is: Jesus Christ laid down his life for us. And we ought to lay down our lives for our brothers and sisters" (3:16). True love involves sharing material possessions with those who need them: "If anyone has material possessions and sees a brother or sister in need but has no pity on them, how can the love of God be in that person? Dear children, let us not love with words or speech but with actions and in truth" (3:17–18). Christian love must be practical; otherwise it is like faith without deeds (Jas 2:26).

Christ Gives Eternal Life

A key theme in the Gospel of John is eternal life (John 20:31). And as we read 1 John, the concept of eternal life forms an enclosure. According to 1 John 1:2, "The life appeared; we have seen it and testify to it, and we proclaim to you the eternal life, which was with the Father and has appeared to us." Jesus is the life that appeared, also called "the Word of life" (1:1). And John brings up eternal life at the end of this letter, "I write these things to you who believe in the name of the Son of God so that you may know that you have eternal life" (5:13). Eternal life is what the Father promises (2:25). This eternal life is in Christ Jesus (5:20).

Questions for Review and Application

1. What are the dominant themes in 1 John?
2. What does it mean to walk in the light?
3. What is the Christological error of the false teachers in 1 and 2 John?
4. How is true love demonstrated?
5. What is the meaning of eternal life in 1 John? How do we come to know that we have eternal life?
6. In what ways can we apply the messages of the three letters of John to the church in Africa?
7. How do 1, 2, and 3 John draw you closer to God?

23

Drums of Redemption in Revelation

Evil always dresses itself up as good, and the worst looks like the best.

John Stott[1]

Do not be afraid of what you are about to suffer. I tell you, the devil will put some of you in prison to test you, and you will suffer persecution for ten days. Be faithful, even to the point of death, and I will give you life as your victor's crown.

Revelation 2:10

Then I saw "a new heaven and a new earth," for the first heaven and the first earth had passed away, and there was no longer any sea. I saw the Holy City, the new Jerusalem, coming down out of heaven from God, prepared as a bride beautifully dressed for her husband. And I heard a loud voice from the throne saying, "Look! God's dwelling place is now among the people, and he will dwell with them. They will be his people, and God himself will be with them and be their God. 'He will wipe every tear from their eyes. There will be no more death' or mourning or crying or pain, for the old order of things has passed away."

Revelation 21:1–4

---

1. Stott says that it is the distinctive office of the Holy Spirit to grant signs and wonders in order to confirm the gospel (Rom 15:18–19). Stott, *Men with a Message*, 151. But the second beast in the book of Revelation takes up this role of performing signs in order to deceive the nations into worshiping the first beast and to act as a false prophet on his behalf (Rev 19:20; 20:10).

Synopsis of the Book of Revelation

The book of Revelation is attributed to John, the apostle of our Lord Jesus Christ. He received his visions while he was in exile on the Island of Patmos at the time of Emperor Domitian. John was banished to the island "because of the word of God and the testimony of Jesus" (Rev 1:9). There he received messages for the seven churches in Asia Minor. His messages contain "what you have seen, what is now and what will take place later" (Rev 1:19).[2]

Stott says that the book of Revelation "has been the playground of cranks ever since it was written – and still is. Is there any way of assuring ourselves that we are reading the book as John intended?"[3] Similarly, Johnson says, "Few writings in all of literature have been so obsessively read with such generally disastrous results as the Book of Revelation."[4] Therefore, this work is intended to provide some basic understanding regarding the theological focus of the book of Revelation.

Basically, Revelation was written to show that history involves spiritual war.[5] The book is the drum beat of the triumph of the Lamb and his bride, the church. In other words, the book deals with the problem of evil and God's visitation on the world with judgment and the ushering in of his kingdom. G. K. Beale rightly says,

> As in John's Gospel, so in John's apocalypse, the death and defeat of Christ are, in reality, his victory over Satan. . . . The Lamb's followers are to recapitulate the model of his ironic victory in their own lives: by *enduring* through *tribulation* they reign in the invisible *kingdom* of the Messiah."[6]

Therefore, the primary purpose of the book is to give a message of hope and comfort to the believers in the light of the church's final victory over evil.

Revelation, like Daniel in the Old Testament, falls within a group of literature called "apocalyptic," from a Greek word that means to "unveil," or "uncover," or "reveal." In other words, the book of Revelation reveals

---

2. G. K. Beale, *The Book of Revelation: A Commentary on the Greek Text*, NIGTC, ed. I. Howard Marshall and Donald A. Hagner (Grand Rapids: Eerdmans, 1999), 152. According to Beale, the understanding of many interpreters that Rev 1:19 is the key verse that provides the structure and interpretation of the whole Apocalypse is debatable.

3. Stott, *Men with a Message*, 146.

4. Johnson, *Writings of the New Testament*, 573.

5. Vern S. Poythress, *The Returning King: A Guide to the Book of Revelation* (Phillipsburg: P&R, 2000), 23.

6. Beale, *Book of Revelation*, 171, emphasis original.

something that has been veiled, covered, or hidden in the past. Against this understanding, however, J. Ramsey Michaels observes that because the word "revelation" does not occur again after 1:1, and that "every other time the book refers to itself, it is a *prophecy* . . . or 'a book of prophecy' . . . revelation should be understood in much the same sense as in 1 Corinthians 14:6, 26."[7] Michaels means that "revelation" in John's book should be regarded as "the things prophets in early Christian congregations received from God in the Spirit – along with knowledge, prophecy, teaching (v. 6), a psalm, a teaching, a tongue, an interpretation (v. 26)."[8] This means that God gave the church this book so that they may understand his mind concerning the church, the problem of evil, and his final triumph over evil.

Prominent images, metaphors, figures, and features in the book of Revelation include the following: Son of Man, angels, the church, thrones,[9] scrolls, seals, multitudes, trumpets, witnesses, woman, dragons, beasts, the Lamb, harvest, plagues, judgment, wrath, the harlot, Babylon, horses (and their riders), Satan, the new Jerusalem, book of life, and the river of life. Similarly, numbers play significant roles in the book of Revelation. The number seven seems to indicate completeness, such as "the seven lampstands," or "the seven spirits of God" (Rev 1:12; 3:1; 4:5; 5:6). The seven spirits (5:6) "represent the fullness of the divine Spirit, sent out from the presence of God."[10]

According to Revelation, Jesus's primary interest is in what the church does as God's witness and light in the dark and corrupt world that opposes God and his people. This interest is seen in the letters to the seven churches. But let us look at some characteristics of this book and apocalyptic writings in general.

1. Apocalyptic is usually written in times of suffering or distress.[11]

---

7. J. Ramsey Michaels, *Revelation*, The IVP New Testament Commentary, ed. by Grant R. Osborne, D. Stuart Briscoe, and Haddon Robinson (Downers Grove: InterVarsity, 1997), 46, emphasis original.

8. Michaels, *Revelation*, 46.

9. Randy Alcorn says God's throne is mentioned forty times in the book of Revelation, "appearing in sixteen of the twenty-two chapters." Randy Alcorn, *Heaven* (Carol Stream: Tyndale House, 2004), 233. This number underscores the significance of the throne in heaven.

10. Richard Bauckham, *The Theology of the Book of Revelation*, New Testament Theology (Cambridge: Cambridge University Press, 1993), 118.

11. Peter-Ben Smit says, "Suffering is a major theme in the Apocalypse of John, as are questions of control and power; both those following the Lamb and those following others, such as a variety of beasts and other apocalyptic adversaries of the Lamb and its followers, suffer." Peter-Ben Smit, "Sadomasochism and the Apocalypse of John: Exegesis, Sensemaking and Pain," *Biblical Interpretation* 26 (2018): 91.

2. The message is conveyed or carried by means of signs, symbols,[12] dreams, and visions.

3. Apocalyptic gives promises of the eventual victory of good over evil.

Scholars have thought about the best methods for interpreting the book of Revelation. Four ways are suggested.

1. The preterist view is that the events described in the book are virtually in the past which is during the first century, and have nothing to do with the present or future church.

2. The historicist view is that the book merely gives a picture of the conflict between the church and the world from the beginning of the church to the end of the world. This view sees the book as an "almanac to world history."[13] The conflict is energized by Satan, the dragon, and the unfolding drama represents events in the world.

3. The futurist approach is that apart from chapters 1–3, the whole book is understood as talking about the future.

4. Finally, the timeless symbolic approach is that the events in the book cannot be tied to literal history. Instead, the book is understood as dealing with the spiritual conflict between God and Satan or good and evil. This approach "treats the book as a series of parables."[14]

But another helpful hint for understanding Revelation is seeing the major divisions based on the visions. The first vision is in the form of messages to seven churches in Asia Minor (Rev 1:9–3:22). These churches, as Onesimus Ngundu well says, were not the only churches in Asia Minor, nor were the letters intended for them alone. The symbolic number seven was used for completeness; therefore, the seven churches represent "the whole of the believing community of God."[15] In the letters, the spiritual condition of each

---

12. Beale, *Book of Revelation*, 69. According to Beale, "The symbols have a parabolic function and are intended to encourage and exhort the audience. They portray a transcendent new creation that has penetrated the present old world through the death and resurrection of Christ and the sending of the Spirit at Pentecost." Accordingly, "the literary form of symbolic parable appears whenever ordinary warnings are no longer heeded, and no warning will ever be heeded by those who are spiritually stiff-necked and intent on continuing in disobedience." Beale, 69.

13. Stott, *Men with a Message*, 147.

14. Stott, 147.

15. Onesimus Ngundu, "Revelation," in *Africa Bible Commentary*, ed. Tokunboh Adeyemo (Nairobi: WordAlive, 2006), 1548.

church is revealed. These messages "mix encouragement with threat, and scolding with praise."[16]

In the second vision three series of judgments on the earth are described, and each of the judgments has seven components (Rev 4:1–16:22). This vision is about the magnitude of God's wrath. As the judgments take place, some parenthetical events are interjected within the same time sequence.

The third vision is on the victory of Christ over evil (Rev 17:1–21:8). He triumphs over the harlot and the beast of Babylon, the beast and the false prophets, Satan and the rebels of the earth, and unrepentant humankind. This victory prepares the way for the new heaven and the new earth. The fourth vision is about the new heaven and the new earth (Rev 21:9–22:5). It is the climax of the book, picturing the glorious triumph of God's children and their place with him.

Finally, the book of Revelation contains a few interpretative keys for understanding some of its images, metaphors, symbols, and figures. The reader will do well to hold on to these important keys. Some are given in Revelation 1:20; 5:8; 6:1–8; 17:1–12, 18. For example, the woman in Revelation 17:1–12, 18 who is dressed in purple and scarlet "sitting on a scarlet beast that was covered with blasphemous names and had seven heads and ten horns" (17:3) is also known as "the great prostitute" (17:1) and "Babylon the Great" (14:8; 16:19). This woman "is the great city that rules over the kings of the earth" (17:18). Since Rome was the great city that ruled a large portion of the world in John's day, this woman is unmistakably Rome (cf. 1 Pet 5:13).

Key Theological Themes in the Book of Revelation

According to Beale, John's biblical theology concerns suffering and victory, the throne, the new creation, and the place of Christians in the world.[17] These key theological themes revolve around messages of judgment to oppressors and comfort for the oppressed, culminating in the dawn of the new kingdom and the new creation.

The Witness of Christ and His Church

Jesus, along with God the Father, is transcendent and unique as "the Alpha and Omega" and "the First and the Last" (Rev 1:8, 17; 21:6; 22:13). Theologically,

---

16. Michaels, *Revelation*, 65.
17. Beale, *Book of Revelation*, 171–76.

the book of Revelation speaks about the witness of Jesus and his church to the effect that "the witness of Jesus is the spirit of prophecy."[18] According to Johnson, "Christians continue and imitate the witness first presented by Jesus. He was the faithful and true witness (1:5; 3:14) who came into the world to 'bear witness to the truth' (John 18:37)."[19] The world rejected Jesus's witness and even killed him, "and his witness was therefore sealed with his blood (1:5; 5:9; 7:14; 19:13)."[20] The church has assumed the witness of Jesus through the Holy Spirit's abiding presence in the lives of believers (Rev 19:10). The Holy Spirit makes the voice of Jesus known to the believers. "And it is the Spirit who equips them for faithful witness after the pattern of Jesus (11:11; 19:10). This witness is manifest both within the churches and to the world at large."[21] Christians maintain their witness through their obedience to God.

Revelation shows that Christians witness in the midst of tribulation and temptation (Rev 2:1–3:22). Similarly, the visions of John show that the witness of the believers can lead to persecution and death, that is, the shedding of their blood (6:9–10; 7:14–16; 12:10–11; 16:5–6; 17:6; 18:24).[22] Christian witness is the imitation of Christ's witness "who was the faithful and true witness (1:5; 3:14)."[23]

The Message from the Throne Room

According to Alcorn, "Revelation isn't primarily a book about the Antichrist or Tribulation; it's a book about God reigning. He reigns over the fallen universe now, and will reign uncontested over the new universe, with mankind reigning by his side."[24] And God reigns from his throne in heaven along with the believers as his delegates. Revelation 4:1–5:14 presents to us the heavenly throne. John sees "a door standing open in heaven" and hears a familiar voice, the voice he heard before, "speaking like a trumpet" (4:1). The voice summons him to come, and he is carried in the Spirit. He is lifted to the place where he sees a throne "with someone sitting on it" (4:2). Although the one seated on the throne is not yet identified, the unfolding revelation of the book is

---

18. Johnson, *Writings of the New Testament*, 584.
19. Johnson, 584.
20. Johnson, 584.
21. Marshall, Travis, and Paul, *Exploring the New Testament*, 314.
22. Johnson, *Writings of the New Testament*, 585–88.
23. Johnson, 584.
24. Alcorn, *Heaven*, 233.

"Salvation belongs to our God, who sits on the throne, and to the Lamb" (7:10). This glorious throne is surrounded by twenty-four other thrones (seats), "and seated on them were twenty-four elders. They were dressed in white and had crowns of gold on their heads" (4:4).[25] Also "In the center, around the throne, were four living creatures, and they were covered with eyes, in front and in back" (4:6). Standing at the center of the throne is the Lamb, "looking as if it had been slain" (5:6).

Like the prophet Ezekiel (Ezek 1:4–28), John sees God's throne. It is impossible to describe the one who sits on the throne because "no one has ever seen God" (John 1:18; 1 John 4:12; cf. Exod 33:20).[26] But Revelation 5:13 seems to unravel the mystery: "To him who sits on the throne and to the Lamb" suggest that God the Father and the Son occupy the throne. What is unmistaken at the throne in heaven is worship (4:8–11; 5:9–14; 14:1–3; 19:4–8). God is the Creator who receives the worship of both the believers and angelic beings in heaven. Therefore, "In spite of all the sufferings which are part and parcel of life in this world . . . the church is safe, 'sealed' with a mark of ownership from God, who rules with unassailable power from the throne of the universe."[27]

The Messages of Judgment to the Oppressors

In the throne room in heaven, God is the Creator and Sustainer of the world he has made. But as the book of Revelation unfolds, we see Satan, the adversary. The demons have "as king over them the angel of the Abyss, whose name in Hebrew is Abaddon, and in Greek, Apollyon (that is, Destroyer)" (Rev 9:11). Apollyon has emissaries who work together in tormenting and attempting to destroy the people of God. Satan's work is destruction, and his primary targets of destruction are the followers of the Lamb, the church of Jesus Christ.

Thankfully, Revelation reveals that God's wrath is reserved for the adversary and his agents, both human and demonic. Therefore, Revelation speaks with a megaphone on the problem of evil in the world (theodicy). "Like Matthew 24:15ff. and 2 Thessalonians 2:3ff., it tells of an evil personage who will be satanically inspired and empowered, who openly defies God and demands that

---

25. For more on these twenty-four elders in heaven, see Rev 4:10–11; 5:6, 8, 11, 14; 7:11–14; 11:16–18; 14:3; 19:4–5.

26. Michaels, *Revelation*, 91.

27. Stott, *Men with a Message*, 154.

people worship him rather than God."[28] Revelation shows that "the Christian's outer body is vulnerable to persecution and suffering."[29] The main adversary is identified in Revelation 2:10:

> Do not be afraid of what you are about to suffer. I tell you, the devil will put some of you in prison to test you, and you will suffer persecution for ten days. Be faithful, even to the point of death, and I will give you life as your victor's crown.

Remarkably, the slain Lamb is entrusted with the judgment of the earth (Rev 14:14–16). He is the "KING OF KINGS AND LORD OF LORDS" (19:16). He has the authority over the seals and the power to judge the entire world (5:5; 16:1).

The Messages of Comfort and Hope to the Oppressed

Persecuted Christians in Northern Nigeria and other parts of the world who are going through perilous times cry out like the souls under the altar in Revelation 6:10, "How long, Sovereign Lord, holy and true, until you judge the inhabitants of the earth and avenge our blood?" But the message of Revelation is "living in the light of God's triumph."[30] The book not only presents the problem of evil but also announces God's final verdict on this monster that has plagued and bewildered humankind throughout the ages. Therefore, the primary purpose of the book is to give the message of hope and comfort to believers in Christ by showing that the present state of things is not final. Every trouble that has an impending expiry date is endurable.

Moreover, Revelation reveals that God is a just God. The seven seals (6:1–8:5), the seven trumpets (8:6–11:19), and the seven bowls of God's wrath (15:1–16:21) all show that God is the God of justice for the church that has been oppressed. For example when the third angel pours out his bowl on the rivers and the springs of water, and they turn to blood, John hears the angel in charge of the waters say: "You are just in these judgments, O Holy One, you who are and who were; for they have shed the blood of your holy people and your prophets" (Rev 16:5–6). Therefore, the series of judgments are in response to the believers' cries for justice.

---

28. Ladd, *Theology of the New Testament*, 675.
29. Beale, *Book of Revelation*, 171.
30. deSilva, *Introduction to the New Testament*, 884.

The dragon and the two beasts, one out of the sea and the other out of the earth, are the main tormentors of the world (Rev 12:1–17; 13:1–18). The dragon gives the beasts their power. But the judgment and fall of "Babylon the Great the mother of prostitutes" (17:5) signals the near final victory of God's people.[31] For "God remembered Babylon the Great and gave her the cup filled with the wine of the fury of his wrath" (Rev 16:19).

According to Revelation 20:2: "he seized the dragon, that ancient serpent, who is the devil, or Satan, and bound him for a thousand years." He will be thrown in the Abyss which will be locked "to keep him from deceiving the nations anymore until the thousand years were ended" (20:3). After this he is set free for a short time, and he "will go out to deceive the nations in the four corners of the earth – Gog and Magog – and gather them for battle" (20:8). Satan will gather his followers against the Lord. "But fire came down from heaven and devoured them. And the devil, who deceived them, was thrown into the lake of burning sulfur, where the beast and the false prophet had been thrown. They will be tormented day and night for ever and ever" (20:9–10). And this is the fatal end of Satan.

The great white throne of God marks the final judgment of the world.

> Then I saw a great white throne and him who was seated on it. The earth and the heavens fled from his presence, and there was no place for them. And I saw the dead, great and small, standing before the throne, and books were opened. Another book was opened, which is the book of life. The dead were judged according to what they had done as recorded in the books. The sea gave up the dead that were in it, and death and Hades gave up the dead that were in them, and each person was judged according to what they had done. Then death and Hades were thrown into the lake of fire. The lake of fire is the second death. Anyone whose name was not found written in the book of life was thrown into the lake of fire. (Rev 20:11–15)

The throne we saw in the beginning (4:2) reappears, not to commence judgment of the world but to finalize it. The candidates for judgment are the dead, great and small. Books that contain the record of their deeds and the book of life will be opened. The judgment is according to what everyone did,

---

31. Babylon is mentioned in Revelation 14:8; 16:19; 17:1–5; 18:1–24. Most interpreters see Babylon as a pseudo name for the city of Rome, capital of the empire under which the church was persecuted and which ruled much of the world.

as Paul says, "For we must all appear before the judgment seat of Christ, so that each of us may receive what is due us for the things done while in the body, whether good or bad" (2 Cor 5:10).

The Coming of the New Heaven and the New Earth

Revelation 20:1–8 serves as a beautiful prelude for the consummation of the kingdom of God. The coming of the kingdom is preceded by a one-thousand-year reign of Christ, which theologians refer to as the millennial reign of Christ. "Millennium" is the Latin word for one thousand. The concept of the millennium remains complex because it lacks backing from other biblical sources. Theologically, there are three views regarding the millennium – premillennialism, postmillennialism, and amillennialism. The first two views hold that there will be a future literal one thousand years of Christ's reign on earth. Premillennialists believe that the one thousand years of Christ's reign will happen when Christ returns, and we cannot expect the millennium until Christ returns. But postmillennialists believe that the one thousand years will occur before the second coming of Christ.

It is believed that the millennial reign of Christ will be characterized by unprecedented peace and prosperity on earth. This is possible because Satan and his emissaries will be bound for one thousand years and will not be able to cause trouble again until the one thousand years are over. Some theologians see Isaiah 11:6–9 as a foreshadowing of the millennium as envisaged by the prophet Isaiah:

> The wolf will live with the lamb,
>   the leopard will lie down with the goat,
> the calf and the lion and the yearling together;
>   and a little child will lead them.
> The cow will feed with the bear,
>   their young will lie down together,
>   and the lion will eat straw like the ox.
> The infant will play near the cobra's den,
>   and the young child will put its hand into the viper's nest.
> They will neither harm nor destroy
>   on all my holy mountain,
> for the earth will be filled with the knowledge of the LORD
>   as the waters cover the sea.

Amillenialists, however, do not believe that the millennial reign of Christ will be a specific time in human history. They hold that the concept of the millennium should be understood figuratively and symbolically, like many of the concepts in Revelation. Therefore, believers are not to expect a literal one thousand years of Christ's reign on earth.

But the climax of redemption is the gathering of the redeemed into the kingdom of God. This is revealed in John's final and glorious vision (Rev 21:1–27). This vision is "the church's union with Christ."[32] According to Johnny V. Miller, "The history of salvation begins in a garden, Eden, and two people communicating with God. It ends in a city, the New Jerusalem, paradise regained."[33] The coming of the kingdom of God or the new heaven and the new earth mark the final triumph of the people of God. The coming kingdom will usher in a time of peace never known to humankind. Nothing pictures this time better than the words of Revelation 21:1–4:

> Then I saw "a new heaven and a new earth," for the first heaven and the first earth had passed away, and there was no longer any sea. I saw the Holy City, the new Jerusalem, coming down out of heaven from God, prepared as a bride beautifully dressed for her husband. And I heard a loud voice from the throne saying, "Look! God's dwelling place is now among the people, and he will dwell with them. They will be his people, and God himself will be with them and be their God. "He will wipe every tear from their eyes. There will be no more death" or mourning or crying or pain, for the old order of things has passed away.

Therefore, "Blessed are those who wash their robes, that they may have the right to the tree of life and may go through the gates into the city" (Rev 22:14).

Questions for Review and Application

1. What would you consider to be the central message of the book of Revelation?
2. How does the book of Revelation show that history involves spiritual warfare?

---

32. Stott, *Men with a Message*, 155.
33. Johnny V. Miller, "Mission in Revelation," in *Mission in the New Testament: An Evangelical Approach*, ed. William J. Larkin, Jr. and Joel F. Williams (Maryknoll: Orbis, 2005), 227.

3. What does the book of Revelation say about the wicked?
4. How does the book of Revelation bring comfort to the oppressed believers in Africa and other parts of the world?
5. How does the book of Revelation draw you closer to God?

Bibliography

Achtemeier, Paul J., Joel B. Green, and Marianne Meye Thompson. *Introducing the New Testament: Its Literature and Theology.* Grand Rapids: Eerdmans, 2001.

Adam, A. K. M. *Making Sense of New Testament Theology: "Modern" Problems and Prospects.* Studies in American Biblical Hermeneutics 11. Macon: Mercer University Press, 1995.

Adamo, David T. *Reading and Interpreting the Bible in African Indigenous Churches.* Benin, Nigeria: Justice Jeco, 2005.

Aernie, Jeffrey W. *Is Paul Also Among the Prophets? An Examination of the Relationship between Paul and the Old Testament Prophetic Tradition in 2 Corinthians.* Maiden Lane: T&T Clark International, 2012.

Afriyie, Ernestina. "A Christian Response to Homosexuality." *West African Journal of Higher Education.* God, the Bible and Human Sexuality 6 (2017): 34–45.

Agang, Sunday Bobai. *No More Cheeks to Turn?* Nairobi: WordAlive, 2017.

Alcorn, Randy. *Heaven.* Carol Stream: Tyndale House, 2004.

Alpha-Omega Ministries. *Colossians: The Teachers' Outline and Study Guide.* Chattanooga: Leadership Ministries Worldwide, 1994.

———. *Galatians: The Teachers' Outline and Study Guide.* Chattanooga, TN: Leadership Ministries Worldwide, 1994.

Amolo, Hope. "Paul's View of Same Sex as Sexual Deviation." *West African Journal of Higher Education.* God, the Bible and Human Sexuality 6 (2017): 80–111.

Andria, Solomon. "Colossians." In *Africa Bible Commentary.* Edited by Tokunboh Adeyemo. Nairobi: WordAlive, 2006.

Arnold, Clinton E. *Acts.* Grand Rapids: Zondervan, 2002.

———. *Power and Magic: The Concept of Power in Ephesians.* Eugene: Wipf & Stock, 1989.

Ashby, Ernest G. "Colossians." In *New International Bible Commentary.* Edited by F. F. Bruce, H. L. Ellison, and G. C. D. Howley, 1451–1459. Grand Rapids: Zondervan, 1979.

Aslan, Reza. *Zealot: The Life and Times of Jesus of Nazareth.* New York: Random House, 2013.

Ayala, Francisco J. *Am I a Monkey? Six Big Questions about Evolution.* Baltimore: John Hopkins University Press, 2010.

Baker, David L. *Two Testaments, One Bible: The Theological Relationship Between the Old and the New Testaments,* 3rd ed. Downers Grove: InterVarsity, 2010.

Balla, Peter. *Challenges to New Testament Theology.* Peabody: Hendrickson, 1997.

Barclay, William. *The Letter to Timothy, Titus, and Philemon,* rev. ed. Philadelphia: Westminster, 1975.

Bauckham, Richard. *Bible and Mission: Christian Witness in a Postmodern World.* Grand Rapids: Baker Academic, 2003.

———. *Jesus and the Eye Witnesses: The Gospels as Eyewitness Testimony.* Grand Rapids: Eerdmans, 2006.

———. *The Theology of the Book of Revelation.* New Testament Theology. Cambridge: Cambridge University Press, 1993.

Beale, G. K. *The Book of Revelation: A Commentary on the Greek Text.* NIGTC. Edited by I. Howard Marshall and Donald A. Hagner. Grand Rapids: Eerdmans, 1999.

———. *Handbook on the New Testament Use of the Old Testament: Exegesis and Interpretation.* Grand Rapids: Baker Academic, 2012.

———. *A New Testament Biblical Theology: The Unfolding of the Old Testament in the New.* Grand Rapids: Baker Academic, 2011.

Bird, Michael F. *A Bird's Eye View of Paul: The man, his mission and his message.* Nottingham: Inter-Varsity, 2008.

Boa, Kenneth. *Conformed to His Image: Biblical and Practical Approaches to Spiritual Formation.* Grand Rapids: Zondervan, 2001.

Bock, Darrell L. *Luke.* The IVP New Testament Commentary. Edited by Grant R. Osborne, D. Stuart Briscoe, and Haddon Robinson. Downers Grove: Inter-Varsity, 1994.

———. "The Son of Man in Luke 5:24." *Bulletin for Biblical Research* 1 (1991): 109–21.

———. "A Theology of Luke-Acts." *A Biblical Theology of the New Testament.* Edited by Roy B. Zuck. Chicago: Moody, 1994: 87–166.

Boer, Harry. *A Short History of the Early Church.* Ibadan, Nigeria: Daystar, 1976.

Boice, James Montgomery. *Ephesians: An Expositional Commentary.* Grand Rapids: Baker Academic, 1998.

———. "Galatians." *The Expositor's Bible Commentary,* abridged ed. Edited by Kenneth L. Barker and John R. Kohlenberger, III, 703–47. Grand Rapids: Zondervan, 1994.

Boring, M. Eugene. *1 Peter.* Abingdon New Testament Commentaries. Nashville: Abingdon, 1999.

Bounds, E. M. *E. M. Bounds on Prayer.* New Kensington: Whitaker House, 1997.

Brannon, M. Jeff. *The Heavenlies in Ephesians: A Lexical, Exegetical and Conceptual Analysis.* New York: T&T Clark International, 2011.

Breytenbach, Cilliers. *Versöhnung: Eine Studie zur paulinischen Soteriologie.* Wissenschaftliche Monographien zum Alten und Neuen Testament 60. Neukirchen-Vluyn: Neukirchener Verlag, 1989.

———. "Versöhnung, Stellvertretung, und Sühne." *New Testament Studies* 39 (1993): 59–79.

Briscoe, Stuart. *1 Peter: Holy Living in a Hostile World.* Understanding the Books Series. Chicago: Harold Shaw, 1993.

Brown, Raymond E. *An Introduction to the New Testament,* ABRL. New York: Doubleday, 1997.

Brown, Rick. "Delicate Issues in Mission: Explaining the Biblical Term 'Son(s) of God' in Muslim Contexts." *International Journal of Frontier Mission* 2, no. 3 (Fall 2005): 91–96. http://biblicalmissiology.org/wp-content/uploads/2012/02/91-96Brown_SOG.pdf.

Brown, Steve. *A Scandalous Freedom: The Radical Nature of the Gospel.* New York: Howard, 2004.

Bruce, F. F. *The New Testament Documents: Are They Reliable?* Sixth edition. Nottingham: Inter-Varsity, 2000.

Bujo, Bēnēzet. *African Theology in Its Social Context.* Nairobi: Paulines Publications Africa, 1992.

Bultmann, Rudolf. *Jesus and the Word.* New York: Charles Scribner's Sons, 1958.

———. *Theology of the New Testament.* Translated by Kendrick Grobel. New York: Scribner, 1951.

Cara, Robert J. *Cracking the Foundation of the New Perspective on Paul: Covenantal Nomism versus Reformed Covenantal Theology*, rev. ed. Ross-shire: Mentor, 2017.

Cardin, H. E. "The Synoptic Gospels." Unpublished manuscript, last modified 12 May 2010. PDF.

Carpenter, John B. "The Parable of the Talents in Missionary Perspective: A Call for an Economic Spirituality." *Missiology: An International Review* 25, no. 2 (April 1997): 165–181.

Carson, D. A. *The Gagging of God: Christianity Confronts Pluralism.* Leicester: Apollos, 1996.

———. *Jesus the Son of God: A Christological Title Often Overlooked, Sometimes Misunderstood, and Currently Disputed.* Wheaton: Crossway, 2012. https://divinity.tiu.edu/wp-content/uploads/sites/4/2013/04/Carson-jesus-the-son-of-god-download.pdf. Accessed 25 August 2018.

———. *The Sermon on the Mount: An Exposition of Matthew 5–7.* Carlisle: Paternoster, 2013.

Carson, D. A., and Douglas J. Moo. *An Introduction to the New Testament*, 2nd ed. Leicester: Apollos, 2005.

Carson, D. A., Peter T. O'Brien, and Mark A. Seifrid, eds. *Justification and Variegated Nomism.* Vol. 1. *The Complexities of Second Temple Judaism.* Tübingen, Mohr Siebeck/Grand Rapids: Baker, 2001.

———. *Justification and Variegated Nomism.* Vol. 2. *The Paradoxes of Paul.* Tübingen, Mohr Siebeck/Grand Rapids: Baker, 2001.

Chapell, Bryan. *Ephesians.* Reformed Expository Commentary. Phillipsburg: P&R, 2009.

Christensen, Sean. "Reborn Participants in Christ: Recovering the Importance of Union with Christ in 1 Peter." *JETS* 61, no. 2 (2018): 339–54.

Ciampa, Roy E. "The History of Redemption." In *Central Themes in Biblical Theology: Mapping Unity in Diversity.* Edited by Scott J. Hafemann and Paul R. House, 254–308. Nottingham: Apollos, 2007.

Climenhaga, Alison Fitchett. "Pursuing Transformation: Healing, Deliverance, and Discourse of Development among Catholics in Uganda." *Journal of the International Association for Mission Studies* 35, no. 2 (2018): 204–24.

Cole, R. Alan. *Galatians*, rev. ed. Tyndale New Testament Commentaries. Grand Rapids: Eerdmans, 1989.

———. *The Gospel According to Mark: An Introduction and Commentary.* Tyndale New Testament Commentaries, rev. ed. Leicester: Inter-Varsity, 1989.

Colson, Charles. *The Good Life: Seeking Purpose, Meaning, and Truth in Your Life.* Wheaton: Tyndale House, 2005.

Cooper, Aaron. "No Longer Invisible: Gay and Lesbian Jews Build a Movement." In *Homosexuality and Religion.* Edited by Richard Hasbany, 83–94. New York: Harrington Park, 1989.

Coulibaly, Issiaka. "2 Corinthians." In *Africa Bible Commentary.* Edited by Tokunboh Adeyemo, 1339–1412. Nairobi: WordAlive, 2006.

Cray, Graham. *Disciples and Citizens: A Vision for Distinctive Living.* Nottingham: Inter-Varsity, 2007.

Daille, John. *An Exposition of the Epistle to the Colossians.* Marshallton, DE: National Foundation for Christian Education, 1972.

Datiri, Dachollom. "1 Corinthians." In *Africa Bible Commentary.* Edited by Tokunboh Adeyemo, 1376–98. Nairobi: WordAlive, 2006.

Davids, Peter H. *The Epistle of James: A Commentary on the Greek Text.* Grand Rapids: Eerdmans, 1982.

Davies, W. D., and Dale C. Allison. *The Gospel According to Matthew.* The New International Critical Commentary on the Holy Scriptures of the Old and New Testaments. London: T&T Clark, 1997.

Daw, Carl P., Jr. "God the Spirit, Guide and Guardian." In *Sing to the Lord: Church of the Nazarene Hymnal.* Kansas City: Lillenas, 1993.

Dempster, Stephen G. "The Servant of the Lord." In *Central Themes in Biblical Theology: Mapping Unity in Diversity.* Edited by Scott J. Hafemann and Paul R. House, 128–78. Nottingham: Apollos, 2007.

deSilva, David A. *An Introduction to the New Testament: Contexts, Methods and Ministry Formation.* Leicester: Apollos, 2004.

Dodd, C. H. *The Interpretation of the Fourth Gospel.* Cambridge: Cambridge University Press, 1970.

Doriani, Daniel N. *Matthew.* Vol. 1. *Matthew 1–13.* Reformed Expository Commentary. Phillipsburg: P&R, 2008.

Dryden, J. De Wa Al. *Theology and Ethics in 1 Peter: Strategies for Christian Character Formation.* Tübingen: Mohr Siebeck, 2006.

Dunn, James D. G. *Christianity in the Making.* Vol. 1: *Jesus Remembered.* Grand Rapids/Cambridge: Eerdmans, 2003.

———. *The Epistle to the Galatians.* Black's New Testament Commentaries. London: A&C Black, 1993.

———. *Jesus and the Spirit: A Study of Religious and Charismatic Experience of Jesus and the First Christians as Reflected in the New Testament.* Grand Rapids: Eerdmans, 1997.

———. *The New Perspective on Paul*, rev. ed. Grand Rapids: Eerdmans, 2008.

———. *New Testament Theology: An Introduction.* Nashville: Abingdon, 2009.

———. *The Theology of Paul the Apostle.* Grand Rapids: Eerdmans, 1998.

Dunn, James D. G., and James P. Mackey. *New Testament Theology in Dialogue: Christology and Ministry.* Philadelphia: Westminster, 1987.

Erdmann, Martin. "Mission in John's Gospel and Letters." In *Mission in the New Testament: An Evangelical Approach.* Edited by William J. Larkin, Jr. and Joel F. Williams, 207–26. Maryknoll: Orbis, 2005.

Erickson, Millard J. *Christian Theology*, 2nd ed. Grand Rapids: Baker Academic, 1998.

———. *Where is Theology Going: Issues and Perspectives on the Future of Theology.* Grand Rapids: Baker, 1994.

Esler, Philip F. *New Testament Theology: Communion and Community.* Minneapolis: Fortress, 2005.

Falako, Francis O. "Heterosexuality in Traditional African Culture: Peculiarities, Modern Concerns and Implications for the Church." *West African Journal of Higher Education.* God, the Bible and Human Sexuality 6 (2017): 46–63.

Fee, Gordon D. *God's Empowering Presence: The Holy Spirit in the Letters of Paul.* Peabody: Hendrickson, 1994.

Ferch, Arthur J. "The Apocalyptic 'Son of Man' in Daniel 7." Dissertation, Andrews University, Seventh-day Adventist Theological Seminary, April 1979. https://digitalcommons.andrews.edu/cgi/viewcontent.cgi?article=1047&context=dissertations.

Filson, Floyd V. *A Commentary on the Gospel according to St Matthew*, 2nd ed. London: Black, 1975.

Fisk, Bruce N. *A Hitchhiker's Guide to Jesus: Reading the Gospels on the Ground.* Grand Rapids: Baker Academic, 2011.

Frame, John M. *The Doctrine of the Christian Life.* Phillipsburg: P&R, 2008.

France, R. T. *The Gospel of Matthew.* The New International Commentary on the New Testament. Grand Rapids: Eerdmans, 2007.

Gamble, Robin. *The Irrelevant Church.* Eastbourne: Monarch, 1991.

Gathercole, Simon. "'Sins' in Paul." *New Testament Studies* 64 (2018): 143–61.

———. *Where Is Boasting? Early Jewish Soteriology and Paul's Response in Romans 1–5.* Grand Rapids: Eerdmans, 2002.

Getui, Mary N., Tinyiko Maluleke, and Justin Ukpong, eds. *Interpreting the New Testament in Africa.* Nairobi: Action, 2001.

Goodacre, Mark. *The Synoptic Problem: A Way Through the Maze.* New York: Sheffield Academic, 2001.

Goppelt, Leonhard. *Typos: The Typological Interpretation of the Old Testament in the New.* Translated by Donald H. Madvig. Grand Rapids: Eerdmans, 1982.

Graham, Franklin. *Billy Graham in Quotes*. Nashville: Thomas Nelson, 2011.
Greenlee, J. Harold. *Introduction to New Testament Textual Criticism*, rev. ed. Peabody: Hendrickson, 1995.
Grudem, Wayne. *Systematic Theology: An Introduction to Biblical Doctrine*. Leicester: Inter-Varsity/Grand Rapids: Zondervan, 1994.
Gundry, Robert H. *Matthew: A Commentary on His Literary and Theological Art*. Grand Rapids: Eerdmans, 1982.
Guthrie, Donald. *New Testament Introduction*. Leicester: Apollos, 1990.
———. *New Testament Theology*. Leicester: Inter-Varsity, 1981.
———. *The Pastoral Epistles*. Tyndale New Testament Commentaries, rev. ed. Leicester: Inter-Varsity, 1990.
Hagner, Donald. "How 'New' Is the New Testament? Continuity and Discontinuity Between the Old Testament (Formative Judaism) and the New Testament (Early Christianity)." *AJPS* 19, no. 2 (2016): 99–107.
Hale, Thomas. *The Applied New Testament Commentary*. Colorado Springs: Victor, 1996.
Hanson, R. P. C. *The Search for the Christian Doctrine: The Arian Controversy, 318–381*. Edinburgh: T&T Clark, 1988.
Hardy, John D. *Anointed with the Spirit: The Holy Spirit's Empowering Presence*. Phillipsburg: P&R, 2008.
———. "Mission in Matthew." In *Mission in the New Testament: An Evangelical Approach*. Edited by William J. Larkin, Jr. and Joel F. Williams, 119–36. Maryknoll: Orbis, 2005.
Harpur, George E. "Ephesians." In *New International Bible Commentary*. Edited by F. F. Bruce, H. L. Ellison, and G. C. D. Howley, 1428–39. Grand Rapids: Zondervan, 1979.
Harris, R. Laird. "Canonicity." In *The Zondervan Pictorial Bible Dictionary*. Edited by Merrill C. Tenney, 144–46. Grand Rapids: Zondervan, 1963.
Harrison, Everett F. *Colossians: Christ-All Sufficient*. Chicago: Moody, 1971.
———. *Introduction to the New Testament*, rev. ed. Grand Rapids: Eerdmans, 1971.
Harrison, Everett F., Geoffrey W. Bromiley, and Carl F. H. Henry, eds. *Baker's Dictionary of Theology*. Grand Rapids: Baker, 1960.
Hasel, Gerhard. *New Testament Theology: Basic Issues in the Current Debate*. Grand Rapids: Eerdmans, 1978.
Hayford, Jack W., and David P. Seemuth. *Ephesians and Colossians*. Spirit-Filled Life Commentaries. Nashville: Thomas Nelson, 2005.
Hays, Richard B. *The Moral Vision of the New Testament: A Contemporary Introduction to New Testament Ethics*. Waterloo: T&T Clark, 1996.
Hendricksen, William, and Simon J. Kistemaker. *Exposition of Thessalonians, the Pastorals, and Hebrews*. New Testament Commentary. Grand Rapids: Baker, 1996.
Hendriksen, William. *1 & 2 Thessalonians, 1 & 2 Timothy, Titus*. Edinburgh: Banner of Truth Trust, 1972; reprint, 2001.

Hernando, James D. *Dictionary of Hermeneutics: Concise Guide to Terms, Names, Methods and Expressions.* Springfield: Gospel, 2005.

Hill, David. *The Gospel of Matthew.* The New Century Bible Commentary. Grand Rapids: Eerdmans, 1972; reprint, 1990.

Hoehner, Harold W. *Ephesians: An Exegetical Commentary.* Grand Rapids: Baker Academic, 2002.

Holladay, Carl R. *Introduction to the New Testament*, ref. ed. Waco: Baylor University Press, 2017.

Holmes, Christopher T. "Gestures to the priesthood: Exploring Jesus' priestly function in 1 John." *R&E* 114, no. 4 (2017): 564–73.

House, Paul R. "The Day of the Lord." In *Central Themes in Biblical Theology: Mapping Unity in Diversity.* Edited by Scott J. Hafemann and Paul R. House, 179–224. Nottingham: Apollos, 2007.

Hunt, John P. T. *An Introduction to Romans: A Resource for the Nigerian Church.* Kaduna, Nigeria: Prudent Universal, 2020.

———. *Understanding and Applying Romans: A Commentary for the Nigerian Church.* Kaduna, Nigeria: Prudent Universal, 2020.

Hurtado, Larry W. *God in New Testament Theology.* Library of Biblical Theology. Nashville: Abingdon, 2010.

Ijatuyi-Morphé, Randee O. *Africa's Social Quest: A Comprehensive Survey and Analysis of the African Situation.* Jos, Nigeria: Hokma House, 2011.

———. *Community and Self-Definition in the Book of Acts.* Bethesda: Academica Press, 2004.

Ilori, J. A. *Moral Philosophy in African Context*, 2nd ed. Zaria, Nigeria: Ahmadu Bello University Press, 1994.

Isaak, Jon M. *New Testament Theology: Extending the Table.* Eugene: Cascade, 2011.

Isaak, Paul John. "Luke." In *Africa Bible Commentary.* Edited by Tokunboh Adeyemo, 1203–50. Nairobi: WordAlive, 2006.

Johnson, Luke Timothy. *The Writings of the New Testament: An Introduction*, rev. ed. Minneapolis: Fortress, 1999.

Kaiser, Walter C., Jr. *Toward Rediscovering the Old Testament.* Grand Rapids: Zondervan, 1987.

Kapolyo, Joe. "Matthew." In *Africa Bible Commentary.* Edited by Tokunboh Adeyemo, 1105–1170. Nairobi: WordAlive, 2006.

Kasali, David M. "Romans." In *Africa Bible Commentary.* Edited by Tokunboh Adeyemo, 1349–76. Nairobi: WordAlive, 2006.

Kato, Byang H. "Theological Issues in Africa." *Bibliotheca Sacra*, 133, no. 530 (April-June 1976): 142–52.

———. *Theological Pitfalls in Africa.* Kisumu, Kenya: Evangel, 1975.

Kearsley, R. "Repentance." In *New Dictionary of Theology.* Edited by Sinclair B. Ferguson and David F. Wright, 580–81. Downers Grove: InterVarsity, 1988.

Keener, Craig S. *Acts: An Exegetical Commentary*. Vol. 3. Grand Rapids: Baker Academic, 2014.

———. *1–2 Corinthians*. NCBC. Cambridge: Cambridge University Press, 2005.

———. *The IVP Bible Background Commentary: New Testament*. Downers Grove: InterVarsity, 1993.

Koester, Craig R. *The Word of Life: A Theology of John's Gospel*. Grand Rapids: Eerdmans, 2008.

Kösteberger, Andreas J. *John*. BECNT. Edited by Robert Yarbrough and Robert H. Stein. Grand Rapids: Baker Academic, 2004.

Kreitzer, L. J. "Adam and Christ." In *Dictionary of Paul and His Letters*. Edited by Gerald F. Hawthorne, Ralph P. Martin, and Daniel G. Reid, 9–15. Downers Grove: InterVarsity, 1993.

Kroeger, Catherine Clark. "The Classical Concept of *Head* as 'Source.'" In Gretchen G. Hull, *Equal to Serve: Women and Men in the Church and Home*, 267–83. Westwood: Revell, 1987.

Kümmel, Werner Georg. *Introducing the New Testament*, rev. ed. London: SCM, 1975.

———. *Theology of the New Testament According to Its Major Witnesses: Jesus – Paul – John*. Nashville/New York: Abingdon, 1973.

Kunhiyop, Samuel Waje. *African Christian Ethics*. Nairobi: WordAlive, 2008.

———. *African Christian Theology*. Nairobi: Hippo, 2012.

———. *Christian Conversion in Africa: The Bajju Experience*. Jos: ECWA Productions, 2005.

Kwame, Bediako. *Jesus in Africa: The Christian Gospel in African History and Experience*. Akropong-Akuapem, Ghana: Regnum Africa, 2000.

Laansma, Jon C., Grant Osborne, and Ray Van Neste. *New Testament Theology in Light of the Church's Mission: Essays in Honor of I. Howard Richard*. Eugene: Cascade, 2011.

Labberton, Mark. *Called: The Crisis and Promise of Following Jesus*. Downers Grove: InterVarsity, 2014.

———. *The Dangerous Act of Worship: Living God's Call to Justice*. Downers Grove: InterVarsity, 2007.

Ladd, G. E. *The Presence of the Future: The Eschatology of Biblical Realism*, rev. ed. Grand Rapids: Eerdmans, 1974.

———. *A Theology of the New Testament*, rev. ed. edited by Donald A. Hagner. Grand Rapids: Eerdmans, 1993.

Laney, J. Carl. "Gender Based Boundaries for Gathered Congregations: An Interpretive History of 1 Corinthians 14:34–35." *Journal for Biblical Manhood and Womanhood* 7, no. 1 (Spring 2002): 4–13.

Larkin, William J., Jr. *Acts*. The IVP New Testament Commentary Series. Edited by Grant R. Osborne, D. Stuart Briscoe, and Haddon Robinson. Downers Grove: InterVarsity, 1995.

Lea, Thomas D. *The New Testament: Its Background and Message*. Nashville: Broadman and Holman, 1996.

Lewis, C. S. *The Screwtape Letters*. New York: Macmillan, 1961.

Lewis, Nicolas Denzey. "A New Gnosticicism: Why Simon Gathercole and Mark Goodacre on the *Gospel of Thomas* Change the Field." *JSNT* 36, no. 3 (March 2014): 240–50.

Liebscher, Banning. *Jesus Culture: Living a Life that Transforms the World*. Shippensburg: Destiny Image, 2009.

Lieu, Judith M. "Faith and the Fourth Gospel: A Conversation with Teresa Morgan." *JSNT* 40, no. 3 (February 2018): 289–98. http://journals.sagepub.com/doi/abs/10.1177/0142064X18755931.

Lim, D. S. "Fullness." In *Dictionary of Paul and His Letters*. Edited by Gerald F. Hawthorne, Ralph P. Martin, and Daniel G. Reid, 319–20. Downers Grove: InterVarsity, 1993.

Lloyd-Jones, D. Martyn. *Studies in the Sermon on the Mount*. Nottingham: Inter-Varsity, 1976; repr. 2009.

Loba-Mkole, Jean-Claude. "Bible Translation and Inculturation Hermeneutics." In *Biblical Texts and African Audiences*. Edited by Ernst R. Wendland and Jean-Claude Loba-Mkole, 37–58. Nairobi: Action, 2004.

———. "New Testament and Intercultural Exegesis in Africa." *JSNT* 30, no. 1 (September 2007): 7–28.

Longenecker, Bruce W., and Mikeal C. Parsons, eds. *Beyond Bultmann: Reckoning a New Testament Theology*. Waco, TX: Baylor University Press, 2014.

Lowery, David K. "A Theology of Mark." *A Biblical Theology of the New Testament*. Edited by Roy B. Zuck, 65–86. Chicago: Moody, 1994.

———. "A Theology of Paul's Missionary Epistles." In *A Biblical Theology of the New Testament*. Edited by Roy B. Zuck, 243–96. Chicago: Moody, 1994.

Lucas, Dick, and Christopher Green. *The Message of 2 Peter and Jude*. The Bible Speaks Today. Leicester: Inter-Varsity, 1995.

Luz, Ulrich. *The Theology of the Gospel of Matthew*. Translated by J. Bradford Robinson. Cambridge: Cambridge University Press, 1995.

MacArthur, John, Jr. *Our Sufficiency in Christ: Three Deadly Influences that Undermine Our Spiritual Life*. Dallas: Word, 1991.

Machen, J. Gresham. *Christianity and Liberalism*. Grand Rapids: Eerdmans, 1923; reprint, 2002.

Macleod, Donald. *The Person of Christ: Contours of Christian Theology*. Downers Grove: InterVarsity, 1998.

Maigadi, Barje S. *Divisive Ethnicity in the Church in Africa*. Kaduna, Nigeria: Baraka, 2006.

Marshall, I. Howard. *A Concise New Testament Theology*. Nottingham: Inter-Varsity, 2008.

———. *I Believe in the Historical Jesus*. Grand Rapids: Eerdmans, 1977.

———. *New Testament Theology: Many Witnesses, One Gospel*. Downers Grove: InterVarsity, 2004.

Marshall, I. Howard, Stephen Travis, and Ian Paul. *Exploring the New Testament*. Vol. 2: *The Letters and Revelation*. London: SPCK, 2002.

McCain, Danny. *Notes on Acts of the Apostles*. Bukuru, Jos: Africa Christian Textbooks, 2001.

McGrath, Alister E. *Christian Theology: An Introduction*, 3rd ed. Oxford: Blackwell, 2001.

McKenzie, John L. "The Gospel According to Matthew." In *The Jerome Biblical Commentary*, 2 vols. Edited by Raymond E. Brown, Joseph A. Fitzmyer, and Roland E. Murphy, 62–114. Englewood Cliffs: Prentice Hall, 1968.

Michaels, J. Ramsey. *Revelation*. The IVP New Testament Commentary. Edited by Grant R. Osborne, D. Stuart Briscoe, and Haddon Robinson. Downers Grove: InterVarsity, 1997.

Miller, Johnny V. "Mission in Revelation." In *Mission in the New Testament: An Evangelical Approach*. Edited by William J. Larkin, Jr. and Joel F. Williams, 227–31. Maryknoll: Orbis, 2005.

Mitchell, John G. *Let's Revel in John's Gospel*. West Linn: Glory, 2000.

Mitton, C. Leslie. *Ephesians*. The New Century Bible Commentary. Grand Rapids: Eerdmans, 1973; reprint London: Marshall, Morgan & Scott, 1989.

Mohler, R. Albert, Jr. *Culture Shift: The Battle for the Moral Heart of America*. Colorado Springs: Multnomah, 2011.

Molyneux, K. Gordon. *African Christian Theology: The Quest for Selfhood*. San Francisco: Mellen Research University Press, 1993.

Moreland, J. P., and William Lane Craig. *Philosophical Foundations for a Christian Worldview*. Downers Grove: IVP Academic, 2003.

Morgan, Robert. *The Nature of New Testament Theology: The Contribution of William Wrede and Adolf Schlatter*. Naperville: SCM, 1973.

Morris, Leon. *Gospel According to Matthew*. Pillar of the New Testament Commentary. Grand Rapids/Cambridge: Eerdmans, 1992.

———. *New Testament Theology*. Grand Rapids: Academic Books, 1986.

———. *Revelation*. Tyndale New Testament Commentaries, rev. ed. Leicester: InterVarsity, 1987.

———. *1 and 2 Thessalonians*. Tyndale New Testament Commentaries, rev. ed. Grand Rapids: Eerdmans, 1984.

Mounce, William D. *Mounce's Complete Expository Dictionary of Old and New Testament Words*. Grand Rapids: Zondervan, 2006.

———. *Pastoral Epistles*. Word Biblical Commentary. Nashville: Thomas Nelson, 2000.

Newton, John. "Amazing Grace." In *Sing to the Lord: Church of the Nazarene Hymnal*. Kansas City: Lillenas, 1993.

Ng, Esther Yue L. "Matthew 5:17–22 and 'A Tale of Two Missions.'" In *New Testament Theology in the Light of the Church's Mission: Essays in Honor of I. Howard Marshall*.

Edited by Jon C. Laansma, Grant R. Osborne, and Ray Van Neste, 103–121. Eugene: Cascade, 2011.

Ngewa, Samuel. "Galatians." In *Africa Bible Commentary*. Edited by Tokunboh Adeyemo, 1413–24. Nairobi: WordAlive, 2006.

Ngundu, Onesimus. "Revelation." In *Africa Bible Commentary*. Edited by Tokunboh Adeyemo, 1543–79. Nairobi: WordAlive, 2006.

Ngwewa, Samuel, Mark Shaw, and Tite Tienou, eds. *Issues in African Christian Theology*. Nairobi: East African Educational Publishers, 1998.

Nihinlola, Emiola. *Theology Under the Mango Tree: A Handbook of African Christian Theology*. Ikeja, Lagos: Fine Print & Manufacturing, 2013.

Njoroge, Nyambura J. "The Role of Women in the Church." In *Africa Bible Commentary*. Edited by Tokunboh Adeyemo, 1471. Nairobi: WordAlive, 2006.

Nkansah-Obrempong, James. "Theological Heresy." In *Africa Bible Commentary*. Edited by Tokunboh Adeyemo, 1553. Nairobi: WordAlive, 2006.

Obeng, Emmanuel A. "Emerging Concerns for Biblical Scholarship in Ghana." In *Interpreting the New Testament in Africa*. Edited by Mary N. Getui, Tinyiko Maluleke, and Justin Ukpong, 31–41. Nairobi: Action, 2001.

O'Brien, Peter T. *The Letter to the Ephesians*, Pillar New Testament Commentary. Grand Rapids: Eerdmans, 1999.

O'Donovan, Wilbur. *Biblical Christianity in Modern Africa*. Carlisle: Paternoster, 2000.

Ortlund, Dane C. "What Does It Mean to Fall Short of the Glory of God? Romans 3:23 in Biblical-Theological Perspective." *WTJ* 80 (2018): 121–40.

Palmer, Timothy. *Christian Theology in an African Context*. Bukuru, Nigeria: Africa Christian Textbooks, 2015.

Peabody, David B., ed., with Lamar Cope and Allan J. McNicol. *One Gospel from Two: Mark's Use of Matthew and Luke: A Demonstration by the Research Team of the International Institute for Renewal of Gospel Studies*. New York: Trinity Press International, 2002.

Perrin, Norman. *Parable and Gospel*. Edited by K. C. Hanson. Minneapolis: Fortress, 2003.

Pester, John. "The Building of the Church as the Reality of the Kingdom of the Heavens Through the Heavenly Ministry of Christ in the Gospel of Matthew." *Affirmation & Critique: A Journal of Christian Thought* 23, no. 1 (Spring 2018): 23–36.

Philips, John. *Exploring Hebrews: An Expository Commentary*. The John Philips Commentary Series. Grand Rapids: Kregel, 2002.

Phillips, Richard D. *Hebrews*. Reformed Expository Commentary. Phillipsburg: P&R, 2006.

Piper, John, "Praise for *Culture Shift*." In R. Albert Mohler, Jr., *Culture Shift: The Battle for the Moral Heart of America*. Colorado Springs: Multnomah, 2011.

———. *What Jesus Demands from the World*. Wheaton: Crossway, 2006.

Platt, David. *Counter Culture: A Compassionate Call to Counter Culture in a World of Poverty, Same-Sex Marriage, Racism, Sex Slavery, Immigration, Abortion, Persecution, Orphans, and Pornography*. Carol Stream: Tyndale House, 2015.

Poythress, Vern S. *The Returning King: A Guide to the Book of Revelation*. Phillipsburg: P&R, 2000.

———. *The Shadow of Christ in the Law of Moses*. Philipsburg: P&R, 1991.

Prime, Derek. *Let's Study 2 Corinthians*. Edinburgh: Banner of Truth Trust, 2000.

Proffitt, T. D., III. "Ephesians." In *Missional and Messianic Bible Commentary: New Testament, Gospels, and Acts*. Vol. 2. Fullerton: fritzvoncoella.net, 2020; pre-publication draft, 2018.

Punt, Jeremy. "Cross-Purpose in Paul? Violence of the Cross, Galatians, and Human Dignity." *Scriptura* 102 (2009): 446–62.

Puskas, Charles B. *Introduction to the New Testament*. Peabody: Hendrickson, 1987.

Räisänen, Heikki. *Beyond New Testament Theology: A Story and a Program*. London: SCM, 1990.

Rauschenbusch, Walter. *Christianity and the Social Crisis*. Louisville: Westminster John Knox, 1991.

Reformed Books Online. "New Testament Theology." https://reformedbooksonline.com/new-testament-theology/.

Reymond, Robert L. *Paul: Missionary Theologian*. Ross-shire: Christian Focus, 2000.

Roberts, Mark D. "The Birth of Jesus: Hype or History?" Mark D. Roberts (blog) 2011. http://www.patheos.com/blogs/markdroberts/series/the-birth-of-jesus-hype-or-history/.

Ross, Mark E. *Let's Study Matthew*. Edinburgh: Banner of Truth Trust, 2009.

Ryken, Philip Graham. *When You Pray: Making the Lord's Prayer Your Own*. Phillipsburg: P&R, 2000.

Sacks, Rabbi Jonathan. *To Heal a Fractured World: The Ethics of Responsibility*. New York: Schocken, 2005.

Sanders, E. P. *Paul: The Apostle's Life, Letters, and Thought*. Minneapolis: Fortress, 2015.

———. *Paul and Palestinian Judaism: A Comparison of Patterns of Religion*. London: SCM/Philadelphia: Fortress, 1977.

Sarma, Bitrus A. *Blessed New Humanity in Christ*. Carlisle: Hippo Books, 2021.

———. *Hermeneutics of Mission in Matthew: Israel and the Nations in the Interpretative Framework of Matthew's Gospel*. Carlisle: Langham Monographs, 2015.

———. *Jesus Is Lord: Proclaiming the Supremacy of Christ in Africa from the Book of Colossians*. Jos, Nigeria: Yakson, 2015.

———. *People of the Kingdom: Spiritual Leadership Formation for Holistic Transformation in Africa*. Jos, Nigeria: Yakson, 2014.

———. *Pursuing the Ultimate Goal: An Exposition of Philippians for Today*. Jos, Nigeria: Yakson, 2015.

———. *Reading the Bible in Africa: Understanding and Applying the Bible*. Jos, Nigeria: Yakson, 2015.

———. *Worthy of Worship: Beholding the Beauty of the Lord.* Jos, Nigeria: Yakson, 2014.
Satinover, Jeffrey. *Homosexuality and the Politics of Truth.* Grand Rapids: Baker, 1996.
Saucy, Mark. "The Kingdom-of-God Sayings in Matthew." *Bibliotheca Sacra* 151 (April-June 1994): 175–197.
Schnabel, Eckhard J. *Paul the Missionary: Realities, Strategies and Methods.* Downers Grove: IVP Academic, 2008.
Schnelle, Udo. *Apostle Paul: His Life and Theology.* Translated by M. Eugene Boring. Grand Rapids: Baker Academic, 2005.
Schreiner, Thomas R. *The Law and Its Fulfilment: A Pauline Theology of Law.* Grand Rapids: Baker, 1993.
———. *Magnifying God in Christ: A Summary of New Testament Theology.* Grand Rapids: Baker Academic, 2010.
———. *New Testament Theology: Magnifying God in Christ.* Nottingham: Apollos, 2008.
Schweizer, Eduard. *The Letter to the Colossians.* Translated by Andrew Chester. London: SPCK, 1982.
Shillington, V. George. *2 Corinthians.* Believers Church Bible Commentary. Waterloo, ON: Herald, 1998.
Silva, Moisés. *Philippians.* BECNT, 2nd ed. Grand Rapids: Baker Academic, 2005.
Sindima, Harvey J. *Drums of Redemption: An Introduction to African Christianity.* Westport, CT/London: Greenwood, 1994.
Smalley, S. S. "Conversion." In *New Dictionary of Theology.* Edited by Sinclair B. Ferguson and David F. Wright, 167–68. Downers Grove: InterVarsity, 1988.
Smiles, Vincent M. *The Gospel and the Law in Galatia: Paul's Response to Jewish-Christian Separatism and the Threat of Galatian Apostasy.* Collegeville, MN: Liturgical Press, 1998.
Smit, Peter-Ben. "Sadomasochism and the Apocalypse of John: Exegesis, Sensemaking and Pain." *Biblical Interpretation: A Journal of Contemporary Approaches* 26 (2018): 90–112.
Smith, Barry D. *Jesus' Twofold Teaching about the Kingdom of God.* New Testament Monograph, 24. Edited by Stanley E. Porter. Sheffield: Sheffield Phoenix, 2009.
Snodgrass, Klyne R. *Stories with Intent: A Comprehensive Guide to the Parables of Jesus.* Grand Rapids: Eerdmans, 2008.
Stedman, Ray C. *Hebrews.* The IVP New Testament Commentary Series. Edited by Grant R. Osborne. Downers Grove: InterVarsity, 1992.
———. *Waiting for the Second Coming: Studies in Thessalonians.* Grand Rapids: Discovery House, 1990.
Stott, John. *Men with a Message: An Introduction to the New Testament and Its Writers.* Revised by Stephen Motyer. Suffolk: Evangelical Literature Trust, 1994.
Strecker, George. *Theology of the New Testament.* Edited by Friedrich Wilhelm Horn. Translated by M. Eugene Boring. Louisville: Westminster John Knox, 2000.
Strobel, Lee. *The Case for Christ: A Journalist's Personal Investigation of the Evidence for Jesus,* rev. ed. Grand Rapids: Zondervan, 2016.

Stuhlmacher, Peter. *How to Do Biblical Theology*. Allison Park: Pickwick, 1995.
Sumney, Jerry L. *Philippians: A Greek Student's Intermediate Reader*. Peabody: Hendrickson, 2007.
Swartley, Willard M. *Covenant of Peace: The Missing Peace in New Testament Theology and Ethics*. Grand Rapids: Eerdmans, 2006.
Thielicke, Helmut. *Our Heavenly Father*. Grand Rapids: Baker, 1980.
Thielman, Frank S. "The Atonement." In *Central Themes in Biblical Theology: Mapping Unity in Diversity*. Edited by Scott J. Hafemann and Paul R. House, 102–27. Nottingham: Apollos, 2007.
Thiselton, Anthony C. *The First Epistle to the Corinthians: A Commentary on the Greek Text*. Edited by I. Howard Marshall and Donald A. Hagner. Grand Rapids: Eerdmans/Cambridge: Paternoster, 2000.
Tidball, Derek. *The Voices of the New Testament: Invitation to a Biblical Roundtable*. Downers Grove: IVP Academic, 2016.
Tongue, D. H. "The Concept of Apostasy in the Book of Hebrews." *TynB* 5–6 (April 1960): 19–27.
Tozer, A. W. *The Pursuit of God*. Camp Hill: Christian Publications, 1993.
Trevethan, Thomas L. *Our Joyful Confidence: The Lordship of Jesus in Colossians*. Downers Grove: InterVarsity, 1981.
Turaki, Yusufu. "Ephesians." In *Africa Bible Commentary*. Edited by Tokunboh Adeyemo, 1425–38. Nairobi: WordAlive, 2006.
———. "Homosexuality." In *Africa Bible Commentary*. Edited by Tokunboh Adeyemo, 1355. Nairobi: WordAlive, 2006.
———. *Tainted Legacy: Islam, Colonialism and Slavery in Northern Nigeria*. Mclean, VA: Isaac Publishing, 2010.
———. *The Trinity of Sin*. Nairobi: WordAlive, 2011.
Turner, David L. *Matthew*. BECNT. Edited by Robert W. Yarbrough and Robert H. Stein. Grand Rapids: Baker Academic, 2008.
Twelftree, Graham. "Demon, Devil, Satan." In *Dictionary of Jesus and the Gospels*. Edited by Joel B. Green, Scott McKnight, and I. Howard Marshall, 163–72. Downers Grove: InterVarsity, 1992.
———. *Jesus the Miracle Worker*. Downers Grove: InterVarsity 1999.
———. *People of the Spirit: Exploring Luke's View of the Church*. Grand Rapids: Baker Academic, 2009.
Ukpong, J. "Developments in Biblical Interpretations in Africa: Historical and Hermeneutical Directions." In *The Bible in Africa: Translations, Trajectories, and Trends*. Edited by Gerald O. West and Musa W. Dube, 11–28. Leiden/Boston/Köln: Brill, 1998.
Vaughan, Curtis. "Colossians." In *The Expositor's Bible Commentary*. Abridged. Edited by Kenneth L. Barker and John R. Kohlenberger, III, 812–42. Grand Rapids: Zondervan, 1994.

Vawter, Bruce. "The Gospel According to John." In *The Jerome Biblical Commentary*, 2 vols. Edited by Raymond E. Brown, Joseph A. Fitzmyer, and Roland E. Murphy, 414–66. Englewood Cliffs: Prentice Hall, 1968.
Via, Dan O. *What is New Testament Theology?* Minneapolis: Fortress, 2002.
Volf, Miroslav. "Johannine Dualism and Contemporary Pluralism." *Modern Theology* 21, no. 2 (March 2005): 189–217. https://onlinelibrary.wiley.com/doi/10.1111/j.1468-0025.2005.00282.x.
Walls, Andrew F. *The Missionary Movement in Christian History: Studies in the Transmission of Faith.* Maryknoll: Orbis, 1996; reprint, 2009.
Weeks, Noel. *The Sufficiency of Scripture.* Carlisle: Banner of Truth Trust, 1977.
Wenham, David, and Steve Walton. *Exploring the New Testament.* Vol. 1. *The Gospels and Acts.* London: SPCK, 2001.
Wiersbe, Warren W. *Wiersbe's Expository Outlines on the New Testament.* Colorado Springs: David C. Cook, 1992.
Williams, Jay G. *Judaism.* Wheaton: Theosophical Publishing House, 1980.
Witherington, Ben, III. *New Testament Theology and Ethics.* Vol. 1. Downers Grove: IVP Academic, 2016.
———. *New Testament Theology and Ethics.* Vol. 2. Downers Grove: IVP Academic, 2016.
Witmer, Daryl E. "Isn't the virgin birth of Jesus Christ mythological and scientifically impossible?" Christian Answers.net (2011). https://christiananswers.net/q-aiia/virginbirth.html.
Woods, Paul. "First Among Equals: Christian Theology and Modern Philosophy." *Transformation: International Journal of Holistic Mission Studies* 34, no. 3 (2016): 165–75.
Wright, Christopher J. H. *The Mission of God: Unlocking the Bible's Grand Narrative.* Nottingham: Inter-Varsity, 2006.
Wright, N. T. *Jesus and the Victory of God.* Vol. 2. *Christian Origins and the Question of God.* London: SPCK, 1996.
———. *The Resurrection of the Son of God.* London: SPCK, 2003.
———. *What Paul Really Said: Was Paul of Tarsus the Real Founder of Christianity?* Oxford: Lion, 1997.
Yamsat, Pandam. *An Exposition of First Corinthians.* Bukuru, Nigeria: Africa Christian Textbooks, 2004.
Yong, Amos. *Renewing Christian Theology: Systematics for a Global Christianity.* Waco, TX: Baylor University Press, 2014.
Zink-Sawyer, Beverly. "The Word Purely Preached and Heard: The Listeners and the Homiletical Endeavor." *Interpretation: A Journal of Bible and Theology* 51 (1977): 342–57.
Zuck, Roy B., ed. *A Biblical Theology of the New Testament.* Chicago: Moody, 1994.

www.ingramcontent.com/pod-product-compliance
Lightning Source LLC
Chambersburg PA
CBHW060942230426
43665CB00015B/2037